THE
CIVIL WAR
READER

THE
CIVIL WAR
READER

The Union Reader
The Confederate Reader

Edited by Richard B. Harwell

**MALLARD
PRESS**

MALLARD PRESS
An imprint of BDD Promotional Book Company, Inc.
666 Fifth Avenue
New York, N.Y. 10103

Mallard Press and its accompanying design and logo
are trademarks of BDD Promotional Book Company, Inc.

Reprinted by special arrangement by William S. Konecky Associates, Inc.

This edition first published in the United States of America
in 1991 by The Mallard Press

ISBN 0-7924-5601-7

Printed in the United States of America

The Union
Reader

For
RUTH FOREMAN MOORE
and
LAUREN FOREMAN

Acknowledgment

To the Henry E. Huntington Library belongs, almost as completely as in Aesop's fable, the lion's share of the acknowledgments for this book. Not only is every item included in the volume present in the magnificent Civil War collections there, but the editor is indebted to the Huntington for making his search for appropriate selections thoroughly pleasant. His debt is to the whole library and the whole staff, but it is particularly great to Mr. John E. Pomfret, Director; Mr. Leslie Bliss, Librarian; Mr. Carey S. Bliss, Miss Mary Isabel Fry, Miss Gertrude Ruhnka, and Mr. Erwin F. Morkisch. For the graciousness which only a considerate publisher can display he is grateful to Mr. John L. B. Williams of New York. He is thankful for the generous help given by Floyd Cammack and Robert L. Talmadge. And for relief from the infinite troubles of typing and transcription he must thank Miss Elaine Mitchell.

RICHARD BARKSDALE HARWELL

October 8, 1958

Contents

One of the Strangest Naval Combats   101

> The War in the United States, Report to the Swiss
> Military Department; Preceded by a Discourse to the
> Federal Military Society Assembled at Berne, Aug.
> 18, 1862, by Ferdinand LeComte, Lieutenant-Colonel,
> Swiss Confederation . . . New York, D. Van Nos-
> trand, 1863. 148 p.

Shiloh   111

> The Battle Field of Shiloh. [n.p., 1862]. 6 p.

But You Must Act   122

> The President to General McClellan. [Washington,
> 1862]. *Broadside.*

Unfit for Human Beings   125

> One Year's Soldiering, Embracing the Battles of Fort
> Donelson and Shiloh and the Capture of Two Hun-
> dred Officers and Men of the Fourteenth Iowa Infan-
> try, and Their Confinement Six Months and a Half in
> Rebel Prisons, [by] F. F. Kiner, Chaplain Fourteenth
> Iowa Infantry. Lancaster, E. H. Thomas, Printer,
> 1863. 219 p.

The Capture and Occupation of New Orleans   137

> General Orders from Headquaraters Department of
> the Gulf, Issued by Major-General B. F. Butler, from
> May 1st, 1862, to the Present Time. New-Orleans, E.
> R. Wagener, Printer and Stationer, 1862. 35 p.

A Change in Virginia   144

> Soldiers of the Army of the Potomac! [Address of
> Major General George B. McClellan, June 2, 1862.
> Camp Near New Bridge, Va., 1862] [1] p. Soldiers of
> the Army of the Potomac! [address of Major General
> George B. McClellan, July 4, 1862. Camp Near Harri-
> son's Landing, Va., 1862]. [1] p. and To the Officers

1863

1865

Introduction

As the national memory of the American Civil War is dimmed with time the vision of the war is, more and more, portrayed in great bold strokes. We remember Sumter, Bull Run, and Gettysburg—that greatest of battles. We remember a farmhouse at Appomattox, tensed to silence and formality in marking the end of an era of noisy politics and noisier battle. We remember Lincoln and the giant shadow his figure has cast on American history. We remember Grant and Sherman, and Seward and Stanton. And John Wilkes Booth. We remember the Confederates: the nobility of Lee, the zeal of Jackson, the daring of Stuart.

But so much we forget.

The war was more than Lincoln and his generals and his Cabinet, more than battles and heroes. For more than four years war was our national life. War was the climactic event of a generation—of a century—of American life. It was, as its great leader said at the cemetery in Gettysburg, the test of the United States' national existence.

The story of the war has been told many times. Its vast literature still grows by, conservatively, a book a week. With the reports from the two contending sides in the same language and with the motivations of the two sections still influencing sectional thinking, this is a war which has a con-

tinuing interest and reality to Americans. Though historians'
interpretations of the war have changed from generation to
generation, shifting according to the emphasis of an out-
standing historian or according to the fashionable thinking
of a time, the facts of the war have not changed. Nearly a
century after the fighting the closest we can come to those
facts is still in the writings of the people of its own time.
It is in their words that the war is fixed in print and on paper,
for us as it was for them. Even if their facts may sometimes
be wrong, even if their writings may often be crude or incomplete or prejudiced, who can gainsay what they wrote?
What they described was the war as they saw it and lived
it. This was the war they fought.

"The War of the Southern Rebellion," wrote J. B. Rogers,
chaplain of the Nineteenth Wisconsin Volunteers in his *War
Pictures* (Chicago, 1863), "is destined to create a literature
of its own. Its history will be written by many hands, while
its incidents and leading characteristics, above all the principles involved in it, will supply themes for discussion for
a long time to come. The material for all reliable accounts
of this great struggle must be furnished, in no small degree,
by the testimony of eye-witnesses."

The Union Reader is a history by many hands. In nearly
every case the writers were eyewitnesses, even participants
in the events they described. In every case they were participants in the time, eyewitnesses to the most eventful days of
American history. In their words lies the documentation of
America at war—of Sumter, Bull Run, Port Royal, Shiloh,
Seven Days, and on down the long list of battles. Equally
the words of women working in the hospitals, of soldiers
suffering the boredom of inactivity, of prisoners enduring
far greater hardships are documentation of the times. As
Chaplain Rogers wrote: "It is not altogether of battles that

thoughtful people wish to read, even in the history of wars. Especially is this the case with those who read with some view to learn what war really is."

As were their opponents at the South, the Northerners of the sixties were tremendously conscious of their moment in history. There was, it would seem, a national urge to record the experiences of the war at every level of activity. These contemporary accounts as much as the work of later historians and the publication of the official records of the war make the American Civil War the best documented of all wars.

America in 1861 was still a new country. Just as the war was a test of democratic principle it was a test of democratic education. Never before had there been so literate an army. Such a soldiery was ready, and proud, to relate its experiences. Such a soldiery was capable of understanding printed orders and explanations. Nor, in the newness of universal education, was this country "with," as Henry Ward Beecher noted, "books and newspapers thick as leaves in our own forests, with institutions sprung from the people and peculiarly adapted to their genius" inured to the uses of propaganda. It was ripe for the printed word to be used in shaping the course of its history with especial freshness and effectiveness.

Unlike their Southern contemporaries, the Northerners were not impoverished for the materials of printing as the war progressed. Printing did not disappear in the South, but it survived against difficulties that seriously hampered its effectiveness. In the North supplies of paper, presses, and printers were readily available throughout the war. The publishing business was not nearly so concentrated in the big cities of the East as it would be later. The selections in *The Union Reader* include items from books printed in Muscatine, Iowa; Madison, Wisconsin; Denver; and occupied New Orleans; from governmental pamphlets issued at Santa Fe, and at Frederick, Maryland; and from ephemeral sheets produced from the Peninsula of Virginia to Fort Riley, Kansas. Presses were quickly adapted to camp use so that many units had their own regimental papers and every major command had its own field press. In his report to the Swiss Military Department Ferdinand LeComte, an observer with General McClellan's Army of the Potomac, noted: "There is not a village which has not its printing press and its journal. A head-quarters, as populous as many a village, might well pretend to the same privilege. I subjoin here, Mr. Counsellor, a specimen of the elegant pamphlets which our printers executed for us in the marshy woods of the environs of Yorktown. I should add that these pamphlets . . . simplify greatly the labor of the staff department."

Nor was the North impoverished of authors. Though little of literary note was published during the war, there was a wealth of talent among the practicing writers of the time. Some of this talent, such as Walt Whitman's, was redirected into active participation in the war effort. Other was used for purposes of literary propaganda. Even Bret Harte, in far-away California, wrote a special poem for *The Sanitary Commission Bulletin*. Edmund Clarence Stedman reported the war for the New York *World* and wrote topical poetry. Others who contributed to the anthologies of the day included Thomas Bailey Aldrich, Oliver Wendell Holmes, Charles G. Leland, James Russell Lowell, Fitz James O'Brien, and John Greenleaf Whittier. The novels were undistinguished, but there was a plenty of them. And the magazines—*Leslie's, Harper's*, the *Atlantic*—flourished. J. W. DeForest, later to achieve a distinguished reputation as a novelist, wrote reports from the armies for *Harper's*, and the *Atlantic* printed one of its most enduringly popular stories when it published Edward Everett Hale's *The Man without a Country*. Stephen Foster, Henry Clay Work, George F. Root, Patrick Gilmore, and a host of other professional song writers supplied the songs for the soldiers, but the amateurs helped too, particularly Julia Ward Howe with the great "Battle Hymn of the Republic." Of one collection of songs Hale wrote, in *James Russell Lowell and His Friends*: "Eager in everything in the way of public spirit, Professor [F. J.] Child made it his special duty to prepare a 'Song Book' for the soldiers who were going to the field. . . . He made everybody who could, write a war song, and he printed a little book of these songs, with the music, which he used to send to the front with every passing regiment." And, of course, the war was thoroughly documented in the publications of Congress, the personal and private reports of generals, and in the publication in the newspapers of every scrap of information their reporters with the armies could uncover.

General Sherman may or may not have said, "War is hell." It is certain that he wrote, in his letter of September 12, 1864, to the Mayor of Atlanta, "War is cruelty," and proceeded to prove it. War is cruelty, but it is also many more things. It is bravery and heroism, boredom and bombast, starvation and suffering. It is politics. It is tactics. It is fighting. But in the total General Sherman was right. War is cruelty. War is hell. If there is any lesson which should come out of the record of our own Civil War, it is summarized in that statement. And yet it is a lesson still to be learned.

The testimony of the participants in the days of '61 to '65 is vastly interesting. It is this testimony which makes up *The Union Reader*. It is not all here, far from it. Only bits and pieces can be encompassed in one volume. But these bits and pieces catch the spirit of the times from the fall of Fort Sumter to the reraising of the United States flag over its ruin. Each was written and published during the war itself, and many helped form the public opinion that, in turn, helped shape the further course of the war.

Few familiar pieces are included. Lincoln's *Gettysburg Address* and his *Second Inaugural* are known to every literate American. But almost none of the millions who have read Louisa May Alcott's *Little Women* know her charming *Hospital Sketches,* a chapter of which is reproduced here. Even fewer of those who know John Greenleaf Whittier's "Barbara Frietchie" have ever read the report of Dr. Lewis H. Steiner, inspector for the U.S. Sanitary Commission, which relates the incident in more prosaic form. Only the most fully initiated Civil War buff is likely to know that frank and truly remarkable regimental history from the Far West, Ovando Hollister's *History of the First Regiment of Colorado Volunteers,* or the broadside tirade against the Texans addressed to the citizens of New Mexico by their territorial governor in 1862. There is suffering in the prison narratives of F. F. Kiner and Prescott Tracy, heroism in the story of Fort Sumter, pure soldiering in the boyish account of the battlefield of Shiloh. The testimony of *The Union Reader* is, in fact, the essence of war itself.

"Blood ain't so cool as ink, John," wrote James Russell Lowell in 1862 in an admonition to Britain after the Trent Affair nearly precipitated war. But the words of those who participated in our Civil War run with blood as well as with ink. In these words, hot from the heart, that the Americans of another day wrote for each other their day remains alive. This, then, is their own story, the story of the war they fought. This is *The Union Reader.*

1861

Within Fort Sumter

ABRAHAM LINCOLN himself might well have written an
introduction for *The Union Reader*. He summarized
the background for war succinctly in an open letter
written June 12, 1863, to Erastus Corning and other
Democrats of Albany, New York, on the case of Clement
L. Vallandigham and arbitrary arrests. "Prior to my in-
stallation here," he stated, "it had been inculcated that
any State had a lawful right to secede from the national
Union, and that it would be expedient to exercise that
right whenever the devotees of the doctrine should fail
to elect a President to their own liking. I was elected
contrary to their liking; and, accordingly, so far as it was
legally possible, they had taken seven States out of the
Union, had seized many of the United States forts, and
had fired upon the United States flag, all before I was
inaugurated, and, of course, before I had done any official act whatever. The Rebellion thus begun soon ran
into the present Civil War; and, in certain respects, it
began on very unequal terms between the parties. The
insurgents had been preparing for it for more than thirty

3

years, while the Government had taken no steps to resist them."

This was the official point of view, and not without foundation. Southerners had certainly planned, propagandized, and prepared for secession. It is easy to overestimate, however, their preparations for war. The South wanted to "go in peace." Though some secessionists undoubtedly foresaw war and realized the desirability of preparing for it, to prepare for war would have canceled the propaganda of their position that secession was legal and that they could peaceably leave the Union. Had they made the war preparations implied by secession there might well have been no secession, no war.

It can be argued that the South lost its chance to achieve independence and establish the Confederate States when Fort Sumter was fired upon. If the South could not leave the Union in peace, she could not leave at all. For, once the war potential of the North could be mobilized, the South had little chance. Initial defeat or victory could hardly matter; in time the North could win by bringing to bear its might in arms and men, in matériel and technical achievement.

"The first gun that spat its iron insult at Fort Sumter," declared Oliver Wendell Holmes in a Fourth of July oration in Boston, 1863, "smote every loyal American full in the face. As when the foul witch used to torture her miniature charge, the person it represented suffered all that she inflicted on his waxen counterpart, so every buffet that fell on the smoking fortress was felt by the sovereign nation of which that was the representative.

Robbery could go no farther, for every loyal man was despoiled in that single act as much as if a footpad had laid hands upon him to take from him his father's staff and his mother's Bible. Insult could go no farther, for over those battered walls waved the precious symbol of all we most value in the past and most hope for in the future,—the banner under which we became a nation, and which, next to the cross of the Redeemer, is the dearest object of love and honor to all who toil or march or sail beneath its waving folds of glory."

Within Fort Sumter is a small book published in 1861 which purported to be "By One of the Company." Actually it was written by a Miss A. Fletcher, but her representation of life in the fort is sound and is corroborated by other accounts. Printed here is her story of the battle that began the war.

At two o'clock on Thursday, April 11th, a formal demand was sent by General Beauregard to Major Anderson for the evacuation of Fort Sumter. The Major's reply was as follows:

"SIR:—I have the honor to acknowledge the receipt of your communication, demanding the evacuation of this Fort, and to say in reply thereto that it is a demand with which I regret that my sense of honor and my obligations to my Government prevent my compliance.

"ROBERT ANDERSON."

The reception of this answer was immediately followed by a deputation from General Beauregard urging Major Anderson to evacuate, and proposing the most honorable terms, upon which he should be allowed to do so; but the Major, feeling his own strength, besides expecting the fleet from Washington, determined to hold out, and the deputation, after a long interview, in which they earnestly sought to persuade the Major to accept the offered terms, returned to Charleston to report their failure.

It was late on Thursday night when this interview closed; and at half past three o'clock, on Friday morning, the boat with its white flag, shrouded in darkness and mist, again drew up to the walls of Fort Sumter. It conveyed three of General Beauregard's Aid-de-camps, bearing the following notice:

"*Major Anderson:*
"By virtue of Brigadier General Beauregard's command, we have the honor to notify you that he will open the line of his batteries on Fort Sumter in one hour from this time."

Punctual to the minute, at half past four o'clock, the first gun was fired on Fort Sumter.

It was a dark, cloudy morning, not a star was visible, while a heavy mist covered earth and sea; but as through the sombre gloom came the brilliant flash of exploding shells from the batteries all around the bay, while the deep hoarse tones of talking cannon echoed over the waters, the scene was sublimely grand, and sensations wildly inspiriting swelled in every heart.

Major Anderson alone was calm, though the swollen veins of his temples, the dilating nostrils, the nervous lip, told that his great heart beat as ardently as any there.

He would allow of no hurry: he wished that his command

should husband their strength as it would all be needed. With this view he desired that they should breakfast before proceeding to action.

Their simple meal was soon prepared. For a week they had been on short rations of salt pork, biscuit and coffee, with a little rice. This rice, the last they had received, had reached them through a rough sea, and, the boat being leaky, had become saturated with salt water. It had then been spread out in an empty room of the barracks to dry, with the expectation of its being very acceptable when the biscuit should give out. That extremity was reached now. The last few biscuits were divided, and the cook was ordered to boil some rice; but, lo! the very first fire had shattered the windows of the room where the precious article was spread, and particles of glass were thickly strewn amongst the grain —the food was useless.

But they still had a little pork and plenty of coffee; and, thankful for this same, the brave fellows eat and drank, then filed in order to their places in the casements.

And all this time the enemy's shot rattled, thick and fast, around our stronghold, which did but little execution beyond affording the Major an opportunity of observing the efficiency of each battery employed against him, and of tracing the plan which he had to oppose.

At five o'clock day began to break; but the heavy masses of clouds which obscured the sky, the sullen swell of the dark waters, the grey mist which hung, like a sombre veil, over nature's face, only became more apparent as the gathering light increased.

Shortly after the huge clouds burst, and a deluge of rain rushed down upon the scene, as if commissioned to quench the matricidal fire leveled against Columbia's breast. But all in vain. The moaning wind—the splashing shower were scarcely heeded, or made but feeble sounds, while the hoarse bellowing of deep-mouthed cannon still rolled fiercely on. An hour, and the elements ceased to strive, the wailing storm was hushed, and a still but troubled sky looked down upon the scene.

Meanwhile the Fort Sumter garrison coolly prepared for action. Major Anderson divided his command into three reliefs of four hours each, for service at the guns; the first under charge of Captain Doubleday, assisted by Dr. Crawford and Lieutenant Snyder; the second under charge of Captain Seymour, assisted by Lieutenant Hall; and the third under charge of Lieutenant Davis and Lieutenant Meade. The laborers, over forty of whom were in the fort, were appointed to carry ammunition, help make cartridges and assist the gunners where their aid could be available.

All was now ready, every man was in his place, and still, before giving the word to fire, our kind commander walked around to administer his last charge.

"Be careful," he said, "of your lives; make no imprudent exposure of your persons to the enemy's fire; do your duty coolly, determinedly and *cautiously*. Indiscretion is not valor; reckless disregard of life is not bravery. Manifest your loyalty and zeal by preserving yourselves from injury for the continued service of our cause; *and show your love to me by guarding all your powers to aid me through this important duty.*"

This admonition, delivered in sentences, with anxious brow and broken voice, will long be remembered by those who heard it:—no doubt it was the fulcrum sustaining and steadying the power which cast such deadly force from Sumter's walls.

It was just within ten minutes of seven o'clock when the order was given to fire. The first shot was from a forty-two pounder directed against the battery at Cumming's Point. Three of our guns bore upon this point and seven on Fort Moultrie. The famous floating battery—which, by the way, did not float at all, but stuck fast on a point of Sullivan's Island—also received some attention, besides a new battery in the same neighborhood, which had only been unmasked the day previous.

Before our firing commenced—when the storm had cleared off sufficiently to enable us to see around us—we discovered a fleet, which we supposed to be our long-expected succor, outside the bar. The Major signaled them, but the shoals being heavy and the tide low, they could not possibly cross. Shortly after this a fragment of a shell struck and cut through one [of] the flag halliards; but the flag, instead of falling, rose on the wind, and, with a whirl, flung the remaining halliard round the topmast, by which it was held securely all day:— Long live our gallant ensign!

To return. Major Anderson having opened fire continued to pour it forth with good effect. Almost every ball went home. One of the Fort Moultrie guns was soon disabled; the roofs and sides of the building were penetrated by shot; the flag-staff was struck and the flag cut. The floating battery was struck seventeen times; its roof was penetrated, and several shots were sent square through it. The iron battery at Cumming's Point was struck several times, but not much impression was made. Two of its guns, however, were dismounted. The forty-two pound Paixhans of our lower tier worked well: not one of them opened her mouth without giving the enemy cause to shrink, while the ten-inch Columbiads of our second tier meant every word they said. The barbette guns were not manned. Early in the engagement three of them had been fired; but the number of shells descending upon the terreplain of the parapet, and the flanks and faces of the work being taken in reverse by the enemy's batteries rendered the danger of serving in the ramparts so imminent that Major Anderson quickly withdrew his men from them, and kept them in the casemates.

When the cartridges became scarce, the men not engaged at the guns were employed to make them; the sheets and bedding from the hospital being brought out and used for that purpose.

Noon came, yet Fort Sumter was not hurt: the proud stronghold had resisted every effort to do it serious injury. A new species of attack, however, was now resorted to. The solid pile which was impervious to cold ball might feel the influence of *hot shot*, especially as the barracks were constructed mainly of timber; and so a red, hissing shower rushed from Fort Moultrie on this treacherous errand.

The officers' quarters soon caught fire;—the roof of this elegant building, being taller than those adjoining, received the assault first, but the bursting of the cistern, on top, which occurred about the same time, prevented the conflagration from spreading. Still down came the fierce hot shot upon the doomed dwellings, and were it not for the leaking cisterns, each of which had been perforated by ball, the whole would have been quickly consumed.

The ball from the enemy's batteries continued to rattle against the fort, and the latter paid back the compliment with interest. A strong, determined will actuated our men, astonishing to find in so small a number, surrounded and hemmed in by an armament of thousands.

"Aye! there's a great crowd o' them against us!" exclaimed one, as he leaned for a minute behind the column of an embrasure, "but it's the Republic they 're fightin'—not us—and, in the name of the Republic, we 're able for them."

"To be sure we are!" was the hearty response, "seventy

true men to seventy thousand traitors, and the true side is the strongest!"

And at it they kept, loading and firing, firing and re-loading, without stopping for food or repose, except an occasional draught of coffee, to wash the powder from their throats, or a short rest for their weary shoulders against an arch or column.

Nor, all through the exciting day, did the officers ever flag in their duty. Cool, firm, and intrepid, with eyes like eagles, ears quick to hear, and limbs of agile motion, they saw every movement of the enemy, heard their leader's lightest command, and directed each action of their charge with a promptness and energy worthy the important occasion.

The day seemed short, too, full as it was with labor and excitement; and the hearts which beat with hope and enthusiasm heeded not the flight of time. They would fain fight on after day had closed; but the sun went down in lowering gloom, night gathered over us murky and chill, and Major Anderson ordered the firing to cease, and the men to eat some supper and to go to bed.

The only supper they had was a little pork and coffee; but this, with a good sleep, would afford them some refreshment, preparatory to the next day's toil; so they took it cheerfully and laid down.

Still the enemy's fire continued. Even when, at seven o'clock, a mighty storm arose, and rain descended with the force of a cataract, an occasional bomb from one of the batteries mingled with the fury of the elements, as if bidding defiance to nature as well as law.

The condition of the fort was now examined, and the injuries sustained were found to be as follows: The crest of the parapet had been broken in many places; the gorge had been struck by shell and shot, and some of these had pene-

trated the wall to the depth of twelve inches. Several of
the barbette guns had been injured; one had been struck by
a ball and cracked; one was dismounted and two had been
thrown over by a recoil. The lower casemates were uninjured, save one or two embrasures a little broken on the
edges.

But the internal structure had received the most damage
—the *wooden* building which had been treated to hot shot.
Nothing saved it from being consumed but the riddling of
the cisterns which sent the water flowing after the fire as
fast as the red balls kindled it; and now the copious rain
came down to quench every spark that might have remained
in wall or roof.

Yet the pretty edifice was in a sad condition: between fire
and water our pleasant quarters were spoiled.

And here we would say, in parenthesis, to military engineers: Never use timber to build the barracks of a fort, nor
raise the roof of your officers' quarters higher than the outer
wall, unless you calculate upon deserting your colors, turning traitor to your cause, and heading a host in attacking
that very fort. In such case you will find that having used that
material will serve your purpose—as did Beauregard.

That we should be again saluted with hot shot was pretty
certain, and, the cisterns empty and the rain storm over,
nothing could save the wood works from destruction. As
much of the officers' effects as could be removed, were, therefore, carried to the casemates—the privates, many of whom
were now sleeping soundly in their barracks, had not much
to lose.

The next morning rose fair and mild. The rain clouds had
discharged their burden, and now a clear, calm sky looked
down upon the scene. As day broke the firing from the enemy's batteries was resumed, and our garrison arose and

prepared to reply to them. The meagre breakfast of pork and coffee was again partaken, and at seven o'clock Fort Sumter opened fire, which was kept up vigorously during the remainder of the contest.

The first few shots directed at Fort Moultrie sent the chimneys off the officers' quarters, and considerably tore up the roof; nearly a dozen shots penetrated the floating battery below the water line, and several of the guns on Morris Island were disabled. The clear state of the atmosphere to-day enables us to see some of the effects of our fire upon the enemy—*all* the effects we do not expect ever to learn.

As anticipated, hot shot was fired again from Moultrie upon the doomed buildings inside Fort Sumter; and at a little after eight o'clock the officers' quarters were ablaze. All the men, not on duty at the guns, exerted themselves to extinguish the fire, but it spread rapidly, igniting here and there, as the red balls continued to drop, until every portion was in flames.

Attention was now directed to the magazines, which were situated at each of the southern corners of the fort, between the officers' quarters and the barracks. An intimacy with the internal arrangements of the fort had, doubtless, suggested to the gentleman in the opposite command the possibility of blowing up the garrison—hence the clever stratagem of firing the officers' quarters with hot shot; but against this danger Major Anderson provided by ordering all the powder to be taken from the upper magazines, and the lower magazines to be shut tight and thick mounds of earth to be heaped round the doors, through which no amount of heat could penetrate.

Afterwards, when the fire had spread through the barracks and reached the casemates, the Major ordered the powder, which had been removed thither from the magazines, to be thrown into the sea, and ninety barrels were thus disposed of.

As the fire increased the situation of the garrison was distressing beyond description. The water from the cisterns, followed by floods of rain, had saturated the riddled and broken buildings so that they burned with a hissing, smoldering flame, sending forth dense clouds of vapor and smoke, which soon filled the whole fort, rendering it difficult to breathe. The men were often obliged to lie down in the casemates, with wet cloths over their faces, to gain temporary relief.

Still the valiant fellows continued to serve their guns, and bomb after bomb, resounding from Sumter's walls, told that the spirit of American loyalty was not to be subdued, even by fire.

About half past twelve o'clock our flag-staff, which had been grazed several times, was shot through and the flag fell. Down, amid burning brands, surrounded by smoke and ruin, our war-worn ensign lay.

It was but a moment, and the next our young Lieutenant, Mr. Hall, rushed through the fire and, dashing all impediments out of his way, seized the prostrate colors. A buzz of admiration, mingled with words of fear for the officer's safety, and every man started forward, straining his eyes through the smoke until the object of quest emerged to view, begrimed with soot, choking and faint, his face and hair singed, his clothes scorched, and holding aloft, with almost spent strength, the rescued flag. A weak, but heartfelt cheer, from parched throats, greeted him as the precious burden was taken from his blistered hands, and he sunk down exhausted.

When the fire was all spent, the gay dwelling in ashes, and the noble fort was silent—standing, proud as ever, in stern,

strong nakedness—Mr. Hall's epaulets were found on the
spot from which he had raised the flag. In rushing through
the fire they had become heated, and, oppressing his shoulders, he tore them off. They were now burnt—all but one
little bunch of gold wire, which was embedded in ashes.
That little relic is in the writer's possession; treasured as
one of the precious trifles belonging to History's store-
house.

In fifteen minutes from the fall of the flag it was up again;
a jury-mast was hastily raised, to which it was nailed, and it
floated out as before. The honor of nailing it up belongs to
Mr. Peter Hart, a New York gentleman, who had come to
Fort Sumter some time before, to visit Major Anderson, with
whom he had served in the Mexican war, and had remained
at the fort as his guest. Though he took no part in the actual
battle, yet he made himself useful to the garrison in many
ways, of which this, recorded, is not the least.

And still the fire raged within and the cannon roared without. The flames increased in strength and volume, the air
became heated all through the fort; but the more the little
garrison suffered the harder they fought, and each ball that
flew from their embrasures performed its errand well.

At about half past one P. M. a boat was seen approaching
from Cumming's Point. Arrived at Fort Sumter a gentleman
sprang from it, and, with a white handkerchief tied to the
point of his sword to represent a flag of truce, he ran up to
a port-hole, which he entered, saying to a soldier, whom he
met,

"I wish to see the commandant—my name is Wigfall, and
I come from General Beauregard."

The soldier went to inform Major Anderson, and Mr. Wigfall passed into the casemate where he met Captain Foster
and Lieutenant Davis. To them he also introduced himself,

stating that he came from General Beauregard. Then he added excitedly:

"Let us stop this firing. You are on fire, and your flag is down—let us quit!"

Mr. Davis replied,

"No, Sir, our flag is not down. Step out here and you will see it waving over the ramparts."

He ran out and looked up, but the smoke filled his eyes and he exclaimed, impatiently extending his sword:

"Here's a white flag,—will any body wave it out of the embrasure?"

Captain Foster said one of the men might do so, and Corporal Bingham, who was present, took it in his hand and jumped into the embrasure. And so the first white flag that waved from Fort Sumter was Senator Wigfall's handkerchief, tied to the point of that gentleman's sword!

But the firing still continued, when Mr. Wigfall said:

"If you will show a white flag from your ramparts, they will cease firing."

Captain Foster replied:

"If you request that a white flag shall appear there while you hold a conference with Major Anderson, and for that purpose alone, Major Anderson may permit it."

Major Anderson, at that moment came up, and the white flag was ordered to be raised.

"Major Anderson," said Mr. Wigfall, "you have defended your flag nobly, Sir. You have done all that is possible for man to do, and General Beauregard wishes to stop the fight. On what terms, Major Anderson, will you evacuate this fort?"

"Terms?" said Major Anderson, raising himself to his full height, and speaking with emphasis, *I shall evacuate on the most honorable terms, or—die here!*"

Mr. Wigfall inclined his head;—respect for the glorious soul in that slight, frail form could not be withheld by even an enemy.

"Will you, Major Anderson," he then asked, "evacuate this fort upon the terms proposed to you the other day?"

"On the terms *last proposed* I will," was the reply.

"Then, Sir, I understand that the fort is to be ours?"

"On those conditions *only*, I repeat."

"Well, Sir, I will return to General Beauregard," said Mr. Wigfall, and, bowing low, he retired.

The white flag was then hauled down, and the American flag run up.

The Major now ordered that the firing should not be renewed, but that the men should take such refreshment as they had and rest a while. Poor fellows! they were nearly exhausted. Those who had not been engaged at the guns had been toiling to subdue the fire; and faint for lack of food, and suffocating with smoke, it was only their giant hearts sustained them through.

When the flames were at the highest the enemy blazed away the faster, in order to cut down the men who were working to extinguish the fire; but a Divine shield was over them, and *not one life of the gallant First was taken by traitor hands.*

Some "own correspondent" stated that the Major sent men outside the fort on a raft to procure water wherewith to quench the fire:—nonsense; there was plenty of water inside for the purpose, if there had only been hands enough to use it; but the guns must be kept manned, so only those who could be spared from that duty gave attention to the burning buildings.

Their exertions, however, were sufficient to prevent explosions and disaster to life. The fire was kept under, and prevented from communicating with the magazines, until every ounce of powder was removed out of our reach also, for, when hostilities ceased, we had but four barrels and three cartridges on hand.

But the fire had done its work, and was now gradually burning out. The barracks and officers' quarters were destroyed; and as the smoke thinned away, so that the eye could penetrate the scene, nothing but charred and smoldering ruins were visible.

About three o'clock P. M. a formal deputation came to Major Anderson from General Beauregard and Governor Pickens, proposing the same terms as had been previously offered, except that they were not willing the Major should salute his flag.

To this Major Anderson would not consent.

About six o'clock came another deputation, consisting of Colonel Pryor, Colonel Miles, Major Jones, and Captain Hartstene, and presented to Major Anderson General Beauregard's final terms. They were as follows. The garrison to march out with their side and other arms, with all the honors, in their own way and at their own time; to salute their flag and take it with them, and to take all their individual and company property; the enemy also agreeing to furnish transports, as Major Anderson might select, to any part of the country, either by land or water.

With all this Major Anderson was satisfied except the last clause. He would not consent to accept traveling accommodations from the enemy beyond the use of a steam-tug to convey him to the Government vessels outside the bar. . . .

And now all was arranged according to the Major's dictation, nothing remained but for the garrison to pack their effects and prepare to depart. This occupied great part of the night, and the next morning a Charleston steamer was in attendance to convey them to the fleet. The baggage was placed on board, then the men were drawn up under arms, on the parade, and a portion told off, as gunners, to salute their flag.

And now came the last solemn ceremony, to end even more solemnly than we expected. The guns began to fire. One after another their loud voices rolled out upon the Sabbath air until fifty were counted, and then—an explosion, a cry, a rush, and every gun was silent. A pile of cartridges, containing eighty pounds of powder, had been laid inside the bomb-proof, on the parapet, convenient to one of the guns. Among these cartridges a spark had fallen, and while the guns were firing, and the soldiers cheering, the powder exploded, tearing the strong sheets of iron, of which the bomb-proof was composed, into fragments, and scattering them abroad like feathers, at the same time sending a shock —a thrill of horror to every heart, for a group of men had been standing round, and Oh! where were they now?

A few moments and anxious faces were gathered to the scene of the disaster:—sad scene!—one of our brave fellows was dead—quite dead—rent almost in two; another was dying —fractured in every limb; another yet so mutilated that the Doctor only shook his head, and six others more or less injured.

The departure of the garrison was, of course, delayed by this accident—the dead and the wounded must be cared for; yet the process of evacuation must be concluded, and so, while with tender hands and moist eyes the soldiers removed their bleeding comrades, the flag, in vindicating whose honor this warm blood was spilt, drooped its proud pinions and slowly descended from the ramparts.

All that men in their circumstances could do was then done by the garrison for the dead and wounded: the former was prepared for decent burial, the latter tended with the kindest care.

The enemy, impatient to take possession of the fort, now arrived. Governor Pickens and General Beauregard with their aids landed and entered, but, seeing what had occurred, immediately tendered every assistance. A minister was accordingly sent for to Charleston, to perform the service for the dead, and physicians to take charge of those whom we should be obliged to leave behind living. Meanwhile a strong coffin was put together, a grave dug in the parade, and, shortly after the clergyman arrived, the funeral proceeded.

With military honors the scarcely cold remains were buried: the Major heading the procession with crape upon his sword. With the rites of the Church the coffin was lowered into the grave, and, awaiting the resurrection, when the justice of every cause shall be righteously proved, Daniel Howe was left sleeping in Fort Sumter.

The wounded men, all but two who were quite unfit to bear the voyage, were then removed to the steamer. These, under promise of the kindest treatment, were trusted to the hospitality of the South Carolinians; one of them, George Fielding was, therefore, conveyed to the Charleston Hospital, the other, Edward Galway, whose hours were numbered, was made as comfortable as possible in the fort.

These sad details arranged, Major Anderson issued his final orders for embarkation; and, carrying their flag and even its shattered mast, with band playing *Yankee Doodle*, the garrison marched out of the fort and went on board the steamer. As the Major emerged from the gate the music changed into *Hail to the Chief*:—simple tribute but no less heart-felt!

It was now late in the afternoon, and the garrison had eaten nothing since their scanty breakfast of pork and coffee;

it would, therefore, have been most desirable to have got out on board the transport without delay; but the state of the tide was such that the little steamer could not move, and all night she lay under the walls of Fort Sumter. Had they had only their own discomforts to think of, they would have felt more the inconveniences of that long delay without food or resting places; but thoughts of their dying comrade in the fort, whose groans almost reached their ears, filled their minds, even to the exclusion of self. Before they left, however, the sufferer was released. An officer came on board the steamer to inform Major Anderson of the death of Edward Galway, and to assure him that the deceased should be buried beside Howe, with the honors due to a brave soldier. . . .

Early on Monday morning, April 15th, with the rising of the tide, the Isabel, on board which our garrison lay, steamed out of the Charleston waters to where the United States vessels lay, waiting to receive the gallant freight. The little band were welcomed with cheers by the fleet, and the Baltic, on board which they were taken, felt honored by their presence. Every preparation had been made for their comfort, and nothing that could be done to atone for their past privation was neglected.

The Sumter flag, which had floated over the Isabel, was immediately hoisted on the Baltic, and a salute fired; and then Major Anderson was observed to bow his head and weep.

What, tears? Yes, Reader, tears! We don't conceal the fact. Great men can *feel*. It was told of Xerxes—why not tell it of our own loved hero? He looked up at his flag, tattered and begrimed, yet free as ever; he looked round at his comrades, wan and weary, but with hearts of stoutest metal, and emotion mastered him—he bowed his head and wept.

The Baltic was soon under weigh; and, after a pleasant run of three days reached Sandy Hook, where she was boarded by the Medical Staff from Staten Island, and quite a crowd of gentlemen who had come in boats, from New York, to meet her.

Here Major Anderson wrote the following dispatch to the War Department.

> "STEAMSHIP BALTIC, off SANDY HOOK,
>   "Thursday, April 18, 1861.

"*Hon. S. Cameron, Secretary of War, Washington, D. C.:*
"SIR:—Having defended Fort Sumter for thirty-four hours, until the quarters were entirely burned, the main gates destroyed by fire, the gorge wall seriously injured, the magazine surrounded by flames, and its door closed from the effect of the heat, four barrels and three cartridges of powder only being available, and no provisions but pork remaining, I accepted terms of evacuation, offered by General Beauregard, being the same offered by him on the 11th instant, prior to the commencement of hostilities, and marched out of the fort, Sunday afternoon, the 14th instant, with colors flying and drums beating, bringing away company and private property, and saluting my flag with fifty guns.

> "ROBERT ANDERSON,
>   "Major First Artillery."

It was a bright, sunny day as the Baltic steamed up New York Harbor, saluted by the firing of cannon from the forts, and by the ringing of bells and waving of flags from the city as she approached. The late garrison of Fort Sumter was drawn up on her quarter-deck, considerably restored in appearance by good food and rest; and the Major, surrounded by his officers, stood on the wheel-house, still looking pale and care-worn, his expressive features quivering with emotion as he acknowledged the salutations of the people.

All is now told—as far as a hasty sketch can tell it—of what transpired within Fort Sumter: of the energy, courage and determined will which sustained that little garrison to the last. And now you talk of promoting Major Anderson:—*promote Major Anderson!*—Could you promote the lion among beasts—the eagle among birds? could you exalt Sorata among mountains, or dignify the Amazon among streams? could you give distinction to the North Star, or brighten the sunbeam? as well might you attempt to elevate one who has arisen on the pinions of his own grand spirit to the hilltop of glory. No, fellow-countrymen, *you can not promote Major Anderson!* You can give no higher rank to the premier of his contemporaries—you can confer no prouder title on the HERO OF CHARLESTON HARBOR.

Cheer, Boys, Cheer

"WHAT A DEARTH we have in America," wrote George F. Noyes in 1863 in his *Bivouac and Battlefield*, "of good common songs! I have heard fire companies returning from a fire actually compelled to sandwich a good old hymn between two bacchanalian refrains, having quite exhausted their favorite melodies. 'We are bound for the land of Canaan' does not flow naturally from a great two-fisted, red-shirted fellow, nor could I ever enjoy hearing a crowd of roughs yelling out at the top of their lungs, 'I want to be an angel,' especially if they qualified each verse with an intermediate dash of oaths. In all seriousness, that man would be a public benefactor who would give our soldiers some simple patriotic songs, each with a good chorus, to lighten their weary marches and cheer their evening camp fires."

Many tried, but it was not until later in the war that Charles Carroll Sawyer, George F. Root, and Henry Clay Work really succeeded. In the meantime there was no dearth of songsters in which every conceivable tune was set with new words for the times. Here is Dan Emmett's

"Dixie" (in 1861 not yet completely a Southern song) with patriotic verses.

VICTORY'S BAND.
Air—*Dixie's Land.*

We're marching under the Flag of Union,
Keeping step in brave communion!
March away! march away! away! Victory's band
Right down upon the ranks of rebels,
Tramp them underfoot like pebbles,
March away! march away! away! Victory's band

CHORUS

Oh! we're marching on to Victory!
Hurrah! hurrah!
In Victory's band we'll sweep the land,
And fight or die for Victory!
Away! away!
We'll fight or die for Victory!

The rebels want a mongrel nation,
Union and Confederation!
March away! march away! away! Victory's band!
But we don't trust in things two-sided,
And go for Union undivided,
March away! march away! away! Victory's band!
Oh! we're marching, etc.

We're marching down on Dixie's regions,
With Freedom's flag and Freedom's legions.
March away! march away! away! Victory's band!
We're rolling down, a "Pending Crisis,"
With cannon-balls for Compromises,
March away! march away! away! Victory's band!
Oh! we're marching, etc.

Along the Border

THE NEW CONFEDERACY hoped to extend its domain over all the slaveholding states. To its first tier of states of the Deep South, Arkansas, Tennessee, North Carolina, and Virginia were added as the spring of 1861 progressed. There were vigorous secession elements in Maryland, Kentucky, and Missouri. Maryland was retained in the Union by forceful political action. Kentucky tried to remain neutral until it was too late for the Southern sympathizers to swing it to the Confederacy. Firm military action in Missouri soon put down the rebellious minority there.

These two pieces demonstrate the state of affairs on the border. First is the *Address to the People of Maryland by the General Assembly* of April 27, 1861. Next are two proclamations of General William S. Harney to the people of Missouri.

TO THE PEOPLE OF MARYLAND.

Resolved, by the Senate and House of Delegates,

That the "extraordinary state of affairs" in Maryland and the Republic, justifies and demands that we should adopt and publish the following Address to the People of Maryland:

Under the Proclamation of your Governor, we have assembled to act, according to our best judgments, for the true interest of Maryland.

That Proclamation has declared the present to be "an extraordinary state of affairs;" and all must admit the correctness of that assertion. We have been convened to do all that we have the constitutional authority and the mental ability of accomplishing, to provide for your safety and welfare during the pendency of the present unfortunate and terrible crisis. At the commencement of our labors, we feel it to be our duty to you and to your General Assembly to solicit your confidence in the fidelity with which our responsibilities will be discharged. We are Marylanders, as you are. We have families, as you have. Our interests are identified with yours. Our duty, our wishes and our hopes will be to legislate for the true interests of all the people of our State.

We cannot but know that a large proportion of the citizens of Maryland have been induced to believe that there is a probability that our deliberations may result in the passage of some measure committing this State to secession. It is, therefore, our duty to declare that all such fears are without just foundation. We know that we have no constitutional authority to take such action. You need not fear that there is a possibility that we will do so.

If believed by us to be desired by you, we may, by legislation to that effect, give you the opportunity of deciding for yourselves, your own future destiny. We may go thus far, but certainly will not go farther.

We know that the present crisis has materially deranged the usual current of business operations in every department. We shall devote ourselves to the duty of making this change as little inconvenient as possible to our constituents. We invite their scrutiny to our every action. If results do not realise our hopes and anticipations, we ask that you will, at least, extend to us the charity of believing that the failure has occurred from lack of ability, but not of will.

JNO. B. BROOKE,	JAMES F. DASHIELL,
THOMAS J. McKAIG,	J. J. HECKART,
COLEMAN YELLOTT,	S. J. BRADLEY,
H. H. GOLDSBOROUGH,	TILGHMAN NUTTLE,
D. C. BLACKISTONE,	F. WHITAKER,
C. F. GOLDSBOROUGH,	OSCAR MILES,
JNO. E. SMITH,	WASHINGTON DUVALL,
ANTHONY KIMMEL,	TEAGLE TOWNSEND,
J. S. WATKINS,	ANDREW A. LYNCH.

MILITARY DEPARTMENT OF THE WEST,
St. Louis, Missouri, May 12, 1861.
To the people of the State of Missouri and the city of
St. Louis:

I have just returned to this post, and have assumed the military command of this department. No one can more deeply regret the deplorable state of things existing here than myself. The past cannot be recalled. I can only deal with the present and the future. I most anxiously desire to discharge the delicate and onerous duties devolved upon me so as to preserve the public peace. I shall carefully abstain from the exercise of any unnecessary powers, and from all interference with the proper functions of the public offi-

cers of the State and city. I therefore call upon the public
authorities and the people to aid me in preserving the public
peace.

The military force stationed in this department by authority of the government, and now under my command, will
only be used in the last resort to preserve the peace.

I trust I may be spared the necessity of resorting to martial law, but the public peace *must be preserved,* and the
lives and property of the people protected.

Upon a careful review of my instructions, I find I have no
authority to change the location of the "Home Guards."

To avoid all cause of irritation and excitement, if called
upon to aid the local authorities in preserving the public
peace, I shall, in preference, make use of the regular army.

I ask the people to pursue their peaceful avocations, and
to observe the laws and orders of their local authorities, and
to abstain from the excitements of public meetings and
heated discussions. My appeal, I trust, may not be in vain,
and I pledge the faith of a soldier to the earnest discharge
of my duty.

WM. S. HARNEY,
Brigadier General U. S. A., Comd'g Department.
HEADQUARTERS DEPARTMENT OF THE WEST,
St. Louis, Missouri, May 13, 1861.

Official copy.

S. WILLIAMS,
Assistant Adjutant General.

MILITARY DEPARTMENT OF THE WEST,
St. Louis, Missouri, May 14, 1861.
To the people of the State of Missouri:

On my return to the duties of the command of this department, I find, greatly to my astonishment and mortification,

a most extraordinary state of things existing in this State, deeply affecting the stability of the government of the United States, as well as the government and other interests of Missouri itself.

As a citizen of Missouri, owing allegiance to the United States, and having interests in common with you, I feel it my duty, as well as privilege, to extend a warning voice to my fellow-citizens against the common dangers that threaten us, and to appeal to your patriotism and sense of justice to exert all your moral powers to avert them.

It is with regret that I feel it my duty to call your attention to the recent act of the general assembly of Missouri, known as the military bill, which is the result, no doubt, of the temporary excitement that now pervades the public mind.

This bill cannot be regarded in any other light than an indirect secession ordinance, ignoring even the forms resorted to by other States. Manifestly its most material provisions are in conflict with the Constitution and laws of the United States. To this extent it is a nullity, and cannot, and ought not, to be upheld or regarded by the good citizens of Missouri. There are obligations and duties resting upon the people of Missouri under the Constitution and laws of the United States which are paramount, and which, I trust, you will carefully consider and weigh well before you will allow yourselves to be carried out of the Union, under the form of yielding obedience to this military bill, which is clearly in violation of your duties as citizens of the United States.

It must be apparent to every one who has taken a proper and unbiased view of the subject, that whatever may be the termination of the unfortunate condition of things in respect to the so-called "Cotton States," Missouri must share the destiny of the *Union*. Her geographical position, her soil, productions, and, in short, all her material interests, point to this result. We cannot shut our eyes against this controlling fact. It is seen, and its force is felt throughout the nation.

So important is this regarded to the great interests of the country, that I venture to express the opinion that the whole power of the government of the United States, if necessary, will be exerted to maintain Missouri in her present position in the Union. I express to you, in all frankness and sincerity, my own deliberate convictions, without assuming to speak for the government of the United States, whose authority, here and elsewhere, I shall at all times, and under all circumstances, endeavor faithfully to uphold.

I desire above all things most earnestly to invite my fellow-citizens dispassionately to consider their true interests as well as their true relation to the government under which we live and to which we owe so much.

In this connexion, I desire to direct attention to one subject which no doubt will be made the pretext for more or less popular excitement. I allude to the recent transactions at Camp Jackson, near St. Louis. It is not proper for me to comment upon the official conduct of my predecessor in command of this department, but it is right and proper for the people of Missouri to know that the main avenue of Camp Jackson, recently under command of General Frost, had the name of *Davis,* and a principal street of the same camp that of Beauregard; and that a body of men had been received into that camp by its commander which had been notoriously organized in the interests of the secessionists, the men openly wearing the dress and badge distinguishing the army of the so-called Southern Confederacy. It is also a notorious fact that a quantity of arms had been received into the camp which were unlawfully taken from the United States arsenal at Baton Rouge, and surreptitiously passed up the river in boxes marked marble.

Upon facts like these, and having in view what occurred at Liberty, the people can draw their own inferences, and it cannot be difficult for any one to arrive at a correct conclusion as to the character and ultimate purpose of that encampment. No government in the world would be entitled to respect that would tolerate for a moment such openly treasonable preparations.

It is but simple justice, however, that I should state the fact that there were many good and loyal men in the camp who were in no manner responsible for its treasonable character.

Disclaiming, as I do, all desire or intention to interfere in any way with the prerogatives of the State of Missouri, or with the functions of its executive or other authorities, yet I regard it as my plain path of duty to express to the people in respectful, but at the same time decided language, that within the field and scope of my command and authority the "*supreme law*" of the land must and shall be maintained, and no subterfuges, whether in the forms of legislative acts or otherwise, can be permitted to harass or oppress the good and law-abiding people of Missouri. I shall exert my authority to protect their persons and property from violations of every kind, and I shall deem it my duty to suppress all unlawful combinations of men, whether formed under pretext of military organizations or otherwise.

WILLIAM S. HARNEY,
Brigadier General United States Army, Commanding.

Rebels Ahead!

THE SPRING OF 1861 was a time of preparation. There were no big battles. Men were being enlisted and trained for war. But they had little idea what was ahead of them.

Real war broke with sudden fury at Manassas in July, 1861. Confident Federal soldiers were turned back by the Confederates in a defeat humiliating for its unexpectedness.

The naïveté of the recruit, new to the army and new to battle, is apparent in this letter Allen A. Kingsbury of Medfield, Massachusetts, wrote his parents shortly after the battle. The wounded soldier did soon receive a leave but returned to the army in September and was killed in the Peninsular campaign the next April. His letters and his journal were printed in 1862 as *The Hero of Medfield*.

ARLINGTON HEIGHTS, JULY 25, 1861.

My Dear Parents:

Yesterday we moved from Camp Banks across the river to this place, which is just below Washington, and between Forts Corcoran and Albany. To-morrow our regiment will go to Fort Albany, which is about a mile from here. It is one of the outposts, and a very pleasant place; it commands the long bridge, the road from Fairfax to Washington, and the Potomac. It is in fact the post of *honor!*

I will now give you a description of our march to the field of battle, and of the battle itself. Tuesday, July 16, orders came to pack our knapsacks, and prepare to march. We rolled our rubber and flannel blankets up together and slung them across our shoulders in light marching order, filled our canteens with water and our haversacks with hard bread and salt pork for three days' rations. I put some coffee and sugar into my pocket for my own use, and it came very convenient, as we shall see. We left our knapsacks in the care of the sick and those who were not able to march. We started from camp about 4, P. M; went past the Michigan regiment's camp; they went with us. There were four regiments, the Mass. 1st, the Michigan 2d and 3d, and the N. Y. 12th. We were under command of Col. Richardson and Gen. Tyler. The first place of interest which we past was the chain bridge across the Potomac. It is quite long; on the hill above it are several cannon, in the centre of the bridge is a draw and a gate covered with wrought iron, with *port holes* through which to fire the cannon. The bridge is also fixed so that when a crowd of rebels get upon it, it can be pulled and precipitate them into the river, which is about thirty feet from the bridge, and is very rocky. As soon as we filed off the bridge our band struck up "Yankee Doodle." As we stepped upon the "sacred soil of Virginia" we marched at quick time, and there was some *cheering* I can tell you; but we little knew what we were to pass through. We marched on, however, over some of the worst roads I ever saw, worse, if possible, than the road to the top of Noon Hill. The roads are full of stones and gullies. Virginia is indeed a desolate country; most of the buildings are built of logs, the logs are hewed on the sides and placed above the other, and the cracks are filled in with mortar or mud; the chimnies are built on the outside, they are composed of large stones. Again I say it is a rough looking country; but I never saw black-berries so thick before. Would frequently "fall out of ranks," hop over the fence (Virginia fence) and pick our tin pots full in a very few moments, and then such large ones, it was perfect fun to pick them, and not at all unpleasant to eat them. We marched till 10, P. M., when we halted for the night. We camped on a low, marshy piece of ground in a place called Vienna, where the rebels fired upon the Ohio volunteers. We got to sleep about 11, P. M., we were so tired we did not eat any supper. We arose at sunrise next morning, prepared our breakfast of hard bread, salt pork, and cold water, but I had a cup of coffee, owing to the fore-sight of putting some in my pocket. We got under way as soon as possible. Saw the cars which contained the above soldiers when they were attacked by the rebels, the cars were riddled with bullet holes. The boys in my tent went out "*grubbing*" and brought in *peaches* and potatoes, so we had *peach sauce,* soft bread and new potatoes; quite a treat for us *half starved men!* We then proceeded on our march; were very much troubled for the want of water. I never suf-fered so much from thirst before. When we came to a brook or spring the soldiers would break their ranks and run for the water, but it was mostly so muddy and rily that it was hardly fit to drink, but yet it was *water!* Our regiment headed the column. As we came upon the top of a hill it was a splendid sight to look as far as we could and see the road filled with soldiers, horses and wagons. We went through places where the rebels had had their camps and where they had felled the trees across the road to prevent us from passing, but they were soon cut away by our pioneers, who went ahead armed with guns and axes. We stopped that afternoon at 3 o'clock, in a fine place where we staid all night; there were 60,000 or 70,000 troops around us. We marched about ten miles that day (Wednesday), and then I had to go on *picket guard* all night; had about *one* hour's sleep; very good after marching all day.

We were placed in a piece of wood with orders to fire upon any one who should not halt and tell who he was. We did not see any one, but could hear people walking about in the woods. We got into camp about sunrise Thursday morning, found the boys all alive and stirring about getting breakfast and preparing to march. I made some nice coffee, which went first rate. At 8, A. M., we started; as we went along saw places where the rebels had had their camp; near noon we came to places where their camp fires were burning. In some places they had cooked dinner, but in their hurry to leave they had thrown it away. In one place a wagon loaded with flour was stuck fast in the mud; they had unloaded it, stove in the heads of the barrels and left the flour in the road. We were hurried forward as fast as we could go. Between 1 and 2, P. M., we stopped to reconnoitre and to send scouts ahead. In about half an hour they returned and reported *rebels ahead!* We were up in a hurry, and two Co.'s of infantry and one of cavalry were sent forward. When we ascended a hill we could see men in a field about a mile distant—we could see the glittering of their bayonets. The General sent back for three pieces of artillery; when they were ready we opened fire upon them; you ought to have seen how they scattered and run into the woods. We fired some three or four rounds among them, when very suddenly a battery opened upon our left about a mile from us. We were then ordered about, and taking a circle came out at the left of our battery. We were then ordered into a field near some woods. Two Co.'s, G. and H., with our pioneers who had been ahead, commenced firing. Our Co. and Co. G. were then ordered into the woods; we did not know what was there, but we soon found out. We had got perhaps three rods into the woods when a murderous fire was opened upon us by the rebels from a masked battery; several of our men were killed and wounded. Three of my comrades fell dead at my side. Our Capt. then ordered us ahead, and on we went. I saw a battery on a small hill. I saw an officer on the embankment beside a cannon; I brought my rifle to my shoulder and fired at him. He threw up his arms and fell headlong down the bank. A perfect volley of rifle shot then rained around me; one bullet struck me on the breast, went through my blanket and hit the eagle on my cross belt, and knocked me down. Another ball cut off my cap box. Our Capt. then ordered a retreat, and we started for the open ground. The balls fell like hailstones around us, but I did not mind them; was as cool as ice. When I had got out of the woods and was walking along, a cannon ball struck the ground about a rod behind me, and rebounding, hit me in the joint of the knee, upon the under side, and knocked me down. I did not know where I was for several minutes. When I got up I could not stand. Two of the N. Y. 69th took me up and carried me to the wagons. I did not think I was hurt much, but I found I could not walk, so I was carried to the hospital at Centreville, where I staid till Sunday, when I went out to join my Co., but they would not let me, so I remained with the wagons. At 5, P. M., an order came for the wagons to retreat back towards Fairfax. I got on board one of the wagons, rode all night, and next morning found myself in Washington. I am quite lame now, so that I don't go round much. I do not know what they will do with me. *I shall try to get home* if I can. No more this time. *Don't worry about me!* Love to all.

ALLEN.

War in the West

Men from the great new states of the Northwest as eagerly volunteered as did the Yankees of New England. Their war was a different war, scattered over the plains west of the Mississippi, but no less war.

Henry O'Conner, in introducing his *History of the First Regiment of Iowa Volunteers,* addressed a letter to the Hon. S. J. Kirkwood, Governor of Iowa. In part, he wrote:

"The news of the fall of Fort Sumpter, on the twelfth of April 1861, although not wholly unexpected, aroused the people to a sense of the deep wrong and insult suffered by the nation and its flag. The proclamation of the President immediately following, called for seventy-five thousand volunteer troops, and apportioned to Iowa one regiment. The patriotism of the people, and the no less patriotic and prompt action of the State Government, furnished the regiment, clothed and ready for the field, at the designated point of rendezvous, (Keokuk,) within thirty days from the date of the President's proclamation; the chief embarrassment of the government and the principal disappointment of our citizens being in the fact that thousands who responded to the call and who have since proven their devotion to the cause of their country, could not then enter the service.

"The regiment, after its organization, spent five weeks in camp at Keokuk, preparing by company and battalion drill and the discipline of camp life, for the brief, severe, but glorious campaign which they afterwards went through in Missouri, with so much credit to themselves and honor to the State of Iowa.

"When General Lyon moved from St. Louis up the Missouri river to meet the rebel forces of Jackson and Price, then in position near Booneville, orders were sent to Iowa for what troops were ready, to proceed to Hannibal and thence across the country to the Missouri river at such point as he might be. Colonel Curtis, with his (the second) regiment, then at Keokuk, having received orders from the War Department for special service on the Hannibal and St. Joseph Railroad, moved on the twelfth of June at mid-night; and on the thirteenth, the day following, with four hours' notice, the First Regiment, under command of Colonel Bates, struck their tents at Camp Ellsworth, and embarked on two steamboats for Hannibal."

How life was in this Western campaign is related in O'Conner's letter of July 16.

CAMP SIGEL, GREEN COUNTY, MISSOURI,
Ten miles N. W. of Springfield, July 16, 1861.

FRIEND MAHIN: I am so much of a stranger to the *Journal* of late, that I scarcely know how to approach it. I am, as you see, very particular in dating my letter, not that there will be anything new to you in what I have to say, but that such of your readers as feel interested in the doings and misdoings of the First Iowa Regiment, may take map in hand and follow us through our long and somewhat tedious march; and perhaps some of them may wish to preserve it. I can vouch for its accuracy—elegance of style, of course, you cannot expect, when you consider that I am sitting *tailor fashion*, with the tail-board of a wagon across my knees for a writing desk, in a noisy camp of six thousand men, and over two thousand horses and mules—drums beating, fifes squealing, mules braying, horses neighing, men swearing, singing, and doing every thing but praying.

We are now encamped near the summit of the Ozark mountains, in a beautiful region, and what is still better, surrounded by a warm-hearted, Union-loving people, who are ready and willing to make any sacrifice for our beloved country. The soil is rich, but full of lime-stones, which show themselves on the surface of the ground about as thick as onions in Scott county, to the great annoyance of plowmen, and the especial annoyance of us poor devils who have to sleep on them every night. However, I must not get in advance of my story.

We left Keokuk, June thirteenth, thence to Hannibal by boat, next moving by rail to Macon City, thence to Renick by rail, thirty miles, where we remained one night, and commenced our march to Booneville. This is the point at which some unfriendly correspondent of the *Gate City* says we took to the woods and got cut off, a statement no less injudicious than erroneous, as I have no doubt it caused many a tear to be shed about our hearth-stones at home. We made the march to Booneville, fifty-eight miles, in two days and three hours, on three meals, and that it was a good one we need no better evidence than General Lyon's expression to Colonel Bates, that he knew of no better march even by regular soldiers. We staid in Camp Cameron, at Booneville, till the morning of the third of July, when, as a part of General Lyon's command, we started on our march for south-western Missouri, to any point where we could lay our hands on the traitor Jackson. We made what is usually denominated forced marches, twenty-four miles a day—except one day, when it poured down a drenching rain on us, we marched eighteen miles—the Iowa boys at the head of the column, with mud and water running off them in the shape of a mixture of rain and sweat—company A in the van singing national airs, under the leadership of that little nightingale from your office, Emerson O. Upham, who, by the way, has shown himself to be one of the toughest and best soldiers in the regiment. When we had marched eighteen miles and left the two Missouri regiments forty-five minutes behind, and their men dropping by the road-side by the score, the surgeon of Colonel Boernstein's regiment rode in a gallop to the head of the column, and told the General that unless he halted the column he would kill all the Missouri men. We halted right in the rain. The rain held up in an hour or two; we built a fire, dried our clothes on us, (the best way always to save taking cold,) got our supper of some healthy crackers and good coffee, ran round like antelopes, and in the evening, to the surprise of every one, and to the terror of the St. Louis boys, we had a skirmish drill. I believe it was at this point that General Lyon, who first called us Gipsies because of our ragged and dirty appearance, christened us the "Iowa Grey Hounds."

At Grand River, in Henry county, we came up with Colonel Sturgis' command, consisting of two volunteer regiments from Kansas, five hundred regulars, and four pieces of artillery, which, joined to our force of twenty-five hundred troops, put General Lyon at the head of a column of six thousand, with ten pieces of artillery. Crossing Grand river with such a force of men, wagons and horses, on a rickety old ferry boat, was, as you can perceive, a tedious process. It was prosecuted night and day, and the whole column taken over without a single accident to man or beast. We marched from there to the Osage river, at a point ten miles south-west of Osceola. Here, again, we had to go through the disagreeable process of crossing the troops on about the meanest thing in the shape of a ferry boat that I ever saw. But General Lyon was there, and the thing had to go ahead.

Just before starting over the river in the evening, some Union men came into camp and gave information to the General of about eight hundred secessionists being encamped at a point about twelve miles off. Colonel Bates was ordered to detail from his regiment a sufficient force to take them or break them up. Five companies—A, C, D, F and K— were accordingly detailed for that purpose, and got all ready to start, under command of Major Porter, silently, as soon as it was dark; when suddenly, and to the great disappointment of the boys, the order was countermanded. It appeared that a messenger had just arrived from Springfield with the intelligence that Colonel Sigel's command, of about fifteen hundred, were in Springfield surrounded by about eight thousand seccessionists, under the lead of Claib. Jackson nominally, but Ben. McCulloch really, for Jackson is not fit to lead a blind horse to water. He is a coward as well as a traitor. This news, of course, stirred up the old General, who seemed to feel sure of his game this time, having missed Jackson at Booneville.

We went on with the crossing, and got our regiment over by four o'clock in the morning; no sleep, with orders to march at five; made fires, hurried up our breakfast, swallowed it, and started at quarter past five. This was our great march, kept up through a hot sun until three o'clock. We camped, got supper, and at half-past five, when we were thinking of fixing our beds, the General's bugle sounded a forward march. Off we started, and after measuring off forty-five miles in twenty-two hours—recollect with the loss of two nights' sleep, and only three hours' rest—we fetched up in a corn-field, on the bank of a pretty stream; corn reeking with heavy dew, ground muddy from recent rains, men shivering, sleepy and hungry. We were ordered to get our breakfasts, what sleep we could, and be ready to march in two hours. Springfield, still thirty-five miles off, must be reached to-night. Of course, in this long march a great many fell back exhausted, but most of our regiment came up within an hour. Many dropped down in the wet and mud and went to sleep; some went to making a fire and stirring round to prevent chilling—myself among the latter. In a little over three hours we had got breakfast, sleep, rest, &c., &c., and were again on our weary, swinging march, but with many sore feet. We thought of nothing, however, but coming up with Jackson, when lo! after we had gone about five miles, the General received the news of Jackson's defeat by Sigel, and his subsequent hasty flight. Of course this rendered any more forced marching unnecessary; so after marching a few miles farther to a good creek, we encamped for the day, cooked, slept, washed ourselves, our shirts, &c. Next day,

Saturday, we marched to this place, where we have rested ever since.

We spend our time very pleasantly. The intervals between drill and parade are spent in looking up some delicacy in the way of bread, butter, chickens, &c. A good many wagons come into camp with those things, and those of the boys who have not gambled off their money have a little left.

I have given you a rough but faithful sketch of our soldiering for the last four or five weeks. How do you like it? It is better to read of, than to be a part of. Like others, perhaps, you will be astonished to hear that your correspondent stood the march all through without giving out or resorting to the wagons. Pretty fair for a soldier weighing only one hundred pounds. Our officers had not a much better time than the men. Captain Cummins is a perfect horse to march. It is rumored that he is going to Washington with a view of a commission in the regular army; or, failing in that, to get a company accepted, and then come home and raise it.

George Satterlee is acting Quartermaster, and on that account is very little with the company. He is unusually popular with the regiment, and his business knowledge and habits fit him admirably for the place.

Ben. Beach is, and always has been, a favorite with the company. Always at his place, wherever that is, impartial, modest and kind-hearted, he is seen and felt, but not often heard. He desires to raise a company and stay in the army, if he has a chance. I predict that he will make his mark as a soldier.

Colonel Bates has gained very much in favor with his men during this march. He evinced an anxiety for the comfort of his men which endeared him to them, and he assumes a respectful independence in the presence of his superiors which the citizen-soldier likes to see.

Lieutenant-Colonel Merritt and Major Porter have always been personally popular with the regiment. We have had none of those disgusting scenes of *whipping, bucking, gagging,* &c., in our regiment, but we have seen too much of it in the others while at Booneville and here, amongst regulars and volunteers—a great deal of it in the St. Louis regiment. In the First Kansas regiment, a young man named Cole was shot on dress parade, for killing a fellow-soldier. Four balls entered his body, and one his neck. He died instantly.

In a wayside grocery and gambling shop near the Osage river, two soldiers belonging to the regulars, were murdered. The grocery and house were burned by order of the General, and the grocery keeper, who proved to be the murderer of at least one of the men, was taken, tried before the General, convicted, sentenced to be hanged, and is now under guard awaiting execution as soon as the General shall order. He deserves his fate richly. He is an old offender. These are incidents of news.

I had almost forgotten to say a word about General Lyon. A man rather below the middle stature, with no surplus flesh, red hair and whiskers, fast ripening to grey, small blue eyes—vigor, energy, fearlessness, and a dogged determination to accomplished his purpose at all hazards, are the prominent traits of his character. Finish the picture yourself—I must close to get this to Springfield.

We expect to be home about the twentieth or twenty-fifth of August, and will be glad to see the people, whether they will to see us or not.   H.

Fort Laramie

ONE OF THE MOST INTRIGUING of all personal narratives of the Civil War is Ovando J. Hollister's *History of the First Regiment of Colorado Volunteers*. Not only is it one of the rarest of Civil War books, it is also one of the freshest and frankest accounts of army life.

Born in Massachusetts in 1835, Hollister nevertheless qualifies as a "first citizen" of three Western states. He farmed on the Kansas frontier in the 1850's, succumbed to the gold fever and moved to Colorado, where he was living in 1861. After the war he removed to Utah, where he died in Salt Lake City in 1892, an honored citizen of the Mormon capital.

The *History of the First Regiment* is wonderful reading, a fine combination of frontier and army narratives. Hollister himself described it in the book's introductory paragraphs: "I propose to write a History of the First Regiment of Colorado Volunteers; its organization and discipline at Camp Weld; campaign in New Mexico, with notices of the most striking features of that Territory, and the conditions and strength of the Regiment at present [1863].

"I make no pretensions to literary merit or taste. The work was originally written for my own amusement, with no thought of publication. The fact that the members of the Regiment wanted it, and were willing to pay for it, induced me to have it published. It is common, in such cases, to beg indulgence for the constant use of the personal pronoun, but as I am a broken down soldier, consequently as low as I can get on the social ladder, I submit my work to the gentle public to judge of as they please. . . . As a record of our marches and fights, should we unfortunately never have any more, it will, I trust, be of some value. It will at least be a tie to bind us together in the days that are to come."

These portions of the book's first three chapters tell the early history of the regiment.

In the latter part of July, 1861, three men were sitting at dinner, round a rough table in a rougher country—the mining district of South Clear Creek. To those familiar with the style of living in the mountain placers, it will perhaps be unnecessary to say that their meal was neither extra in quality nor profuse in quantity. Judging from the appearance of the country and people, mining at that time was not exceedingly inviting or profitable. If they could make grub out of their claims they were satisfied; flattering themselves with the various wild things they *would* do when they struck the pay-streak. Through a strong hope in the future and a stronger faith in luck, the industrious and sanguine persevered in their hard, thankless task, while the bummer and loafer avoided all labor that was not necessitated by the state of their larder. That of our friends was nearly empty, and as this spasmodic gold-digging was intensely disagreeable, they were discussing their bread and beef and the chances of "raising the wind" in some easier way, at the same time.

Casting their eyes about for a new lode, the state of the country, plunged in a gigantic civil war, attracted their attention, and the idea of taking advantage of the patriotic uprising of the nation's heart and of the hard times in the mines, to raise a company of volunteers for the war, thus securing commissions for themselves, struck them as being a lode, which, once open, might be worked with ease and profit. Accordingly, Sam. H. Cook, who was perhaps the most self-reliant and decisive of the three friends, instantly struck off a few advertisements for Volunteers to form a mounted company, proceed to the States and enter the service under Jim Lane, with whom Cook had been somewhat associated in the Kansas war of '56. These bills, which promised service to the admirers of Lane, under the very eyes of their loved chief—an immediate return to America—a sentiment sufficiently powerful of itself to enlist a company—and which chose the mounted arm of the service as the field of the projected company's future action, were posted in conspicuous places through the mines, and owing to the skill with which they were drawn, eighty or more men had engaged in the enterprise by the middle of August.

Cook was to be Captain—the others Lieutenants. One named Nelson, having been in the service before, consequently somewhat posted on military affairs, was to be First —the other, named Wilson, ambitious and energetic, yet lacking the self-reliance with which Cook was so bountifully provided, was to be Second. With this programme they were well pleased, as it was calculated to advance their personal interests.

Soon, advertisements under the auspices of one W. F. Marshall, appeared in the Denver papers, inviting proposals for the transportation of the company to Leavenworth. The expenses of the trip across the plains were to be defrayed by a contribution of five dollars from each enlisted man.

About the 20th of August they all repaired to Denver, expecting to start for the States as soon as the requisite transportation could be procured. But Gov. Gilpin, unwilling to have these men leave the Territory, where he was then recruiting a Regiment of Volunteers, tried to induce them to remain and form one company of the First Colorados. Having pledged his honor that they should be well mounted, armed and equipped, and have active service "till they couldn't rest," they concluded to stay.

They were furnished quarters on Ferry Street, West Denver, and immediately proceeded to elect officers—commissioned and non-commissioned. It seems the W. F. Marshall mentioned above was an old acquaintance of Cook's, and had held a commission as Second Lieutenant in the Kansas Militia, under Lane. For this reason, and his services in enlisting men, he was the Captain's choice for Second Lieutenant, if not for First; but the Company disliking his haughty style and reserved manner, would not have him First nor even Second, until Wilson, at Marshall's earnest entreaty waived his claims and withdrew his name from the canvass.

Wilson became Orderly Sergeant, the hardest and most thankless position in the business. The other non-coms. were indicated by those who had secured the most important positions, rather than elected by the men.

As the Ferry Street quarters became too small for the increasing number of the company they were moved down to the old Buffalo House, where they remained two or three months. A corral just below and across the road contained the company horses, and was used as a guard house. There was no trouble in getting out at the back side, however, and prisoners confined in the corral enjoyed the freedom of the town.

A guard was stationed before the doors of the Captain's and Orderly's rooms, to prevent privates from passing in. Here the non-coms. chiefly congregated, while the privates occupied the upper story. Judging from their appearance, they were well possessed of the idea of their own importance. The finest clothes in market were none too good, and these, with the skill of the barber and tailor, made a very tangible contrast between these fifteen day soldiers, and recruits who were constantly coming in. Collisions between them and the town secesh occurred occasionally, but they never resulted in anything serious. The men were obliged to remain in quarters, a pass being necessary even to go up town.

A picket guard was stationed every night on various routes leading into Denver, to prevent surprise from domestic traitors or Texans, who were supposed to be coming in force. Then again cartridges would be issued and orders published for all to sleep on their arms, ready for action at a moment's notice. The idea of there being any necessity for these precautions was jeered at by us, but the cry of "wolf, wolf," was persisted in, till many no doubt trembled for safety.

Finally the wolf came. The company was put in fighting trim instanter. Time passed, and men breathed hard and quick. Perhaps they thought of home, and the loving ones there awaiting them. Orderlies galloped through the streets as if the fate of empires hung on their movements. Small bodies of troops hurried to their assigned positions, and suspense had become painful, when some enterprising scout came in with the news that the fancied host of Texans was a drove of stock, "Oh! what a fall was there," etc.

At that time the other companies of the Regiment, excepting A and B, were in embryo, and straining every nerve to entice recruits. A sketch of their organization would not perhaps come amiss.

Soon after the war broke out it became patent to every one that some force would be necessary to preserve Colorado to the Union. Gold was first discovered by Georgians, and the Southern element had always been well represented in our society. In view of this fact, and with the idea of strengthening the forts in the lower portion of the Territory, Gov. Gilpin during the summer recruited two companies of volunteers.

After the battle of Bull Run the disaffected in Denver boldly avowed their principles, raised a Secesh flag, which, however, did not fly long, secretly bought up arms, and in various ways commenced marshaling their forces to seize our infant Territory. But the Governor and other public men were alive to the emergency. They knew it would not do to stand idly by while the active, turbulent factionists were preparing to make their deadly spring, *a la* C. F. Jackson, in Missouri. The capture of Forts Bliss and Fillmore, in Arizona, by "Baylor's Babes," and their reported march on Santa Fe, decided the Governor, and in the last days of August J. P. Slough, Captain of Co. A, was appointed Colonel; S. F. Tappan, Captain of Co. B, Lieut. Colonel; J. M. Chivington was commissioned Major . . .

Recruiting offices were opened in Denver, at Gregory, Idaho, and beyond the Range; and in two months the required complement of men was obtained. A site was selected for barracks on the Platte, two miles from the centre of Denver City, and called Camp Weld, in honor of the then Secretary of the Territory. At a cost of $40,000 comfortable and sufficient barracks were constructed, and as fast as the companies were filled they went into quarters there. Notices like the following were occasionally seen in the daily papers.

"Yesterday Capt. S. F. Tappan, with Co. B, numbering 101 men, arrived from the mountains and went into quarters at Camp Weld. The men look hale and hearty, and are in excellent spirits." . . .

By means of drafts on the U. S. Treasury, the Governor defrayed the expense of raising clothing and sustaining his Volunteers, though this irregular proceeding afterwards environed him with trouble and finally cost him his office. Government was slow to endorse his action, and it is said never would have done so but for the meritorious service of the Regiment in Mexico. This idea was prevalent among the men for six months, and caused much lawlessness and insubordination that might otherwise have been avoided.

The men having enlisted with the idea of going to the States and taking an active part in the war, were dissatisfied with the inactivity of Camp Weld, and the idea of something in Gilpin's proceedings which would prevent their entering the service under their present organization, rendered them reckless. They have been publicly accused as "chicken thieves, jayhawkers, turbulent and seditious, a disgrace to themselves and the country." Grant it true. Suppose they plead guilty. Was there not much in the attendant circumstances to palliate their little irregularities? The fact that man's inactivity is the Devil's opportunity, and the prevalent though erroneous idea that they would never be recognized or paid, gave some excuse for the slight peccadilloes of the Volunteers at Camp Weld. Believing that every candid man will view it as I do, I leave the subject with the assertion that notwithstanding all that has been said, east, west, north or south, about their jayhawking proclivities, there is not a manlier, better disposed thousand men in the United States service than the First Colorados.

All the arms in the country were purchased, not so much for the use of the volunteers as to prevent traitors from getting them. Owing to our judicious state of preparation, Colorado escaped the civil convulsions that have desolated portions of our once happy country.

For the better equipment of his Regiment, the Governor had already sent to divert southward a train of arms proceeding from Camp Floyd to the States. This train was known to be in the vicinity, and fears were entertained for its safety. An escort, numbering sixteen, under command of Lieut. Nelson, was sent out to protect it on the way in. They started September 6th, full of the idea of their good fortune in being mounted and on their first service, and of escaping from the restraint imposed in quarters, which, though novel, was disagreeable. They proceeded with light hearts as far as Crow Creek, where they met the train and turned back with it. But danger seeming to thicken, at least to the apprehension of the authorities, another detail of twenty men, under Lieut. Marshall, was sent out on the same errand, on the 10th inst. We furnished ourselves with rations for six days, and a pair of blankets apiece, which we packed on two ponies.

At our first camp, on St. Vrain's Creek, a dispute occurred in the party as to whether bacon, used to oil firearms, would or would not make them rust. Little Hawley had ten dollars that said bacon grease was the best that could be used. Jude, on the other side, would bet ten dollars, but he had not got it with him. He put up five—the balance to be staked at the time of trial. As soon as the money was up, the crowd adjourned to an adjoining grocery, procured two buckets of milk and a gallon of whisky, and bound the bet by drinking the stakes. The betters joined us, and as neither ever mentioned it again, the merits of the case are still in the dark.

Next morning an express passed us. He said a few words to Marshall, probably of an alarming nature, for we left our pack animals on Little Thompson and hurried on. About dark we came in sight of Box Elder, when the orders "Form Fours"—"Trot"—"Gallop"—"CHARGE!" followed in quick succession, and Nelson, alarmed at so unusual an approach, ordered his men under arms, and prepared to give us a warm reception, should we prove enemies. On nearing the sentinels, our column was halted with some difficulty, and after recognition we quietly proceeded into camp.

On the ensuing day we came back to Cache-a-la-Poudre, where a messenger met us, with dispatches from the Governor. They contained orders for Lieut. Marshall to proceed, with his detail, on the Horse Creek route, towards Fort Laramie. It was thought a train of arms had left that place for Denver, on the strength of Gilpin's representations.

As we had only provided for a six days' trip, it seemed hard to start on a six weeks' one; but our newly fledged zeal was mounting as eagles' wings, and made small account of obstacles.

After bidding Nelson's party good bye (fresh friendships are always tender) we pressed a wagon and harness, hitched up our horses and started down the river. We had a good supply of flour, fifteen pounds of bacon and three of coffee. Our culinary department contained two frying-pans—minus handles—two small tin coffee-boilers and a few tin cups. Flour was mixed in the mouth of the sack and baked before the blaze. Thus furnished, we struck across the desert, two hundred miles in extent, between the mouth of Cache-a-la-Poudre and Laramie. Not a man in the party had ever been in the country before, though two citizens of Denver accompanied us as guides.

Our first day's travel was down the Cache-a-la-Poudre.
Though late in the haying season, but little grass had been
cut. It was a good indication of the quality of the soil. Ten
miles below Laporte there is some good bottom, especially
on the north side; but sandy, barren streaks, destitute of
vegetation, are common in the best of it. These are from two
to ten rods wide—the edges as well defined as if a mowing
machine had cut out the barren strips. I thought that was
the case till we passed over some. On the stream, as a whole,
there is much good land—more that is worthless. The small
breadth in crops is heavily burdened. But few people live
here though every claim is occupied by a cabin. We camped
near the mouth of the creek.

Next morning we struck across six or eight miles, to Crow
Creek. There was but one water hole in the lower part of its
course, and we were lucky enough to find it, and a small
quantity of bacon and coffee hanging in a tree. We traveled
up this creek two or three days. The lower part was dry,
with occasional patches of low, scraggy-topped cottonwoods,
among which great inky ravens were always wheeling and
screaming. The upper, was running full of muddy water—the
effect of a heavy storm in that vicinity. Antelope abound in
this region. There was not an hour in the day when they
might not be seen "on a thousand hills."

One day the writer was sent out to get one. He rode along
for a time without success. Having got some distance ahead,
he came to a flock of several hundred, scattered over a large
bottom. Antelope, when scared, first huddle together before
they "skedaddle." Knowing this, our hunter approached as
near as possible under cover, then dashing boldly on them,
his horse at his best speed, his eye on the sight and finger
on trigger, visions of roast venison dancing through his brain,
he had just selected his mark when his horse suddenly

stopped. He went *on* at about the same gait till his momentum became exhausted and he stopped. His gun went a piece farther, discharged itself and it stopped. By the time he had gathered himself, gun and horse together again, the antelope were viewing his outfit over their left shoulders, from a high hill about three miles off. A dog-hole was the innocent cause of this ludicrous finale of his hunt. Owing to the state of our commissary we were anxious to kill some game, but our efforts were uniformly unsuccessful. . . .

Fort Laramie, like all Government posts in the Western Desert, is built with little regard to system or defensive purposes. It consists of the usual accommodations for officers and men, quartermaster and commissary buildings, hospital, sutler's store and stables. It is handsomely situated on the north bank of Laramie Creek, a mile above its junction with the Platte. Beyond, a high ridge, upon the crest of which the gray rocks crop out, supporting here and there a stunted growth of pine, extends nearly to the junction, hiding the Platte from view. On the south the sand-hills approach within rifle-shot, and altogether the situation appears cramped and encroached upon by the desert. There is but little arable land in the vicinity, and that is of a light sandy texture. Nothing but necessity can make the desolate place endurable to white men. Two companies of the Second Dragoons and one of Infantry, form the garrison at present.

When we arrived on the ground the soldiers gathered round, anxious to hear from the world. They, too, had been alarmed by rumors of Texan invasion, and were half minded to take us for enemies. Subsequent usage proved that we were viewed as intruders at least. There were unoccupied quarters in the Post, and plenty of supplies; yet we could get no quarters, no clothing, and only wormy, condemned bacon and hardbread for rations. The soldiers swore that Col. Alexander, commanding the Post, was an old "Secesh," and I guess they were right. He hated us not only as interlopers, in which light Volunteers are detested by all Regulars, rank and file, but as opposed to him politically—enemies on principle—and he treated us accordingly.

We pitched camp on the north side of the Platte, as near the Post as possible. The sand-burs were thick and the feed poor, but it was the best we could do. A fine grove of cottonwoods enhanced the beauty of the place. Sober Autumn, with his nipping frosts and withered leaves dancing down to their burial, while the wild wind moans their requiem through the bare branches, was rapidly advancing—but summer resigned her sceptre with reluctance. A shade was still indispensable to comfort. The river channel averages a hundred yards in width, muddy and shallow, with numerous bars in sight at low water. Fording is hard on account of loose cobbles at the bottom.

They had no transportation at Laramie, and we had to send to Denver for it. As we were to remain here till it returned, we set about enjoying ourselves as well as we could. Sometimes we went over to the Post to see them mount guard, but the cavalry drill was the most interesting. The horses were large and spirited, and in splendid condition. Prancing and curveting from excess of life, when they charged in platoons down banks and over ditches where it seemed they could hardly pass safely in a walk, it required nerve and practice to keep the saddle. Nor did these daring horsemen, who covered themselves with glory on many bloody fields in Mexico, always come off scatheless—two or three men being seriously injured and their horses stove up while we were there. In this school of the trooper we first saw the opening bud that promised danger and excitement enough by the

time it should ripen into the hard and glorious fruit of victory. In camp, a slack-rope was stretched for gymnasts; a
broken iron axle answered for dumb-bells; and foot-racing,
jumping, wrestling, boxing, tumbling, and fishing with a
seine borrowed from the Post, filled the time.

One incident that occurred here will perhaps pay for telling. Lieut. Marshall had bought a lot of tobacco, and the
Sergeant issued it to the men as they needed it, keeping an
account with each. One of the boys, named Frank, draws a
plug or two, and has it charged to another, called Jem. Jem
is a Sucker. How he came to wander so far from the paternal
acres has never ceased to be a wonder. He is not a fool—far
from it—only troubled with a mild type of simplicity. Guile,
or the idea of guile, has never entered his brain. Nothing
can prevent a crowd from having their fun with such a character. Jem soon learned that he was charged with sundry
plugs of tobacco on the Sergeant's books, and as he made no
use of the weed he naturally became wrathy. Hints were
dropped by one and another to bait him until he demanded
a public investigation of the affair. This was what the boys
wanted, and a court-martial was promptly organized for the
trial of suspected persons. Jem's suspicions had been adroitly
directed to Frank as the guilty party, and Frank was accordingly brought before the court. The oath administered to
the witnesses being to the effect that "they wouldn't tell the
truth nor nothing like the truth so help them grog," there
was no difficulty in proving Frank's innocence, and that of
others who were suspected. During the progress of the case,
which was conducted with due solemnity, Jem sat among
the crowd as sober as if he thought himself on trial for his
life. It was finally proved to the satisfaction of the court, that
Jem himself had drawn the tobacco; and when the President
so decided, and fined him four dollars and costs, he looked as

blank as if struck by lightning. The boys told him it was too bad—outrageous—but Frank was mad, and going to maul him for falsely accusing him, unless he paid the fine in "rot" immediately. As the pleasantest alternative thus offered, Jem forked over the four dollars, and a party started to the Post for whiskey. They returned in due time, with two quarts —three parts of it inside of them, however. Jem drank a small swallow, to see how his money tasted. He got excited. "It was his first spree." "D—n the expense." "Who wouldn't get drunk a thousand miles from home, and 'rot' only two dollars a quart?" "He must learn to play cards." "He would be a man or a long-tailed rat.". . .

That evening we had a new sport. The cook threw a burning brand at some one who was molesting him. Its streaming passage through the air suggested the idea. Forthwith, fires appeared in different quarters of the grove, and soon the air was full of brands. It was a picture in miniature, of Farragut below New Orleans. One by one the boys joined in the sport till the whole camp was engaged. Jem was there. He engineered both sides. Was the North in the ascendant? There was Jem pawing fire and bellowing like a Stentor, "Charge! Chester, Charge!" "Down with the rebels." "Give 'em hell." "We'll whip 'em, by G—d we'll whip 'em." Was the South uppermost? Jem had flown, and his lank figure, split to the armpits, stood out boldly from the midst of the blaze, where, with hat and shirt off, arms blackened to the shoulders, the sweat pouring down his smoky face in streams, he scattered fire like Vulcan forging thunderbolts; and ever as the fight lulled were heard his lusty cheerings, "We'll whip 'em—the d—d abolitionists—we'll give 'em Bull Runs till they can't rest." Jem was a tiger that night. The battle ceased towards morning. The South got cleaned out. One by one their men came over to the North, until their chief was left alone. He fought to the last, but was finally disarmed and taken prisoner.

Soon after this occurrence Marshall and Pott contrived a plan for their sport if not for ours. It was evening, and a young moon was beginning to cast shadows. We were ordered to "Fall in," and Marshall drilled us in various motions of the arms and legs, while Pott stretched a rope between two trees close by. Soon Marshall brought us into line near the rope and ordering the "charge," stood by to see the fun. Away went the men at their best speed till their shins struck the rope, when they rolled over and over in the sand-burs. Then we agreed that each should sing, speak, or tell a story. Some, took their turns agreeably. Contumacious subjects were forced to the bar and "compelled to give in evidence." Several popular songs were "did," but—

> "Cot tam dat shnaik vot pites mine Shon,
> He 'sh all over plack, mit fite shpots on;
> He laish in ter grass, and he fistle mit him tail.
> Cot tam dat Cot tam shnaik to Hail,"

carried away the palm. The tune was like a Virginia fence, jagged on both sides. It was rich. But Jude, the laughing, boisterous, buck-eye butcher had gone to bed. His turn came at last. He said he was sick. It was no go—out of bed and away went Jude, with a dozen after him. They lassoed him, after a long race, and brought him on the stage. He was dressed—in a shirt. He began, "Blaze with your serried columns, I will not bow the knee." Poor fellow! he is dead now; died as he lived—laughing. We laughed at first. His theme, his attitudes and gestures—extra-theatrical—were so incongruous with his costume. But as he warmed with his subject, he thundered the old Chief's defiance with such truth that

we forgot he was acting, and almost expected him to leap
among us with a tomahawk, and seal his words with deeds.
Had his skin been a shade or so darker the illusion would
have been perfect. We were satisfied and the curtain fell.

There was a large encampment of Ogalallah Sioux on Laramie Creek, three or four miles above the Post, that we
often visited. They were assembled in Council, preparatory
to taking the war-path against the Pawnees. Their temple of
ceremonies was a large booth, constructed by planting parallel rows of long slender withes in the ground about ten feet
apart. The tops were then bent in and fastened together,
and this frame-work filled in with small brush, basket fashion, was closed up at one end, the entrance festooned with
pine boughs and wild flowers and it was ready for use. First
comes the inevitable smoke. Seated in a circle round the
council fire, the pipe, an iron tomahawk with hollow head
and perforated handle, is filled and lighted. Each in succession takes three whiffs, invariably pouring the smoke
through the nostril, till it is burned out. Then comes the
dance in which all participate. Forming in a circle, facing
inward, hands joined, when the music strikes up they slowly
move round, chanting Ha! ha! ha! Ha! ha! ha! through all
the variations of the scale, though with a certain uniformity
that claims a distant relation to tune. Time is kept by beating tin-pans and gourds. As their wild, untutored music rises
and falls on the breeze, weird shadows from the dark forests
of the east float before you. Readily assimilating, they assume a terrible shape, and midnight massacre alights in the
circle and seems at home. You turn with disgust from the
tawny brutes and wonder if they *are* the descendants of
King Philip and Tecumseh.

Now comes a scene told of in books, but seldom witnessed.
Some young braves are to be initiated. With sharp knives,

they open great gashes in their breasts and shoulders. Two men seize the subject, pierce the quivering flesh between the cuts, with oak splints a half-inch in thickness. A pony is hitched to these and the intervening flesh torn out. Others are suspended in the air by the splints. Scourges are applied till the back and thighs are completely lacerated. During these operations not a muscle betrays their torture. More impassable than the chiefs and warriors who look on, they inflict these cruelties on themselves to prove their fortitude and courage. They are now admitted to the council and war-path as braves.

Such scenes were of daily occurrence while the encampment lasted. Whatever of savage grandeur in the Indian character they conjured from the records of history or romance, was speedily dissipated on entering a lodge. The squaws, miserable and emaciated, were baking human excrement on shingles for food, while the bucks were usually engaged lousing themselves. The squalid misery of these wasted creatures is past belief, and must be seen to be appreciated. Utter and speedy extinction is their only cure. Association with our race injures rather than benefits them. It has already done its work. Their ruin is accomplished.

Battle of Port Royal

IN THE EAST there was continued skirmishing along the battle line in northern Virginia, but no big battle followed that at Bull Run in the remainder of 1861. It was a time of stalemate, of regrouping, of enemies feeling out the positions and the strength of one another.

But Union troops gained an important victory farther south. On November 7, 1861, the Union fleet, under the command of Admiral S. F. DuPont and operating with the army, captured Port Royal, South Carolina, and gained its first foothold on the rebel shore.

The firsthand account of that operation reprinted here is from a small pamphlet published in 1863, *Abstract of the Cruise of the U.S. Steam Frigate Wabash . . . 1861–'62 & '63*, apparently written by a veteran of the crew. Its author is unknown, the pamphlet being signed "Marlinspike."

[October] 29*th*. General Sherman and staff came on board, and were saluted with 13 guns. Got under way, as also the whole fleet, in order of sailing, *Wabash* leading. The fleet consisted of 23 naval vessels, and about 50 transports with troops.

NOVEMBER, 1861

4th. After experiencing a very heavy gale, in which the transports *Governor* and *Peerless* went down, *Union* and *Osceola* ashore, and the crews captured by the rebels, we arrived off Port Royal, most of fleet at anchor, and the rest heaving in sight. The light draft gunboats stood in over the bar to reconnoitre; first shot from enemy's batteries.

5th. Got under way and stood in over the bar, anchoring inside, being greeted with cheer upon cheer from the transports while crossing.

6th. At anchor, preparing for action, sending down topgallant masts, snaking down stays, reefing preventer slings to the yards, and getting everything in readiness, with as much coolness, as if we were going into port to pay off; pay off we certainly meant to, but in a sort of coin that was rather too hot for the recipients to hold, and too heavy to retain. During the preparations several small rebel gunboats were crossing and recrossing the channel apparently landing troops.

BATTLE OF PORT ROYAL

Nov. 7th. At 8.08 A. M., "all hands up anchor." At 8.18 anchor catted and ship under way; 8.50 stopped the engine, the starboard spring being foul of the propeller; 9 propeller clear of hawser. Beat to quarters to engage the enemy, the forts on Hilton Head and Bay Point, and the enemy's steamers lying near the latter; 9.17 all ready for action; stood for the enemy, starboard guns trained well forward on Bay Point; fort called "Fort Beauregard;" 9.27 enemy opened fire

from Hilton Head; fort called "Fort Walker;" shot fell short;
immediately enemy opened from Bay Point; fire answered at
once from our forward pivot gun; shot good; our port broadside was also at once brought to bear upon Hilton Head fort,
and a heavy gun masked about 500 yards below the fort.
At 9.45 *Bienville* ranged alongside on starboard bow; 9.53
ceased firing from the *Wabash* until the ship turned to present the starboard battery at Hilton Head; 10.03 reopened
fire with forward pivot gun; made signal for close action
with fort on Hilton Head; kept up terrific and well-directed
fire from starboard battery; received a shot which cut in
two the starboard lower studdingsail boom, and carried
away jewsharp of sheet anchor; 10.15 a shot carried away
the paunch batten of mainmast; 10.30 none of our guns bearing, we ceased firing. Between 10.15 and 10.30 an 80-pound
rifled shot passed through our mainmast, near the centre,
about 25 feet from the deck; two other shots successively
cut away both mainstays about 25 feet from collars, and a
fourth shot cut away the end of the spanker boom at taffrail;
10.35 resumed firing from our port battery; 10.37 ceased firing except from pivot guns. Ship turned; 10.40 trained starboard battery to play upon Bay Point; our shot fell short;
10.50 ceased firing, ship turned round; 11.15 ship's head
S. S. E.; 11.18 fired the forward pivot gun on the starboard
side at Hilton Head—shot too high. Ship now ran in within
600 yards of Hilton Head; 11.26 opened with all starboard
battery and both pivots; trained, knocked down enemy's
flagstaff. The firing from our guns admirably accurate; 11.40
ceased firing, except from pivot guns; guns no longer bearing
upon the fort; ship turned round; 11.50 reopened fire from
our port battery and pivots. Our jib halliards cut twice, main-
topgallant stay cut away; 11.52 received a heavy shot in
starboard main chains, which carried away the lower dead-

eye and laniard of the maintopmast backstay, topsail halliards, and smashed in the hammock rail. Starboard battery
manned to play upon Bay Point; 11.54 received a heavy shot
through the starboard head-rail, and stranded the port fore
swifter; 11.55 our starboard mizen horse-block shot away,
and upper part of starboard after port badly chipped; also
cut off inside of sheave hole of starboard arm of spare main-
topsail yard; shot came from Hilton Head; 11.56 port battery
manned to bear upon Hilton Head; 11.58 ceased firing from
gun deck; 12 a 42-pound shot from Bay Point, struck the
deck port side at No. 16 gun, knocked a hole in the deck,
wounded four men, carried away forward truck of the gun
and broke into the hammock netting; also Thomas Jackson,
(cox.) captain of the gun, had his leg shot away at the thigh;
was removed to cock-pit, and died within an hour; the others
were injured by splinters; the shot went no farther than the
hammock netting, and was kept by the ex.-officer as a souve-
nir; 12.05 received a spent shot from "Fort Walker" at cop-
per line under port counter; 12.10 ceased firing, ship turning
round; gave biscuit and grog to the crew at their guns. 1.15
reported by signal from gunboat *Ottawa* that "Fort Walker"
was abandoned. 2 P. M. starboard battery manned, ran within
500 yards of the fort, and fired both pivot guns into it; fire
unanswered; ceased firing; 2.12 commander John Rodgers,
(aid to flag-officer,) left the ship in one of our boats, with
flag of truce to visit the fort; 2.15 reported from mast-head
that about 1000 men were in full retreat for the woods; 2.20
the American flag flying upon the enemy's ramparts; 2.45
anchored near and abreast of "Fort Walker," and proceeded
to land our marines, Lieut. Barnes taking a company of 50
small-arm men in the tug *Mercury,* to land at the fort. "Fort
Walker" was taken possession of by Commander C. R. P.
Rodgers of the *Wabash,* and at 5.45 formally turned over to

the command of Brigadier-General Wright and his brigade; at 4 P. M. secured the guns and went to supper. 800 shell and shot were fired from this ship alone.

As we approached the forts the enemy's flotilla was in line of defence on our starboard bow, near Bay Point. At 9.40 the enemy's largest gunboat stood across the head of the bay, evidently to annoy this ship; the forward pivot gun was vigilantly handled to answer from either bow. At 9.45, as the enemy crossed our bow, he discharged a shell which struck very near our port bow. We immediately answered from our pivot gun.

The enemy's gunboats then ran out of range, where they remained until near the close of the engagement, when they disappeared up the river. At 10 P. M., Lieutenant Barnes and his command returned to the ship. The enemy had retreated in utter rout and confusion, without attempting to carry away either public or private property. The ground was covered with the arms of the soldiers, and the officers retired in too much haste to take their swords; even the dinners of both officers and men were left on the fire cooking, and ready to be partaken of by the victors. The scene of the battle must have been grand and terrific to those who had the opportunity of witnessing it from the decks of the transports. The battle was spoken of by men, who had been under fire more than once during their life-time, as terrible, and described the *Wabash* a destroying angel as she hugged the shore, men stationed in the chains, calling the soundings with cool indifference, slowing the engine, as to only give her steerage way, signalizing to the vessels their various evolutions, at the same time raining shells with the precision and calmness of target practice. It can be truly said, that when in close action the men were only getting warm, thinking about going in with a will; what the effect would have been had it lasted an hour longer it is difficult to say, as nearly all the spectators acknowledged they could compare it to nothing but "hell upon earth." The conflict at an end, the usual duties of the ship were resumed as if no such occurrence had happened, as plenty of men can testify in stronger terms than can be written. The weather during the day was

LIST OF VESSELS IN THE ACTION.

Wabash, ... 44 guns.
Susquehanna, ... 18 "
Mohican, ... 7 "
Seminole, ... 6 "
Pawnee, ... 11 "
Unadilla, ... 6 "
Ottawa, ... 5 "
Pembina, ... 4 "
Isaac Smith, guns thrown overboard in gale.
Vandalia, towed by I. Smith, ... 22 "
Bienville, ... 11 "
Seneca, ... 4 "
Curlew, ... 6 "
Penguin, ... 7 "
Augusta, ... 10 "
Mercury, ... 2 "
R. B. Forbes, ... 1 "
Pocahontas, ... 6 "

REBEL SIDE.

Fort Beauregard, ... 20 guns.
    Outwork, ... 5 "
Fort Walker, ... 23 "
    Outwork, ... 1 "

and 5 steamers, from 2 to 3 guns each.

pleasant, light winds from the north-east, and smooth sea. The loss in the whole fleet was eight killed, six wounded seriously, and seventeen slightly.

10*th*. Sent mail and despatches on board United States steamer *Bienville* for New York. After divine service all hands mustered on quarter-deck, and an order from Flag Officer DuPont, thanking the officers and men for their gallantry and skill during the bombardment of the 7th, was read.

19*th*. H. B. M. frigate *Immortalité* came in and anchored; saluted the flag with twenty-one guns and Flag Officer with thirteen, which was duly returned.

On the Sunday following the battle a number of our men went on shore to have a look at the damage that was done by our guns; they found the fort, as a matter of course, in possession of the soldiers, but were greatly surprised to find they were not allowed to go inside without a pass from the commanding officer. Such rules and regulations may be all very well, but it certainly seemed rather hard for those very men who had fought for the place, and were the means of placing the army in the position they then held, to be refused from visiting it. However, be it as it may, some of our shellbacks murmured at it, and one, who was getting rather frosty through servitude and years, determined to see the General himself;—the name of General does not abash Jack in the least; a General to him is no more than any one else, but the case is different when Commodore or Captain is mentioned, he is then all attention and respect, and they are the only titles that he supposes himself bound to take any cognizance of—so our old Barnacle-Back started for the quarters of the General, and bolted right in, demanding to see him. It happened that he alighted in the midst of the General's staff, and himself among them. One of the officers desired to know what he wished? "What do I wish, is it? Well, I wish for a second pass to go into the fort; I did not know before that a man had to have two passes to go to one place." "How, two passes," asked one; "have you had one before?" "No," returned Jack, "I sent one on shore Thursday, in the shape of a nine-inch shell, and I thought it sufficient." Jack got his pass, and visited the fort.

1862

The Enemy Is Texas

IN THE SPARSELY SETTLED Territory of New Mexico the traditional enemies had been, first, the Indians and, second, the Texans. War gave the Texans an opportunity to exercise their ambitions for expansion and, early in 1862, they invaded New Mexico in the name of the Confederate government.

Facundo Pino, President of the Council of the Territory, and J. M. Gallegos, Speaker of the House, issued on January 29 an impassioned plea for resistance. "Now is the day to feel the tinglings of the ancient, and unconquerable Castilian blood, that our ancestors brought to this land. The fire-sparks are deathless in every drop. —Now is the day for the flame, that shall conquer and consume."

The complete text of Pino and Gallegos' "Address of the Legislative Assembly of New Mexico" is printed here. Following it is another section from Hollister's *History of the First Regiment of Colorado Volunteers.*

The New Mexicans unaided were no match for the Texans. Aid was sent from the North. Hollister's narrative for March, 1862, tells of the Coloradans' march to help in New Mexico and the Battle of Glorietta Pass which ended Confederate hopes of conquest to their west. In the battle the Confederates held the field, but the destruction of their train effectually ended their New Mexican campaign.

Interesting and entertaining as it is, Hollister's account must be taken with at least a small grain of salt. Each side exaggerated the importance and the violence of the battle, and each side claimed overwhelming victory. In an undated letter of many years later Hollister wrote book collector John Page Nicholson: "I do not know where a copy of the pamphlet can be found, & saving that it might be of use to you, I sincerely hope there is not one in existence. I was so exceedingly crude, & it is so ditto, that I never think of it without mortification. Some of the incidents are colored, somewhat, to make a story, such as . . . the raiding of Mexican towns, stealing blankets, chickens, &c. In fact there is nothing in the whole book that I can now tolerate, & I wonder that I could have put my name, fool that I was at the time, to such stuff."

ADDRESS OF THE LEGISLATIVE ASSEMBLY OF NEW MEXICO.

MANIFESTO OF

The Council and House of Representatives to the Inhabitants of the Territory of New Mexico.

FELLOW CITIZENS:

Being at the close of the present session of your Legislative Assembly, and knowing from this Capital, the danger that threatens you, we have thought it well, to address you this

MANIFESTO

That a savage tribe of Indians should be your enemies, and plunder and murder, is not a thing new or unexpected. Such has been *their* habits, since our brave ancestors first possessed the Valley of the Rio Grande. But we have now another enemy less excusable than the barbarians, because he has grown in the midst of civilization, and enlightenment.

Without any fault or even offense of yours, your honor and property, your families and children are now in peril, by an enemy you have not injured, and whose invasion of the peace, security, and integrity of your soil and homes, you have not provoked.

This enemy is Texas and the Texans. With their hostile armed regiments, rebels to the Government of the United States, to whose protection and flag, our good faith, our duties, our confidence, interests and hopes turn and belong, they have come upon us, in violation of every principle of right, of justice and friendship. They threaten you with ruin and vengeance.— They strive to cover the iniquity of their marauding inroad, under the pretence, that they are under the authority of a new arrangement they call a Confederacy, but in truth is a rebel organization. But this pretence cannot deceive. They come to subsist upon the substance of our property and industry. They are without money or credit.

They come to destroy the Government under which we have lived, prospered, and been happy, and whose protection and care we need. They come to turn from their places, those in offices and authority among you, and to erect by military despotism alone, a power to oppress, to harrass and crush you. You are free and unmolested in your religion, and they who are in violation of every thing held sacred by our religion pretend to come to protect our religion already protected.

They pretend to relieve you from the expenses of Government, when they have no Government, that can bring into our Territory one dollar of money or credit.

To even eat for a day, they must take and plunder your cattle, your sheep, your wheat, corn and beans. They must plunder from our people, all their living. Could they succeed in their infamous and iniquitous attempts, they have no way of subsisting, but upon the substance of our people. A lawless body of men, banded together, hoping to kill or conquer us, would then be established among us, and our shame, injuries and sufferings, we will not attempt to describe.

May a just and avenging God, not withdraw his arm from us, and leave our people to the insults, wrongs, dishonors, cruelties and oppression, that these Texan invaders will inflict, the moment they shall have the power! We must not forget they are our ancient enemies. Twenty years ago they came with intents like they now come. Then they were overcome, and the integrity of our soil vindicated. In 1849, they strove to set up their power over our people, and sent their agents among our people, to carry out their schemes, but our people stood firm, and the General Government silenced Texan pretension.

Taking advantage of the troubles in the United States, they have now come hoping to succeed. Their long smothered vengeance against our Territory and people, they now seek to gratify.

We are a free people, and our fathers ever abhorred negro slaves and slavery.— Our enemies found their rebellion upon pretences touching the negro, negro slaves and slavery. They have set up their rebel organization upon those elements, and boast in the face of a Christian world, of their skill and wisdom in building upon such foundations.

We have condemned, and put slavery from among our laws. It is not congenial with our history, our feelings or interests. The marauders come to destroy our enactments, and force upon us by the cannon and rifle, slave institutions, against our will, protests and tastes.

We have no interests to promote, by being drawn within the destinies of the rebels and rebellion. All in that direction is danger and ruin. Listen not to their agents or emissaries, whether sent for mischief, or shall be found as traitors, living among us. In the midst of our wrongs and dangers, neutrality is without excuse. He that is not for us, is for the rebels and rebellion, and his sympathies favor the invaders.— The Texans may circulate their seditious papers and proclamations, by traitors to us among our people. Be not deceived by these pretensions. Put far from you, the language and sentiments of treason.— Touch not the poison. A serpent's fang is in it. Expose your loyalty to no suspicions. Look to the Government for reward for your services. Forfeit no claim by giving any favor to the enemy. Trust the justice and generosity of the Government. We are well assured, that we will be relieved from the assessment, placed upon us. The matter is brought to the attention of Congress. We have no doubt of liberality being extended to us. Could our enemies gain advantages and *even* battles, they could not long profit by their success. But success cannot crown so iniquitous, so unholy a cause. Success is impossible where there is not the treachery, the cowardice, weakness or folly, that condemned to undying infamy, the conduct, the affairs and surrender of Fort Fillmore. The time has fully come to wipe out that shame.— The army feels it, the people and the whole government feel it. The means of your complete success, in driving the enemy from our limits, are in our hands, large columns of well armed, well disciplined, and well prepared United States American troops, are ready for the fight. These are commanded by officers, who should know the whole art of war. It is their education and profession. We would recoil from even the approach of the thought, that they have not the spirit, courage, conduct, skill and judgement, that must lead the elements under their command, to victory and glory. May they and their troops, win fame that shall dazzle with its brightness, and honor that shall endure as the mountains. With our native soldiery, and volunteers, our pride, our solicitude and sympathies, are too deep for expression. Side by side as they are, with the veteran regular soldier, they live at a time and are actors in the scenes when they may win wreaths of glory and renown, for themselves, their children, and their children's children's generations.— We know they have spirit and courage.— Let us trust to their love of country, justice and honor.

In one sense, the period and event upon us, is fortunate. The enemy is accustomed to sneer at our valor, and depreciate our force and capacity. Never did time, present to outraged men, a fairer field in which to save a country, punish an enemy, and make a name, that invaders shall ever dread, than now surrounds us. Now is the day to feel the tinglings of the ancient, and unconquerable Castillian blood, that our ancestors brought to this land. The fire-sparks are deathless in every drop.— Now is the day for the flame, that shall conquer and consume. The remains of our intrepid and glorious ancestors, slept in no grave, that did not entomb a hero. Their pride and honor could endure no invader. To violate truth, and to commit cowardice, their high souls scorned and abhorred.— Now is the day to show ourselves worthy of our ancestors. Now is the day in which we can make a bright name, that shall shine throughout the union and through time. Let not the veteran Regular surpass you in daring. Emulate the boldest daring he has the spirit to attempt. Let him who commands know no fear like defeat, no dishonor like flying from the face of the invader. Drive off the audacious invader, and then the Indian marauders can be exterminated. If the invader gets a foothold further within the country, there are many modes of depriving him of any profit by his advance, more than the plunder he will gather. This people will never consent to his rule, his military, his slave despotism. The brave and just from neighboring sections will come to our aid. Already reinforcements of Regiments are organized to march to our assistance. They are coming with strong arms and hearts, and will join us in driving off all enemies. The Texans will be driven from our soil. Let no one despair. Our troops are ready and eager to win their laurels and security.

Let every Mexican in the Territory rally to the brave in the field; your fathers, sons and brothers. Let no discouragement or alarm disturb you. Your deliverance from enemies is at hand. Be true, be faithful, and be courageous; then your native land will be full of songs, in honor of your glorious deeds, and New Mexico blaze with fame, and her sons and daughters glow with pride when wheresoever they may travel hereafter through the Union or other lands, they shall find how great the benefit and distinction will be, in being known as the sons and daughters of New Mexico.

FACUNDO PINO,
PRESIDENT OF THE COUNCIL.

J. M. GALLEGOS,
SPEAKER OF THE HOUSE
[T.]N. M. Jan. 29, 1862

———

We left camp about 8 o'clock, the infantry detachment immediately in advance. The cavalry numbered 210, and marched in the order of their rank, our company being second in the column. Our whole force numbered nearly 400, commanded by Major Chivington. As we advanced leisurely, scouts kept coming in, confirming the intelligence received last night. We thought likely we would meet a force of Texans during the day, but it is doubtful if many realized the issues involved in the meeting. If we had we would have stolen a longer and tenderer look at some of our comrades, whose countenances were soon to be robed in *death*.

We passed Pigeon's Ranche, gained the summit of the divide, and were proceeding down the road, when our picket came charging back with the Lieutenant in command of their artillery a prisoner, crying, "We've got them corralled this time." "Give them h—l, boys." "Hurrah for the Pike's Peakers." Instantly the ranks closed up, the cavalry took open order by fours, and we rushed forward on the double-quick. Knapsacks, canteens, overcoats and clothing of all kinds were flung along the road as the boys stripped for the encounter. How our hearts beat! That tremendous event, the burden of history and song, a *battle*, burst on our hitherto peaceful lives like an avalanche on a Swiss village. Were we worthy of the name we bore? A few minutes would tell. On turning a short bend we entered the canon proper and came full on two howitzers, less than two hundred yards off. These were attended by a company of mounted men, displaying a saucy little red flag emblazoned with the emblem of which Texas has small reason to be proud. San Jacinto expresses all the glory of that arrogant, impotent State, while language is inadequate to describe the narrowness and insolence of her public policy or the moral and intellectual degradation of her outcast society. On seeing these "lions in the path," the infantry divided, a wing flew into either hill, and the fight commenced. Capt. Howland's company parted either way and filed to the rear in confusion, leaving us in front. A couple of shells whizzed over our heads and we instinctively crowded to the left to get out of range. All was confusion. The regular officers in command of the cavalry plunged wildly here and there, and seemed to have no control of themselves or of their men. Every one was talking—no one talking to any purpose. Major Chivington was placing the infantry in position, and Cook's cavalry awaited orders, while the shells went tearing and screaming over them. The Texans soon found their position in the road untenable and retired rapidly with their little red clout a mile or so down the canon, where their infantry was concealed in the rocks on either side, and posted their howitzers to command the road. We followed cautiously until within an eighth of a mile of the battery, which seemed throughout to be more occupied in keeping out of our way than in trying to do us injury. Here we halted behind a projecting point while the infantry were collected from the hills, and together with the mounted men, except Cook's company, deployed right and left to outflank the enemy's new position. Major Chivington, with a pistol in each hand and one or two under his arms, chawed his lips with only less energy than he gave his orders. He seemed burdened with a new responsibility, the extent of which he had never before realized, and to have no thought of danger. Of commanding presence, dressed in full regimentals, he was a conspicuous mark for the Texan sharp shooters. One of their officers taken prisoner averred that he emptied his revolvers three times at the Major and then made his company fire a volley at him. As if possessed of a charmed life, he galloped unhurt through the storm of bullets, and the Texans, discouraged, turned their attention to something else.

At this time, so far as I could judge, the battle was progressing finely. Our flankers were rapidly approaching them, and it was arranged that simultaneously with their attack on the wings, we should charge the centre. True, their battery commanded the road, but we had seen that move before with more celerity than grace, and as the event proved, we had only to go down after it to drive it from the field. The ground was unfavorable for the action of cavalry; the road was rough, narrow and crooked; a deep trench, worn by the water and which the road crossed occasionally, running alongside, rendered it impossible to approach a battery but by column in the fair face of it; our horses were weak and thin, and there was every chance to conceal a heavy support. But obstacles only stimulate the daring and determined. The enemy had a strong natural position, and to dislodge them it was necessary to walk into their affections without ceremony. About four hundred yards below us, the canon bent abruptly to the left, then directly resumed its old course, leaving a high, steep, rocky bluff, like the bastion of a fort, square in our front. On this point the enemy had posted a

full company, and at its base, on a smaller mound, their battery was stationed and had now worked diligently for an
hour. Below this we could not see, but personal observation
of the closest kind soon convinced us that the bluffs and
road were alive with Texans, for some distance. As soon as
the order to charge left the Major's mouth we were on the
wing, fearful lest our company should win no share of the
laurels that were to crown the day. As we approached the
point mentioned above, the old United States musket cartridges, containing an ounce ball and three buck-shot, began
to *zip* by our heads so sharply that many, unused to this
kind of business, took them for shells, and strained their
eyes to see where the spiteful bull-dogs were. There were
none to be seen. Divining our intentions, they had turned
tail again and vamosed. Instead, however, we met a redoubled shower of lead, rained on us from the rocks above. Capt.
Cook was among the first hit. An ounce ball and three buck-
shot struck him in the thigh, but did not unseat him. Forty
rods further down, his horse stumbled and fell on him badly
spraining his ankle, and he got another shot in the foot. As
the battle swept down the canon like a hurricane, he limped
one side and escaped further injury. We still had a leader as
cool and fearless as Cook—Lieut. Nelson. Slightly halting at
the bend in the road where the fire from small arms was
indeed terrific, and discharging a few shots from our revolvers at the rocks above, we dashed around the point, broke
through their centre, trampled down their reserve, and
passed away beyond the fight in pursuit of the coveted artillery. But it was too fleet-footed for us, and we returned in
time to help Lieut. Marshall, with the two rear sections,
clean out the reserve. They had been stationed in the road,
and though somewhat confused and scattered by our sudden
advent among them, made for cover and stood like a tiger

at bay. By this time, the infantry, under Capts. Downing, Wynkoop and Anthony, came down on them like a parcel of wild Indians, cheering at the top of their lungs, regardless of the shower of bullets raining among them. It was a fine evening, and the boys felt like fun; they were full of *vim* as they could hold. The Texans, terrified at the impetuosity of the attack, broke and fled in every direction.

Personal incidents make quite an episode in this hand to hand encounter. Boone and Dixon took fifteen fellows from a house which they could have held against fifty. As they were being disarmed, somebody cried out "Shoot the s——s of b——s." "No, I'm d——d if you do. I'm d——d if you do. You didn't take 'em. I took these prisoners myself, prisoners of wah. Fall in thar, prisoners. Forward, double quick," and away went Boone to the rear with them.

Lowe's horse fell with and partly on him, badly wrenching his knee, in the ditch just around the corner where the fire was hottest. Hastily disengaging himself from his horse, he jumped over a bank to gain some shelter. He was confronted by a stalwart Texan captain, who, with a cocked pistol bearing on him, "guessed Lowe was his prisoner." Lowe sprang on him like a cat, and after a violent struggle disarmed and marched him to the rear.

Logan, already wounded in the face, observing a fellow behind a rock, leveled on him, when he called out that he was wounded and wished to surrender. Logan dropped his aim and advanced to disarm him, when he coolly drew up his pistol and fired. The ball, which was meant for a centre shot passed through Logan's arm. "O, you son of a b——h," exclaimed Logan, "I'll kill you now. G——d d——n you." And suiting the action to the word, put a bullet through his head. He lived long enough to tell his brother that his death-shot had been given after he was wounded and a prisoner. Logan being in the hospital at Pigeon's, which the Texans occupied after the second fight, heard them talking about it, swearing they would hang the perpetrator of the atrocity if they could lay hands on him. Whereupon he informed them he was the man that did it, and gave his reasons. His story, backed by his wounds, proved entirely satisfactory, and he and the Texans were on the best of terms until they were separated.

Dan. Rice, who claims no kin to the great showman, opened a show of his own on the occasion of a certain bone-heap yclept "Rice's Battery," depositing him on the road where the leaden hail fell thickest and there leaving him to his fate. What he did, or rather did not, I cannot tell, but those who saw it say there was humor in it of the broadest kind.

Many of the boys were unhorsed in the charge, and some of the horses escaped entirely, which should be credited no doubt to profit.

We were obliged to make prisoners of some forty or fifty —all there were in the road; for when they found us in their midst, as if descended from the clouds, they forgot that one of them was equal to five of us, and insisted on surrendering.

In half an hour after the charge the enemy had disappeared and the firing ceased. It was too dark to follow them.

Slowly and sadly we gathered our dead and wounded and returned to Pigeon's Ranche, as there was no water in the canon where we were.

A reinforcement of five hundred men, with the howitzer battery, Capt. Claflin, arrived just as we did, and the woods rang for half an hour with their cheering.

No cheers came from me. I was sick at the wounds of Dutro, and spent the night watching his life ebb away.

Thus ended our first battle. We had driven them from their position under every disadvantage; killed and disabled fifty at least, and captured one fourth of their entire number. If we had had two hours more daylight our victory would have been still more decisive. Darkness favored their escape.

The action, though small, was conducted with great spirit and judgment. Officers and men came to the scratch with enthusiasm. The impression made on the enemy paved the way for success in subsequent encounters. They cared little for death—we cared less. By their own admission they never expected to whip us till the last man had bit the dust.

The feelings of men in battle is a subject of interest to people generally. I am persuaded there are but few brave men by nature. Battle brings all speculation to a point. Life and death stare each other in the face. Life, however miserable, against death that ends all. Until actually engaged, the most of men suffer excessively from suspense. In the midst of a fight they partake more or less of the demoniac spirit surrounding them. The "thunder of the captains and the shouting" has an awful inspiration of its own. Man glories in his mad power and fear is forgotten. But the men who go into battle with pleasure, depend upon it, are mighty scattering. Many, whose patriotism is unaffected and pure, would flinch at the last moment but for self-respect. That I believe is the only boon *more* precious than life.

Our loss was 5 killed, 13 wounded and 3 missing. How we escaped so cheaply God only knows, for we rode five hundred yards through a perfect hailstorm of bullets. Many were the men lying behind rocks, almost near enough to knock us off our horses, taking dead rests and firing as we passed. Among the conflicting emotions of that evening, not the weakest was one of disappointment in the character of the foe we had met. "Why, they ought to have killed the last one of us," was in the mouth of every one, as often as they thought of it. Our Second Lieut. Marshall, in breaking a prisoner's gun, shot himself so badly that he died in a few hours. "This was the most unkindest cut of all." True bravery, which not only deserves but compels respect, had elevated him in the estimation of the company and the regiment, and his cruel, unfortunate death cast a shadow athwart the glories of the day.

Capt. Cook, than whom none truer can be found, was all shot to pieces, but his usual fortitude remained with him. The ghastly smile with which he endeavored to make light of his wounds, to cheer his boys, betrayed his agony.

We lost three men—Martin Dutro, Jude W. Johnson and George Thompson. Mart was shot down obliquely through the head, and again through the chest, and lived till near morning. He was a noble hearted, generous fellow, and the boys loved him. As we lowered his remains to their last resting place, all the stoicism I could muster was unsufficient to suppress some bitter tears at his early and cruel death. The other boys died instantly, one shot through the head, the other through the heart. They were among our very best men. Bristol, Pratt, Keel, Hall, Logan and Patterson were wounded, and left in the hospital at Pigeon's Ranche.

After burying our dead, some teams went out and brought in a lot of Texan flour and corn, stored at a short distance. As there was only a well at Pigeon's from which to water our stock, we fell back to our camp at Coslosky's. The prisoners were sent to Union under guard of Lord's company of dragoons.

As near as we could learn, the Texan loss yesterday was 16 killed, 30 to 40 wounded, and 75 prisoners, including 7 commissioned officers.

BATTLE OF PIGEON'S RANCHE.

MARCH TWENTY-EIGHTH.

Late last evening Col. Slough arrived with the reserve, from Vernal Spring. They had heard of the engagement yesterday, and could not be restrained. Companies A, B, E and H, of the First, Jim Ford's of the Second, and A and G of the Fifth Infantry, were detached from the command and sent across the mountains, under Major Chivington, to harass the enemies' rear. Lieut. Falvey, of the dragoons, with forty mounted men, went on a scout towards Galisteo. The balance of the regiment, with two batteries and two small companies of regular cavalry, numbering about six hundred, moved forward again towards Santa Fe, not doubting but that every inch of ground would be stubbornly contested by the Rangers. We knew nothing certainly of their force, either as to strength, disposition or intentions, and consequently were slightly surprised when at Pigeon's our pickets came in somewhat hurriedly and reported the Texans advancing in force, and less than half a mile distant. The men were resting—some visiting the wounded in the hospital, others filling their water canteens. Suddenly the bugles sounded assembly, we seized our arms, fell in and hastened forward perhaps five hundred yards, when their artillery commenced cutting the tree tops over our heads.

The cavalry halted, dismounted and formed to the front, under shelter of a small hill. Both batteries, the large one consisting of two twelve-pound howitzers and two six-pound shot-guns, Capt. Ritter, the small one of four twelve-pound mountain howitzers, Capt. Claflin, were run forward and opened with great spirit. Col. Slough came up, and in a hoarse voice gave his orders. Companies K and C were stationed in the road, sheltered by the brow of the hill, as a support to the batteries; D and I were advanced on either hand as skirmishers; G was on guard perhaps a mile in the rear.

The battle was opened and seemed going well enough, judging from the deafening roar of artillery, the unceasing rattle of small arms, accompanied by all kinds of cheering and yelling from the men, when the Colonel, to draw them out, ordered the cavalry to fall back on Pigeon's. The artillery followed; Claflin's battery took position on a hill on the left, while Ritter's remained in the road near the house. The Texan battery soon slackened its fire till it almost ceased. Companies D and I had picked off all the gunners and one piece was dismounted by our guns. If there had been anybody to support Capt. Downing they never would have taken their artillery from the field.

But these brave boys paid dearly for their temerity. Advancing without support they combated the whole Texan force alone for a few minutes. Having lost one half their men and seen Lieut. Baker fall, severely wounded, they reluctantly gave ground.

Our company was posted on a rocky point opposite Claflin's battery and near the ranche, behind which our horses were sheltered.

Owing to the nature of the ground, rough, hilly, rocky and timbered, cavalry and artillery were almost useless, and it became evident that rifles must decide the contest. We were obliged to remain near our horses, yet many of the boys thought our Sharpes inspired more terror, even at five hundred yards distance, than the battery opposite.

The regular cavalry was of no account at all, for whenever the Texans came in sight they would mount and fall back out of range. Walker's company never discharged a single rifle during the day.

Company G, hearing the rumpus, came up on double-quick. The first platoon, Capt. Wilder, hurried to the support of Downing; the second, Lieut. Hardin, was assigned to Ritter's battery, which had retired three or four hundred yards.

The Texan artillery was again playing a lively tune, and as the thunder reverberated from mountain to mountain we could scarcely tell our guns from theirs—both about equidistant.

The hard breast to breast fighting was mostly confined to the flanks. Outnumbering us three to one they made the preponderance still greater by flocking thither to avoid our artillery, which was well served throughout the day. In this unequal struggle Lieut. Chambers, of C, a brave soldier and a gentleman, was severely wounded in the shoulder and thigh, while electrifying his men by his voice and example.

Downing, Wilder, Baker, Davidson, Kerber and others stubbornly held their ground, only yielding, inch by inch, to an overwhelmingly superior fire. When they were outflanked and nearly surrounded they would deliver a stunning volley and fall back a piece. Thus they were nearly always covered, an advantage which their sparse numbers rendered inestimable.

If the Texans had known how weak we were doubtless they would have ruined us, but the lesson of the day before made them cautious. They would creep along up from tree to tree, and from rock to rock, but as sure as one rose in fair view a dozen balls gave his soul choice in the way of departure.

Doubtless other officers performed their duty gallantly—but not coming under my immediate observation it is not so particularly noticed. Report says, however, that Lieuts.

Cobb and Anderson, on the Colonel's staff, were fearless and prompt in the discharge of their arduous duties.

About noon we were forced to retire our whole line half a mile, as they had discovered our weakness and were endeavoring to surround us. At this juncture about three hundred fresh troops came to their assistance, and with this for a charging column they designed to corral our whole command.

Claflin's battery was posted in the road, some portions of the wings called to its support, the cavalry formed on the left in line of battle, and we were ready for them. Col. Slough came to the front and assisted in the disposition of our handful of men. Robbins, Soule and Hardin were there, every one of them as cool and collected as if on parade. Lieut. Col. Tappan sat on his horse during the charge, leisurely loading and firing his pistols as if rabbit hunting.

The bullets came from every point but the rear, showing that this was an effort to close in and capture us. It was right, of course, if they had the "sand" to do it.

Soon they appeared in front, encouraged and shouted on by as brave officers as live; some in squads, others singly, taking advantage of the timber as much as possible in their approach. Waiting till they came within fifty yards, Claflin's battery opened on them like a regiment of Mexican dogs roused by the stranger at midnight. One man shoved in a charge with his arm, another fired her off, and the four pieces played the liveliest Yankee doodle ever heard—and all the time thud, thud, thud, the bullets coming down off the mountains on each side into the ground.

Claflin's salute appeared to astonish them, but when that ceased and the support fired volley after volley into their faces they concluded they were going the wrong way and turned back. We followed them a ways to see how well they could run.

The time gained by this repulse enabled us to extricate ourselves from our perilous position, move back, and take a new stand. This was immediately done. They closed in, and where they expected to wipe us out they found a few dead and wounded.

We took a new position beyond a large open space; our guns thundered as defiantly as ever, but their firing soon ceased. They had no inclination to come out of the woods and fight on open ground, and we slowly retired to camp.

Though we were obliged to give ground from the commencement yet considering the disparity of our forces (by their own admission they had 1800) we were well satisfied. The Colorados are willing to fight them, man for man, every day in the year.

A flag of truce, which seems to be their best hold, arrived in camp as soon as we did, requesting an armistice of eighteen hours duration, ostensibly to bury their dead and take care of their wounded; really to gain time to return to Santa Fe, which they immediately commenced doing in the greatest confusion.

The cause of this remains to be noticed. Though we had crippled them severely, yet they would undoubtedly have tried us on again whenever we were so disposed had not the Major succeeded in striking a blow which pierced to their vitals and drew from thence the life blood. He left camp in the morning with a force of 450 men, crossed the mountains with no regard to obstacles, routes, or ought else save direction and gained their rear. Scattering their rearguard to the winds, he blew up and destroyed their supply train of seventy wagons, containing all the ammunition, provisions, clothing and other war supplies they had in the

Territory; spiked one six-pounder with a ram-rod and tumbled it down the mountain, and then, every man taking his own course, regained our camp soon after dark without any loss whatever.

On arriving in sight of our camp-fires, the Major, ignorant of the events of the day, characteristically called a halt, and as he gave the command, "Fall in, every man in his place;" "Fix bayonets," only replied to the murmur of inquiry as to whose camp it was, "I don't know whose it is, but if it a'nt ours we'll soon make it so." "Forward," "Keep close," and they started for the camp. On coming within hailing distance of the guard they found it was the Colorados, and reserved their hostility for other occasions.

This was the irreparable blow that compelled the Texans to evacuate the Territory. Its audacity was the principal cause of its success.

Had we known the extent of the injury inflicted, we might have advanced to Santa Fe without firing a gun. Caution, however, seemed to be in the ascendant, and perhaps it will win oftener than it will lose.

Tardy George

THE COUNTRY CHAFED at General George B. McClellan's slowness to move his army into action.

President Lincoln exercised his prerogative as commander in chief to question in early February McClellan's plans:

"*My dear Sir*—You and I have distinct and different plans for a movement of the Army of the Potomac—yours to be down the Chesapeake, up the Rappahannock to Urbanna, and across land to the terminus of the railroad on York River; mine to move directly to a point on the railroad southwest of Manassas. If you will give me satisfactory answers to the following questions I shall gladly yield my plan to yours:

"1. Does not your plan involve a greatly larger expenditure of *time* and *money* than mine?

"2. Wherein is a victory more certain by your plan than mine?

"3. Wherein is a victory *more valuable* by your plan than mine?

"4. In fact, would it not be *less* valuable in this, that

it would break no great line of the enemy's communication, while mine would?

"5. In case of disaster, would not a safe retreat be more difficult by your plan than by mine? Yours truly,

A. Lincoln"

George H. Boker expressed the feeling of the people generally in a satirical poem, "Tardy George."

McClellan secured approval for *his* plan, however, and spoke to his army with confidence and pride in an address to his soldiers in March.

TARDY GEORGE.

What are you waiting for, George, I pray?—
To scour your cross-belts with fresh pipe-clay?
To burnish your buttons, to brighten your guns;
Or wait you for May-day and warm Spring suns?
Are you blowing your fingers because they are cold,
Or catching your breath ere you take a hold?
Is the mud knee-deep in valley and gorge?
What are you waiting for, tardy George?

Want you a thousand more cannon made,
To add to the thousand now arrayed?
Want you more men, more money to pay?
Are not two millions enough per day?
Wait you for gold and credit to go,
Before we shall see your martial show;
Till Treasury Notes will not pay to forge?
What are you waiting for, tardy George?

Are you waiting for your hair to turn,
Your heart to soften, your bowels to yearn
A little more towards "our Southern friends,"
As at home and abroad they work their ends?
"Our Southern friends!" whom you hold so dear
That you do no harm and give no fear,
As you tenderly take them by the gorge?
What are you waiting for, tardy George?

Now that you've marshaled your whole command,
Planned what you would, and changed what you
    planned;
Practiced with shot and practiced with shell,
Know to a hair where every one fell,
Made signs by day and signals by night;
Was it all done to keep out of a fight?
Is the whole matter too heavy a charge?
What are you waiting for, tardy George?

Shall we have more speeches, more reviews?
Or are you waiting to hear the news;
To hold up your hands in mute surprise
When France and England shall "recognize"?
Are you too grand to fight traitors small?
Must you have a Nation to cope withal?
Well, hammer the anvil and blow the forge:
You'll soon have a dozen, tardy George!

Suppose for a moment, George, my friend—
Just for a moment—you condescend
To use the means that are in your hands,
The eager muskets, and guns, and brands;

Take one bold step on the Southern sod,
And leave the issue to watchful God!
For now the Nation raises its gorge,
Waiting and watching you, tardy George!

I should not much wonder, George, my boy,
If Stanton get in his head a toy,
And some fine morning, ere you are out,
He send you all "to the right about"—
You and Jomini, and all the crew
Who think that war is nothing to do
But drill, and cipher, and hammer, and forge—
What are you waiting for, tardy George?
    JANUARY, 1862.

HEADQUARTERS ARMY OF THE POTOMAC,

FAIRFAX COURT HOUSE, VA., *March* 14, 1862.

SOLDIERS OF THE ARMY OF THE POTOMAC!

For a long time I have kept you inactive, but not without
a purpose; you were to be disciplined, armed and instructed;
the formidable artillery you now have, had to be created;
other armies were to move and accomplish certain results.
I have held you back that you might give the death-blow
to the rebellion that has distracted our once happy country.
The patience you have shown, and your confidence in your
General, are worth a dozen victories. These preliminary results are now accomplished. I feel that the patient labors of
many months have produced their fruit; the Army of the
Potomac is now a real Army,—magnificent in material, admirable in discipline and instruction, excellently equipped
and armed;—your commanders are all that I could wish. The

moment for action has arrived, and I know that I can trust in you to save our country. As I ride through your ranks, I see in your faces the sure presage of victory; I feel that you will do whatever I ask of you. The period of inaction has passed. I will bring you now face to face with the rebels, and only pray that God may defend the right. In whatever direction you may move, however strange my actions may appear to you, ever bear in mind that my fate is linked with yours, and that all I do is to bring you, where I know you wish to be,—on the decisive battlefield. It is my business to place you there. I am to watch over you as a parent over his children; and you know that your General loves you from the depths of his heart. It shall be my care, as it has ever been, to gain success with the least possible loss; but I know that, if it is necessary, you will willingly follow me to our graves, for our righteous cause. God smiles upon us, victory attends us, yet I would not have you think that our aim is to be attained without a manly struggle. I will not disguise it from you: you have brave foes to encounter, foemen well worthy of the steel that you will use so well. I shall demand of you great, heroic exertions, rapid and long marches, desperate combats, privations, perhaps. We will share all these together; and when this sad war is over we will all return to our homes, and feel that we can ask no higher honor than the proud consciousness that we belonged to the ARMY OF THE POTOMAC.

GEO. B. McCLELLAN,
Major General Commanding.

One of the Strangest Naval Combats

THE GREAT NAVAL BATTLE at Hampton Roads between the Federal *Monitor* and the Confederate *Virginia* (the renamed *Merrimac*) was, in the words of Swiss observer Ferdinand LeComte, "one of the strangest naval combats." It was also one of the most important. It was the test in an actual military situation of the iron vessels whose adoption would soon revolutionize the navies of the world.

LeComte was most interested in the uses of new tools of war in the army. But the chance to report on such an important military development as these new ships, even to the navy-less Swiss, was one he could not overlook.

His report on the American war was sound and interesting throughout, and it was soon translated and published in New York for the American audience.

Since I am to speak of machinery utilized for the war, I shall be pardoned for saying, also, a few words of one of the most remarkable facts of this war, viz.: the transformation in naval constructions.

We may well wait for what the mechanical genius of this people may realize, having reference to the means of the struggle, as well as the remarkable innovations in other more pacific domains. The results have still surpassed the anticipations. The old wooden navy, those collossi of 120 guns, which made the pride of England and of France, are now only decayed powers in the presence of the heavy calibres and the armored vessels created by the Americans.

The two belligerent parties had from the commencement of the war constructed vessels covered with iron, of various forms, and on each side they hoped to surprise one another. On both sides they found themselves gradually entering the lists with equal arms.

The 6th of March, in Hampton Roads, near Fortress Monroe, one of the strangest naval combats took place—one with which the whole world has resounded. The secession frigate, the *Merrimac*, proceeding from Norfolk, had just attacked, and disabled in a few hours, two powerful frigates of war of the United States, the *Cumberland* and the *Congress*. The next day a vessel equally singular in construction, the *Monitor*, in its turn entered the contest on the side of the Federals, and forced the terrible vanquisher to a retreat.

Having had the advantage of seeing these two vessels, and of visiting the *Monitor* in the very roadstead of the combat, I shall endeavor to give here a brief description of it.

The *Merrimac* has nothing particularly remarkable in fact, except her iron armor and ram. She is an old frigate of the first class, of the United States. She was of very small cost, and made in 1857 her first voyage to England. Anchored at Southampton, she was then remarked upon by critics for her proportions and for the cut of her hull, and provoked controversy amongst seamen and builders.

Sunk by the Federals at the time that they were engaged

in evacuating their maritime arsenal at Norfolk, where she was, she was afterwards put afloat again by the Secessionists. They razed her, and covered her with iron plating, rising by plates superposed one upon the other, in the form of a roof above the deck. They furnished her with ten Armstrong guns: four at each side, one on the prow, and one on the poop. In front was fixed an enormous iron ram; by the port, and by two openings near the chimney, were arranged pipes for throwing boiling water and steam, as a defence against attempts at boarding.

When the *Merrimac* wished to go out, thus armed, for the first time, she could not float, and was obliged to be lightened; but she remained always slow in her movements. Only once was she able to use her ram at pleasure; this was on the occasion of her demonstration against the *Cumberland*, which once experienced her destructive power. Since then, her adversaries have always been able to avoid her blows.

The strength of this vessel, as the engagements at Hampton have demonstrated, consisted chiefly in the resistance which her armor opposed to the enemy's fire, and which permitted her, without fear, to moor herself with broadside presented, at short range. She confronted thus three complete broadsides of the *Cumberland*, a sustained fire from the *Congress* at short distance, and another of the *Monitor*. This last succeeded only in inflicting upon her an injury in front, which caused her to abandon the struggle. To supply the rapidity of movement which she lacked, the *Merrimac* went escorted by two or three steamers and gunboats, performing about her the service of scouts and sharp-shooters.

At a distance, the heavy-looking *Merrimac*, without mast, and with her low chimney, gliding slowly over the sea, had a strange and monstrous aspect, which struck the inhabitants of the coast with superstitious terror.

It is known that this vessel was destroyed the 18th of May, at the time of the capture of Norfolk by the Federals. The Secessionists not being willing to let her fall into the hands of her former proprietors, and not being able to carry her away, inasmuch as she was then receiving repairs, blew her up while evacuating the place. On the other hand, they towed to Richmond the carcass of another *Merrimac*, whose early appearance on the James River has been announced.

The *Monitor*, created by Captain Ericcson [Ericsson], is of a wholly different character. It was constructed after a plan well considered, and with the idea of offering the least possible surface to the blows of the enemy; of giving to this exposed surface a solidity proof against every thing; and of causing the density of the water to operate as a shield for the most delicate parts.

Entirely answering to this plan, the *Monitor* makes but little show, and it was some time before I was able to discover her at Hampton Roads, in the midst of the vessels of every dimension confided to her protection.

Upon the whole, this vessel is a raft, like a body on a level with the water, under which is found a hull, less long and less wide, enclosing the machinery, and with the spiral line of the hull, the anchor, and the helm all below. On the raft is raised a tower, sheltering two Dahlgren cannon of two hundred pounds each. The tower can be moved on a circular framework, and this movement is directed from the interior of the tower. By this means the cannon, while remaining all the while under cover, can be brought to bear in every direction of the horizon.

The raft has a length of about one hundred and seventy feet by a width of forty, and a depth of five, of which three and a half are under water. Her waterline is elliptical.

The lower hull is about one hundred and twenty feet in length, thirty-five in width, and seven in depth. It is perceived then that she is curtailed at the points of the ellipse by fifty feet, and on the sides by five feet, on the full length of the raft. These two parts are of oak, covered with sheets and plates of iron. The tower, wholly of iron, is nine feet high by twenty in diameter, and presents a thickness of metal of nine inches, in eight concentric walls. The two ports are three feet above the deck. Her mechanism for effecting the rotation of the tower is very ingenious, but would demand, in order to give a complete idea of it, a detailed description with drawings, which I have not the means of presenting here. Two men alone suffice to handle the guns. The smoke escapes by traps in the roof of the tower, and also by means of a ventilating apparatus which conducts it to other grated traps under the deck. Apart from the tower, the raft offers no other prominent point except the pilot-house, also of iron, which rises twelve inches above the deck, and has inclined sides. Holes, covered with glass, allow the pilot to direct the vessel, while being fully under cover.

It is thus seen that this battery is theoretically adapted to its object; its delicate portions are covered by a great thickness of water, and its exterior portions, of small surface, strongly protected, and circular, offer little hold for the action of the projectiles. Practical experiment corroborated these calculations of theory. In the combat of the 7th of March the two guns of the *Monitor* contended for two hours against the ten of the *Merrimac*, without other damage than a blow at the look-out of the pilot-house. Several times did the *Monitor*, manœuvring with ease, avoid, without ceasing her fire, the charges of the ram of her antagonist.

Since then the *Monitor* has not been engaged but once, against Fort Darling, below Richmond, and it was admitted

that she required still some improvements, among others
the following:

1st. The arrangement of the guns in the tower does not
permit a sufficient inclination of range;

2d. Her slight elevation above the water-line causes it to
be doubted whether she can bear the open sea. Room would
also fail her for supplies for a long voyage;

3d. The tower has the ordinary inconvenience of casemates; the smoke, and especially the heat, are not dissipated
there with sufficient readiness, and soon become very annoying to the gunners.

These observations, the first two in particular, will appear
the better founded, as Captain Ericsson had not had the
intention of making the *Monitor* any thing else than a coast
battery, designed originally, during the incident of the *Trent,*
to defend the entrance to the harbor of New York. The con-
structor having afterwards solicited the opportunity of proving his battery against the enemy, she was sent in haste to
Fortress Monroe, when the real existence and the approaching sortie of the *Merrimac* were learned. The guns which
were used in the fight were not of the intended calibre; and
Commodore Dahlgren thinks that if his gun, of large calibre,
had been in action, the *Merrimac* would have been pierced
and sunk.

The fight of the 7th of March produced a great sensation
in the United States. The two vessels engaged in the tilt,
which until then had been considered as chimerical constructions, and on which many a jester had exercised his wit,
were surrounded with respect, and on all sides mechanicians,
ship-owners, and engineers put themselves to work to create
and improve vessels of this kind. They used old vessels which
they improved; they constructed new ones; they invented
others, of forms more and more odd; and to-day the navy

of the United States possesses a whole fleet of these formidable engines. The *Naugatuck* and the *Galena* were the first
to join the *Monitor* in the James River. The waters of the
Mississippi bear also a fleet of them, and, very recently, the
Secessionists have put one afloat, the *Arkansas,* which made
her *début* in passing by force the Federal gunboats, in order
to strengthen the defences of Vicksburg.

It is necessary, however, to recognize, that these so improved products of the mechanic arts bear in them defects,
arising from their very excellencies. The smallest error in
time, a slight accident to the machinery, is sufficient, sometimes, to paralyze the action of an immense force, and to
cause disappointments which are so much the more lively
as the hopes excited have been great. It is thus that, at the
attack on Fort Darling, the 15th of May, the Federal flotilla
was unable to obtain any result. The *Galena,* which had been
grounded in ascending the James River, had to be lightened,
and was soon deficient in munitions. The *Naugatuck* saw
her hundred-pound gun burst at the first fire; and the *Monitor* had to remain at long range to get her angle of aim.

At the same time that it was sought to appropriate these
new means of destruction, each party aimed with not less
eagerness at obtaining the corresponding means of preservation. After the poison, the antidote, after the projectile, the
plate: thus is the career of invention pursued. This second
search is also not less interesting than the other.

I give below the facts of the contest which I have heard
the most appreciated, in view of new combats between the
Merrimac and the *Monitor*.

Against the *Merrimac,* the North proposed to employ the
shock, as being the most effectual mode of action. Certain
enormous steamers, of great swiftness, and heavily ballasted,
amongst others the *Vanderbilt* and the *Constitution,* were to

rush, under a full head of steam, upon the *Merrimac*. The latter, less capable of moving, could not avoid the shock of one of these steamers, and, according to the calculations and the laws of dynamics, would necessarily be sunk. With this object, a flotilla of this naval cavalry was for a long while in station below Fortress Monroe, always under steam. While it should have prepared and executed its charges, the *Merrimac* would have been entertained by the fire of the *Monitor* and other armored vessels.

Great success was not expected from boarding, considering the difficulty of throwing men on the inclined sides of the armor, who, besides, could be driven back by jets of boiling water and steam.

Against the *Monitor*, I have heard it said that the seamen of the South thought, amongst others, of three means, which appear in fact susceptible of some efficiency.

They would attempt to board her, and bold men would throw shell into the tower through the ports. But the *Monitor* put herself on guard against this danger by the arrangement of pumps of boiling water discharging at the ports.

Or, they would open the deck and sink her, by a bombshot of heavy calibre, and as vertical as possible. But such a shot it is difficult to make.

Or, to capture her with a chain,—to throw it in the manner of a *lasso* around the tower, and to ground her on the coast.

It is unfortunate that these different means, sufficiently curious, of contest, cannot, perhaps, be put to the proof, in new actions between these same two vessels. But they will be so, without doubt, in others, under conditions very similar.

Upon the whole, the navy of the United States, whether it be by its creations or by its operations, has acquired, and is acquiring still, the greatest honor in this war. It may well console her for the disappointments which the land army has experienced.

The blockade of so great an extent of coast, a blockade which, whatever may be said of it, is as real and as effective as a blockade has ever been, testifies the power and the vigilance of the Federal fleet.

The actions of Fort Pulaski, of Forts Donelson and Henry, of Port Royal, of Hampton, of Vicksburg, of New Orleans, and of other points of the Mississippi; also of Pittsburg Landing, and of Harrison's Landing, show what resources of energy, of precision, and of intrepidity, there are among these brave seamen.

In fine, the frequent transportation of troops, successfully effected at the distance of hundreds of leagues along the coast, the embarkation and disembarkation of the Army of the Potomac, of those of Burnside, Butler, and Sherman, with all their supplies and *matériel* of the heaviest calibre, prove that the most difficult and extensive operations can be seriously undertaken by an army, as well as seconded on all the navigable waters.

At this time an entire fleet of vessels, identical with the *Monitor,* is in course of construction in the various shipyards of the North, without reckoning a great number of others on different models.* When these different vessels shall have taken the sea, that is to say, in a few months only, the United States will possess, for the moment, the greatest military naval force in the world, and will be able to exercise sovereign control over their waters. I have it from a very

---

* Amongst other variations from the system of Capt. Ericsson, is mentioned the system of Whitney, of which a specimen, the *Keokuk,* is at this time being built at New York. As capable of resistance as the Monitors, it will be lighter, inasmuch as wood enters, for a great part, into its construction, and be more manageable. It will have a speed of ten knots an hour.

experienced and impartial seaman, that the famous *Warrior*, or her rival *La Gloire*, would find themselves at a disadvantage against a single Monitor. In return, those vessels are more suitable, it is true, for distant navigation.

In the course of this year, nine new Monitors, constructed under the direction of Capt. Ericsson, ought to be launched, to wit: the *Montauk*, the *Catskill*, and the *Passaic*, in course of construction at Green Point, New York; the *Sangamon* and *Lehigh*, in construction at Chester, Pennsylvania; the *Nantucket* and the *Nahant*, in construction at Boston; the *Weehawken*, in construction at Jersey City; and the *Patapsco*, in construction at Wilmington, Delaware.

At the commencement of the year 1863, the military marine of the North should reckon fifty mailed vessels, on different systems and of different strength.

The South, really very inferior in this respect, and everywhere closely blockaded in her ports, is also making great efforts to establish for herself a navy. It is said that two new Merrimacs are already in advanced construction at Richmond, and that they ought soon to make their appearance in the waters of the James River. Another is expected to contribute to the defence of Vicksburg, on the Mississippi. Others are in construction at Charleston, and still others are receiving their armament in England, designed to give chase to the commercial vessels of the North.

Shiloh

THERE WAS STILL no movement of the army in Virginia, but the army in the West was pressing deep into Confederate territory. Nashville fell in February. Early in April one of the great battles of the war took place, forever changing the meaning of "Shiloh" from "place of peace."

Here is the account of that battle written by a private soldier only a week after the event. It is signed only "W." but, according to John Page Nicholson, the author was W. W. Worthington.

FIELD OF SHILOH, TENNESSEE, APRIL 14th, 1862.

DEAR KING:—I commence writing you a letter, which, I know, you will be glad to get; for I mean to tell you what our battalion did on the 6th and 7th inst., whilst the great battle at this place was progressing. * * * Leaving Columbia, we took up the line of march for Savannah, a distance of eighty-two miles through a country almost uninhabited and barren to the last degree. On Saturday night we en-

111

camped at a place seventeen miles from the latter town. Starting again the next morning, we had proceeded but a little way when the noise of the battle of that disastrous day broke upon our ears. As we advanced the cannonading became each moment more distinct. It was plain that a desperate fight was going on somewhere: but not one of our number dreamed that Grant had been attacked and was at that instant slowly losing ground before the enemy. Indeed the general belief was created by reports brought from the front that our gunboats were attacking some batteries at a place called Hamburg. About noon, however, we began to think it possible that in some way or other our aid might be needed; for we were halted in an old cotton field, our arms were inspected, and rations and ammunition were issued. Still we were ignorant of the terrible conflict then going on, though by this time the ground fairly trembled under our feet with the rapid discharge of artillery. Again pushing on, sweltering in the hot southern sun, travelling over roads almost impassable and fording several streams, about dark we halted for a few hours at a creek three miles inland from Savannah. There we learned for the first time, that instead of a gunboat bombardment, that day had been fought at Pittsburg Landing, the bloodiest battle in which American troops were ever engaged. The accounts of the conflict were most cheering. They represented that Grant had that morning attacked the immense army under Albert Sidney Johnston and Beauregard, completely defeating and routing it after a desperate fight of fifteen hours duration. The cannon we continued to hear at intervals were said to be those hurried forward in pursuit of the flying enemy. You may be sure we were jubilant at this news; although we declaimed somewhat against the selfishness that precipitated the engagement and won the victory before Buell's column had an opportunity to take a part. Little did we dream that so far from having gained a triumph, Grant's force was then defeated and panic-stricken, with an insolent foe occupying most of his camps, and that the morrow would introduce us to scenes of carnage the mere imagination of which sickens the heart.

It was quite dark, though still early in the night, when we moved on again. The men were in the best of spirits, rude witticisms, laughter and snatches of song ran along the whole line. Here and there some fellow boasted of the gallant deeds he would have performed had he been in the day's engagement. The officers, on the other hand, were more quiet than usual. They marched in silence or gathered in little knots and conversed in whispers. At length, the town of Savannah was entered. Every house in the place seemed to be illuminated; for each had been converted into an hospital and was packed from attic to basement with the dying and wounded who had been conveyed thither by the steamer.

Groans and cries of pain saluted our ears from all the buildings we passed. Through the windows, the sash of which were removed to give air to the injured, we could see the surgeons plying their horrid profession. The atmosphere was that of a vast dissecting room. The streets were crowded with ambulances, baggage trains, parties bearing the victims of the fight on stretchers, on rails, on rude litters of muskets and on their shoulders, and with batteries of artillery and long lines of infantry waiting to be taken to the scene of the struggle. The confusion everywhere visible, the shouting, cursing, quarrelling, beggars descriptions. Teams of mules, abandoned by their drivers, ran away trampling down every thing in their course. Quartermasters rode about at furious pace trying to extricate their transportation from the general mass. Doctors, one hand full of instruments, the other of bandages, and covered with blood, wildly rushed through the immense crowd in search of additional subjects of their art. Still, from all that could be gathered, the idea appeared to be that we had achieved a great victory. No one could exactly tell the events of the day; but the fact of our decisive triumph was unquestioned. The falsity of this common opinion every reader of the newspapers already knows.

Getting on board the "Hiawatha," by midnight we were ploughing the turbid Tennessee river *en route* for Pittsburg Landing, by water a distance of fourteen miles. From the officers of the steamer we got other accounts of the battle, which we afterwards ascertained to be correct. Their statements were, that Johnston and Beauregard, hoping to destroy Grant before he was joined by Buell, then close at hand, made a furious attack upon him, in great strength, that Sunday morning immediately after daylight. There is some dispute whether or not we had outposts; those who maintain we had, admit that they were playing cards at the time of the assault. At all events our troops were completely and criminally surprised. Unable to form to resist the onslaught, hundreds of them were mercilessly shot down in their tents and company streets. Those who escaped fled in the greatest terror through the camps in their rear, spreading the panic and closely followed by the successful foe. At least two miles of the ground occupied by our forces was thus abandoned before the regiments near the river could be brought to present a front to the rebels. A temporary check was then given to the enemy's impetuous advance, but being strongly reinforced they pushed our army slowly and surely towards the landing. During the whole day the battle raged with violence. Several corps of our volunteers behaved with great gallantry; but others ran at the first fire, and with those surprised in the morning (at least 10,000 men) could not again be brought into action. But the Secessionists steadily gained upon us. Seven batteries of our light artillery and a large number of our soldiers fell into their hands, as well as thousands of tents, and immense quantities of Commissary and Quartermaster's stores. When night closed upon the struggle we were driven within three hundred yards of the river, and would have been pushed into it had not the spiteful little gunboats then been enabled to come to our relief. Our loss in the engagement was terrible; but it was not all we suffered. At times when the fortune of war was most decidedly against us, the skulkers under the bluff, would rush in crowds to reach the steamers moored in the Tennessee, and by jostling and pushing each other into and struggling together in the water, hundreds of them were drowned. Little pity is felt for their fate, of course; but still these help to swell the casualties of that disastrous day.

Regaled, as we were, during the entire passage from Savannah to Pittsburg Landing, with stories of defeat and forebodings of what would occur the next day, you may be certain that we were not as comfortable as if we were in the old barracks. It was plain to the dullest comprehension that McCook's, Nelson's and Crittenden's divisions of Buell's army, then arrived at the scene of action, would have work enough to do early in the morning, and that too against an enemy flushed with recent victory. It seemed like folly to hope for success; for our strength did not exceed thirty thousand. From Grant's badly beaten and demoralized force we expected nothing, unless it was a mere show of numbers. On the other hand, the rebels were estimated at from 60,000 to 80,000. These considerations did not do much to inspirit, whilst throughout the night our anxiety was kept alive and our consciousness of the immediate presence of the foe not permitted to slumber by the regular firing from the gunboats upon the camps of the enemy close beside those of our own.

At daybreak on Monday the 7th inst. our battalion was disembarked. Forcing its way with difficulty through the vast crowd of fugitives from the previous day's fight gathered on the river bank, we scrambled up the bluff in the best way we could and formed in the camp of the Missouri Artillery. Here there were more refugees, their officers riding among them and urging them to rally, but without the least success. I never witnessed such abject fear as these fellows exhibited. Without a single avenue of escape in the event of defeat, they were unable, even, to muster up the desperation of cornered cowards. It is said that several in high command set them the example of pusillanimity. As we moved among them they inquired "what regiment is that?" "15th Regulars," replied some of our men. "Well, you'll catch regular hell to-day," was their rejoinder. Others said "Boys, it's of no use; we were beaten yesterday and you'll be beaten now." But still our men got into line well, and were marched by the right flank a few hundred yards to the place where the action of the previous day had ended. Here Capt. Swaine and Major King joined us, knapsacks were unslung, and we made the final preparations for the conflict we knew to be imminent. Being informed that we were the reserve of Rousseau's Brigade, we were slowly moved forward in column at half distance, through camps our troops had abandoned in the fight of the 6th inst. Other corps, all the while, were passing us on either side, and disappearing from view in a dip of ground in front, but as yet the engagement had not begun.

Let me try, at this point, to give you as good an idea of the field of battle as I am able. The Tennessee river at Pittsburg Landing describes a considerable curve; in the neck formed by this bend and some distance outside of it were

the camps of Gen. Grant's command. On the morning of the
7th, the rebels were posted some distance inside of the
ground formerly occupied by us, so that the line of conflict
was pretty nearly straight between the two points of the
semi-circle. Nelson's division was on our extreme left, resting
on the river; Crittenden was next to him on his right, then
came McCook in the centre, and joined to him was McCler-
nand, who had other of Grant's generals beyond him. This
order continued unbroken until the struggle was over.

Nelson and Crittenden's commands having passed the left
flank of our battalion speedily became engaged. A few scattering shots were heard from their direction, which were
soon followed by such a heavy firing of small arms that it
was plain our men had found the enemy. The field artillery
also broke in with its thunder, increasing the din already so
great that it was difficult to hear one's self speak. As further
evidence that the battle had begun in earnest, a mounted
officer dashed by, crying, "bring on the ambulances," and
those vehicles were at once taken to the front, to return in a
few minutes laden with mangled freight. Other wounded
men, some on foot, others carried by their comrades, likewise
now came to the rear. From these we learned that Nelson
and Crittenden, although suffering severely, were steadily
pushing the rebels back, a story attested by the frequent
cheers that arose from their gallant fellows.

A sharp firing that now took place almost immediately in
our front, showed that the left and centre of our (McCook's)
division had got into action, and that the battle was rapidly
becoming general. Our battalion was instantly deployed into
line to receive the foe should the troops in advance give way.
While in this position, Generals Buell and Rousseau rode up,
ordered us to proceed to the right of the brigade, which was
the right of the division, and be ready for any emergency,

and to send out at the same time a company of skirmishers to provoke an attack. This converted us from a reserve into an assaulting party.

Forming in column by division on the first, we marched by the right flank to the position we were to occupy, Captain Haughey with his command, being thrown forward to feel the enemy. (I will state here that battalions of the 16th and 19th regiments U. S. Infantry, the whole under Major John H. King, were with us and shared in all our operations.) At this place we again deployed, then moved by the right of companies to the front, until a little hill between us and the rebels was surmounted, when we were again brought into line. Rapid discharges of small arms forward of our left flank, now showed that our skirmishers were successful in their search. Again we were advanced, until having gained some distance, we were ordered to lie close to the ground. Immediately we were exposed to a cannonade and fire of musketry, whose severity defies description. From three batteries and their strong support of infantry just before us, masked by the underbrush, came a shower of grape, canister, spherical case, rifle balls, &c., that would have swept every one of us away had we been standing on our feet. An examination I have since made of the ground exhibits the fact that every tree and sapling bears the marks of shot. Protecting ourselves as we did, our loss was still severe. Among the injured were Capt. Acker of the 16th, killed, and Capt. Peterson of the 15th, wounded in the head. As yet, as I have said before, the foe was concealed in the thick woods so that we could not see them; but now emboldened, perhaps, by what they supposed their irresistible attack, they emerged from their cover. Never did they commit a more fatal mistake. Our men, restrained by their officers, had not discharged a piece up to this time. But now each coolly marked his man; and when

Capt. Swaine, in a voice that could be heard along the whole line, gave the command to fire, our Springfield rifles dealt a destruction that was awful. After pelting the rebels a little while longer, we again moved forward to the sound of the bugle, taking to the earth once more when the enemy opened upon us. Here Lieut. Mitchell of the 16th was killed, and Lieut. Lyster of the 19th, and 1st Sergeants Williams and Kiggins of the 15th dangerously wounded. Halting a few moments to reply, we moved down upon the traitors a third time, subjected the while to a fearful storm of missiles, by which Capt. Curtiss and Lieut. Wykoff of the 15th were very severely hurt, and 1st Sergeant Killink of the same corps instantly killed. But at length the artillery of the enemy, that had been playing upon us so long, came in sight. Hastily fixing bayonets, we charged upon it at a double-quick. Capt. Keteltas of the 15th being then shot through the body. Unable to withstand our desperate assault, the rebel cannoneers abandoned their guns, and with the infantry supports fled across an open space into the woods beyond. An opportunity offered at this point to ascertain the havoc we had done. Every horse in each piece and caisson lay dead in his harness, and the ground was covered with the killed and dying. Among the latter was the Chief of the Artillery. As we came up he said, "You have slain all my men and cattle, and you may take the battery and be damned." But we had not leisure to stop and talk with him or any other person; for we were already being fired upon from the new covert of the foe. Pushing forward amid great danger across the field, we gained the edge of the timber and continued the fight in which we had then been engaged for more than five hours.

The foregoing was the state of affairs at high noon. Let us pause a moment to see what was the condition of the battle field at that hour. There was no fighting on the right of the centre; indeed it had not been severe in that quarter during the day. On the left, Nelson and Crittenden having repulsed the enemy, were resting on their arms; for the foe in their front had mysteriously disappeared. Our three battalions were our only troops then hotly engaged. You inquire, "where were the rest of the rebels?" That is just what I propose telling you. Leaving only enough of men before the other divisions to mask their purpose, they were engaged massing their troops, those that had been engaged as well as their reserves, for an overwhelming onslaught upon the right of our centre, where we had contested all morning without support. I think it possible that Gen. Rousseau suspected their scheme; for whilst we strove in the edge of the timber, two regiments of volunteers took position on our right, and a section of a battery quietly unlimbered on our left. Scarcely were these dispositions completed, when down upon us came the enemy, pouring in a withering, staggering fire, that compelled the regiments just mentioned to break and fly, in such confusion that they could not be rallied again. This panic not only left us alone to sustain the dreaded onset, but in addition, put us in extraordinary peril by the total exposure of our left flank. The occasion was indeed critical. But before the enemy could take any advantage of the condition of things, Capt. Swaine averted the danger by causing our battalion to charge front, thus giving the 15th, 16th and 19th the form of two sides of a triangle. Here we fought for a time that seemed interminable, holding the rebel force in check, until Col. Gibson's brigade, hastily brought up to our relief, assisted by a flanking attack from Nelson and Crittenden's divisions started the foe in the retreat, that shortly became a rout. Falling back, then, only long enough to replenish our ammunition, we joined in the pursuit, keeping it up, notwithstanding our exhausted condition, until we got beyond the line of the camps captured from our troops the day before.

I do not undertake to say what body of troops engaged in the battle of Shiloh, is entitled to the most honor. But I unhesitatingly assert that the 1st Battalion of the 15th U. S. Infantry did its whole duty. For seven hours it fought without ceasing, that, too, after it had marched seventeen miles the day before, and been deprived of sleep the night previous. And when the dreadful attack upon our centre was made, which caused Willich's German veterans to scatter like cattle upon a thousand hills, it still stood up to its work as though there was no such word as defeat in its lexicon. Throughout the struggle, Major King, Capt. Swaine and the company officers conducted themselves with great gallantry. In our company, nine men are killed and wounded. The loss of the command is sixty-three. Curtenius escaped without a scratch.

Dr. Parry informs me that our loss in killed and wounded, will not fall short of nine thousand men, and may exceed that number. From what I have seen myself, I give the fullest credence to his statement. On the evening of the engagement, the dead were everywhere. There never has been such carnage on this continent. I trust I may never again see anything of the kind.

The battle was fought in the woods, which were as serviceable to the enemy as fortifications. You may travel for a day around here and you will scarcely find a tree, sapling or twig, that has not been struck by a bullet. How any of us escaped is more than I can imagine.

W.

But You Must Act

IN HIS REPORT praising the army for its efficient use of printing presses Ferdinand LeComte commented also on the telegraph as an efficient method of conducting military business. But he added a caveat. "In many circumstances," he wrote, "it would have been very desirable for the army to have fewer telegrams at its command, and to be more independent of the political fluctuations of Washington."

With victory at Shiloh flushing Union ambitions, there was more reason than ever for the President to be impatient at General McClellan's continued inactivity. His letter of April 9 expressed that impatience unequivocally.

WASHINGTON, *April* 9, 1862.
To MAJOR-GENERAL McCLELLAN:
My Dear Sir—Your dispatches, complaining that you are not properly sustained, while they do not offend me, pain me very much. Blenker's Division was withdrawn before you left here, and you know the pressure under which I did

it, and, as I thought, acquiesced in it, certainly not without
reluctance. After you left, I ascertained that less than 20,-
000 unorganized men, without a field battery, were all you
designed should be left for the defence of Washington and
Manassas Junction, and part of this even was to go to Gen.
Hooker's old position. Gen. Banks's corps, once designed for
Manassas Junction, was divided and tied up on the line of
Winchester and Strasburg, and could not leave that position
without again exposing the Upper Potomac and the Baltimore and Ohio Railroad.

This presented, or would present, when McDowell and
Sumner should be gone, a great temptation for the enemy
to turn back from the Rappahannock and sack Washington.
My explicit directions that Washington, sustained by the
judgment of all the commanders of corps, should be left
secure, had been entirely neglected. It was precisely this
that drove me to detain McDowell. I do not forget that I
was satisfied with your arrangement to leave Banks at Manassas Junction. But when that arrangement was broken up,
and nothing was substituted for it, of course I was not satisfied. I was constrained to substitute something for it myself.
And now allow me to ask you, do you really think I could
permit the line from Richmond, via Manassas Junction, to
this city, to be entirely open, except what resistance could
be presented by less than 20,000 unorganized troops? This
is a question which the country will not allow me to evade.

There is a curious mystery about the number of troops
now with you. I telegraphed you on the 6th, saying that you
had over 100,000 with you. I had just obtained from the
Secretary of War a statement taken, as he said, from your
own returns, making 108,000 then with you and en route to
you. You now say you will have but 85,000 when all en route
to you shall have reached you. How can this discrepancy of

35,000 be accounted for? As to Gen. Wool's command, I understand that it is doing precisely what a like number of your own would have to do if that command was away. I suppose the whole force which has gone forward to you is with you by this time; and if so, I think it is the precise time for you to strike a blow.

By delay, the enemy will readily gain on you; that is, he will gain faster by fortifications and re-enforcements than you can by re-enforcements alone. And once more let me tell you, it is indispensable to you that you strike a blow. I am powerless to help. This you will do me the justice to re-member—I was always opposed to going down the Bay in search of a field, instead of fighting at or near Manassas, as only shifting and not surmounting a difficulty; that we would find the same enemy and the same or equal entrenchments at either place. The country will not fail to note—is noting now—that the present hesitation to move upon an intrenched enemy is but the story of Manassas repeated.

I beg leave to assure you that I have never written or spoken to you in greater kindness of feeling than now, nor with a fuller purpose to sustain you so far as in my most anxious judgment I consistently can. But you must act.

Yours, very truly,

A. LINCOLN.

Unfit for Human Beings

THERE IS A MULTITUDE of accounts of prison life behind Confederate lines. One of the best is one of the
least known, Chaplain F. F. Kiner's narrative of his experiences in the prison pen at Macon, Georgia.

Food is always an item near the surface of a soldier's
thinking. Prison fare was guaranteed not to be good, but
the utter badness of it is a fact that is remarked again
and again in the accounts of Federal soldiers. Kiner was
no exception. It is worthy of note that he mentions that
the prisoners' fare was not too different from that of
their guards and that the Confederate citizens were so
short of food that the prisoners sold to them food they
rejected as inedible.

The forenoon of May 4th, 1862, found us in Macon, Georgia. We were taken from the cars and marched to a fair-
ground, called Camp Oglethorpe, which was about fifteen
or twenty acres in extent, enclosed by a picket fence. In the
north-west corner was a very nice grove of pine trees which

formed a most beautiful shade, and served as an excellent retreat in the hot summer days; without this I know not how we could have lived, under the burning sun. In connection with the grove were three large frame buildings, being nothing more than the frames weather-boarded; one of the three, I think, was ceiled, or partly so at least; besides these were two small frame buildings, one of which we used for a doctor shop, the other for a cook house for the hospital; the best of the three large buildings was the hospital. Excepting a row of stalls made for horses in time of fairs, there were no other buildings. There was also, an ever running spring in the camp but the water was not of the best quality. In addition to this was a well of water, about the centre of the grove, and a stronger stream in a well I never saw; fourteen hundred men supplied themselves from it daily and never exhausted it. Sometimes it got very low and muddy, but in a short time gained its usual depth. Here was the first place since our imprisonment that we had an opportunity to wash our bodies and clothes, and you may be sure we were anything but tidy in appearance. When we first went into this camp we had something over eight hundred men, but many of these soon took sick, and a number died.

For the first two months we did not seem to fare so badly, and the food we got was reasonably good. The ration during the month of May was one pound of flour or meal per day; three quarters of a pound of pork; some rice, sugar, molasses, rye for coffee, a small portion of hard soap, &c. So we got along pretty well and began to feel as though we had made a very lucky change. Another advantage was that we had a good chance to exercise, such as walking, playing ball and moving around in various ways, which was very beneficial to our health, and gave relief to our minds by drawing them away from our condition as prisoners, and from the anxious hearts at home. Nothing of any particular note occurred until about the 22nd of June, when orders were received to parole all the privates belonging to the Shiloh prisoners, but to retain the commissioned and non-commissioned officers. This was truly good news to the privates.

On the 24th, they were called into line and took the oath not to take up arms until they were exchanged or otherwise discharged. Thus they bid adieu to us who ranked just enough above them to stay in prison, and took their journey northward by way of Atlanta and Chattanooga, and joined our forces in Gen. Mitchel's command. All that left our camp were accepted; but for some reason, there were five hundred that had been kept at Montgomery, Ala., rejected, and sent back into prison. I presume, however, that Mitchell was acting under proper authority from the War Department. But it looked very hard to see these poor soldiers sent back again; some died upon the way, who had hoped to live long enough to see the Union lines once more; but such is the uncertainty of human expectations. In connection with these five hundred, they kept bringing in prisoners during the summer, until our number increased to twelve or fourteen hundred. We had prisoners from over one hundred and forty different regiments, representing almost every loyal state in the Union. Quite a number of these were captured while hunting blackberries and whisky, and prowling around away from their commands and duty; this they told us themselves. Such persons, I think, are to a certain extent censurable for such conduct.

But let us now notice more particularly our life in this camp during the balance of the summer. After they had paroled the privates, we had only about one hundred left. At this time the guards came and took all the cooking utensils from us, except what were sufficient for this number of men. These were the same that we had got in Mobile, and we never got them back again. When our number was increased to fourteen hundred, we had but the same amount of cooking implements, and we never could get any more for either love or money. Things became worse and worse with us; the nights were always cold, and having no covering, the poor soldiers began to get sicker, and diseases got more fatal. Our flour was now changed to corn or rice meal. The corn meal was of the coarsest kind, having often pieces of cob in it, and whole grains of corn, and this unsifted. This meal we had to bake as best we could, there being but few skillets or ovens. Many, yes very many, had to gather up any old piece of tin or sheet iron, or any piece of flat iron they could find, and make plates and pans. We would stir the meal up in any old thing we could get to hold it. Sometimes we could buy a little saleratus at two dollars and a half per pound, and scarce at that. As for salt, they issued us about a tablespoonful to the man for seven days; sometimes we bought it at the rate of ten cents per spoonful. At these rates our cakes had often neither salt nor soda, and baked in every kind of shape. You could see men baking at almost all hours of the day or night; this was because of the scarcity of things to bake in. It really looked pitiable to see hungry men, young and old, holding an old piece of tin or iron over a smoking fire, with a batch of coarse corn dough upon it, trying to bake it, and perhaps when done, it was so sad, or burnt and smoked, that it was not fit for a dog to eat. But what could we do? we had no better. For plates we used any old scrap of tin we could find, while some made them out of a pine board or shingle. A few of us however, had good tin plates. As for knives and forks the fingers answered all purposes. The bread however, was the best part of our living compared to the meat. They would call us all into line and give us printed tickets good for seven days' rations, which were gathered up by our quartermaster, who drew rations for the number of tickets; these they hauled into the yard under the trees. The meal was brought in barrels, or old sugar hogsheads; the meat was thrown out upon the ground and literally crawled with maggots. They put guards around these rations till they were issued, and we often told them it was necessary to guard it to keep it from crawling off. Some of these hams and sides of meat were so badly spoiled that we could push a finger through and through them, as if they were mince meat. In fact, that was what was the matter with it, the worms had minced it too much. It had spoiled mostly from want of salt, for the grease we got from it was not salt enough to use for gravy. Of this rotten stuff, we got one half pound to the man per day, The maggots upon it were of the largest kind; perhaps I should call them skippers, for they could skip about and jump several feet at one leap; from their size I judged the climate agreed with them. There was, however, a kind much smaller, which worked into the meat, though it looked middling good, similar to those in cheese, and we could not see them until the meat was cooked, when they made their appearance on the top of the water in the pot, and floated around like clever sized grains of rice.

After thus describing our cookery ware, bread and meat, let us see what kind of dinner we could get up, and just such a dinner as this I have eaten many a time: When the cook pronounced dinner ready, we arranged our plates upon boards stuck up on four sticks, or perhaps on the ground just as the case might be; some plates were made by the tinner, some of wood, &c., while our spoons, knives and forks were of the same material and manufacture. This was all well so far, but when the soup came round was the time to talk of delicacies; it was immaterial whether you called it rice or maggot soup. Dear reader, I have seen men almost starving, refuse to eat it, while others with myself, took our spoons and lifted these poor unfortunate victims from the dish, and with the remainder tried to satisfy our craving appetites; and this was not only once, but an every day occurrence with some. I have taken my meat and fried it, when there would be a dozen maggots in the pan, and in trying to get them out many would go to pieces, when, to avoid the sight, I would stir in corn meal and eat the whole mess together. Thus have we spent our time in prison, living upon what any decent man or woman in the North would feel ashamed to offer to a dog. This was not my case alone, it was the case of hundreds with me, who to-day are living witnesses to this fact. A few days ago, while conversing with one of my own regiment who was in prison with me, he stated that he saw a joint of ham or shoulder, cooked while there in prison and the soup from it eaten; when they went to divide the meat, in the joint connecting the bones was a small spoonful of these maggots. I am aware that many will not feel inclined to believe this story, thinking I am taking the extreme side of the matter, and making it the excuse for this history. All I have to say is, that these are facts I wish I had never experienced; and I further say, that there is no writer's pen can do justice to this matter, in describing our wants and sufferings while in this camp of Tophet.

It is not pretended that all of our pork was of this description, but I am certain that I am in the bounds of reason when I say that at least one-third of it was unfit for use. This percentage was too much to lose from our scanty allowance, and as a matter of necessity we had to make use of some of the rancid article. During the latter part of our stay in this camp, we were allowed to sell our pork to the citizens, or as much of it as we did not wish to use ourselves, or could not use on account of its spoiled condition. For this meat they would give us at first twenty, and at last as high as forty cents per pound; and so eager were they to get it that they would come beforehand and try to engage it, and upon the day of issuing rations sent buyers to come and gather it up; sometimes they furnished money to one of our men to buy it for them, and often there was quite a competition in this branch of our trade. The money we got from the sale of the bacon we invested in yams, sweet potatoes, tomatoes, onions, peaches, or anything of the vegetable kind we could get hold of; but everything seemed very scarce among them except sweet potatoes. Irish potatoes were exceedingly scarce. I do not think we had over five bushels during the whole summer, and what few we did get, cost from twenty to twenty-five cents a quart, making about eight dollars a bushel. After we commenced selling our unhealthy meat and used sweet potatoes, we got along much better. They became the principal article of our food during the remainder of our stay in prison. Sometimes beef was brought in to sell to us; this was generally second rate, and what did not sell well among the citizens. They usually brought in the head, horns and all, and the leg below the knee, containing the hoof—in fact, every part that could be used as soup pieces or in any other way. Once in a while we could get a good piece that eat very well; for this we paid about fifteen cents per pound; the head and hoofs we bought by the piece. I have every reason to believe that food was scarce among them, and in fact they told us frequently that they hardly knew how to keep us for want of food. Their own soldiers that guarded us lived as we did, except that they had a better article, while we of course, got the second rate. I am convinced that these mountain arabs in the South can live on food that Northern laboring men would consider unfit for use. Flour was then forty dollars a barrel; meat forty to fifty cents per pound; sugar from thirty-five to fifty cents per pound; salt one hundred and ten to one hundred and forty dollars per sack; coffee and tea not to be had at any price, and other things in proportion. Clothing was also very high. A good wool hat, eight dollars; coarse shoes, eight to twelve dollars a pair; calf skin boots, from twenty-five to forty dollars a pair. As a matter of course, the clothes we had on were worn out, and we had none to take their place, or to wear while we washed our filthy rags. There was a small stream of water running through one side of the camp, in which we bathed and washed; some would strip off their clothes and wash them, then hang them on the picket fence and pass the time in the water till they were dry enough to put on again. When the clothes needed boiling, they borrowed from each other if they could, till their own were done, or tied an old blanket around them while they washed and boiled their proper dress. We managed every style we could think of to get along, yet very many towards the last, had nothing but a piece of an old shirt and an old pair of drawers, or pants with the knees and seats worn out, and torn in shreds every way. Our patching and mending was very limited, having nothing to do it with. Muslin, woolen, tarpaulin, oil cloth, linen, and all kinds were sewed together to hide nakedness and stop the rents in worn out clothing. During the six months' imprisonment we never received from the Southern Confederacy over three hundred coarse, cotton shirts, for all the men that were in camp, and this was all we got of any kind except a few old clothes brought in to the hospital for the sick by the citizens. So there will be no wonder that we were bad off for something to put upon our bodies. This part of our destitution was the cause of much suffering among us, resulting in sickness and death. We used all the vacant buildings, sheds and stalls to sleep in, but they were too small to contain all, and the balance had to lie out under the trees; this brought disease and speedy death on many of the soldiers—it could not be otherwise. It was a pitiable sight to see so many of our brave boys lying out under the trees, with nothing but shirt and drawers, bare headed and bare footed, shivering in every nerve. Though it may be properly said that we were in the sunny South, yet I never passed one night in it but that I needed at least one good blanket, to get which was out of the question with many.

Our hospital contained about one hundred sick, who for the greater part of the time had to lay upon the floor; some were furnished mattresses; a few weeks before we left they got bunks made to lay the sick on. But for want of a proper change of clothing, their beds soon became filthy, as well as their bodies. There were two young doctors in attendance every day, who were, I think, fine young men, and did the best they could, but often had no medicine. We generally had a quantity of medicine sent to us to last a certain time, and if it was exhausted before that time expired, we had to do without. Under these circumstances, many of the sick would sell their scanty rations of food and send out and buy some from the druggist in the town, and we also would get leave to go with an escort of guards into the woods and get such barks as we thought contained medical properties and tonics, for ourselves; every man to a certain extent had to be his own doctor, and as a matter of course there were very many quite strange prescriptions given; some were recommended with miraculous faith. Many were afflicted with swelled feet and legs, having the appearance of dropsy, caused by weakness and diseased constitutions. I have known them to dig holes in the ground and bury their feet and legs knee deep for hours, hoping that the application of fresh

ground might do them good; and it occurs to me that numbers had some faith in the operation. There were four or five
hundred men for medicine every morning, and often none to
be had. Towards the latter part of the summer the mortality
among us became great, and with few exceptions we had
every day from one to seven of our men to bury. I have
known them to get so poor that their thighs were no larger
than a man's arm, and they were really nothing more than
living skeletons, yet they would try to keep about until in
many cases they would drop dead from their feet. Others
would die sitting against a tree, or anywhere, while many
would die so easily upon their beds, without a groan or a
sigh, that even the nurses were not aware of it. . . .

While in prison, we furnished nurses of our own men to
wait upon the sick; every morning a fresh set of nurses would
relieve the ones that went on duty the day before. All our
hospital duties were unpleasant; not because we cared
nothing for the sick, nor felt it our duty to do all in our power
for them, but because our feelings were so mortified to see
the poor beings suffering for the want of something to nour-
ish or make them comfortable which we were unable to
furnish. Often there was but one candle in the entire building by which to give medicine. But let us leave these sad
reflections for a short time, (for our lives were a continued
scene of misery), and notice our various occupations. Even
in this place of confinement Yankee ingenuity and industry
must be engaged. Many of the younger would play marbles;
others, benefit themselves by exercising in playing ball,
pitching horse shoes, &c., but the most popular as well as
the most profitable employment was the manufacture of
bone jewelry, which was carried on very extensively by
nearly all classes in prison, the only exceptions being those
who had no taste or tact for the business. We managed to

get files of different sizes and styles, and made saws out of
common table knives, with which we sawed beef bones into
whatever shape we desired to have them—either for finger
rings, breastpins, slides, watch seals, or, in fact, anything
almost that could be thought of. These pieces of bone we
filed off very smooth, and to the exact shape desired, and then
polished them off with sand paper, after which we drew
with a pencil, all kinds of letters, flowers, figures, &c.; these
marks we carved out with the sharp pointed blade of a
pocket knife, and filled the crevices with sealing wax of different colors; by this means we got up some most beautiful
jewelry, for which we found ready sale, or at least for a
great deal of it. The citizens, both ladies and gentlemen,
from far and near, came to purchase relics from the Yankees.
I think I can safely say, that we sold several thousand dollars
worth of it. This money helped us to increase our diet of
vegetables and improved our living very much; indeed very
many did not live on anything else than what they bought
in this way. The Confederates were very much astonished at
our ingenuity, and gave us credit for being a go-ahead kind
of people, and for turning everything into some use. Old
bones got to be quite in demand among us, and we used to
give little boys a ring for bringing us in an armful; sometimes
we paid the money for them. These articles sold for various
prices, according to the style in which they were gotten up;
generally the rings brought from twenty-five cents to one
dollar; the other articles, such as breastpins and seals, several dollars. They paid us altogether in Southern money,
some of which was issued by states, others by various associations, or companies, and some by individuals. They were
very scrupulous about using the bills issued by different
companies, associations, or individuals of any other state,
because these parties were liable to be dissolved, or perhaps

broken up at any time, and could not be considered as permanent. Another of our daily duties was to see to our personal comfort. I have already spoken of washing and boiling our clothes, but now we had another enemy to combat with, which our boys knew by the name of "graybacks." They were very troublesome and with all the care we could take, made inroads upon our peace, and increased in numbers so rapidly that our buildings and camp soon became full of them. They seemed as numerous as when they paid Pharaoh a visit in Egypt, and all the execution we could do did not seem to diminish their number. It became one of our regular daily duties, mostly in the morning, to hunt a shady place and make a general search for these intruders, and seldom failed to secure a large number of captives. These we executed upon the spot as guerrillas, and never considered them as entitled to the rights of prisoners of war, although they undoubtedly belong to both the regular and volunteer army.

The Capture and Occupation of
New Orleans

THE SPRING OF 1862 brought a great naval victory on
the Mississippi when Admiral David G. Farragut's
fleet stormed past the forts protecting New Orleans and
forced the surrender of the largest Confederate city.

The Confederates had believed the defenses of the
lower Mississippi impregnable. They had overestimated
the strength of Forts Jackson and St. Philip and, because
of pressing needs in other areas, had in fact neglected
properly to defend New Orleans.

Farragut bombarded the forts for nearly a week, succeeded in breaking the chain stretched across the river
to close the channel, and took his fleet into the unforti-
fied area between the forts and the city. He had brought
with him a land army under command of Major General
Benjamin F. Butler. These men were successfully landed
and Confederate General Mansfield Lovell had no
choice but to leave New Orleans and permit its surrender.

Butler became famous as a military despot. He ruled
the city with an iron hand, caring little for the opinions

of the New Orleanais or of the world. Most famous is his General Orders No. 28, in which he "ordered that hereafter when any female shall, by word, gesture or movement, insult or show contempt for any officer or soldier of the United States, she shall be regarded and held liable to be treated as a woman of the town plying her avocation."

Equally as harsh, and controlling nearly every facet of New Orleans life, was his very first pronouncement, his Proclamation of May 1, 1862, which established military rule in the city.

PROCLAMATION.

HEADQUARTERS DEPARTMENT OF THE GULF, *New-Orleans, May 1, 1862.*

The City of New-Orleans and its environs, with all its interior and exterior defenses, having been surrendered to the combined naval and land forces of the United States, and having been evacuated by the rebel forces in whose possession they lately were, and being now in occupation of the forces of the United States, who have come to restore order, maintain public tranquility, enforce peace and quiet under the Laws and Constitution of the United States, the Major-General commanding the forces of the United States in the Department of the Gulf, hereby makes known and proclaims the object and purposes of the Government of the United States in thus taking possession of the City of New-Orleans and the State of Louisiana, and the rules and regulations by which the laws of the United States will be for the present and during a state of war enforced and maintained, for the plain guidance of all good citizens of the United States, as well as others who may heretofore have been in rebellion against their authority.

Thrice before has the City of New-Orleans been rescued from the hand of a foreign government, and still more calamitous domestic insurrection, by the money and arms of the United States. It has of late been under the military control of the rebel forces, claiming to be the peculiar friends of its citizens, and at each time, in the judgment of the Commander of the military forces holding it, it has been found necessary to preserve order and maintain quiet by the administration of Law Martial. Even during the *interim* from its evacuation by the rebel soldiers and its actual possession by the soldiers of the United States, the civil authorities of the city have found it necessary to call for the intervention of an armed body known as the "European Legion," to preserve public tranquility. The Commanding General, therefore, will cause the city to be governed until the restoration of Municipal Authority, and his further orders, by the Law Martial, a measure for which it would seem the previous recital furnishes sufficient precedents.

All persons in arms against the United States are required to surrender themselves, with their arms, equipments and munitions of war. The body known as the "European Legion," not being understood to be in arms against the United States, but organized to protect the lives and property of the citizens, are invited still to co-operate with the forces of the United States to that end, and, so acting, will not be included in the terms of this order, but will report to these Headquarters.

All flags, ensigns and devices, tending to uphold any authority whatever, save the flag of the United States and the flags of foreign Consulates, must not be exhibited, but suppressed. The American Ensign, the emblem of the United States, must be treated with the utmost deference and respect by all persons, under pain of severe punishment.

All persons well disposed towards the Government of the United States, who shall renew their oath of allegiance, will receive the safeguard and protection, in their persons and property, of the armies of the United States, the violation of which, by any person, is punishable with death.

All persons still holding allegiance to the Confederate States will be deemed rebels against the Government of the United States, and regarded and treated as enemies thereof.

All foreigners not naturalized and claiming allegiance to their respective Governments, and not having made oath of allegiance to the supposed Government of the Confederate States, will be protected in their persons and property as heretofore under the laws of the United States.

All persons who may heretofore have given their adherence to the supposed Government of the Confederate States, or have been in their service, who shall lay down and deliver up their arms and return to peaceful occupations and preserve quiet and order, holding no further correspondence nor giving aid and comfort to the enemies of the United States, will not be disturbed either in person or property, except so far, under the orders of the Commanding General, as the exigencies of the public service may render necessary.

The keepers of all public property, whether State, National or Confederate, such as collections of art, libraries, museums, as well as all public buildings, all munitions of war, and armed vessels, will at once make full returns thereof to these Headquarters; all manufacturers of arms and munitions of war, will report to these Headquarters their kind and places of business.

All rights of property, of whatever kind, will be held inviolate, subject only to the laws of the United States.

All inhabitants are enjoined to pursue their usual avocations; all shops and places of business are to be kept open in the accustomed manner, and services to be had in the churches and religious houses as in times of profound peace.

Keepers of all public houses, coffee houses and drinking saloons, are to report their names and numbers to the office of the Provost Marshal; will there receive license, and be held responsible for all disorders and disturbances of the peace arising in their respective places.

A sufficient force will be kept in the city to preserve order and maintain the laws.

The killing of an American soldier by any disorderly person or mob, is simply assassination and murder, and not war, and will be so regarded and punished.

The owner of any house or building in or from which such murder shall be committed, will be held responsible therefor, and the house will be liable to be destroyed by the military authority.

All disorders and disturbances of the peace done by combinations and numbers, and crimes of an aggravated nature, interfering with forces or laws of the United States, will be referred to a military court for trial and punishment; other misdemeanors will be subject to the municipal authority, if it chooses to act. Civil causes between party and party will be referred to the ordinary tribunals. The levy and collection of all taxes, save those imposed by the laws of the United States, are suppressed, except those for keeping in repair and lighting the streets, and for sanitary purposes. Those are to be collected in the usual manner.

The circulation of Confederate bonds, evidences of debt, except notes in the similitude of bank notes issued by the

Confederate States, or scrip, or any trade, in the same, is strictly forbidden. It having been represented to the Commanding General by the city authorities that these Confederate notes, in the form of bank notes, are, in a great measure, the only substitute for money which the people have been allowed to have, and that great distress would ensue among the poorer classes if the circulation of such notes were suppressed, such circulation will be permitted so long as any one may be inconsiderate enough to receive them, till further orders.

No publication, either by newspaper, pamphlet or handbill, giving accounts of the movements of soldiers of the United States within this Department, reflecting in any way upon the United States or its officers, or tending in any way to influence the public mind against the Government of the United States, will be permitted; and all articles of war news, or editorial comments, or correspondence, making comments upon the movements of the armies of the United States, or the rebels, must be submitted to the examination of an officer who will be detailed for that purpose from these Headquarters.

The transmission of all communications by telegraph will be under the charge of an officer from these Headquarters.

The armies of the United States came here not to destroy but to make good, to restore order out of chaos, and the government of laws in place of the passions of men, to this end, therefore, the efforts of all well-disposed persons are invited to have every species of disorder quelled, and if any soldier of the United States should so far forget his duty or his flag as to commit any outrage upon any person or property, the Commanding General requests that his name be instantly reported to the Provost Guard, so that he may be punished and his wrongful act redressed.

The municipal authority, so far as the police of the city and crimes are concerned, to the extent before indicated, is hereby suspended.

All assemblages of persons in the streets, either by day or by night, tend to disorder, and are forbidden.

The various companies composing the Fire Department in New-Orleans, will be permitted to retain their organization, and are to report to the office of the Provost Marshal, so that they may be known and not interfered with in their duties.

And, finally, it may be sufficient to add, without further enumeration, that all the requirements of martial law will be imposed so long as, in the judgment of the United States authorities, it may be necessary. And while it is the desire of these authorities to exercise this government mildly, and after the usages of the past, it must not be supposed that it will not be vigorously and firmly administered as occasion calls.

By command of   MAJOR-GENERAL BUTLER.
   GEO. C. STRONG, A. A. G., Chief of Staff.

A Change in Virginia

PRESIDENT LINCOLN had called for action in Virginia. He now got it.

"Stonewall" Jackson conducted a whirlwind campaign in the Valley of Virginia that secured his military fame forever. The Confederates withdrew up the Peninsula, relinquishing Yorktown and being defeated at Williamsburg early in May. By the end of May McClellan had crossed the Chickahominy and was threatening Richmond. In a bloody action near Fair Oaks Station May 31 and June 1 each side lost over forty thousand men. Confederate General Joseph E. Johnston was wounded on the first day of the battle, and, on the next, General R. E. Lee was appointed to command the Confederate troops facing McClellan. Costly as it was, Fair Oaks was indecisive. A little over two weeks later Confederate General J. E. B. Stuart rode around McClellan's army in his famous Chickahominy Raid. There was no further major action till the end of the month, when the great Seven Days' Battles began June 26. Repulsed with heavy loss after battles at Mechanicsville, Gaines' Mill, Allen's Farm, Savage's Station, Glendale, and Malvern Hill,

McClellan nevertheless succeeded in withdrawing to a new base at Harrison's Landing on the banks of the James River. Though Confederate losses had exceeded Federal, the Union Army had failed in its grand attempt on the Confederate capital. General Henry W. Halleck was appointed to the command of all United States land forces on July 11, and withdrawal of the Army of the Potomac from the Peninsula was begun. On July 14 General John Pope took command of the Federal Army of Virginia.

Three army circulars are milestones in the progress of the campaign, General McClellan's addresses to his army on June 2 and July 4 and General Pope's message on his assumption of command.

HEAD-QUARTERS, ARMY OF THE POTOMAC.

CAMP NEAR NEW BRIDGE, VA., *June 2d*, 1862.
SOLDIERS OF THE ARMY OF THE POTOMAC!

I have fulfilled at least a part of my promise to you; you are now face to face with the rebels, who are at bay in front of their Capital. The final and decisive battle is at hand. Unless you belie your past history, the result cannot be for a moment doubtful. If the troops who labored so patiently, and fought so gallantly at Yorktown, and who so bravely won the hard fights at Williamsburg, West Point, Hanover Court House and Fair Oaks, now prove worthy of their antecedents, the victory is surely ours. The events of every day prove your superiority; wherever you have met the enemy you have beaten him; wherever you have used the bayonet he has given way in panic and disorder. I ask of you now one last crowning effort. The enemy has staked his all on the issue of the coming battle. Let us meet and crush him here in the very centre of the rebellion.

Soldiers! I will be with you in this battle, and share its dangers with you. Our confidence in each other is now founded upon the past. Let us strike the blow which is to restore peace and union to this distracted land. Upon your valor, discipline and mutual confidence that result depends.

GEO. B. McCLELLAN,

Major General Commanding.

———

HEAD-QUARTERS, ARMY OF THE POTOMAC.

Camp near Harrison's Landing, Va., *July 4th.* 1862

SOLDIERS OF THE ARMY OF THE POTOMAC!

Your achievements of the last ten days have illustrated the valor and endurance of the American Soldier! Attacked by vastly superior forces, and without hope of reinforcements, you have succeeded in changing your base of operations by a flank movement, always regarded as the most hazardous of military expedients. You have saved all your material, all your trains, and all your guns, except a few lost in battle, taking in return guns and colors from the enemy. Upon your march you have been assailed day after day with desperate fury by men of the same race and nation, skillfully massed and led; and under every disadvantage of numbers, and necessarily of position also, you have in every conflict beaten back your foes with enormous slaughter. Your conduct ranks you among the celebrated armies of history. No one will now question that each of you may always say with pride: "I belonged to the Army of the Potomac!" You have reached this new base, complete in organization and unimpaired in spirit. The enemy may at any moment attack you. We are prepared to receive them. I have personally established your lines. Let them come, and we will convert their repulse into a final defeat. Your Government is strengthening you with the resources of a great people.

On this our Nation's Birthday we declare to our foes, who are rebels against the best interests of mankind, that this Army shall enter the Capital of their so-called Confederacy; that our National Constitution shall prevail; and that the Union which can alone insure internal peace and external security to each State must and shall be preserved, cost what it may in time, treasure and blood.

> GEO. B. McCLELLAN,
> Major General Commanding.

HEADQUARTERS, ARMY OF VIRGINIA,

WASHINGTON, D. C., *July* 14, 1862.

To THE OFFICERS AND SOLDIERS
    OF THE ARMY OF VIRGINIA:

By special assignment of the President of the United States, I have assumed the command of this Army. I have spent two weeks in learning your whereabouts, your condition, and your wants; in preparing you for active operations, and in placing you in positions from which you can act promptly and to the purpose. These labors are nearly completed, and I am about to join you in the field.

Let us understand each other. I have come to you from the West, where we have always seen the backs of our enemies; from an Army whose business it has been to seek the adversary and to beat him when he was found; whose policy has been attack and not defence. In but one instance has the enemy been able to place our western armies in defensive attitude. I presume that I have been called here to pursue the same system, and to lead you against the enemy. It is my purpose to do so, and that speedily. I am sure you long for an opportunity to win the distinction you are capable of achieving. That opportunity I shall endeavor to give you. Meantime I desire you to dismiss from your minds certain phrases which I am sorry to find much in vogue amongst you. I hear constantly of taking "strong positions and holding them," of "lines of retreat," and of "bases of supplies." Let us discard such ideas. The strongest position a soldier should desire to occupy is one from which he can most easily advance against the enemy. Let us study the probable lines of retreat of our opponents, and leave our own to take care of themselves. Let us look before us, and not behind. Success and glory are in the advance; disaster and shame lurk in the rear. Let us act on this understanding, and it is safe to predict that your banners shall be inscribed with many a glorious deed, and that your names will be dear to your countrymen forever.

JNO. POPE,
Major General Commanding.

We Must Learn Righteousness

THE EXTENT to which slavery was a cause of the Civil War has been debated ever since the war began. If it was not a principal cause, agitation over slavery was certainly the catalyst that precipitated war.

By the fall of 1862 the moral issue of slavery had achieved greater importance than ever. From many sides there was pressure on President Lincoln to promulgate a proclamation which would end slavery. Typical of such pressure is the Memorial issued by a meeting of citizens in Chicago, September 7. Prominent citizens had been called together "to take measures to memorialize the President to issue a Proclamation of National Emancipation."

A delegation was appointed to carry the Memorial to Washington and present it to the President. It was published and circulated widely with the admonition:

"Read it! read it carefully! Call your Christian fellow citizens together without distinction of sect, and adopt it or something like it, and send it to the President. The united voice of the Christians of this whole land should go up to the Executive Mansion, calling for justice to the oppressed. We must as a Nation learn righteousness, or our poor bleeding, imperiled Country is undone! Religious men everywhere, at such a time as this, should act and speak fearlessly and promptly. They should also pray unceasingly that God would incline our President to do that great act of justice and mercy, which this Memorial implores."

There follows the "Memorial of the Christian Men of Chicago. To His Excellency, Abraham Lincoln, President of the United States."

MEMORIAL
OF THE
PUBLIC MEETING OF THE CHRISTIAN MEN OF CHICAGO.

To His Excellency, Abraham Lincoln, President of the
United States:

Your memorialists of all Christian denominations in the city of Chicago, assembled in solemn meeting to consider the moral aspects of the war now waging, would utter their deepest convictions as to the present relation of our country and its rulers to the government and providence of Almighty God; and would respectfully ask a hearing for the principles and facts deemed fundamental to a right judgment of this appalling crisis. And to this we are encouraged by the frequency with which, on various public occasions, you have officially recognized the dependence of the country and its chief magistrate upon the Divine favor.

We claim, then, that the war is a Divine retribution upon our land for its manifold sins, and especially for the crime of oppression, against which the denunciations of God's Word are so numerous and pointed.

The American nation, in this its judgment-hour, must acknowledge that the cry of the slave, unheeded by man, has been heard by God and answered in this terrible visitation. The time has at length come of which Jefferson solemnly warned his countrymen, as he declared that the slaves of America were enduring "a bondage, one hour of which is fraught with more misery than ages of that which occasioned the war of the Revolution," and added, "When the measure of their tears shall be full, when their tears shall have involved heaven itself in darkness, doubtless a God of justice will awaken to their distress, by diffusing a light and liberality among their oppressors, or at length by his exterminating thunder, manifest his attention to things of this world, and that they are not left to the guidance of blind fatality."

The slave oligarchy has organized the most unnatural, perfidious and formidable rebellion known to history. It has professedly established an independent government on the avowed basis of slavery, admitting that the Federal Union was constituted to conserve and promote liberty. All but four of the slave states have seceded from the Union, and those four (with the exception of Delaware, in which slavery but nominally exists) have been kept in subjection only by overwhelming military force. Can we doubt that this is a Divine retribution for national sin, in which our crime has justly shaped our punishment?

Proceeding upon this belief, which recent events have made it almost atheism to deny, your memorialists avow their solemn conviction, deepening every hour, that there can be no deliverance from Divine judgments *till slavery ceases in the land*. We cannot expect God to save a nation that clings to its sin. This is too fearful an hour to insult

God, or to deceive ourselves. National existence is in peril: our sons and brothers are falling by tens of thousands on the battle-field: the war becomes daily more determined and destructive. While we speak the enemy thunders at the gates of the capital. Our acknowledged superiority of resources has thus far availed little or nothing in the conflict. As Christian patriots we dare not conceal the truth, that these judgments mean what the divine judgments meant in Egypt. They are God's stern command—"LET MY PEOPLE GO!"

This work of national repentance has been inaugurated by the abolition of slavery in the District of Columbia, and its prohibition in the territories, as also by encouragement to emancipation in the border slave states, offered by Congress at the suggestion of the President.

But these measures do not meet the crisis as regards either the danger of the country or the national guilt. We urge you, therefore, as the head of this Christian nation, from considerations of moral principle, and, as the only means of preserving the Union, to proclaim, *without delay*, NATIONAL EMANCIPATION.

However void of authority in this respect you might have been in time of peace, you are well aware, as a statesman, that the exigences of war are the only limits of its powers, especially in a war to preserve the very life of the nation. And these exigences are not to be restricted to what may avail at the last gasp prior to national death, but are to be interpreted to include all measures that may most readily and thoroughly subdue the enemy. The rebels have brought slavery under your control by their desperate attack upon the life of the republic. They have created a moral, political and military necessity, which warrants the deed, and now God and a waiting world demand that the opportunity be used. And surely the fact that they have placed in our power a system which, while it exposes them, is itself the grossest wickedness, adds infinitely to the obligation to strike the blow.

In this view of a change of power involving an equal change in duty, we will not conceal the fact that gloom has filled our hearts at every indication that the war was regarded as simply an issue between the Federal authorities and the rebel states; and that therefore slavery was to be touched only to the extent that the pressure of rebel success might absolutely necessitate. Have we not reason to *expect* rebel success on that policy? Are we to omit from our calculations the necessary conditions of Divine favor? Has the fact no moral force, that the war has suddenly placed within the power of the President, the system that has provoked God's wrath? Is there not danger that while we are waiting till the last terrible exigency shall force us to liberate the slave, God may decide the contest against us, and the measure that we would not adopt on principle, prove too late for our salvation? We claim that justice, here as everywhere, is the highest expediency.

At the time of the national peril of the Jews under Ahasuerus, Mordecai spake in their name to Queen Esther, who hesitated to take the step necessary to their preservation, in these solemn words: "Think not with thyself that thou shalt escape in the king's house, more than all the Jews. For if thou altogether holdest thy peace at this time, then shall there enlargement and deliverance arise to the Jews from another place; but thou and thy father's house shall be destroyed; and who knoweth whether thou art come to the kingdom for such a time as this?" And your memorialists believe that in Divine Providence you have been called to the Presidency to speak the word of justice and authority which shall free the bondman and save the nation. Our prayer to God is, that by such an act the name of ABRAHAM LINCOLN may go down to posterity with that of GEORGE WASHINGTON, as the second SAVIOR OF OUR COUNTRY.

RESOLUTIONS.

Resolved, That universal emancipation seems pointed out by Providence as the most effectual, if not the only means of saving our country.

That in the appalling loss of blood and treasure, and repeated reverses to our arms, pressing the nation to the verge of destruction should be heard the voice that sounded above the wail of desolated Egypt—"Let my people go."

That universal emancipation as a mere act of *political* justice would be without a parallel in the annals of the world.

That it would be the abandonment of a wrong long perpetuated against the oppressed race, to the contravention of impartial liberty, the reproach of free institutions and the dishonor of our country.

That it would be a consummation of the expectations of the founders of the republic, who, deploring while tolerating slavery, anticipated its early disappearance from the continent.

That it would accord with the world's convictions of justice, and the higher teachings of Christianity.

That we should not expect national deliverance till we rise at least to the moral judgment of Jefferson who, in view of slavery exclaimed: "I tremble for my country when I reflect that God is just; that his justice cannot sleep forever; that considering numbers, nature, and natural means only, a revolution of the wheel of fortune, an exchange of situation, is among possible events, that it may become probable by supernatural interference! The Almighty has no attribute which can take side with us in such a contest."

That all assumed right to slavery under the Constitution is forfeited by open and persistent rebellion; and therefore, emancipation, to preserve the republic, would only vindicate and honor the Constitution.

That, as slavery is a principal reliance of the rebellion, conserving its property, tilling its plantations, feeding and clothing its armies, freeing the slaves would take away its support, recall its armies from the field, demoralize its conspiracy, and organize in its midst a power for its overthrow.

That, putting down this rebellion is as obvious a Christian duty as prayer, preaching, charity to the poor, or missions to heathen.

That the postponement of emancipation jeopards countless treasure, the best blood and the *existence* of the nation.

That no evils apprehended from emancipation are comparable to those that would arise from the overthrow of the republic, and they would fall upon those madly provoking the catastrophe.

That as the perpetuation and extension of slavery were a primary aim of this rebellion, its overthrow would seem a fitting and signal retribution upon its authors—like hanging Haman upon the gallows he erected for Mordecai.

That it were better for this generation to perish than that the American Union should be dissolved; and it is a delusion that those disloyal and belligerent under the Constitution and traditions of their fathers, would become peaceable citizens, observant of treaties and oaths in rival states.

L. B. OTIS, *Chairman,*
E. W. BLATCHFORD, *Secretary.*

Maryland Invaded

A SECOND FEDERAL DEFEAT at Bull Run had ended General John Pope's career as a field commander and paved the way for Confederate invasion of Maryland. General McClellan resumed command and prepared to face his old enemies again.

Dr. Lewis H. Steiner, an inspector for the Sanitary Commission, was a native of Frederick, Maryland. He was thus qualified by both duty and natural interest as a particularly appropriate reporter of the occupation of that town.

The occupation of Frederick is famous out of proportion to its importance because it inspired one of the best loved of American poems, John Greenleaf Whittier's "Barbara Frietchie." As it may well be that Steiner's account was the source of Whittier's inspiration (the story was relayed to him, possibly already embellished by the popular novelist, Mrs. E. D. E. N. Southworth), it is appropriate to point out here how history and myth become interwoven and how the reality of history can disappear in the stronger truth of fiction.

Steiner's factual version appears as a single paragraph

in his report. Whittier's poem was published the next year. In a perceptive article, "The Yankee Muse in History," in the fall of 1863 the Richmond *Examiner* (quoted in *The Record of News, History and Literature* for November 26, 1863) prophesied the future of the piece.

"Verse is stronger than prose," wrote the anonymous Richmond reporter, "and history is powerless in competition with the popular ballad. . . . Late Yankee papers bring us a ballad fresh from the mint, which is so remarkable in itself, and destined to play such havoc with Southern histories of the war, that we cannot refrain from inserting it entire. . . .

"A likely story, truly. Frederick City, fair as a garden of the Lord to famished rebels; Jackson at the head of his columns, ordering his men to fire on a Dutch dame, ninety years old, because she hung a flag out of the garret window, and then blushing for shame because the bullets cut the flag clean away from the staff, and the nimble old harridan catches it as it fell, leans far out the window sill and shakes it forth with a royal will, careless of the danger of losing her center of gravity and pitching headlong into the street. See the noble nature within him stirred at Dame Barbara's deed and word, and hear him thunder

'Who touches a hair of yon gray head,
Dies like a dog! March on!' he said.

"Think, too, of the loyal winds upholding the flag they loved so well. The sunset light, bidding the flag good night, in pure Yankee accents, and drop a tear on

Stonewall's bier for old Frietchie's sake, if you can; and if you cannot, employ a loyal onion to aid you in the pathetic task.

"The uncultivated may pronounce the poem so much unadulterated and self-evident nonsense, but the wise, the gifted, the good, know that it will outlive and disprove all histories, however well authenticated."

REPORT.

FREDERICK L. OLMSTED, Esq.,
    Secretary U. S. Sanitary Commission:

IN accordance with your request, I have the honor to transmit an account of my operations as Sanitary Inspector during the last month. The engagements which crowd so thickly upon me just now, prevent that careful preparation which a report, including incidents of such deep interest to every American, should receive from the reporter. The best that I can do is to give you as faithful an account as my diary and recollections, and the reports of other officers of the Commission, will enable me, in as few words as possible, deprecating all criticism of its style and finish. . . .

Friday, September 5.—Left Washington at 6 o'clock, under the impression that the Confederate army had crossed the Potomac the preceding evening and were then in Frederick. Anxiety as to the fate of my friends, as well as to the general treatment my native place would receive at rebel hands, made the trip by no means a pleasant one.

Along the road, at different stopping-places, reports reached us as to the numbers of the Confederates that had crossed into Maryland. The passengers began to entertain fears that the train would not be able to reach Frederick. These were, however, quieted by a telegram received at a station near Monrovia, which announced the road open. Arriving at 12 o'clock, M., I found the town full of surmises and rumors. Such information had been received by the Post Quarter Master and the Surgeon in charge of Hospital, that they were busy all the afternoon making arrangements to move off their valuable stores. The citizens were in the greatest trepidation. Invasion by the Southern army was considered equivalent to destruction. Impressment into the ranks as common soldiers, or immurement in a *Southern* prison— these were not attractive prospects for quiet, Union-loving citizens!

Towards nightfall it became pretty certain that a force had crossed somewhere about the mouth of the Monocacy. Telegrams were crowding rapidly on the army officers located here, directing that what stores could not be removed should be burned, and that the sick should as far as possible be sent on to Pennsylvania. Here began a scene of terror seldom witnessed in this region. Lieut. Castle, A. Q. M., burned a large quantity of his stores at the depot. Assist. Surg. Weir fired his store-house on the Hospital grounds and burned the most valuable of his surplus bedding contained in Kemp Hall, in Church street near Market. Many of our prominent citizens, fearing impressment, left their families and started for Pennsylvania in carriages, on horseback, and on foot. All the convalescents at the Hospital that could bear the fatigue, were started also for Pennsylvania, in charge of Hospital Steward Cox. The citizens removed their trunks containing private papers and other valuables from the bank-vaults, under the firm belief that an attack would be made on these buildings for the sake of the specie contained in them.

About 1½ o'clock, A.M., it was ascertained that Jackson's force—the advance guard of the Southern army—was encamped on Moffat's farm, near Buckeystown, and that this force would enter Frederick after daylight; for what purpose no one knew. Having possession of this amount of information, I retired about two o'clock, being willing to wait the sequel, whatever it might be.

Saturday, September 6.—Found, on visiting the market in the morning, that a very large number of our citizens had "*skedaddled*" (i. e. retired rapidly in good order) last night. Every mouth was full of rumors as to the numbers, whereabouts, and whatabouts of the Confederate force. One old gentleman, whose attachment to McClellan has become proverbial, declared that it was an impossibility for the rebels to cross the Potomac; and another, who looks upon Banks as the greatest of generals, declared that Banks' force had been taken for Confederates, and that the supposed enemies were friends.

At length uncertainty was changed into certainty. About nine o'clock two seedy-looking individuals rode up Market street as fast as their jaded animals could carry them. Their dress was a dirty, faded gray, their arms rusty and seemingly uncared for, their general appearance raffish or vagabondish. They shouted for Jeff. Davis at the intersection of Patrick and Market street, and then riding to the intersection of Church and Market, repeated the same *strange* jubilant shout. No one expressing an opinion as to the propriety or impropriety of this proceeding, they countermarched and trotted down the street. Then followed some fifty or a hundred horsemen, having among them Bradley T. Johnson, *soi-disant* Colonel C.S.A. These were received with feeble shouts from some secession-sympathizers. They said, "the time of your deliverance has come." It was plain that the deliverance they meant was from the rule of law and order. The sidewalks were filled with Union-loving citizens, who felt keenly that their humiliation was at hand, and that they had no course but submission, at least for a time.

As this force of cavalry entered the town from the south, Capt. Yellot's company retreated west from the town, and disappeared no one knew whither. One ruffian cavalry soldier rode up to Sergt. Crocker (in charge of hospital stores in Kemp Hall) and accosted him with "Sa-ay, are you a Yankee?" "No, I am a Marylander." "What are you doing in the Yankee army?" "I belong to the United States army," said the old man, proudly. "If you don't come along with me, I'll cut your head off." Having waved his sabre over the *unarmed* old man's head, he demanded his keys, and rode off with the sergeant as a prisoner. This display of chivalry did not infuse great admiration of the Southern army into the hearts of the bystanders.

A force of cavalry entered the hospital grounds and took possession of hospital and contents. All the sick were carefully paroled, not excepting one poor fellow then in a moribund condition. After some hours, the medical officers and hospital stewards were allowed to go about town on passes.

At ten o'clock Jackson's advance force, consisting of some five thousand men, marched up Market street and encamped north of the town. They had but little music; what there was gave us "My Maryland" and Dixie in execrable style. Each regiment had a square red flag, with a cross, made of diagonal blue stripes extending from opposite corners: on these blue stripes were placed thirteen white stars. A dirtier, filthier, more unsavory set of human beings never *strolled* through a town—marching it could not be called without doing violence to the word. The distinctions of rank were recognized on the coat collars of officers; but all were alike

dirty and repulsive. Their arms were rusty and in an unsol-
dierly condition. Their uniforms, or rather multiforms, corre-
sponded only in a slight predominance of gray over butter-
nut, and in the prevalence of filth. Faces looked as if they
had not been acquainted with water for weeks; hair, shaggy
and unkempt, seemed entirely a stranger to the operations
of brush or comb. A motlier group was never herded
together. But *these* were the chivalry—the deliverers of
Maryland from Lincoln's oppressive yoke.

During the afternoon a Provost Marshal was appointed
for the town, and he occupied the same office which had
been the headquarters of the U. S. Provost Marshal. Guards
were posted along our streets, and pickets on the roads leading from Frederick. Our stores were soon thronged with
crowds. The shoe stores were most patronized, as many of
their men were shoeless and stockingless. The only money
most of them had was Confederate scrip, or shinplasters
issued by banks, corporations, individuals, etc.—all of equal
value. To use the expression of an old citizen "the notes de-
preciated the paper on which they were printed." The
crowded condition of the stores enabled some of the chivalry
to *take* what they wanted, (confiscate is the technical expression,) without going through the formality of even
handing over Confederate rags in exchange. But guards
were placed at the stores wherever requested, and only a
few men allowed to enter at a time. Even this arrangement
proved inadequate, and the stores were soon necessarily
closed. The most intense hatred seems to have been encouraged and fostered in the men's hearts towards Union people,
or *Yankees* as they style them; and this word *Yankee* is employed with any and every manner of emphasis possible to
indicate contempt and bitterness. The men have been made
to believe that "to kill a Yankee" is to do a duty imperatively

imposed on them. The following incident will illustrate this: A gentleman was called aside, while talking with some ladies, by an officer who wished information as to shoes. He said he was in want of shoes for his men, that he had United States money if the dealers were so foolish as to prefer it, or he would procure them gold; but if they wouldn't sell he was satisfied to wait until they reached Baltimore, where he had no doubt but that shoes in quantity could be procured. No reply was made. Changing the subject, he inquired how the men were behaving. The answer was *very well;* there was no complaint, although some few had been seen intoxicated on the street. "Who gave them the liquor," said the officer. "Townsmen who sympathize with you and desire to show their love for you." "The only way to do that," said the officer, "is to kill a Yankee: kill a Yankee, sir, if you want to please a Southerner." This was uttered with all imaginable expression of vindictiveness and venom.

Our houses were besieged by hungry soldiers and officers. They ate everything offered them with a greediness that fully sustained the truth of their statement, that their entire subsistence lately had been *green corn, uncooked, and eaten directly from the stalk.* Union families freely gave such food as they had. "If thine enemy hunger, feed him," seemed the principle acted on by our good people. But few of our secession citizens aided them. They seemed ashamed of their Southern brethren. The Union people stood out for their principles, and took care to remind them that they were getting their food from those they had come to destroy. A gentleman relates the following: "In the evening, after having had one of their officers to tea—one whom I had known in former days—two officers came to the door and begged that something might be given them for which they wished to pay. On giving them the last biscuits in the house, one of them offered *pay*. The reply was, 'No, sir, whenever you meet a Federal soldier wanting food, recollect that a Union man in Frederick gave you the last morsel of food in his house when *you* were famishing.' The officer's face flushed up, and he replied, 'You are right, sir, I am very, very much obliged to you.' The coals of fire had been heaped on his head."

Outrages were committed on the National flag whenever one fell into the hands of the soldiers. These simply strengthened the Union feeling, and made the men and women of Frederick more attached than ever to the National cause for which their fathers had fought and died. Stauncher, stouter, stronger did Unionism in Frederick grow with each passing hour. We were conquered, not enslaved,—humiliated greatly with the thought that rebel feet were pressing on our soil, but not disposed to bow the knee to Baal.

An attack on the *Examiner* Printing Office being anticipated, a small guard was placed at the door. About nine o'clock, P.M., a rush was made on the guard by some of the Southern soldiers, the door was driven in and the contents of the office thrown into the street. W. G. Ross, Esq., a prominent lawyer of Frederick, called on the Provost Marshal, who soon arrived with a strong force, suppressed the riot, and, having obliged the rioters to return every thing belonging to the office, put them in the guard-house. During the continuance of this disturbance, the oaths and imprecations were terrific. Every one in the neighborhood expected that a general attack would be made on the Union houses. Fortunately, a quiet night ensued.

Sunday, September 7.—The rebels obliged most of our shoe-stores to be kept open during the day so that their men could obtain shoes. The reign of terror continued, although no personal violence was done to any citizen. Pickets are posted miles out of town. The main body of rebel troops is said to be encamped about Urbana. General Robert E. Lee is in command, and there are three divisions or, it may be, four, commanded by Jackson, Longstreet, D. H. Hill, and some one else. Forage is obtained by taking it and offering Confederate notes in payment.

At the Evangelical Reformed Church, the pastor, Rev. Dr. Daniel Zacharias, offered up prayers for the President of the United States, notwithstanding the presence of a number of Confederate officers. In the evening General Jackson was seen *asleep* in the same church.

The Commissioner for the Enrolment of the State Militia was seized to-day and made to hand over the enrolment-books. No further requirement was made of him, except that he should report himself daily at the office of the Provost-Marshal.

During the afternoon one of those incredible incidents oc-curred, which have been occasionally reported in our papers, but have always been disbelieved by those who have faith in the humanity of rebels. Several young ladies were standing in front of the house of one of our prominent citizens, when a rebel officer rode up and, halting his horse, said, "Ladies, allow me to make you a present. This is a ring made from *the bone of a dead Yankee*." A gentleman, near the curb, seized the article before the officer had finished speaking and handed it to the ladies, who quickly answered, "Keep your present for those who appreciate *such* presents." The only reply of the chivalry was, "Ah! I supposed you were *Southern* ladies!" This incident is instructive.

Monday, September 8.—General Robert E. Lee issues a proclamation, announcing that the Southern Army enters Maryland to restore her to freedom, that she has been down-trodden for a long time, and that her Sister States of the

Southern Confederacy have sworn to set her free from the influence of Northern bayonets,—free to decide for herself whether she will go with the South or no,—and promising protection to all of whatever opinion. Colonel B. T. Johnson, emulating the example of his superior officer, calls upon the citizens to unite in forming companies and regiments to join the Confederate States Army. Captain E. V. White announces that he is empowered to raise a regiment of cavalry. Mr. Heard (former Editor of the *Frederick Herald*—a secession paper) issues a card calling for recruits to a company he is forming. Thus we are flooded with proclamations. . . .

The supplies in our stores having nearly given out, some of the Union merchants resolutely closed their stores to the soldiers, and sending for their customers asked them to take what they required at the usual rates. The wealthiest grocer in the town raised the price of coffee to seventy-five cents, and brown sugar to forty cents per pound, to be paid in gold or in our own currency. This outrageous attempt to take advantage of the troublous condition of the community has excited considerable indignation in a quiet way all around.

We are still importuned by the rebels for food. It is furnished whenever asked, but the Union citizens take care to inform them that they are fed by their opponents. How the rebels manage to get along no one can tell. They are badly clad. Many of them without shoes. Uncleanliness and vermin are universal. The odor of clothes worn for months, saturated with perspiration and dirt, is intense and all-pervading. They look stout and sturdy, able to endure fatigue, and anxious to fight in the cause they have espoused, willingly or unwillingly. The movement they have now made is believed by them to be a desperate one, and they must "see it through." They all believe in *themselves* as well as in their generals, and are terribly in earnest. They assert that they have never been whipped, but have driven the Yankees before them whenever they could find them. They have killed so many Yankees and have gloried therein to such an extent that one would almost think them veritable Thugs. Bragging is a favorite game with them, and they do it well. Their army is plainly intended for an advance into Pennsylvania, and they speak freely of their intention to treat Pennsylvania very differently from Maryland. I fear there will be great destruction of property as they move forwards. Many a citizen will lose his all of this world's goods in this raid, for devastation is meant to be the order or disorder of their march when they cross the border.

Tuesday, September 9.—Recruiting goes on slowly in the town. We are told that three companies are to be raised here. It may be so, but one "can't see it." If ever suicide were contemplated by any one it must be by those civilians who propose to attach themselves to Jackson's corps. His men have become inured to hardships by long training, and are now on one of their most difficult undertakings. New recruits, taken from the comforts of social life, altogether unused to hardships, will readily sink under the fatigue of camp and field life.

A clergyman tells me that he saw an aged crone come out of her house as certain rebels passed by trailing the American flag in the dust. She shook her long, skinny hands at the traitors and screamed at the top of her voice, "My curses be upon you and your officers for degrading your country's flag." Her expression and gesture as described to me were worthy of Meg Merilies.

The Confederates have been seizing horses from our farmers, tendering Confederate scrip in payments. They allege military necessity in justification of this seizure. Military necessity is a convenient cloak for any outrage whatever.

As an offset to these operations of the rebels may be mentioned the sale of a horse to a Confederate by a *smart* Frederick boy. He had purchased a condemned Government horse for thirteen dollars, with the hope that by careful feeding he might so improve the animal's condition that he would command a profit. Food and care, however, proved vain. The horse refused to eat for two days, and was manifestly "sinking." A rebel asked the youth if he had a horse to sell. "Well, yes; I have a very fine horse, worth two hundred dollars to any man who can prize a good horse."

The rebel proposed entering the stable to examine the horse. "No sir! he is a spirited animal and might do a stranger some injury. Let me bring him out for you." By some special stimulus the horse was induced to come out, and the proprietor stated that on reflection he would let his valuable animal go for eighty dollars in *money*—not Confederate scrip. The rebel remarked that the horse held one foot off the ground, resting the weight of his body on three legs. He inquired as to the cause of this phenomenon. "Why, Lord bless you! don't you understand that? He is a *natural racker; all* natural rackers stand on three legs that way—always." The enunciation of this physiological law settled the question. The money was paid over. The rebel mounted his newly-purchased steed and rode away, somewhat to the seller's astonishment. He remarked to the by-standers, "I pledge you my word, gentlemen, he will last about three quarters of an hour at least. Any other gentleman wanting a natural racker can be accommodated at the shortest notice, if he will only call on me."

Wednesday, September 10.—At four o'clock this morning the rebel army began to move from our town, Jackson's force taking the advance. The movement continued until eight o'clock P.M., occupying sixteen hours. The most liberal calculations could not give them more than 64,000 men. Over 3,000 negroes must be included in this number. These were clad in all kinds of uniforms, not only in cast-off or captured United States uniforms, but in coats with Southern buttons, State buttons, etc. These were shabby, but not shabbier or seedier than those worn by white men in the rebel ranks. Most of the negroes had arms, rifles, muskets, sabres, bowie-knives, dirks, etc. They were supplied, in many instances, with knapsacks, haversacks, canteens, etc., and were manifestly an integral portion of the Southern Confederacy Army. They were seen riding on horses and mules, driving wagons, riding on caissons, in ambulances, with the staff of Generals, and promiscuously mixed up with all the rebel horde. The fact was patent, and rather interesting when considered in connection with the horror rebels express at the suggestion of black soldiers being employed for the National defence.

Some of the rebel regiments have been reduced to 150 men; none number over 500. The men are stout and ragged, anxious to "kill a Yankee," and firm in their belief that *Confederate notes* are as good as gold. Their marching is generally very loose. They marched by the flank through the streets of Frederick. Some few houses had rebel flags, to which one enthusiastic admirer of secession had added a white cross on a red ground. Some handkerchiefs waved, but all felt there was no genuine enthusiasm. The movement to Frederick had proved a failure. Their friends were anxious to get rid of them and of the penetrating ammoniacal smell they brought with them. Union citizens had become stronger in their faith. Rebel officers were unanimous in declaring that "Frederick was a d——d Union hole." The ill-suppressed expressions of delight on the countenances of the citizens could not be interpreted into indication of sympathy with Secession. They manifested only profound delight at the prospect of its speedy departure.

This force had about 150 guns with the letters U. S. This rebel army seemed to have been largely supplied with transportation by some United States Quartermaster. Uncle Sam's initials were on many of its wagons, ambulances, and horses. One neat spring-wagon was lettered "*General Casey's Headquarters.*" Each regiment was supplied with but one or two wagons. The men were mostly without knapsacks; some few carried blankets, and a *tooth-brush* was occasionally seen pendant from the button-hole of a private soldier, whose reminiscences of home-life were not entirely eradicated.

Their apologies for regimental bands were vile and excruciating. The only real music in their column to-day was from a bugle blown by a negro. Drummers and fifers of the same color abounded in their ranks. The men seemed generally disinclined to insult our citizens. But there were conspicuous exceptions. A drunken, bloated blackguard on horseback, for instance, with the badge of a Major-General on his collar, understood to be one *Howell Cobb,* formerly Secretary of the United States Treasury, on passing the house of a prominent sympathizer with the rebellion, removed his hat in answer to the waving of handkerchiefs, and reining his horse up, called on "his boys" to give three cheers. "Three more, my boys" and "three more!" Then, looking at the silent crowd of Union men on the pavement, he shook his fist at them, saying, "Oh you d——d long-faced Yankees! Ladies, take down their names and I will attend to them personally when I return." In view of the fact that this was addressed to a crowd of unarmed citizens, in the presence of a large body of armed soldiery flushed with success, the prudence—to say nothing of the bravery—of these remarks, may be judged of by any man of common sense.

Some of the citizens have been encouraging the Confederate soldiers by assuring them of the sympathy of Maryland, and urging them to push on northward with their offensive operations. One gray-haired man, who had escaped from the military authorities twelve months since by taking the oath of allegiance, was overheard saying to a rebel Colonel, "Make them feel the war when you reach Philadelphia."

Thursday, September 11.—General Hill's division, numbering about eight thousand men, marched through the streets, on their route westward, this morning. This division showed more of military discipline than either of its predecessors; the men marched in better order, had better music and were fairly clothed and equipped. This division moves more rapidly than either of the others. This was held to indicate the approach of the National army.

Three of the buildings on the hospital grounds were taken possession of by the Confederates for the accommodation of their sick. These soon threw themselves on the beds, with their filthy clothing and boots. In a few hours a marked contrast could be noticed between the neatness of the wards containing the Union soldiers and those occupied by the rebels. The secessionists collected the ladies of their order of thinking, and, for the first time since the breaking out of the rebellion, the fair forms of female secessionists were seen within the walls of the Frederick hospital, ministering to the wants of suffering humanity. I must confess that they seemed to work with a will. The Union ladies, whenever they found their supplies more than sufficient for our own sick, freely gave them to sick rebels. Charity knows neither party nor religious creed as a limit to its blessed work.

Rumors of a strong Federal force moving towards Frederick prevailed during the evening. Old and young prayed with fervor that these rumors might be based on truth. The

Union citizens were not harboring vindictive feelings towards their secession neighbors, but they longed for the old flag. Bright eyes were growing dim and rosy cheeks pale from anxious watching, day and night, for the coming of our National army. Hope deferred had made the heart sick, but still it was clung to with wondrous tenacity. Dreams of "blue-coats" were the attendants of such sleep as met their eyelids —dreams of a happy restoration to the rights of the old Union. Would they never be realized!

Friday, September 12.—Stewart's [Stuart's] cavalry passed through town to-day, on their way towards Hagerstown. It is said to be composed of Ashby's Cavalry and the Hampton Legion. The men are more neat and cleanly than the infantry that preceded them, and their horses, of good stock, are well-groomed and fed. Bragging is the order of the day with the cavalry. They boast that they never met more than one Federal regiment that dared to cross sabres with them, and that was the First Michigan Cavalry. Stewart has been visiting some of our sympathizers with the rebellion. Meeting Hospital Steward Fitzgerald, he asked him to state to the commanding officer of the Federal troops that might come to Frederick, that he would inflict severe punishment on Union men, wherever he could find them, if any punishment was meted out to the Southern sympathizers in Frederick by such officer. The steward answered that he, as a warrant-officer of the United States Army, could carry no such message, and suggested that General Stewart should remain to deliver it himself. The General did *not* act on this suggestion.

The joyous news at last reached town that the Federal troops were near at hand. Union people looked up their National flags. Two companies of Stewart's men, still in town, were stationed at the intersection of Market and Patrick streets. Cannonading was heard in the distance. Hearts were beating with joyous expectation. Our Union citizens were assembling at different points, discussing the probable results of the skirmish then taking place. It was evident that nothing more than a skirmish would take place, for the enemy, notwithstanding his boast that our troops would not meet him in a fair fight, was retreating westward towards the mountains. The advance cavalry of our National Army charged into our streets, driving the rebels before them. They were met by a counter-charge of Stewart's men, made in grand style. Saddles were emptied on both sides. Stewart's men fell back, carrying with them seven of our men as prisoners, and leaving many of their own men wounded on the ground. The accidental discharge of a cannon caused the death of seven horses and the wounding of a few men. Martial music is heard in the distance; a regiment of Ohio volunteers makes its appearance and is hailed with most enthusiastic demonstrations of joy. Handkerchiefs are waved, flags are thrown from Union houses, and a new life appears infused into the people. Burnside enters amid vociferous plaudits from every one, and the citizens, with enthusiastic eagerness, devote themselves to feeding the troops and welcoming them to their houses, as their *true* deliverers from a bondage more debasing than that of the African slave.

A little incident connected with the charge referred to is worthy of note. The wife of one of our prominent Union men threw out the National flag from her window just as Stewart's men dashed by the house. It seemed peculiarly fitting that a member of the *Washington* family should first unfurl her country's banner as our victorious troops entered a place which had been infested with the armed supporters of treason.

Saturday, September 13.—The town was effervescent with

joy at the arrival of the Union troops,—no business was done. Every one felt jubilant, and congratulated himself and neighbor that the United States troops were once more in possession. General McClellan with his staff rode through, about nine o'clock, and was received on all sides with the most unlimited expressions of delight. Old and young shouted with joy; matrons held their babes towards him as their deliverer from the rule of a foreign army, and fair young ladies rushed to meet him on the streets, some even throwing their arms around his horse's neck. It was a scene difficult to realize in this matter-of-fact age, but deep-seated feelings of gratitude found expression in every possible form. The reality of the joy constituted the poetry of the reception. Years of obloquy and reproach might have been considered compensated for by such a reception. The army, as well as its loved general, was welcomed with enthusiasm. To Frederick belongs the high honor of having given the *first* decided, enthusiastic, whole-souled reception which the Army had met since its officers and men had left their families and homes to fight the battles of their country. It is true that companies and regiments on their way to join the Army had been received with shouts of approval in the towns through which they passed, but the Army, as such, had always trudged along its accustomed line of duty without one word from the people in the way of satisfaction or commendation. But in Frederick it was received as a band of brothers, fighting for the welfare of the whole country and, whether successful or unsuccessful, entitled to the warmest demonstrations of good feeling possible.

I Think He Should Be Engaged

ONCE AGAIN General McClellan did not move with the alacrity and forcefulness President Lincoln felt he should. Success in turning back the Confederates at Antietam was not enough. It had enabled Mr. Lincoln to announce the Emancipation Proclamation on the heels of Federal victory, but the country clamored for greater victories still. First there was a letter of admonition, then another change of command. Here are the President's letter and addresses to the troops by Generals George B. McClellan and Ambrose E. Burnside respectively.

EXECUTIVE MANSION, WASHINGTON, *Oct. 13, 1862.*
My dear Sir—You remember my speaking to you of what I called your overcautiousness. Are you not overcautious when you assume that you can not do what the enemy is constantly doing? Should you not claim to be at least his equal in prowess, and act upon the claim?

As I understand, you telegraphed Gen. Halleck that you

can not subsist your army at Winchester, unless the railroad
from Harper's Ferry to that point be put in working order.
But the enemy does now subsist his army at Winchester at
a distance nearly twice as great from railroad transportation
as you would have to do without the railroad last named.
He now wagons from Culpepper [Culpeper] Court House,
which is just about twice as far as you would have to do
from Harper's Ferry. He is certainly not more than half as
well provided with wagons as you are. I certainly should
be pleased for you to have the advantage of the railroad
from Harper's Ferry to Winchester; but it wastes all the remainder of the autumn to give it to you, and in fact ignores
the question of *time*, which can not and must not be ignored.

Again, one of the standard maxims of war, as you know,
is, "to operate upon the enemy's communications as much
as possible, without exposing your own." You seem to act
as if this applies *against* you, but can not apply in your *favor*.
Change positions with the enemy, and think you not he
would break your communication with Richmond within
the next twenty-four hours? You dread his going into Pennsylvania. But if he does so in full force, he gives up his communications to you absolutely, and you have nothing to do but
to follow and ruin him; if he does so with less than full
force, fall upon and beat what is left behind all the easier.

Exclusive of the water line, you are now nearer Richmond
than the enemy is by the route that you *can* and he *must*
take. Why can you not reach there before him, unless you
admit that he is more than your equal on a march? His route
is the arc of a circle, while yours is the chord. The roads
are as good on yours as on his.

You know I desired, but did not order, you to cross the
Potomac below instead of above the Shenandoah and Blue
Ridge. My idea was, that this would at once menace the

enemy's communications, which I would seize if he would permit. If he should move northward, I would follow him closely, holding his communications. If he should prevent our seizing his communications, and move toward Richmond, I would press closely to him, fight him if a favorable opportunity should present, and at least try to beat him to Richmond on the inside track. I say, "try"; if we never try, we shall never succeed. If he make a stand at Winchester, moving neither north nor south, I would fight him there, on the idea that if we can not beat him when he bears the wastage of coming to us, we never can when we bear the wastage of going to him. This proposition is a simple truth, and is too important to be lost sight of for a moment. In coming to us, he tenders us an advantage which we should not waive. We should not so operate as to merely drive him away. As we must beat him somewhere, or fail finally, we can do it, if at all, easier near to us than far away. If we can not beat the enemy where he now is, we never can, he again being within the intrenchments of Richmond. Recurring to the idea of going to Richmond on the inside track, the facility of supplying from the side, away from the enemy, is remarkable, as it were by the different spokes of a wheel, extending from the hub toward the rim, and this whether you move directly by the chord or on the inside arc, hugging the Blue Ridge more closely. The chord-line, as you see, carries you by Aldie, Haymarket, and Fredericksburg, and you see how turnpikes, railroads, and finally the Potomac, by Aquia Creek, meet you at all points from Washington. The same, only the lines lengthened a little, you press closer to the Blue Ridge part of the way. The gaps through the Blue Ridge I understand to be about the following distances from Harper's Ferry, to wit: Vestal's, five miles; Gregory's, thirteen; Snicker's, eighteen; Ashby's, twenty-eight; Manassas, thirty-eight; Chester, forty-five; and Thornton's, fifty-three. I should think it preferable to take the route nearest the enemy, disabling him to make an important move without your knowledge, and compelling him to keep his forces together for dread of you. The gaps would enable you to attack if you should wish. For a great part of the way you would be practically between the enemy and both Washington and Richmond, enabling us to spare you the greatest number of troops from here. When, at length, running to Richmond ahead of him enables him to move this way; if he does so, turn and attack him in the rear. But I think he should be engaged long before such point is reached. It is all easy if our troops march as well as the enemy, and it is unmanly to say they can not do it. This letter is in no sense an order. Yours, truly,   A. LINCOLN.

Major-Gen. McCLELLAN.

HEAD-QUARTERS, ARMY OF THE POTOMAC,

CAMP NEAR RECTORTOWN, VA., *Nov.* 7, 1862.

OFFICERS AND SOLDIERS OF THE
    ARMY OF THE POTOMAC:

An order of the President devolves upon Major General BURNSIDE the command of this Army.

In parting from you I cannot express the love and gratitude I bear to you. As an army you have grown up under my care. In you I have never found doubt or coldness. The battles you have fought under my command will proudly live in our nation's history. The glory you have achieved, our mutual perils and fatigues, the graves of our comrades fallen in battle and by disease, the broken forms of those whom wounds and sickness have disabled,—the strongest associations which can exist among men,—unite us still by an indissoluble tie. We shall ever be comrades in supporting the Constitution of our country and the nationality of its people.

GEO. B. McCLELLAN,

Major General U. S. A.

HEAD-QUARTERS, ARMY OF THE POTOMAC,

WARRENTON, VA., *November* 9, 1862.

General Orders, ⎫
   No. 1. ⎭

In accordance with General Orders, No. 182, issued by the President of the United States, I hereby assume command of the Army of the Potomac.

Patriotism and the exercise of my every energy in the direction of this army, aided by the full and hearty co-operation of its officers and men, will, I hope, under the blessing of God, ensure its success.

Having been a sharer of the privations and a witness of the bravery of the old Army of the Potomac in the Maryland campaign, and fully identified with them in their feeling of respect and esteem for General McCLELLAN, entertained through a long and most friendly association with him, I feel that it is not as a stranger that I assume their command.

To the 9th Corps, so long and intimately associated with me, I need say nothing; our histories are identical.

With diffidence for myself, but with a proud confidence in the unswerving loyalty and determination of the gallant army now entrusted to my care, I accept its control with the steadfast assurance that the just cause must prevail.

A. E. BURNSIDE,

Major General Commanding.

Battle of Fredericksburg

Humorists of the day, both Yankee and Confederate, parodied Dan Emmett's "Jordan Is a Hard Road to Travel" as "Richmond Is a Hard Road to Travel." General Burnside learned that lesson quickly. On December 13 he threw his troops against the Confederates across the natural breastwork of a sunken road at the base of Marye's Hill. The Federal loss of over ten thousand nearly doubled Confederate losses, and the attack was not renewed. Burnside retired, soon to be relieved by General Joe Hooker.

The letter following relates the story of the Battle of Fredericksburg as it concerned one New York regiment. It was written by an unidentified private and quoted in William P. Maxson's *Camp Fires of the Twenty-Third*.

Camp "Paul" (Nowhere), *December 21st, 1862.*
Dear M——: On the night before the bombardment we bivouacked in a dense thicket of pines near the old camp-ground known as "Rufus King." We were not long in gather-

ing the cedar boughs, always abundant, and spreading this bed of down over the floor of our little tents. As darkness came on, the huge camp-fires gave a charming outline and feature to this little fairy city of white roofs. Their bright light in long diverging rays beat back the dark, and showed in relief the graceful tapering trunks of the pines, gray and dusky. Their boughs arch and form deep, dark aisles of nature's grand old cathedral filled with dim and spectral shadows. Around the fires groups of hardy soldiers were telling stories.

Aside from the deep, wild interest of battle, the shock of armies, when death is wantonly swooping into the gulf of ruin so many precious lives, there is a peculiar something in camp-life that may challenge comparison in interest to any other. . . . This noble band of men have come together to defend liberty with their lives, and a cord of sympathy ties the knot around the cheerful camp-fires. The rude jostling of these great hearts together, as they talk of their mutual dangers, hair-breadth escapes, noble deeds of comrades and the sacred cause, unites them one in purpose, one in action. To be sure, there is a lack of polish of manner and speech about all this (camp dialect is blunt), but it has the plain outspoken manhood, a smack of truth and honor, that atones for much of refinement. We are compelled to look upon it in this light. Such thoughts are born of such a life, no matter how uncultivated the soldier or rude the thought.

The pontoon bridges had been pushed nearly to the opposite shore under cover of darkness, and ere the faintest ray of dawn had streaked the east, the quick, sharp rattle of musketry broke the stillness. The engineers laying the last plank were charged upon, and a bloody struggle followed. Ought not that blood to doom that proud and ancient city? It certainly cries to Heaven for vengeance. A shaft of flame leaps out from the opposite shore, the earth trembles, the air breaks with a deafening roar, and a huge shell, with a shriek like a demon, speeds out upon its errand of destruction. Another followed, and another, till the storm of iron crushed through the walls and set the town on fire. All day long the incessant thunder of the bombardment shook the hills and rent the air. Our brigade moved down near to the river during the day and awaited orders. When the sun sunk darkly into the smoke of burning, the rebels on the opposite hills looked down upon the wreck of their proud city.

On the following morning the sun strove in vain to dispel the mountains of fog that covered the two armies like a shroud, and the mist held the river till after noon. Under this kindly cover we crossed the river. As we reached the level of the plain, a rebel battery opened upon the division while *en masse,* and with surprising accuracy dropped the shell in our midst, but to very little effect. One man in the regiment was slightly wounded. The advance was thrown briskly forward and a footing for the army obtained. Night now closed in upon the opposing armies, and they await the morrow.

The morrow came, and with it the conflict. It was evident that the enemy must be driven from the plain to his stronghold on the heights, and these heights must be stormed. The forces were disposed in order of battle before the mists of morning had been dispersed by the rising sun. Our brigade, now commanded by Colonel Rogers, of the Twenty-first New York Volunteers, held the extreme left, and had the supreme satisfaction of driving the vanguard of the enemy from that part of the field. Batteries B and L made it decidedly too warm for them.

The fight opened fiercely. The great wave of battle surged across the plain and up the rugged heights, swallowing up

in its bloody tide regiments, brigades, divisions of brave and
heroic men who went down before that death-storm to bite
the dust. Great men, men of promise, the sturdy oaks of
society as well as the brushwood, were swept by its fury into
a soldier's grave. Fortune seemed to favor us, the rebel lines
gave way, and our forces drove them up the slope of the
heights. But an avalanche awaited them. A flame of fire
leaped from the now uncovered supports, and our columns
melted before it like dew before the morning sun. The tide
of battle changed and rolled back upon the plain.

It was at this point that Lieutenant-Colonel N. M. Crane,
as inspector-general of General Reynolds' staff, seeing the
Pennsylvania reserves in full retreat, rode up to General
Reynolds and said:

"See yonder, General! the 'reserves' have broken."

"My God! Colonel," said the General, "can't you go and
stop them!"

Colonel Crane dashed into the midst of the flying mob,
and by threats, persuasion, and praise of their former deeds
of valor, succeeded in rallying a small battalion of them in
the face of the storm of lead that followed them.

It was here also that General Reynolds, failing to get immediate support from the right, sent in haste to General
Doubleday for a brigade. Colonel Rogers was ordered up, and
with cheerfulness and spirit the entire brigade moved forward double quick, and in perfect line, though the field was
continually raked by cannon-shot. Files of men were swept
away without a waver in the lines. The expected support
arrived before we reached the ground, and the brigade returned to its post. The day had been almost lost, but the
veteran regiments were thrown heavily against the triumphant host, and quivering under the awful blow it was beaten
back with equal loss. Night at last approached. The sunset

was gorgeously beautiful. Nature seemed to laugh at the great calamity. Fighting did not cease till late, and when at last we thought of sleep, we were kept awake by grape and canister.

Sunday morning dawned bright and beautiful, and as calm as though the earth had not groaned and the heavens been rent by a scene of carnage seldom equaled in history. Slight cannonading and skirmishing occupied the day, and as we lay down at night with the sky for our cover, Aurora flung out the grand banner of the heavens, "red, white, and blue," bespangled by the everlasting stars. Its beautiful folds floated up and covered one half of the arch. As we gazed upon it with delight, we felt that the national emblem had not been dishonored by act of ours, and we worshiped in silence the starry banner.

Another day of anxious expectation, of skirmishing, and it became evident that our position was untenable. With masterly skill of plan and execution General Burnside placed his army on the east side of the Rappahannock during the night of the 15th, much to the chagrin and disappointment of the foe.

In this engagement the Twenty-third lost two killed and sixteen wounded. There were instances of especial coolness and courage, but to point out these in a regiment where a want of courage is the exception and not the rule, would be unjust to others. Each man, in whatever capacity, did his duty nobly. You will of course guess by this letter that your friend came off whole, not damaged. Yours,

P—— S——.

A Day in a Hospital

EVERY BATTLE produced more work for already over-
loaded hospitals. Here is Louisa May Alcott's
sprightly account of a day of hospital service shortly
after the Battle of Fredericksburg.

"THEY'VE come! they've come! hurry up, ladies—you're
wanted."

"Who have come? the rebels?"

This sudden summons in the gray dawn was somewhat
startling to a three days' nurse like myself, and, as the thundering knock came at our door, I sprang up in my bed, prepared

"To gird my woman's form,
And on the ramparts die,"

if necessary, but my room-mate took it more coolly, and, as
she began a rapid toilet, answered my bewildered question.—

"Bless you, no, child; it's the wounded from Fredericksburg; forty ambulances are at the door, and we shall have
our hands full in fifteen minutes."

"What shall we have to do?"

185

"Wash, dress, feed, warm and nurse them for the next three months, I dare say. Eighty beds are ready, and we were getting impatient for the men to come. Now you will begin to see hospital life in earnest, for you won't probably find time to sit down all day, and may think yourself fortunate if you get to bed by midnight. Come to me in the ball-room when you are ready; the worst cases are always carried there, and I shall need your help."

So saying, the energetic little woman twirled her hair into a button at the back of her head, in a "cleared for action" sort of style, and vanished, wrestling her way into a feminine kind of pea-jacket as she went.

I am free to confess that I had a realizing sense of the fact that my hospital bed was not a bed of roses just then, or the prospect before me one of unmingled rapture. My three days' experiences had begun with a death, and, owing to the defalcation of another nurse, a somewhat abrupt plunge into the superintendence of a ward containing forty beds, where I spent my shining hours washing faces, serving rations, giving medicine, and sitting in a very hard chair, with pneumonia on one side, diphtheria on the other, five typhoids on the opposite, and a dozen dilapidated patriots, hopping, lying, and lounging about, all staring more or less at the new "nuss," who suffered untold agonies, but concealed them under as matronly an aspect as a spinster could assume, and blundered through her trying labors with a Spartan firmness, which I hope they appreciated, but am afraid they didn't. Having a taste for "ghastliness," I had rather longed for the wounded to arrive, for rheumatism wasn't heroic, neither was liver complaint, or measles; even fever had lost its charms since "bathing burning brows" had been used up in romances, real and ideal; but when I peeped into the dusky street lined with what I at first had inno-

cently called market carts, now unloading their sad freight
at our door, I recalled sundry reminiscences I had heard
from nurses of longer standing, my ardor experienced a sudden chill, and I indulged in a most unpatriotic wish that I
was safe at home again, with a quiet day before me, and no
necessity for being hustled up, as if I were a hen and had
only to hop off my roost, give my plumage a peck, and be
ready for action. A second bang at the door sent this recreant
desire to the right about, as the little woolly head popped in,
and Joey, (a six years' old contraband,) announced—

"Miss Blank is jes' wild fer ye, and says fly round right
away. They's comin' in, I tell yer, heaps on 'em—one was
took out dead, and I see him,—ky! warn't he a goner!"

With which cheerful intelligence the imp scuttled away,
singing like a blackbird, and I followed, feeling that Richard
was *not* himself again, and wouldn't be for a long time to
come.

The first thing I met was a regiment of the vilest odors
that ever assaulted the human nose, and took it by storm.
Cologne, with its seven and seventy evil savors, was a posy-
bed to it; and the worst of this affliction was, every one had
assured me that it was a chronic weakness of all hospitals,
and I must bear it. I did, armed with lavender water, with
which I so besprinkled myself and premises, that, like my
friend, Sairy, I was soon known among my patients as "the
nurse with the bottle." Having been run over by three excited surgeons, bumped against by migratory coal-hods,
water-pails, and small boys; nearly scalded by an avalanche of
newly-filled tea-pots, and hopelessly entangled in a knot of
colored sisters coming to wash, I progressed by slow stages
up stairs and down, till the main hall was reached, and I
paused to take breath and a survey. There they were! "our
brave boys," as the papers justly call them, for cowards could

hardly have been so riddled with shot and shell, so torn and shattered, nor have borne suffering for which we have no name, with an uncomplaining fortitude, which made one glad to cherish each as a brother. In they came, some on stretchers, some in men's arms, some feebly staggering along propped on rude crutches, and one lay stark and still with covered face, as a comrade gave his name to be recorded before they carried him away to the dead house. All was hurry and confusion; the hall was full of these wrecks of humanity, for the most exhausted could not reach a bed till duly ticketed and registered; the walls were lined with rows of such as could sit, the floor covered with the more disabled, the steps and doorways filled with helpers and lookers on; the sound of many feet and voices made that usually quiet hour as noisy as noon; and, in the midst of it all, the matron's motherly face brought more comfort to many a poor soul, than the cordial draughts she administered, or the cheery words that welcomed all, making of the hospital a home.

The sight of several stretchers, each with its legless, arm-less, or desperately wounded occupant, entering my ward, admonished me that I was there to work, not to wonder or weep; so I corked up my feelings, and returned to the path of duty, which was rather "a hard road to travel" just then. The house had been a hotel before hospitals were needed, and many of the doors still bore their old names; some not so inappropriate as might be imagined, for my ward was in truth a *ball-room*, if gun-shot wounds could christen it. Forty beds were prepared, many already tenanted by tired men who fell down anywhere, and drowsed till the smell of food roused them. Round the great stove was gathered the dreari-est group I ever saw—ragged, gaunt and pale, mud to the knees, with bloody bandages untouched since put on days before; many bundled up in blankets, coats being lost or

useless; and all wearing that disheartened look which proclaimed defeat, more plainly than any telegram of the Burnside blunder. I pitied them so much, I dared not speak to
them, though, remembering all they had been through since
the rout at Fredericksburg, I yearned to serve the dreariest
of them all. Presently, Miss Blank tore me from my refuge
behind piles of one-sleeved shirts, odd socks, bandages and
lint; put basin, sponge, towels, and a block of brown soap
into my hands, with these appalling directions:

"Come, my dear, begin to wash as fast as you can. Tell
them to take off socks, coats, and shirts, scrub them well, put
on clean shirts, and the attendants will finish them off, and
lay them in bed."

If she had requested me to shave them all, or dance a
hornpipe on the stove funnel, I should have been less staggered; but to scrub some dozen lords of creation at a moment's notice, was really—really——. However, there was
no time for nonsense, and, having resolved when I came to
do everything I was bid, I drowned my scruples in my wash-
bowl, clutched my soap manfully, and, assuming a business-
like air, made a dab at the first dirty specimen I saw, bent on
performing my task *vi et armis* if necessary. I chanced to
light on a withered old Irishman, wounded in the head,
which caused that portion of his frame to be tastefully laid
out like a garden, the bandages being the walks, his hair the
shrubbery. He was so overpowered by the honor of having
a lady wash him, as he expressed it, that he did nothing but
roll up his eyes, and bless me, in an irresistible style which
was too much for my sense of the ludicrous; so we laughed
together, and when I knelt down to take off his shoes, he
"flopped" also and wouldn't hear of my touching "them dirty
craters. May your bed above be aisy, darlin', for the day's
work ye are doon!—Whoosh! there ye are, and bedad, it's

hard tellin' which is the dirtiest, the fut or the shoe." It was; and if he hadn't been to the fore, I should have gone on pulling, under the impression that the "fut" was a boot, for trousers, socks, shoes and legs were a mass of mud. This comical tableau produced a general grin, at which propitious beginning I took heart and scrubbed away like any tidy parent on a Saturday night. Some of them took the performance like sleepy children, leaning their tired heads against me as I worked, others looked grimly scandalized, and several of the roughest colored like bashful girls. One wore a soiled little bag about his neck, and, as I moved it, to bathe his wounded breast, I said,

"Your talisman didn't save you, did it?"

"Well, I reckon it did, marm, for that shot would a gone a couple a inches deeper but for my old mammy's camphor bag," answered the cheerful philosopher.

Another, with a gun-shot wound through the cheek, asked for a looking-glass, and when I brought one, regarded his swollen face with a dolorous expression, as he muttered—

"I vow to gosh, that's too bad! I warn't a bad looking chap before, and now I'm done for; won't there be a thunderin' scar? and what on earth will Josephine Skinner say?"

He looked up at me with his one eye so appealingly, that I controlled my risibles, and assured him that if Josephine was a girl of sense, she would admire the honorable scar, as a lasting proof that he had faced the enemy, for all women thought a wound the best decoration a brave soldier could wear. I hope Miss Skinner verified the good opinion I so rashly expressed of her, but I shall never know.

The next scrubbee was a nice looking lad, with a curly brown mane, and a budding trace of gingerbread over the lip, which he called his beard, and defended stoutly, when the barber jocosely suggested its immolation. He lay on a bed, with one leg gone, and the right arm so shattered that it must evidently follow; yet the little Sergeant was as merry as if his affliction were not worth lamenting over, and when a drop or two of salt water mingled with my suds at the sight of this strong young body, so marred and maimed, the boy looked up, with a brave smile, though there was a little quiver of the lips, as he said,

"Now don't you fret yourself about me, miss; I'm first rate here, for it's nuts to lie still on this bed, after knocking about in those confounded ambulances, that shake what there is left of a fellow to jelly. I never was in one of these places before, and think this cleaning up a jolly thing for us, though I'm afraid it isn't for you ladies."

"Is this your first battle, Sergeant?"

"No, miss; I've been in six scrimmages, and never got a scratch till this last one; but it's done the business pretty thoroughly for me, I should say. Lord! what a scramble there'll be for arms and legs, when we old boys come out of our graves, on the Judgment Day: wonder if we shall get our own again? If we do, my leg will have to tramp from Fredericksburg, my arm from here, I suppose, and meet my body, wherever it may be."

The fancy seemed to tickle him mightily, for he laughed blithely, and so did I; which, no doubt, caused the new nurse to be regarded as a light-minded sinner by the Chaplain, who roamed vaguely about, informing the men that they were all worms, corrupt of heart, with perishable bodies, and souls only to be saved by a diligent perusal of certain tracts, and other equally cheering bits of spiritual consolation, when spirituous ditto would have been preferred.

"I say, Mrs.!" called a voice behind me; and, turning, I saw a rough Michigander, with an arm blown off at the shoulder, and two or three bullets still in him—as he afterwards mentioned, as carelessly as if gentlemen were in the habit of carrying such trifles about with them. I went to him, and, while administering a dose of soap and water, he whispered, irefully:

"That red-headed devil, over yonder, is a reb, damn him! You'll agree to that, I'll bet? He's got shet of a foot, or he'd a cut like the rest of the lot. Don't you wash him, nor feed him, but just let him holler till he's tired. It's a blasted shame to fetch them fellers in here, along side of us; and so I'll tell the chap that bosses this concern; cuss me if I don't."

I regret to say that I did not deliver a moral sermon upon the duty of forgiving our enemies, and the sin of profanity, then and there; but, being a red-hot Abolitionist, stared fixedly at the tall rebel, who was a copperhead, in every sense of the word, and privately resolved to put soap in his eyes, rub his nose the wrong way, and excoriate his cuticle generally, if I had the washing of him.

My amiable intentions, however, were frustrated; for, when I approached with as Christian an expression as my principles would allow, and asked the question— "Shall I try to make you more comfortable, sir?" all I got for my pains was a gruff—

"No; I'll do it myself."

"Here's your Southern chivalry, with a witness," thought I, dumping the basin down before him, thereby quenching a strong desire to give him a summary baptism, in return for his ungraciousness; for my angry passions rose, at this rebuff, in a way that would have scandalized good Dr. Watts. He was a disappointment in all respects, (the rebel, not the blessed Doctor,) for he was neither fiendish, romantic, pathetic, or anything interesting; but a long, fat man, with a head like a burning-bush, and a perfectly expressionless face: so I could hate him without the slightest drawback, and ignored his existence from that day forth. One redeeming trait he certainly did possess, as the floor speedily testified; for his ablutions were so vigorously performed, that his bed soon stood like an isolated island, in a sea of soap suds, and he resembled a dripping merman, suffering from the loss of a fin. If cleanliness is a near neighbor to godliness, then was the big rebel the godliest man in my ward that day.

Having done up our human wash, and laid it out to dry, the second syllable of our version of the word war-fare was enacted with much success. Great trays of bread, meat, soup and coffee appeared; and both nurses and attendants turned waiters, serving bountiful rations to all who could eat. I can call my pinafore to testify to my good will in the work, for in ten minutes it was reduced to a perambulating bill of fare, presenting samples of all the refreshments going or gone. It was a lively scene; the long room lined with rows of beds, each filled by an occupant, whom water, shears, and clean raiment, had transformed from a dismal ragamuffin into a recumbent hero, with a cropped head. To and fro rushed matrons, maids, and convalescent "boys," skirmishing with knives and forks; retreating with empty plates; marching and counter-marching, with unvaried success, while the clash of busy spoons made most inspiring music for the charge of our Light Brigade:

> "Beds to the front of them,
> Beds to right of them,
> Beds to the left of them,
>   Nobody blundered.
> Beamed at by hungry souls,
> Screamed at with brimming bowls,
> Steamed at by army rolls,
>   Buttered and sundered.

With coffee not cannon plied,
Each must be satisfied,
Whether they lived or died;
All the men wondered."

Very welcome seemed the generous meal, after a week of
suffering, exposure, and short commons; soon the brown
faces began to smile, as food, warmth, and rest, did their
pleasant work; and the grateful "Thankee's" were followed
by more graphic accounts of the battle and retreat, than any
paid reporter could have given us. Curious contrasts of the
tragic and comic met one everywhere; and some touching
as well as ludicrous episodes, might have been recorded that
day. A six foot New Hampshire man, with a leg broken and
perforated by a piece of shell, so large that, had I not seen
the wound, I should have regarded the story as a Munchau-
senism, beckoned me to come and help him, as he could not
sit up, and both his bed and beard were getting plentifully
anointed with soup. As I fed my big nestling with corresponding mouthfuls, I asked him how he felt during the
battle.

"Well, 'twas my fust, you see, so I aint ashamed to say I
was a trifle flustered in the beginnin', there was such an all-
fired racket; for ef there's anything I do spleen agin, it's
noise. But when my mate, Eph Sylvester, caved, with a bullet through his head, I got mad, and pitched in, licketty cut.
Our part of the fight didn't last long; so a lot of us larked
round Fredericksburg, and give some of them houses a
pretty consid'able of a rummage, till we was ordered out of
the mess. Some of our fellows cut like time; but I warn't
a-goin to run for nobody; and, fust thing I knew, a shell
bust, right in front of us, and I keeled over, feelin' as if I
was blowed higher'n a kite. I sung out, and the boys come

back for me, double-quick; but the way they chucked me
over them fences was a caution, I tell you. Next day I was
most as black as the darkey yonder, lickin' plates on the sly.
This is bully coffee, ain't it? Give us another pull at it, and
I'll be obleeged to you."

I did; and, as the last gulp subsided, he said, with a rub
of his old handkerchief over eyes as well as mouth:

"Look a here; I've got a pair of earbobs and a handkercher
pin I'm a goin' to give you, if you'll have them; for you're
the very moral o' Lizy Sylvester, poor Eph's wife: that's why
I signalled you to come over here. They aint much, I guess,
but they'll do to memorize the rebs by."

Burrowing under his pillow, he produced a little bundle of
what he called "truck," and gallantly presented me with a
pair of earrings, each representing a cluster of corpulent
grapes, and the pin a basket of astonishing fruit, the whole
large and coppery enough for a small warming-pan. Feeling
delicate about depriving him of such valuable relics, I accepted the earrings alone, and was obliged to depart, somewhat abruptly, when my friend stuck the warming-pan in
the bosom of his night-gown, viewing it with much compla-
cency, and, perhaps, some tender memory, in that rough
heart of his, for the comrade he had lost.

Observing that the man next him had left his meal untouched, I offered the same service I had performed for his
neighbor, but he shook his head.

"Thank you, ma'am; I don't think I'll ever eat again, for
I'm shot in the stomach. But I'd like a drink of water, if you
aint too busy."

I rushed away, but the water-pails were gone to be refilled,
and it was some time before they reappeared. I did not forget my patient patient, meanwhile, and, with the first mug-
ful, hurried back to him. He seemed asleep; but something

in the tired white face caused me to listen at his lips for a
breath. None came. I touched his forehead; it was cold: and
then I knew that, while he waited, a better nurse than I had
given him a cooler draught, and healed him with a touch. I
laid the sheet over the quiet sleeper, whom no noise could
now disturb; and, half an hour later, the bed was empty. It
seemed a poor requital for all he had sacrificed and suffered,
—that hospital bed, lonely even in a crowd; for there was
no familiar face for him to look his last upon; no friendly
voice to say, Good bye: no hand to lead him gently down
into the Valley of the Shadow; and he vanished, like a drop
in that red sea upon whose shores so many women stand
lamenting. For a moment I felt bitterly indignant at this
seeming carelessness of the value of life, the sanctity of
death; then consoled myself with the thought that, when the
great muster roll was called, these nameless men might be
promoted above many whose tall monuments record the
barren honors they have won.

All having eaten, drank, and rested, the surgeons began
their rounds; and I took my first lesson in the art of dressing
wounds. It wasn't a festive scene, by any means; for Dr. P.,
whose Aid I constituted myself, fell to work with a vigor
which soon convinced me that I was a weaker vessel, though
nothing would have induced me to confess it then. He had
served in the Crimea, and seemed to regard a dilapidated
body very much as I should have regarded a damaged gar-
ment; and, turning up his cuffs, whipped out a very unpleasant looking housewife, cutting, sawing, patching and piecing,
with the enthusiasm of an accomplished surgical seamstress;
explaining the process, in scientific terms, to the patient,
meantime; which, of course, was immensely cheering and
comfortable. There was an uncanny sort of fascination in
watching him, as he peered and probed into the mechanism

of those wonderful bodies, whose mysteries he understood
so well. The more intricate the wound, the better he liked it.
A poor private, with both legs off, and shot through the lungs,
possessed more attractions for him than a dozen generals,
slightly scratched in some "masterly retreat;" and had any
one appeared in small pieces, requesting to be put together
again, he would have considered it a special dispensation.

The amputations were reserved till the morrow, and the
merciful magic of ether was not thought necessary that day,
so the poor souls had to bear their pains as best they might.
It is all very well to talk of the patience of woman; and far
be it from me to pluck that feather from her cap, for, heaven
knows, she isn't allowed to wear many; but the patient endurance of these men, under trials of the flesh, was truly
wonderful; their fortitude seemed contagious, and scarcely
a cry escaped them, though I often longed to groan for them,
when pride kept their white lips shut, while great drops
stood upon their foreheads, and the bed shook with the
irrepressible tremor of their tortured bodies. One or two
Irishmen anathematized the doctors with the frankness of
their nation, and ordered the Virgin to stand by them, as if
she had been the wedded Biddy to whom they could administer the poker, if she didn't; but, as a general thing, the work
went on in silence, broken only by some quiet request for
roller, instruments, or plaster, a sigh from the patient, or a
sympathizing murmur from the nurse.

It was long past noon before these repairs were even partially made; and, having got the bodies of my boys into
something like order, the next task was to minister to their
minds, by writing letters to the anxious souls at home; answering questions, reading papers, taking possession of
money and valuables; for the eighth commandment was reduced to a very fragmentary condition, both by the blacks

and whites, who ornamented our hospital with their presence. Pocket books, purses, miniatures, and watches, were
sealed up, labelled, and handed over to the matron, till such
times as the owners thereof were ready to depart homeward
or campward again. The letters dictated to me, and revised
by me, that afternoon, would have made an excellent chapter for some future history of the war; for, like that which
Thackeray's "Ensign Spooney" wrote his mother just before
Waterloo, they were "full of affection, pluck, and bad spell-
ing;" nearly all giving lively accounts of the battle, and ending with a somewhat sudden plunge from patriotism to
provender, desiring "Marm," "Mary Ann," or "Aunt Peters,"
to send along some pies, pickles, sweet stuff, and apples, "to
yourn in haste," Joe, Sam, or Ned, as the case might be.

My little Sergeant insisted on trying to scribble something
with his left hand, and patiently accomplished some half
dozen lines of hieroglyphics, which he gave me to fold and
direct, with a boyish blush, that rendered a glimpse of "My
Dearest Jane," unnecessary, to assure me that the heroic
lad had been more successful in the service of Commander-
in-Chief Cupid than that of Gen. Mars; and a charming little
romance blossomed instanter in Nurse Periwinkle's romantic fancy, though no further confidences were made that
day, for Sergeant fell asleep, and, judging from his tranquil
face, visited his absent sweetheart in the pleasant land of
dreams.

At five o'clock a great bell rang, and the attendants flew,
not to arms, but to their trays, to bring up supper, when a
second uproar announced that it was ready. The new comers
woke at the sound; and I presently discovered that it took a
very bad wound to incapacitate the defenders of the faith
for the consumption of their rations; the amount that some
of them sequestered was amazing; but when I suggested the

probability of a famine hereafter, to the matron, that motherly lady cried out: "Bless their hearts, why shouldn't they eat? It's their only amusement; so fill every one, and, if there's not enough ready to-night, I'll lend my share to the Lord by giving it to the boys." And, whipping up her coffee-pot and plate of toast, she gladdened the eyes and stomachs of two or three dissatisfied heroes, by serving them with a liberal hand; and I haven't the slightest doubt that, having cast her bread upon the waters, it came back buttered, as another large-hearted old lady was wont to say.

Then came the doctor's evening visit; the administration of medicines; washing feverish faces; smoothing tumbled beds; wetting wounds; singing lullabies; and preparations for the night. By eleven, the last labor of love was done; the last "good night" spoken; and, if any needed a reward for that day's work, they surely received it, in the silent eloquence of those long lines of faces, showing pale and peaceful in the shaded rooms, as we quitted them, followed by grateful glances that lighted us to bed, where rest, the sweetest, made our pillows soft, while Night and Nature took our places, filling that great house of pain with the healing miracles of Sleep, and his diviner brother, Death.

1863

The Grand Terpsichorean Festival

Early in 1862 General Burnside had led an expedition which secured a Federal beachhead at Roanoke Island, North Carolina. From there Federal control was extended over much of the coastal plain of the state, and a major command centered around the old Carolina town of New Bern. There was sporadic activity between these occupation troops and the Confederates, marked chiefly by battles at Kinston, Whitehall, and Goldsboro in December, 1862. But the soldiers' chief enemy when their principal duty is that of occupation is boredom.

To help relieve the boredom in eastern North Carolina the soldiers of the Forty-fourth Massachusetts Regiment got up their own entertainments. In the winter of 1863 they amused themselves with improvised dances. To one they announced that none but those in costume would be admitted, but "the restriction was of little avail. Those who failed to pass the door keepers entered at the ventilators." Here is Zenas T. Haines's account of the "grand Terpsichorean Festival" of January 20, 1863.

203

NEWBERN, N. C., JAN. 23, 1863.

The first grand Terpsichorean festival of the New Year in our regiment transpired on the evening of the 20th instant, in the barracks of Co. D. The much lamented absence of the feminine element was in part atoned for by female apparel donned for the occasion by a number of young men with smooth faces and an eye to artistic effect. If Jenkins had been present his pencil would have waxed eloquent over the superb attire and tasteful colors of the magnificent blonde, Miss C. D. N. His page would have glowed with lover-like panegyrics of the tall and peerless, white-robed queen of the night, Miss G. F. B. Good taste, however, might have suggested that the former was a little too *en bon point,* as well as too demonstrative in her personal decorations, and that the latter was a trifle tall for the breadth of her raiment. But when Jenkins came to the Misses C. F. W., J. H. W., W. G. R. and especially to Miss C. W. S., of East Boston, he would assuredly have "slopped over" in his characteristic manner. Not, however, because these Hebes were less faulty in toilet than the others, for a critical eye might have suggested dresses higher in the neck, longer in skirt, and less protuberant in the rear; less suggestive, in short, of those gay and festive occasions which have rendered Joe Clash and North street immortal the world over. Some of the gallants of the young women were scarcely less stunning in their make up. The insignia of military office, from that of Major Generals to Lieutenants, extensively prevailed. Dancing, of course, was the order of the night; a fiddler was engaged, and

"When music arose with its voluptuous swell,
Soft eyes looked love to eyes which spake again,
And all went merry as a marriage bell."

The following is the

ORDER OF DANCES.

1. SICILIAN CIRCLE, ... March to Tarboro'.
2. QUADRILLE, ... New England Guards.
3. POLKA QUADRILLE, ... Kinston Gallop.
4. QUADRILLE, ... Yankee Doodle.

INTERMISSION.
Waltz, Polka Redowa, Schottische.

5. QUADRILLE, ... Bloody 44th Quickstep.
6. LES LANCIERS, ... Connecticut 10th March.
7. QUADRILLE, ... Lee's March.
8. CONTRA (*Virginia Reel*), ... Rebels' Last Skedaddle.

In this connection I will introduce the managerial card, which was as follows:

GRAND BALL.

SIR:—The pleasure of your company, with ladies, is respectfully solicited at a Grand Ball, to be held in the Grand Parlor of the FIFTH AVENUE HOTEL, (No. 4 Newbern.) on TUESDAY EVENING, January 20th, 1863.

The Management beg leave to state that nothing will be left undone on their part to make it *the* party of the season.

MANAGERS.
C. H. DEMERITT,   W. HOWARD,   J. E. LEIGHTON.

COMMITTEE OF ARRANGEMENTS.

Benj. F. Burchsted,	W. G. Reed,
W. E. Savery,	F. M. Flanders,
J. B. Gardner,	Charles Adams,
C. D. Newell,	H. D. Stanwood,
F. A. Sayer,	H. Howard,
Joe Simonds,	G. W. Hight.

MUSIC.

Quintzelbottom's Grand Quadrille and Serenade Band,
(*One Violin.*)

TICKETS $00.03 EACH, TO BE HAD OF THE MANAGERS.
☞ *No Postage Stamps or Sutler's Checks taken
in payment.*

N. B. LADIES will be allowed to smoke.

Persons wishing carriages will please apply to LIEUT.
WHITE, of the Ambulance Corpse.

Persons wishing anything stronger than Water are referred
to the "Sanitary."

The managers were decorated with official rosettes, a solid
square of hard tack forming the centre of each. Even some
of the belles of the evening were resplendent with pendant
jewels cut from the same tenacious mineral.

That nothing might be wanting to revive the memories
of Clash's Hall, a bar was improvised inside the sliding door
where we get our rations, and here the cooks busily regaled
the dancers with water, and molasses and water, from a
bottle and a single tumbler, while announcing, by means
of placards over the window, "Splendid New Drinks," in the
shape of quinine and diarrhœa mixture No. 3, names forever
associated with and articulate in the surgeon's matutinal
bugle-call. The bar soon began to show its effects in the
shape of cocked hats, awry toilets, loud-mouthed contro-
versies, and, at last, fighting. The intervention of an active
but diminutive policeman was invoked. He was a little man,
but chewed tobacco with a serious determination, which
boded danger to evil doers. His services in keeping back the
crowd and quelling disturbances in the vicinity of the bar
were in constant requisition. Not unfrequently his badge was
seen tossing in the midst of a riotous crowd, and he was re-

ported to be once seen skedaddling before a slightly superior force. He was noticed as being very familiar with your reporter, whom he furnished with considerable doubtful information about his own operations.

At the proper hour refreshments were served. "A beautiful slave," in the person of Mr. West Williams . . . entered with two trays containing severally hard tack and salt horse. His advent was hailed with the same shouts and swaying of the crowd as usually attend the administration of our rations. The tack and horse vanished, and the dance proceeded with various divertisements to the end.

We had many visitors, including Colonel Lee and staff, all of whom evinced their intense satisfaction with what they heard and saw.

It is expected that other balls, including a masquerade, will succeed this affair.

A soldier's life is one of curious contrasts. Although *not* always gay, it has the jolliest kind of episodes. It affords the two emotional extremes. One day finds him in the midst of hilarity and social enjoyment, the next in the blood and carnage of battle, with friends falling all about him

"Thick as autumnal leaves in Valambrosa."

But an hour or two before the festivities recounted above, a slow-moving procession with muffled drum and reversed arms, moved from our lines with the remains of a much-loved comrade suddenly stricken down with the malarious fever. His name was Boynton, of Company G. A day or two previously, Corporal Upham of the same company died of the same disease.

Chancellorsville

THE THIRD SPRING of the war brought renewed activity on the front in Virginia. General Hooker moved the Federal troops once more south of the Rappahannock in an "on to Richmond" campaign. In the great battle of his career as commander of the Army of the Potomac, Federals and Confederates met at Chancellorsville, May 3 and 4.

General orders are notorious for representing the best possible point of view. As Hooker's order points out they are "the guardian of [the army's] own history and its own fame." This order of May 6 describes Chancellorsville as if it might have been an overwhelming victory. Actually it was a severe defeat, the Federals losing 17,287 men and the Confederates 12,423. But it was too costly a victory for the Confederates. They could ill afford to win with such heavy losses, and their loss included General "Stonewall" Jackson, shot down by his own troops on the evening of May 3.

HEAD-QUARTERS, ARMY OF THE POTOMAC,

CAMP NEAR FALMOUTH, VA., *May* 6, 1863.

General Orders,⎫
   No. 49. ⎭

The Major General Commanding tenders to this Army his congratulations on its achievements of the last seven days. If it has not accomplished all that was expected, the reasons are well known to the Army. It is sufficient to say they were of a character not to be foreseen or prevented by human sagacity or resource.

In withdrawing from the south bank of the Rappahannock before delivering a general battle to our adversaries, the Army has given renewed evidence of its confidence in itself and its fidelity to the principles it represents. In fighting at a disadvantage, we would have been recreant to our trust, to ourselves, our cause and our country.

Profoundly loyal, and conscious of its strength, the Army of the Potomac will give or decline battle, whenever its interest or honor may demand. It will also be the guardian of its own history and its own fame.

By our celerity and secrecy of movement, our advance and passage of the rivers were undisputed, and on our withdrawal not a rebel ventured to follow.

The events of the last week may swell with pride the heart of every officer and soldier of this Army. We have added new lustre to its former renown. We have made long marches, crossed rivers, surprised the enemy in his entrenchments, and whenever we have fought, have inflicted heavier blows than we have received.

We have taken from the enemy five thousand prisoners, captured and brought off seven pieces of artillery, fifteen colors, placed *"hors de combat"* eighteen thousand of his chosen troops, destroyed his depots filled with vast amounts of stores, deranged his communications, captured prisoners within the fortifications of his capital, and filled his country with fear and consternation.

We have no other regret than that caused by the loss of our brave companions, and in this we are consoled by the conviction that they have fallen in the holiest cause ever submitted to the arbitrament battle.

BY COMMAND OF MAJOR GENERAL HOOKER:

S. WILLIAMS,
Assistant Adjutant General.

OFFICIAL:

Captain, A D C.

The Second Louisiana

THE USE OF NEGRO TROOPS was questioned in the North
and damned in the South. But more and more, as
the war grew longer, were colored soldiers accepted into
the Federal armies. Not only were Negroes in the North
trained as soldiers (under white officers), freed slaves in
the South were accepted for military service. Such a
unit was the Second Louisiana, a part of the command
of General Nathaniel P. Banks.

General Banks had first come to fame as the adversary
of "Stonewall" Jackson in the Valley of Virginia. Soundly
outgeneraled there, he became known as "Commissary"
Banks, from the army stores that Jackson's men captured
from his troops. He succeeded General Butler in command at New Orleans and conducted an unsuccessful
campaign on the Red River in the spring of 1863. By the
end of May he was back on the Mississippi, operating
against Port Hudson in part of the campaign which centered on Vicksburg. It was in this campaign that his
Second Louisiana Regiment proved its mettle.

Secretary William H. Seward praised the colored soldiers in a pamphlet published as *Secretary Seward's Re-*

view of Recent Military Events. "As the national armies advanced into the insurrectionary territories," he wrote, "slaves in considerable numbers accepted their freedom and came under the protection of the national flag. Amidst the great prejudices and many embarrassments which attend a measure so new and so divergent from the political habits of the country, freedmen with commendable alacrity enlisted in the Federal army. There was in some quarters a painful inquiry about their moral capacity for service. That uncertainty was brought to a sudden end in the siege of Port Hudson. The newly raised regiments exhibited all necessary valor and devotion in the military assaults which were made, with desperate courage, and not without fearful loss, by General Banks."

Here is General Banks's own appraisal of his troops in a letter to General H. W. Halleck. It is reprinted from a propaganda pamphlet, *Washington and Jackson on Negro Soldiers,* compiled by Henry Carey Baird and published in Philadelphia in 1863.

HEADQUARTERS ARMY OF THE GULF,
BEFORE PORT HUDSON, May 30, 1863.
Major-General H. W. Halleck, General-in-Chief,
    Washington.

GENERAL:—Leaving Sommesport on the Atchafalaya, where my command was at the date of my last dispatch, I landed at Bayou Sara at 2 o'clock on the morning of the 21st.

A portion of the infantry were transported in steamers,

and the balance of the infantry, artillery, cavalry, and wagon train moving down on the west bank of the river, and from this to Bayou Sara.

On the 23d a junction was effected with the advance of Major-General AUGUR and Brigadier-General SHERMAN, our line occupying the Bayou Sara road at a distance five miles from Port Hudson.

Major-General AUGUR had an encounter with a portion of the enemy on the Bayou Sara road in the direction of Baton Rouge, which resulted in the repulse of the enemy, with heavy loss.

On the 25th the enemy was compelled to abandon his first line of works.

General WEITZEL's brigade, which had covered our rear in the march from Alexandria, joined us on the 26th, and on the morning of the 27th a general assault was made upon the fortifications.

The artillery opened fire between 5 and 6 o'clock, which was continued with animation during the day. At 10 o'clock WEITZEL's brigade, with the division of General GROVER, reduced to about two brigades, and the division of General EMORY, temporarily reduced by detachments to about a brigade, under command of Colonel PAINE, with two regiments of colored troops, made an assault upon the right of the enemy's works, crossing Sandy Creek, and driving them through the woods to their fortifications.

The fight lasted on this line until 4 o'clock, and was very severely contested. On the left, the infantry did not come up until later in the day; but at 2 o'clock an assault was opened on the centre and left of centre by the divisions under Major-General AUGUR and Brigadier-General SHERMAN.

The enemy was driven into his works, and our troops moved up to the fortifications, holding the opposite sides of the parapet with the enemy on the right. Our troops still hold their position on the left. After dark the main body, being exposed to a flank fire, withdrew to a belt of woods, the skirmishers remaining close upon the fortifications.

In the assault of the 27th, the behavior of the officers and men was most gallant, and left nothing to be desired. Our limited acquaintance of the ground and the character of the works, which were almost hidden from our observation until the moment of approach, alone prevented the capture of the post.

On the extreme right of our line I posted the first and third regiments of negro troops. The First regiment of Louisiana Engineers, composed exclusively of colored men, excepting the officers, was also engaged in the operations of the day. The position occupied by these troops was one of importance, and called for the utmost steadiness and bravery in those to whom it was confided.

It gives me pleasure to report that they answered every expectation. Their conduct was heroic. No troops could be more determined or more daring. They made, during the day, three charges upon the batteries of the enemy, suffering very heavy losses, and holding their position at nightfall with the other troops on the right of our line. The highest commendation is bestowed upon them by all the officers in command on the right. Whatever doubt may have existed before as to the efficiency of organizations of this character, the history of this day proves conclusively to those who were in a condition to observe the conduct of these regiments, that the Government will find in this class of troops effective supporters and defenders.

The severe test to which they were subjected, and the determined manner in which they encountered the enemy, leave upon my mind no doubt of their ultimate success. They require only good officers, commands of limited numbers, and careful discipline, to make them excellent soldiers.

Our losses from the 23d to this date in killed, wounded, and missing, are nearly 1000, including, I deeply regret to say, some of the ablest officers of the corps. I am unable yet to report them in detail.

I have the honor to be, with much respect,

Your obedient servant,

N. P. BANKS, *Major-General Commanding.*

Our Present Duty to Our Country

B<small>Y</small> 1863 <small>THE WAR</small> seemed interminable. Each side had expected a quick victory. Instead, the Confederates had been unable to follow up military victories, and the Federals had been unable to conclude campaigns which struck deep into enemy territory with a definitive defeat of the Southerners.

In the South there was disaffection in East Tennessee, and the western counties of Virginia had early in the war formed themselves into a new state, but the tenor of Confederate opinion and nearly the whole of its manpower supported the war. The North was able (and this should have been an indication of the eventual result) to continue its interests in other affairs—international relations, the development of newly opened areas in the West, the building of a transcontinental railroad. Opposition to the war, therefore, was widely and freely expressed. Antiwar men in the Old Northwest were ready and willing to let the South stay out of the Union, to end the war and turn to business closer to home. The Copperheads and the Knights of the Golden Circle were dangerous to public opinion as enemies of the war. Their

216

spokesman in national circles was Clement L. Vallandigham of Ohio. Vallandigham was arrested and banished outside Union lines. President Lincoln explained: "Mr. Vallandigham avows his hostility to the War on the part of the Union; and his arrest was made because he was laboring, with some effect, to prevent the raising of troops; to encourage desertions from the army; and to leave the Rebellion without an adequate military force to suppress it. He was not arrested because he was damaging the political prospects of the Administration, or the personal interests of the Commanding General, but because he was damaging the Army, upon the existence and vigor of which the life of the Nation depends."

But for every Copperhead there were many more loyal soldiers. Here is the admonition to the soldiers with which Norman Gunnison, of the Second New Hampshire Volunteers, concluded his little book *Our Stars* in the spring of '63.

The war has now reached its culminating point; henceforth its progress must be to the Union cause a course of victory and ultimate triumph, or a course of irretrievable reverse. The indecisive battles of the war have been fought. Victory and defeat have alternated, but whether we have attained victory or suffered defeat, the result has fallen far short of our expectations; were we defeated, our rout was not utter; were we victorious, the fruits of our victory were neither great nor lasting. At this time the rebellion has assumed an entirely new moral phase. The monster is in its

death agonies, but it is only the more deadly. Never is the
leviathan of the deep more dangerous than when in its death
throes. The traitors have collected all their energies for the
final struggle. Treason in the South, treason abroad, and,
worst of all, treason in our own homes, uplifts its hand, red
with fratricidal blood, and braces anew its nerves for the
last despairing effort. As if it were not enough that slavery's
minions in the South should seek to strangle the liberty which
on the American Continent found a fitting birthplace, its
parasites in the North and Northwest—men who were
suckled at the very breast of Freedom—are forming in our
midst secret organizations with the view of aiding and abet-
ting their brother traitors in arms. If the local authorities
have lost the power to suppress and crush out such combinations, will not our soldiers in the field speak out, and emulating the noble soldiery of Illinois, rebuke the monster which,
in their distant homes, by their deserted hearthstones, is now
rearing its hydra-heads? The leaders of these organizations,
using and desecrating the sacred name of Peace, clamor for
a cessation of hostilities; in our Halls of Legislation oppose
and throw stumbling-blocks in the way of the Administration, and embarrass and render of no avail the movements
of our Generals. Soldiers of the Union! when leaving home
and its allurements, you went forth to do battle for our country; you thought not of the vipers you left behind to poison
your own nests. To you I appeal! Men who have passed
through the fire of battle, who have stood in the van at Williamsburg, Yorktown and Manassas, show yourselves equal
to the present emergency! Speak out in the might of your
fire-tried souls, and the reverberations of your voice shall
shake the pillars of the rebellion—whether at the North or
South—from centre to foundation! Remember this: the Administration is struggling to maintain our national existence,

and he who, at this hour, opposes the Administration—be he
Democrat or Republican—Seymour or Greeley—stamps his
soul forever with the indelible, damning stain of treason! Our
duty as men and soldiers is to our present rulers. We do not
ask for their political antecedents; we only ask, will they,
with the aid of God, save our country? In the past, our army
in Virginia has labored under many discouragements: the
mismanagement of Generals, the scheming of politicians,
the imbecility or covert treason of Quarter Masters, has
rendered their bravery and self-sacrifice of no avail. In the
Southwest we have experienced a succession of victories,
and yet the men have not fought more bravely, the *morale*
of the Southwestern army is not better, and no braver hearts
lie buried at Donelson or Murfreesboro., than now lie in their
last repose before the walls of Richmond. Never has a more
determined, self-sacrificing spirit been evinced than at
Gaines' Mills and Fredericksburg. Where, then, does the
fault lie? On *you*, base, scheming politician, *you*, General,
more anxious for your own personal aggrandizement than
for your country's good. *I charge* the sin of our past failures;
the blood of our noblest and truest, from the soil of Virginia,
cries out against you. Men of the North! men who, unwilling
or unable to take the field, have remained in your peaceful
homes, I ask of *you* to lay aside for a time your party bicker-
ings, and come forward cordially to the support of our noble
ones in the field. How can they fight with traitors in their
rear? Knights of the Golden Circle, members of other secret
societies in the North and North-west, are you so lost to all
sense of honor, to the common dictates of humanity, as to
dip your hands in the blood of your fathers, brothers and
sons, as you are now doing, and hold them, reeking with
kindred gore, to the world? If you cannot aid us, we ask,
at least, that you will not impede us. But, rest assured, if

you will persist in your course, there is coming a day of retribution when the Arnolds of to-day shall take rank with *the* Arnold of the Revolution. You cry peace, but do you fully understand the meaning of the peace you crave? A peace bought by a nation's dishonor is more dangerous than the sword. A peace with *you* means a division—the giving up of our inalienable rights as freemen—the acknowledgement that the South is too strong for us. True it is that our army of Virginia is in a discontented state at present; but give them but your cordial support, let them know that every heart at home battles for them, and with the prestige of victory resting upon their banners, they will yet go forward, "conquering and to conquer," until this unholy rebellion shall be as the things that were. Allowing, however, that we were to desire peace upon *your* terms, could we divide our Union and mete out an heritage of graves? Will the South give up its share in Bunker Hill? or the North its part in Yorktown's closing fight? Will *you*—breathing the air of Freedom, and calling yourselves men—allow the hallowed shades of Mount Vernon to pass into the hands of traitors, who are fighting against the very principles for which the Father of our Country fought and suffered? The geographical configuration of our country precludes the possibility of disintegration. The hopes of the future, the memories of the past, cry out against it; and did they not, those old bones that, for three-quarters of a century, have whitened at Princeton and Fort Moultrie, would arise from their very graves, and, with out-stretched arms, curse the degenerate sons, who could yield, while life remained, their fathers' dearest birthright. But I do not, *will* not believe that the day will ever come when we shall be willing to accept peace on such terms. With prophetic vision, I look forward to the time when the North and South shall again strike hands. I see our banner waving upon every Southern hill. I see, in the coming day, a vast Republic, stretching from the shores of the Atlantic to the coast of the Pacific—from the frozen regions of Hudson's Bay to the sunny clime of the tropical South, embracing Mexico in its limits, having its centre at New Orleans, and with its power controlling the world, whilst over all, the calm stars of our banner soar triumphant, lighting our Nation's pathway to glory. It needs but a united effort, and this rebellion will be crushed; only let our troops be not trammeled by the traitors of the North, and in the coming campaign they will mark for our country a page of glory.

At the head of our army in Virginia we have now a leader who knows no party where his country is concerned, one who is incapable of forming plans for personal aggrandizement, whose soul is in the cause, and whose valor upon the field, and discretion in council, have been tried and not found wanting. When he moves forward it will be to victory. Let us give to him our entire co-operation. The time to strike is near at hand, and our men in the field—the men who are to bear suffering, wounds, and perhaps death—should have to the utmost, the aid and the sympathy of every man who, in this land of freedom, can raise aloft his hand to Heaven, *and thank God that he is free!* The crisis of the war is now at hand. It is said that propositions of peace have already been made. If we yield to them, we, as a nation, are lost, with our national honor, national pride, everything but life sacrificed, what will remain to us: separated into petty republics, obliged to keep a standing army upon our borders, our form of government will degenerate into a military despotism, and we will present to the world that most pitiable of objects—a nation fallen—a people degenerated. Angels might weep over the picture, but even the tears of the angels would not blot from the records of freedom, the stain of that damning cowardice which would cause our downfall. If, on the other hand, the present contingency is met with the firmness of purpose which becomes a great people whose swords are unsheathed in the sacred cause of freedom, we are saved, and our heritage of liberty will descend to posterity as pure as we received it from the hands of the revolutionary fathers.

Though the ark of our national salvation may only come to us over an ocean of blood, still let us pray—God speed its coming.

Gettysburg

L EE's VICTORY at Chancellorsville cleared the way for an offensive move on the part of the Confederates. A march north into Pennsylvania could threaten Washington and the big cities of the East. It would remove the Confederate Army from a home ground swept clean of supplies to an enemy area of rich farms and towns well stocked with stores. And it would be a vast boost to Confederate morale.

The Confederate campaign reached its climax, and the climax of the war, at Gettysburg. Gettysburg is one of the most fully described battles of all history. It is not necessary to record its military development here. Instead, two general orders and excerpts from a straightforward account by a woman who lived in Gettysburg throughout the invasion are printed here as accurate reflections of the times.

HEAD-QUARTERS, ARMY OF THE POTOMAC,

June 28, 1863.

General Orders,⎱
   No. 67. ⎰

By direction of the President of the United States, I hereby assume command of the Army of the Potomac.

As a soldier, in obeying this order—an order totally unexpected and unsolicited—I have no promises or pledges to make.

The country looks to this Army to relieve it from the devastation and disgrace of a hostile invasion. Whatever fatigues and sacrifices we may be called upon to undergo, let us have in view, constantly, the magnitude of the interests involved, and let each man determine to do his duty, leaving to an all-controlling Providence the decision of the contest.

It is with just diffidence that I relieve in the command of this Army, an eminent and accomplished soldier, whose name must ever appear conspicuous in the history of its achievements; but I rely upon the hearty support of my companions in arms to assist me in the discharge of the duties of the important trust which has been confided to me.

GEORGE G. MEADE,
Major General Commanding.

OFFICIAL:

———

DIARY.

JUNE 15, 1863.—To-day we heard that the Rebels were crossing the river in heavy force, and advancing on to this State. No alarm was felt until Governor Curtin sent a telegram, directing the people to move their stores as quickly as possible. This made us begin to realize the fact that we were in some danger from the enemy, and some persons, thinking the Rebels were near, became very much frightened, though the report was a mistake.

JUNE 16.—Our town had a great fright last night between 12 and 1 o'clock. I had retired, and was soundly asleep, when my child cried for a drink of water. When I got up to get it, I heard so great a noise in the street that I went to the window, and the first thing I saw was a large fire, seemingly not far off, and the people were hallooing, "The Rebels are coming, and burning as they go." Many left town, but, having waited for the fire to go down a little, I returned to bed and slept till morning. Then I learned that the fire was in Emmettsburg [Emmitsburg], ten miles from here, just over the Maryland line, and that the buildings were fired by one of her townsmen. Twenty-seven houses were burned, and thirty-six families made homeless, all effort to stop the flames being useless, as, owing to everything being so dry, they spread with great rapidity. . . .

JUNE 19.—Another excitement to-day. The 87th Pennsylvania Volunteers is composed of men from this and adjacent counties, one company from our town being of the number. Word came that the captain, both lieutenants, and nearly all the officers and men had been killed or captured. Such a time as we had with those having friends in the regiment! At 10 o'clock it was rumored that some of the men were coming in on the Chambersburg pike, and not long after about one dozen of those who lived in town came in, and their report and presence relieved some and agonized others. Those whose friends were not of the party, were in a heart-rending plight, for these returned ones could not tell of the others; some would say, This one was killed or taken prisoner, and others, We saw him at such a place, and the Rebels may have taken him; and so they were kept in suspense.

JUNE 20.—The report of to-day is that the Rebels are at Chambersburg and are advancing on here, and refugees begin to come in by scores. Some say the Rebels number from twenty to thirty thousand, others that Lee's whole army is advancing this way. All day we have been much excited. . . .

JUNE 22. *Sunday.*—The report now is that a large force is in the mountains about eighteen miles away, and a call is made for a party of men to go out and cut down trees to obstruct the passages of the mountains. About fifty, among them my husband, started. I was very uneasy lest they might be captured, but, they had not gone half way, when the discovery was made that it was too late; that the Rebels were on this side of the mountain, and coming this way. Our men turned back, uninjured, though their advance, composed of a few men, was fired upon. About seventy of the Rebels came within eight miles, and then returned by another road to their main force. They stole all the horses and cattle they could find, and drove them back to their encampment. We did not know but that the whole body would be down upon us, until 11 o'clock, when a man came in and said that he had seen them, and that they had recrossed. I shall now retire, and sleep much better than I had expected an hour since.

JUNE 23.—This has been the most quiet day since the excitement began. I expect news to-morrow, for it has been too quiet to last long.

JUNE 24.—As I expected, the Rebels have, several times, been within two or three miles, but they have not yet reached here. Two cavalry companies are here on scouting duty, but they can be of little use, as they have never seen service.

Deserters come in every little while, who report the enemy near in large force. This morning early a despatch was received, saying that a regiment of infantry was coming from Harrisburg. We do not feel much safer, for they are only raw militia. The train bringing them came within ten miles, when it ran over a cow, which threw the cars off the track. No one was hurt, and they are now encamped near the place of the accident. The town is a little quieter than on yesterday. We are getting used to excitement, and many think the enemy, having been so long in the vicinity without visiting us, will not favor us with their presence. They have carried off many horses. Some, who had taken their stock away, returned, supposing the Rebels had left the neighborhood, and lost their teams.

JUNE 25.—To-day passed much as yesterday did. Every one is asking, Where is our army, that they let the enemy scour the country and do as they please? It is reported that Lee's whole army is this side of the river, and marching on Harrisburg; also, that a large force is coming on here, to destroy the railroad between there and Baltimore. Our militia did not come to town, but remain encamped where they were yesterday.

JUNE 26.—Our militia passed through town this morning about 10 o'clock, and encamped about three miles to the west. Before they had unpacked their baggage, a scout came in with a report, which proved true, that the enemy were quite near. Our men then had to retreat and get off the best way they could. About two hundred were captured. The town was quiet after our men retreated, until about 2 o'clock P.M., when a report spread that the Rebels were only two miles from town. No one believed this, for they had so often been reported as just coming, and had as often failed to appear, and little attention was now paid to the rumor.

When, however, the wagons of the militia came thundering through the streets, and the guard stated that they had been chased back, we began to realize that the report was a fact. In about half an hour the entrance of Jenkins' Rebel cavalry began, and they came with such horrid yells that it was enough to frighten us all to death. They came in on three roads, and we soon were surrounded by them. We all stood in the doors whilst the cavalry passed, but when the infantry came we closed them, for fear they would run into our houses and carry off everything we had, and went up stairs and looked out of the windows. They went along very orderly, only asking every now and then how many Yankee soldiers we had in town. I answered one that I did not know. He replied: "You are a funny woman; if I lived in town I would know that much." The last regiment stacked arms, on both sides of the street in front of our door, and remained for an hour. They were a miserable-looking set. They wore all kinds of hats and caps, even to heavy fur ones, and some were barefooted. The Rebel band were playing Southern tunes in the Diamond. I cannot tell how bad I felt to hear them, and to see the traitors' flag floating overhead. My humiliation was complete when I saw our men marching behind them surrounded by a guard. Last of all came an officer, and behind him a negro on as fine a horse as I ever saw. One, looking up, and noticing my admiration of the animal, said: "We captured this horse from General Milroy, and do you see the wagons up there? we captured them, too. How we did whip the Yankees, and we intend to do it again soon." I hope they may not.

JUNE 27.—I passed the most uncomfortable night of my life. My husband had gone in the cars to Hanover Junction, not thinking the Rebels were so near, or that there was much danger of their coming to town, and I was left entirely alone, surrounded by thousands of ugly, rude, hostile soldiers, from whom violence might be expected. Even if neighbors were at hand, it was not pleasant, and I feared my husband would be taken prisoner before he could return, or whilst trying to reach me. I was not disturbed, however, by anything except my fears, and this morning when I got up I found that the Rebels had departed, having, on the night of the 27th, burned the railroad bridge over Rock Creek, just outside of the town, and the cars that had brought up the militia, and had torn up the track and done other mischief. I became more uneasy about my husband, and I went to see some of the railroad hands to find out what I could relating to him. They told me that he had been captured and paroled, and that he had gone to Harrisburg; so I feel easier, and hope to rest to-night. Three of our scouts came in this morning just after the Rebels left, and report a large force of our soldiers near, making all feel much safer.

June 28. *Sunday.*—About 10 o'clock a large body of our cavalry began to pass through town, and we were all busy feeding them as they passed along. It seemed to me that the long line would never get through. I hope they may catch the Rebels and give them a sound thrashing. Some say we may look for a battle here in a few days, and others say it will be fought near Harrisburg. There is no telling where it will be.

June 29.—Quiet has prevailed all day. Our cavalry came up with the Rebels at Hanover, fourteen miles from here, and had quite a spirited fight, driving them through the town. Their infantry had reached York and had taken possession, as they did here, and demanded goods, stores, and money; threatening, if the demand was not complied with, to burn the town. Dunce-like, the people paid them $28,000, which they pocketed, and passed on to Wrightsville. A company of our militia, guarding the Columbia bridge over the Susquehanna, retreated on the approach of the Rebels, and fired the bridge, which was entirely consumed, preventing the enemy from setting foot on the east bank, and ending their offensive movements for a time.

JUNE 30.—My husband came home last night at 1 o'clock, having walked from Harrisburg, thirty-six miles, since 9 o'clock of yesterday morning. His return has put me in good spirits. I wonder that he escaped the Rebels, who are scouring the country between here and there. Fatigue is all the ill that befell him. This morning the Rebels came to the top of the hill overlooking the town on the Chambersburg pike, and looked over at our place. We had a good view of them from our house, and every moment we expected to hear the booming of cannon, and thought they might shell the town. As it turned out, they were only reconnoitring the town preparatory to an advance if no force opposed them. We were told that a heavy force of our soldiers was within five miles, and the Rebels, learning that a body of cavalry was quite near, retraced their steps, and encamped some distance from town. It begins to look as though we will have a battle soon, and we are in great fear. I see by the papers that General Hooker has been relieved, and the change of commanders I fear may give great advantage to the enemy, and our army may be repulsed.

JULY 1.—I got up early this morning to get my baking done before any fighting would begin. I had just put my bread in the pans when the cannons began to fire, and true enough the battle had begun in earnest, about two miles out on the Chambersburg pike. What to do or where to go, I did not know. People were running here and there, screaming that the town would be shelled. No one knew where to go or what to do. My husband advised remaining where we were, but all said we ought not to remain in our exposed position, and that it would be better to go to some part of the town farther away from the scene of the conflict. As our neighbors had all gone away, I would not remain, but my husband said he would stay at home. About 10 o'clock the shells began to "fly around quite thick," and I took my child and went to the house of a friend up town. As we passed up the street we met wounded men coming in from the field. When we saw them, we, for the first time, began to realize our fearful situation, and anxiously to ask, Will our army be whipped? Some said there was no danger of that yet, and pointed to Confederate prisoners who began to be sent through our streets to the rear. Such a dirty, filthy set, no one ever saw. They were dressed in all kinds of clothes, of all kinds and no kind of cuts. Some were barefooted and a few wounded. Though enemies, I pitied them. I, with others was sitting at the doorstep bathing the wounds of some of our brave soldiers, and became so much excited as the artillery galloped through the town, and the infantry hurried out to reinforce those fighting, that for a time we forgot our fears and our danger. All was bustle and confusion. No one can imagine in what extreme fright we were when our men began to retreat. A citizen galloped up to the door in which we were sitting and called out, "For God's sake go in the house! The Rebels are in the other end of town, and all will be killed!" We quickly ran in, and the cannonading coming nearer and becoming heavier, we went to the cellar, and in a few minutes the town was full of the filthy Rebels. They did not get farther, for our soldiers having possession of the hills just beyond, shelled them so that they were glad to give over the pursuit, and the fighting for the day was ended. We remained in the cellar until the firing ceased, and then feared to come out, not knowing what the Rebels might do.

How changed the town looked when we came to the light. The street was strewn over with clothes, blankets, knapsacks, cartridge-boxes, dead horses, and the bodies of a few men, but not so many of these last as I expected to see. "Can we go out?" was asked of the Rebels. "Certainly," was the answer; "they would not hurt us." We started home, and found things all right. As I write all is quiet, but O! how I dread to-morrow.

JULY 2.—Of course we had no rest last night. Part of the time we watched the Rebels rob the house opposite. The family had left some time during the day, and the robbers must have gotten all they left in the house. They went from the garret to the cellar, and loading up the plunder in a large four-horse wagon, drove it off. I expected every minute that they would burst in our door, but they did not come near us. It was a beautiful moonlight night, and we could see all they did.

JULY 2.—The cannonading commenced about 10 o'clock, and we went to the cellar and remained a little while until it ceased. When the noise subsided, we came to the light again, and tried to get something to eat. My husband went to the garden and picked a mess of beans, though stray firing was going on all the time, and bullets from sharpshooters or others whizzed about his head in a way I would not have liked. He persevered until he picked all, for he declared the Rebels should not have one. I baked a pan of shortcake and boiled a piece of ham, the last we had in the house, and some neighbors coming in, joined us, and we had the first quiet meal since the contest began. I enjoyed it very much. It seemed so nice after so much confusion to have a little quiet once more. We had not felt like eating before, being worried by danger and excitement. The quiet did not last

long. About 4 o'clock P.M. the storm burst again with terrific
violence. It seemed as though heaven and earth were being
rolled together. For better security we went to the house
of a neighbor and occupied the cellar, by far the most comfortable part of the house. Whilst there a shell struck the
house, but mercifully did not burst, but remained embedded
in the wall, one half protruding. About 6 o'clock the cannonading lessened, and we, thinking the fighting for the day
was over, came out. Then the noise of the musketry was
loud and constant, and made us feel quite as bad as the
cannonading, though it seemed to me less terrible. Very soon
the artillery joined in the din, and soon became as awful as
ever, and we again retreated to our friend's underground
apartment, and remained until the battle ceased, about 10
o'clock at night. I have just finished washing a few pieces
for my child, for we expect to be compelled to leave town
to-morrow, as the Rebels say it will most likely be shelled.
I cannot sleep, and as I sit down to write, to while away
the time, my husband sleeps as soundly as though nothing
was wrong. I wish I could rest so easily, but it is out of the
question for me either to eat or sleep under such terrible
excitement and such painful suspense. We know not what
the morrow will bring forth, and cannot even tell the issue
of to-day. We can gain no information from the Rebels, and
are shut off from all communication with our soldiers. I think
little has been gained by either side so far. "Has our army
been sufficiently reinforced?" is our anxious question. A few
minutes since we had a talk with an officer of the staff of
General Early, and he admits that our army has the best position, but says we cannot hold it much longer. The Rebels
do so much bragging that we do not know how much to
believe. At all events, the manner in which this officer spoke

indicates that our troops have the advantage so far. Can they keep it? The fear they may not be able causes our anxiety and keeps us in suspense.

July 3.—To-day the battle opened with fierce cannonading before 4 o'clock A.M. Shortly after the battle began we were told to leave this end of the town, for likely it would be shelled. My husband declared he would not go while one brick remained upon another, and, as usual, we betook ourselves to the cellar, where we remained until 10 o'clock, when the firing ceased. We could not get breakfast on account of our fears and the great danger. During the cessation we managed to get a cold bite. Again, the battle began with unearthly fury. Nearly all the afternoon it seemed as if the heavens and earth were crashing together. The time that we sat in the cellar seemed long, listening to the terrific sound of the strife; more terrible never greeted human ears. We knew that with every explosion, and the scream of each shell, human beings were hurried, through excruciating pain, into another world, and that many more were torn, and mangled, and lying in torment worse than death, and no one able to extend relief. The thought made me very sad, and feel that, if it was God's will, I would rather be taken away than remain to see the misery that would follow. Some thought this awful afternoon would never come to a close. We knew that the Rebels were putting forth all their might, and it was a dreadful thought that they might succeed. Who is victorious, or with whom the advantage rests, no one here can tell. It would ease the horror if we knew our arms were successful. Some think the Rebels were defeated, as there has been no boasting as on yesterday, and they look uneasy and by no means exultant. I hope they are correct, but I fear we are too hopeful. We shall see to-morrow. It will be the 4th of July, and the Rebels have promised us a glorious day. If it only ends the battle and drives them off it will be glorious, and I will rejoice.

July 4.—This morning, about 6 o'clock, I heard a great noise in the street, and going to the door I saw a Rebel officer on horseback hallooing to some soldiers on foot, to "Hurry up, the Yankees have possession of the town and all would be captured." I looked up street and saw our men in the public square, and it was a joyful sight, for I knew we were now safe. Soon after, the Rebels sent in a flag of truce, but what was communicated we did not know, and, in consequence, the people were more scared than ever, the report spreading that it was to give notice to remove the women and children before shelling the town. As soon as the flag of truce had gone, our sharpshooters were pushed out to this side of town, and were all around us. We were between two fires, and were kept close prisoners all day, not daring either to go out, or even look out of the windows, on account of the bullets fired at every moving object. The people of other parts of the town could go where they pleased. It has been a dreadfully long day. We know, however, that the Rebels are retreating, and that our army has been victorious. I was anxious to help care for the wounded, but the day is ended and all is quiet, and for the first time in a week I shall go to bed, feeling safe.

July 5.—What a beautiful morning! It seems as though Nature was smiling on thousands suffering. One might think, if they saw only the sky, and earth, and trees, that every one must be happy; but just look around and behold the misery made in so short time by man. Early this morning I went out to the Seminary, just outside of town, and which, until the retreat, was in the hands of the enemy. What horrible sights present themselves on every side, the roads being strewn with dead horses and the bodies of some men, though the dead have nearly all been buried, and every step of the way giving evidence of the dreadful contest. Shall we—for I was not alone—enter the building or return home? Can we endure the spectacle of hundreds of men wounded in every conceivable manner, some in the head and limbs, here an arm off and there a leg, and just inside a poor fellow with both legs shot away? It is dreadful to behold, and, to add to the misery, no food has been served for several days. The little we have will not go far with so many. What can we do? is the only question, and the little we brought was distributed. It is heart-sickening to think of these noble fellows sacrificing everything for us, and saving us, and it out of our power to render any assistance of consequence. I turned away and cried. We returned to town to gather up more food if possible, and to get soft material to place under their wounded limbs, to help make them more comfortable. As we returned, our cavalry was moving out to follow the Rebels, and the street was all in an uproar. When I reached home, I found my husband's brother, who had passed through the battle unhurt, and had come to see us. I rejoiced at seeing him, for we feared he had fallen, and at once set to work to prepare a meal to appease his hunger. As I was baking cakes for him, a poor prisoner came to the door and asked me to give him some, for he had had nothing to eat for the past two or three days. Afterward more joined him, and made the same statement and request. I was kept baking cakes until nearly noon, and, in consequence, did not return to the Seminary. The poor fellows in my house were so hungry that they could hardly wait until the cakes were baked.

HEAD-QUARTERS, ARMY OF THE POTOMAC,

July 4th, 1863.

General Orders,}
    No. 68.

  · The Commanding General, in behalf of the country, thanks the Army of the Potomac for the glorious result of the recent operations.

An enemy superior in numbers and flushed with pride of a successful invasion, attempted to overcome and destroy this Army. Utterly baffled and defeated, he has now withdrawn from the contest. The privations and fatigue the Army has endured, and the heroic courage and gallantry it has displayed will be matters of history to be ever remembered.

Our task is not yet accomplished, and the Commanding General looks to the Army for greater efforts to drive from our soil every vestige of the presence of the invader.

It is right and proper that we should, on all suitable occasions, return our grateful thanks to the Almighty Disposer of events, that in the goodness of his Providence He has thought fit to give victory to the cause of the just.

BY COMMAND OF MAJOR GENERAL MEADE:

S. WILLIAMS,
Assistant Adjutant General.

OFFICIAL:

The Fall of Vicksburg

As HURTFUL to Confederate hopes as the failure of the invasion of Pennsylvania—and more immediately apparent in its results—was the Union capture of Vicksburg. Triumph there secured the length of the Mississippi River to Federal control and separated the eastern states of the Confederacy from its trans-Mississippi west.

Vicksburg had repulsed one siege in 1862. In 1863 it could not withstand the long assault of General U. S. Grant. After a valiant and desperate resistance Confederate General John C. Pemberton surrendered the city on July 4.

Here is a Federal soldier's report, a letter written by George W. Driggs on July 5 and published in his history of the Eighth Wisconsin Volunteers, *Opening of the Mississippi.*

YOUNG'S POINT, LA., SUNDAY, July 5th, 1863.

In strange contrast with the startling scenes of carnage, and the deafening roar of artillery around us, is the calm,

238

sweet serenity of this beautiful Sabbath morning. So quiet that a feeling of loneliness creeps around the heart of one accustomed to hearing the constant booming of cannon and the sharp crack of musketry, and why have the iron throats of these savage monsters been hushed? Is it because it is the Sabbath day of rest that this holy calm pervades the hitherto exciting scenes around us?

No, the tumultuous chaos of two great contending armies have ceased their struggles, and the Federal arms have gained another victory over the wily foe. Vicksburg, as you have long ere this been informed, has surrendered, after being besieged for forty-seven days. It was a gala day for our troops, I assure you, and the 4th of July was never before celebrated in Vicksburg with such a right hearty good feeling as on yesterday. The mortars on the point opposite the city, with the accompanying chorus from the distant gunboats had kept our ears in a perfect hum for many long weeks, until they became like household words, familiar to the ear, and no longer a terror, as at its introduction. But the sound of battle strife has ceased for a while, and our army now breathes the pure air of freedom once again. Victory is perched upon our blood-stained and tattered banners, and the heart of the great North, which has evinced so much restlessness and anxiety for the result of our success, may now leap for joy, and smile at the happy and successful achievements of the Federal arms. And though we regret that so much of noble blood has been sacrificed in the attempt to reduce this stronghold, yet such is the fate of war, and he whose misfortune it has been to fall while in the discharge of his duty, will receive the praise and honor due a brave and noble patriot. Peace and honor to the departed dead— we honored them for their deeds of bravery while living, we will now sing a requiem o'er their graves, and entwine around their head-stones a garland of honor, that their friends may receive the consolation that they are not forgotten by their comrades in arms.

There had been but little firing on either side during the day previous to the surrender, and many were the surmises as to what was the cause of the unusual cessation. It was whispered around in military circles, that Grant intended to celebrate the anniversary of our National Independence in the city—that our approaches were sufficient to warrant another desperate assault upon the enemy's works, and that we were to take the place by storm sometime during the following day. This, I am convinced, was Gen. Grant's intention, and was so believed among his subordinates. It was also surmised, from the appearance of a flag of truce which made its appearance early in the afternoon of Friday the 3d, that Grant and Pemberton were having an interview relative to the surrender of the city, and all waited in breathless suspense the cheering announcement that Vicksburg was ours. While in this suspense, the silence was broken by the appearance of Gen. Pemberton and staff, who approached our lines bearing in his hand a flag of truce, which was received by Gen. Grant with all the courtesy due from one high in rank. They met with a smile, each recognizing the other as old class-mates at West Point—shook hands and dismounted, and while Gen. Grant's staff entertained the gentlemanly officers of Pemberton's staff, the two distinguished generals proceeded arm in arm to the shade of an old oak tree near by—throwing themselves leisurely upon the grassy ground beneath the old shade tree, they reviewed the past in all kindness, and laughed as jocosely as if they had been daily associates and friends, instead of deadly foes. Grant reverted to the national troubles, and regretted that so gross an evil existed between this once prosperous people, and while

Grant sat coolly chewing away upon a stub of a cigar, (one of his peculiar traits,) Pemberton amused himself pulling up tufts of grass, much to the amusement of those that were permitted to gain a peep at long range upon the scene. Pemberton finally broke in upon the point at issue, by stating that he had often been desirous of meeting him since he started his *Correll,* and had called upon him at this time with a view of delivering over the city of Vicksburg—that he had run the thing till the *mule beef* had "gin out," and didn't propose to take charge of the place any longer under the peculiar auspices of the present occasion. Grant agreed to relieve him of his command, and after taking a "chaw of tobacco" in unison, they separated to meet again the following day in the city.

At 11 a. m., yesterday—the 4th of July—Gen. Logan's Division marched into the city, with banners flying and music playing, and at noon the stars and stripes were unfurled from the top of the Court House. It was not long before the city was swarming with Federal soldiery, and the city once more assumed the appearance of life and animation. Admiral Porter, with his fleet, came "rounding to," and soon the shore was closely hemmed in by the steamers which now lined the levee. Bands were playing, troops were marching to and fro through the streets, and the cannon opened the National salute at noon, which was kept up by the gunboats till after 2 o'clock, p. m. Gen. Logan was immediately placed in command of the post, and the prisoners were kept under close guard. The force taken was over 27,000 prisoners, and between 4,000 and 5,000 non-combatants. There were also taken 103 field pieces, 30 siege guns, 5,000 stands of arms, ammunition in vast quantities, locomotives, cars, and 87 stands of colors. Among the distinguished prisoners captured are Lieut. Gen. Pemberton, Major Generals Smith, Forney,

Bowen and Stephenson, fourteen or fifteen brigadier generals, and about one hundred and thirty colonels. Only 15,000 of the garrison are reported able for duty, about 5,000 being sick and wounded in hospitals. Nearly every building in the town is used as a hospital, and great destitution prevailed among them, previous to the surrender, which induced them, no doubt, to surrender the sooner. They were actually reduced to *mule meat!* I am convinced that they could not have maintained their position much longer.

The terms of capitulation allow the officers and men to be paroled here. The former are to retain their side arms, horses and personal property. They are being furnished with subsistence, and rations have been issued to all the prisoners for three days. They seem to take hold of "hard tack" with a hearty good will. The ladies—of whom there are not a few in the city—are quite amused at the rescue; but the officers, when interrogated as to the result, rather disdain the idea of being considered captives. They claim that the surrender was not unconditional, when Gen. Grant, out of courtesy, for their noble defense of the city, allowed them the honors of war to retain their side arms, horses, etc.

Of the surrender. No event since the commencement of the rebellion has caused the nation to rejoice so much as the fall of Vicksburg. It has been universally regarded as the most impregnable point we have been compelled to work against, and many were the doubts of its being reduced, yet, while Gen. Grant was allowed to command the helm, our faith was strong and we only looked for final success, if he was allowed time and means. He has accomplished a great and magnanimous work. Take his movements since our forces left Milliken's Bend on the first of May last; trace his footsteps across the country to the Mississippi river at Grand Gulf, his victories at that point, his march through the en-

emy's country, capture of Port Gibson, his fight at Champion
Hills and later at Raymond, capture of the city of Jackson,
Miss., of his victories on the Black river, by driving a superior
rebel force from their chosen position, of the fights at Me-
chanicsburg, Yazoo City and Richmond, and finally, the
crowning wreath of his laurels, the capture of Vicksburg on
the glorious 4th of July. Gen. Grant has won the confidence
of the entire army, as being a general of no ordinary attain-
ments, and should receive the praise of the whole nation.

The Draft

UNTIL 1863 THE UNITED STATES ARMY had been supported by voluntary enlistments. In March the first
draft had been enacted by Congress. Many people considered it downright un-American. As a whole it worked
smoothly, but there were riots against it in Rutland, Vermont; Portsmouth, New Hampshire; Wooster, Ohio;
Boston, and New York. The riots in New York assumed
major proportions and resulted in a thousand casualties
and heavy property damage.

Here are two items relating to the draft. The first records the words of Henry Clay Work's song "Grafted
into the Army"; Americans could laugh even at things
they did not like. Following the song is President Lincoln's letter to Governor Seymour answering a communication in which the Governor had suggested a suspension of the draft until its legality could be tested before
the Supreme Court.

GRAFTED INTO THE ARMY

Our Jimmy has gone for to live in a tent,
They have grafted him into the army;
He finally pucker'd up courage and went,
When they grafted him into the army.
I told them the child was too young, alas!
At the captain's forequarters, they said he would
    pass—
They'd train him up well in the infantry class—
So they grafted him into the army.

Oh Jimmy farewell! Your brothers fell Way down in
    Alabarmy;
I thought they would spare a lone widder's heir,
But they grafted him into the army.

Drest up in his unicorn—dear little chap;
They have grafted him into the army;
It seems but a day since he sot in my lap,
But they grafted him into the army.
And these are the trousies he used to wear—
Them very same buttons—the patch and the tear—
But Uncle Sam gave him a bran new pair
When they grafted him into the army;

Now in my provisions I see him revealed—
They have grafted him into the army;
A picket beside the contented field,
They have grafted him into the army.
He looks kiner sickish—begins to cry—
A big volunteer standing right in his eye!
Oh what if the ducky should up and die
Now they've grafted him into the army?

———

EXECUTIVE MANSION, WASHINGTON, *Aug.* 7, 1863.
HIS EXCELLENCY, HORATIO SEYMOUR, GOVERNOR OF NEW
　YORK, ALBANY, N. Y.:

Your communication of the 3d instant has been received
and attentively considered. I can not consent to suspend the
draft in New York, as you request, because, among other
reasons, TIME is too important. By the figures you send,
which I presume are correct, the twelve districts represented
fall in two classes of eight and four respectively.

The disparity of the quotas for the draft in these two
classes is certainly very striking, being the difference between an average of 2,200 in one class, and 4,864 in the other.
Assuming that the districts are equal, one to another, in entire population, as required by the plan on which they were
made, this disparity is such as to require attention. Much
of it, however, I suppose will be accounted for by the fact
that so many more persons fit for soldiers are in the city
than are in the country, who have too recently arrived from
other parts of the United States and from Europe to be
either included in the census of 1860, or to have voted in
1862. Still, making due allowance for this, I am yet unwilling to stand upon it as an entirely sufficient explanation of
the great disparity. I shall direct the draft to proceed in all
the districts, drawing, however, at first from each of the four
districts—to wit, the Second, Fourth, Sixth, and Eighth—
only 2,200, being the average quota of the other class. After
this drawing, these four Districts, and also the Seventeenth
and Twenty-ninth, shall be carefully re-enrolled—and, if you
please, agents of yours may witness every step of the process.
Any deficiency which may appear by the new enrollment
will be supplied by a special draft for that object, allowing
due credit for volunteers who may be obtained from these
districts respectively during the interval; and at all points,

so far as consistent with practical convenience, due credits shall be given for volunteers, and your Excellency shall be notified of the time fixed for commencing a draft in each district.

I do not object to abide a decision of the United States Supreme Court, or of the Judges thereof, on the constitutionality of the draft law. In fact, I should be willing to facilitate the obtaining of it. But I can not consent to lose the time while it is being obtained. We are contending with an enemy who, as I understand, drives every able-bodied man he can reach into his ranks, very much as a butcher drives bullocks into a slaughter-pen. No time is wasted, no argument is used. This produces an army which will soon turn upon our now victorious soldiers already in the field, if they shall not be sustained by recruits as they should be. It produces an army with a rapidity not to be matched on our side, if we first waste time to re-experiment wth the volunteer system, already deemed by Congress, and palpably, in fact, so far exhausted as to be inadequate; and then more time to obtain a Court decision as to whether a law is constitutional which requires a part of those not now in the service to go to the aid of those who are already in it; and still more time to determine with absolute certainty that we get those who are to go in the precisely legal proportion to those who are not to go. My purpose is to be in my action just and constitutional, and yet practical, in performing the important duty with which I am charged, of maintaining the unity and the free principles of our common country. Your obedient servant,

A. LINCOLN.

The Gettysburg Address

THE SHORT SPEECH Abraham Lincoln made November 19, 1863, at the dedication of the National Cemetery at Gettysburg is one of the most familiar as well as one of the greatest documents of American history.

DEDICATORY ADDRESS
OF
PRESIDENT LINCOLN.

FOURSCORE and seven years ago our fathers brought forth upon this continent a new nation, conceived in Liberty, and dedicated to the proposition that all men are created equal.

Now we are engaged in a great civil war, testing whether that nation, or any nation so conceived and so dedicated, can long endure. We are met on a great battle-field of that war. We are met to dedicate a portion of it as the final resting-place of those who here gave their lives that that nation might live. It is altogether fitting and proper that we should do this.

But in a larger sense we cannot dedicate, we cannot consecrate, we cannot hallow this ground. The brave men, living and dead, who struggled here, have consecrated it far above our power to add or detract. The world will little note nor long remember what we say here, but it can never forget what they did here. It is for us, the living, rather to be dedicated here to the unfinished work that they have thus far so nobly carried on. It is rather for us to be here dedicated to the great task remaining before us,—that from these honored dead we take increased devotion to the cause for which they here gave the last full measure of devotion,—that we here highly resolve that the dead shall not have died in vain, that the nation shall, under God, have a new birth of freedom, and that the government of the people, by the people, and for the people, shall not perish from the earth.

The Battle of Chattanooga

THE WESTERN ARMIES, with General U. S. Grant gaining greater reputation each step of the way, made their way slowly but surely into the heartland of the Confederacy. They were defeated in September at Chickamauga, but the Confederates were unable to follow up their victory, and the Federals retired to Chattanooga. Confederate General Bragg held them under siege there till late November. The siege was broken in the brilliant battles at Lookout Mountain and Missionary Ridge. Grant's pursuit of the Confederates was halted at Ringgold Gap, Georgia, and the Union troops retired once more to Chattanooga, but no longer under siege. Here is Quartermaster General Montgomery C. Meigs's report of the Battle of Chattanooga.

HEADQUARTERS U. S. QUARTERMASTER'S
DEPARTMENT,

IN THE FIELD,

CHATTANOOGA, TENN., *November 26, 1863.*

HON. E. M. STANTON,
Secretary of War, Washington, D. C.:

SIR: On the 23d, at 11¼, a. m., General Grant ordered a demonstration against Mission [Missionary] Ridge, to develop the force holding it. The troops marched out, formed in order, advanced in line of battle, as if on parade. The rebels watched the formation and movement from their picket lines and rifle pits, and from the summits of Mission Ridge, five hundred feet above us, and thought it was a review and drill, so openly, so deliberately, so regularly was it all done.

As the line advanced, preceded by skirmishers, and at 2, p. m., reached our picket lines, they opened a rattling volley upon the rebel pickets, which replied and ran into their advanced line of rifle pits. After them went our skirmishers, and into them, along the centre of the line of twenty-five thousand troops, which General Thomas had so quickly displayed.

Until we opened fire, prisoners assert that they thought the whole movement was a review and general drill, and then it was too late to send to their camps for reinforcements and they were overwhelmed by force of numbers. It was a surprise in open daylight.

At 3, p. m., the important advanced position of "Orchard Knob" and the lines right and left were in our possession, and arrangements were ordered for holding them during the night.

The next day at daylight General Sherman had five thousand men across the Tennessee, established on its south bank, and commenced the construction of a pontoon bridge about six miles above Chattanooga.

The rebel steamer "Dunbar," repaired at the right moment, rendered effective aid in this crossing, ferrying over some six thousand men.

By nightfall General Sherman had seized the extremity of Mission Ridge nearest the river, and was entrenching himself.

General Howard, with a brigade, opened communication with him from Chattanooga on the south side of the river.

Skirmishing and cannonading continued all day on the left and centre. General Hooker scaled the slopes of Lookout Mountain from the valley of Lookout Creek, drove the rebels around the point, captured some two thousand prisoners, and established himself high up the mountain side, in full view of Chattanooga. This raised the blockade, and our steamers were ordered from Bridgeport to Chattanooga. They had run only to Kelly's Ferry, whence ten miles of hauling over mountain roads and twice crossing the Tennessee on pontoon bridges brought us our supplies.

All night the point of Mission ridge, on the extreme left, and the side of Lookout Mountain, on the extreme right, blazed with the camp fires of loyal troops. The day had been one of driving mists and rains, and much of Hooker's battle was fought above the clouds, which concealed him from our view, but from which his musketry was heard.

At nightfall the sky cleared, and the full moon, the "hunter's moon," shone upon the beautiful scene.

Till 1, a. m., twinkling sparks upon the mountain side showed that picket skirmishing was still going on; then it ceased.

A brigade sent from Chattanooga crossed Chattanooga

creek and opened communication with Hooker soon after nightfall.

General Grant's headquarters during the afternoon of the 23d and the day of the 24th were in Wood's redoubt, except when in the course of the day we rode along the advanced lines, visiting the headquarters of the several commanders in Chattanooga valley.

At daylight on the 25th the stars and stripes were discerned on the peak of Lookout. The rebels had evacuated the mountain. Hooker moved to descend the mountain, and, striking Mission Ridge at the Rossville Gap, to sweep it on both sides and on its summit.

The rebel troops were seen as soon as it was light enough streaming by regiments and brigades along the narrow summit of Mission Ridge, either concentrating on their right to overwhelm Sherman or marching for the railroad and raising the siege. They had evacuated the valley of Chattanooga, would they abandon that of the Chickamauga?

The 30-pounders and 4½-inch rifles of Wood's redoubt opened on Mission Ridge. Orchard Knob sent its compliments to the ridge, which with rifled Parrotts answered, and the cannonade thus commenced continued all day. Shot and shell screamed from Orchard Knob to Mission Ridge, from Mission Ridge to Orchard Knob, and from Wood's redoubt, over the heads of General Grant and General Thomas and their staffs, who were with us in this favorable position, whence the whole could be seen as in an amphitheater.

Headquarters were under fire all day long. Cannonading and musketry were heard from General Sherman. Howard marched the 11th Corps to join him.

Thomas sent out skirmishers, who drove in the rebel pickets, and even shook them in their entrenchments at the foot of Missouri [Missionary] ridge.

Sherman sent an assault against Bragg's right, entrenched on a high knob, next to that on which Sherman himself lay fortified.

The assault was gallantly made, reached the edge of the crest, held its ground for what seemed to me an hour; but was then bloodily repulsed by reserves.

A general advance was ordered, and a strong line of skirmishers, followed by a deployed line of battle, some two miles in length, at the signal of six cannon shots from the headquarters on Orchard Knob, moved rapidly and orderly forward.

The rebel pickets discharged their muskets and ran into their rifle-pits; our skirmishers followed on their heels; the line of battle was not far behind; and we saw the gray rebels swarm out of the long line of rifle-pits in numbers which surprised us, and spread over the base of the hill. A few turned and fired their pieces, but the greater number collected into the various roads which creep obliquely up its steep face, and went on to the top. Some regiments pressed on and began to swarm up the steep sides of the ridge. Here and there a color was advanced beyond the line. The attempt appeared most dangerous; but the advance was supported, and the whole line ordered to storm the heights, upon which not less than forty pieces of artillery, and no one knew how many muskets stood ready to slaughter the assailants.

With cheers answering to cheers, the men swarmed upwards. They gathered to the lines of least difficult ascent and the line was broken. Color after color was planted on the summit, while musketry and cannon vomited their thunder upon them. A well-directed shot from Orchard Knob exploded a rebel caisson on the summit. A gun was seen galloping to the right, its driver lashing his horses. A party of our soldiers intercepted him, and the gun was captured with cheers.

A fierce musketry fight broke out to the left where, between Thomas and Sherman, a mile or two of the ridge, was still occupied by the rebels. Bragg left the house in which he had held his headquarters, and rode to the rear, as our troops crowned the hill on each side of him.

General Grant proceeded to the summit, and then only did we know its height.

Some of the captured artillery was put into position, artillerists were sent for to work the guns, caissons were searched for ammunition. The rebel log breastworks were torn to pieces and carried to the other side of the ridge, and used in forming barricades across it. A strong line of infantry was formed in the rear of Baird's line, hotly engaged in a musketry contest with the rebels to the left, and a secure lodgment was soon effected.

The other assault to the right of our centre gained the summit, and the rebels threw down their arms and fled. Hooker coming in from Rossville swept the right of the ridge and captured many prisoners.

Bragg's remaining troops left early in the night and the battle of Chattanooga, after three days of manœuvring and fighting was won. The strength of the rebellion in the centre was broken; Burnside relieved from danger in East Tennessee; Kentucky, and Tennessee redeemed; Georgia and the southeast threatened in the rear, and another victory added to the chaplet of Unconditional Surrender Grant.

To-night the estimate of captures is several thousand prisoners and thirty pieces of artillery. Loss for so great a victory not severe. Bragg is firing the railroad as he retreats towards Dalton, Sherman is in hot pursuit.

To-day I visited the battle-field, which extends for six

miles along Mission Ridge, and for several miles on Lookout Mountain.

Probably no so well directed, so well ordered a battle has been delivered during the war. But one assault was repulsed, but that assault, by calling to that point the reserves prevented their repulsing any of the others.

A few days since Bragg sent to General Grant a flag of truce to advise him that it would be prudent to remove any non-combatants who might be still in Chattanooga. No reply has been returned, but, the combatants having been removed from this vicinity, it is probable that the non-combatants can remain without imprudence.

May I suggest that your visit to Louisville, with the measures there inaugurated have done the cause in this quarter much good. It would be well to visit us here and also for the President to review an army which has done so much for the country, and which has not yet seen his face.

(Signed.)   M. C. MEIGS,
                            Quartermaster General.

1864

Fresh from Abraham's Bosom

As Lincoln grew in stature as President, popular interest in him grew in proportion, particularly in the election year of 1864. The President was roundly criticized by some for his habit of telling jokes. But his readiness with an anecdote endeared him to the masses of Americans who were his greatest supporters. Collections of his jokes and stories were eagerly read. It did not matter that most of the tales they repeated were old jokes revised with an application to Lincoln. The President himself was not averse to putting an old story to new use, and a good laugh is always a good laugh.

In this section is a sketch of "Mr. Lincoln's Daily Life" from *Old Abe's Jokes, Fresh from Abraham's Bosom.* The other items are from *Lincolniana; or, The Humors of Uncle Abe.*

Mr. Lincoln's Daily Life.

Mr. Lincoln is an early riser, and he thus is able to devote two or three hours each morning to his voluminous private correspondence, besides glancing at a city paper. At nine he breakfasts—then walks over to the war office, to read such war telegrams as they give him, (occasionally some are withheld,) and to have a chat with General Halleck on the military situation, in which he takes a great interest. Returning to the white house, he goes through with his morning's mail, in company with a private secretary, who makes a minute of the reply which he is to make—and others the President retains, that he may answer them himself. Every letter receives attention, and all which are entitled to a reply receive one no matter how they are worded, or how inelegant the chirography may be.

Tuesdays and Fridays are cabinet days, but on other days visitors at the white house are requested to wait in the ante-chamber, and send in their cards. Sometimes, before the President has finished reading his mail Louis will have a handful of pasteboard, and from the cards laid before him Mr. Lincoln has visitors ushered in, giving precedence to acquaintances. Three or four hours do they pour in, in rapid succession, nine out of ten asking offices, and patiently does the president listen to their application. Care and anxiety have furrowed his rather homely features, yet occasionally he is "reminded of an anecdote" and good humored glances beam from his clear, grey eyes, while his ringing laugh shows that he is not "used up" yet. The simple and natural manner in which he delivers his thoughts makes him appear to those visiting him like an earnest, affectionate friend. He makes little parade of his legal science, and rarely indulges in speculative propositions, but states his ideas in plain Anglo-saxon, illuminated by many lively images and pleasing allusions, which seem to flow as if in obedience to a resistless impulse of his nature. Some newspaper admirer attempts to deny that the President tells stories. Why, it is rarely that any one is in his company for fifteen minutes without hearing a good tale, appropriate to the subject talked about. Many a metaphysical argument does he demolish by simply telling an anecdote, which exactly overturns the verbal structure.

About four o'clock the President declines seeing any more company, and often accompanies his wife in her carriage to take a drive. He is fond of horseback exercise, and when passing the summers' home used generally to go in the saddle. The President dines at six, and it is rare that some personal friends do not grace the round dining table where he throws off the cares of office, and reminds those who have been in Kentucky of the old school gentleman who used to dispense generous hospitality there.— From the dinner table the party retire to the crimson drawing room, where coffee is served, and where the President passes the evening, unless some dignitary has a special interview. Such is the almost unvarying daily life of Abraham Lincoln, whose administration will rank next in importance to that of Washington in our national annals.

Uncle Abe on the Whisky Question.

A committee, just previous to the fall of Vicksburg, solicitous for the *morale* of our armies, took it upon themselves to visit the President and urge the removal of General Grant.

"What for?" asked Uncle Abe.

"Why," replied the busy-bodies, "he drinks too much whisky."

"Ah!" rejoined Uncle Abe, "can you inform me, gentlemen, where General Grant procures his whisky?"

The committee confessed they could not.

"Because," added Uncle Abe, with a merry twinkle in his

eye, "If I can find out, I'll send a barrel of it to every General in the field!"

The delegation retired in reasonable good order.

A Touching Incident.

The following incident, which occurred at the White House, will appeal to every heart. It reveals unmistakably the deep kindness of Uncle Abe's character:

"At a reception recently at the White House, many persons present noticed three little girls poorly dressed, the children of some mechanic or laboring man, who had followed the visitors into the house to gratify their curiosity. They were passed from room to room, and were passing through the reception room with some trepidation, when Uncle Abe called to them: 'Little girls, are you going to pass me without shaking hands?' Then he bent his tall, awkward form down, and shook each little girl warmly by the hand. Everybody in the apartment was spellbound by the incident, so simple in itself, yet revealing of so much of Uncle Abe's character."

Bushwhackers

THE WAR WOULD BE DECIDED in its Eastern theaters, but it was no less intense in the West. Each battle was supremely important to the men who engaged in it. The Federals slowly restricted Confederate resistance to the confines of Texas, Louisiana, and Arkansas, and territorial inroads were made even into those states. But pro-Southern elements along the border caused flurries of military activity. In August, 1863, William Clarke Quantrill had led a band of Missouri guerrillas into Lawrence, Kansas, and virtually destroyed the town. It was necessary to guard against any possible repetition of such a massacre.

Stationed at Fort Riley, Kansas, were the men of the Second Colorado Cavalry. Even at this isolated post energetic soldiers managed to produce and circulate their own newspaper. Here is a portion of the story of the Second Colorado and its war against the bushwhackers as told in the columns of the *Soldier's Letter*.

The Counties of Jackson, Cass, Bates, and part of Vernon —forming the 4th Sub-District, District Central Mo. had been infested by a set of outlaws, consisting in part—of Deserters from the Rebel army, and partly of rebels, who— from cowardice, or some other motive, had failed to join the army—and preferred wreaking their vengeance upon the few persons who were so unfortunate as to be Union citizens. As indicative of their cowardly dispositions, their actions were attended with stealth, seldom daring to risk an open contest, unless vastly superior to the opposing force— in point of numbers; but confining their actions, principally to the bushes—ambushing small parties, and individuals, robbing all who fell into their hands, and showing no quarter to Union Soldiers:—hence, from this mode of warfare, and highway robberies—were termed "Bushwhackers." Sometimes their depredations extended to all parties; but as a general rule, the Union people were the greatest sufferers.

These marauders, or banditti became so numerous, and bold in their nefarious transactions—and such difficulty was experienced in apprehending and punishing the guilty—that it was deemed necessary in order to insure justice to all parties—to cause the immediate abandonment by the inhabitants of these counties; about the 23d of September, 1863, the order was issued by General Ewing, giving them 15 days to leave the Counties, which was speedily obeyed by the inhabitants; troops were stationed in the different parts of the Sub.-District, and the country overrun: houses burned to the ground; grain and farms destroyed—causing the country to resemble a wilderness—with "homes deserted, fields of ground, abandoned by the faithful plow."

On the 14th of January, 1864, Gen. Brown—who was at that time in command of the District of Central Missouri, issued an order—(General Order No. 2 Hd.-Qrs. Dist. Central Mo.) allowing all loyally disposed citizens who had been driven from their homes, to return—on conditions—viz: that they should ever be ready to assist the Government in its endeavors to put down the Rebellion, and protect themselves, and their homes, from all enemies; the same General Order assigned Colonel James H. Ford, Second Colorado Cavalry, to the command of the 4th Sub.-District District of Central Missouri, Hd-Qrs. at Kansas City, Mo. Col. Ford assumed command on the 18th of February, and appointed Lieut. E. L. Berthoud, Co. E, (now Captain Co. D,) Acting Assistant Adjutant-General, and Capt. J. C. W. Hall, Co. B, Assistant Provost Marshal. On assuming command, Colonel Ford proceeded to distribute his forces throughout the Sub District, in such a manner as would be best calculated to conduct the campaign against the squads of Bushwhackers, and at the same time, be able to concentrate his forces, with little delay, on the appearance of a superior force of the enemy. Among the Stations announced, were the following: Kansas City, Independence—eight miles east—Westport, three miles south, Hickman's Mills—16 miles south; Pleasant Hill—thirty-five miles south-east; and Harrisonville—about 45 miles south from Kansas City.

At this time, the Bushwhackers were comparatively quiet, confining their efforts to an occasional midnight assassination, or robbery; evidently deferring operations on a large scale, until the leaves came out on the trees—to afford them protection in their fiendish work; nevertheless, the troops at the different stations were not idle, but were actively engaged in scouring the country, and becoming acquainted with its geographical position, the roads and by-ways, as well the inhabitants—who consisted chiefly of "widows" (!) whose husbands had gone to the war—and who were strictly loyal to the Government of the—Southern Confederacy! So much diligence was exercised by the troops, that, by the 1st of June, there was scarcely a locality, road, or bypath through the country, including the famous "Sni Hills"—with which they were not thoroughly familiar; a very important feature, in hunting Bushwhackers. . . .

On the 29th of April, a detachment of our troops, under command of Lieut. Spencer, pursued on the trail of a party of *Bushwhackers,* between Lone Jack and the Sni Hills; coming up with them, they charged them, but the *Bandits* were well mounted, and succeeded in escaping unharmed, after the first fire, which killed Geo. Wells, Private of K Company, and wounding John Freestone, of Company G, whose horses had led them far in advance of the others.

On the 13th of June, Sergeant-Major Hennion, with an escort of 8 men, and a six mule team in charge, was attacked about 5 o'cl'k in the afternoon, about four miles southwest of Westport, on the Hickman's Mill road, by a band of 25 or 30 *Bushwhackers,* under the infamous desperado, Dick Yeager; the first volley fired, although not over 20 feet distant, had no other effect than the wounding of Hennion slightly in the ankle, and the complete surprise of our little party, who fired several hurried shots, and took to the brush, closely pursued; at the second discharge from the enemy, Hennion's horse was killed, and the cylinder blown from his revolver at the same time; but he succeeded in making his escape into the brush, where he lay until 10 o'clock that night, and reached Kansas City the next morning at 6, a. m., with three bullet-holes in his jacket, and one through his pants. The rest of the party succeeded in getting away unharmed—two of them, who were in the advance, hastened forward to Hickman's Mill for reinforcements, and one of the party lay out during the night and reached Hickman's Mill the next day.

The *Banditti* captured the team, unloaded some goods belonging to Mrs. Johnson of Company L, and directed her to
a house near by, where she could stay until relief would
come; they then set fire to the wagon, killed two of the
mules, and wounded a third one, which they left; the other
three they appropriated to their own use. Some days afterward, a fresh grave was found near the spot, supposed to
be that of a *Bushwhacker* killed in the encounter. The frequency of these attacks, and the increasing temerity of the
assassins, required energetic action, on the part of our troops
—consequently—Colonel Ford, ordered the Regiment into
the field, and established its Head-Quarters near a deserted
village, called Raytown, situated on the Independence and
Hickman's Mill road, and 16 miles distant from Kansas City:
from this point, the troops, under Majors Smith and Pritch-
ard, and other officers of the Regiment, scoured the country,
in every direction—sometimes mounted, and at other times
dismounted—which had the desired effect, of driving these
marauders from that portion of the country, to seek a safer,
and more congenial latitude; during one of these scouts,
Corporal Martin, Co. H. with 10 men, some two miles east
of camp, were quietly passing along, when hearing a noise
as if some persons talking in the distance; quickly concealing themselves in the brush, our party awaited the approach
of the other party, who, approaching within 50 yards, were
discovered to be Bushwhackers—five in number—and were
immediately fired upon by the scout; a ball from the gun of
private Jones, of H Company, passed through the hips of
one of the enemy named Young—wounding him severely,
but his horse carried him off: pursuing the course taken by
them, and coming up to a house, the alarm was given by
some one who acted as sentinel, and out rushed the same
party, and after a hurried exchange of shots, disappeared

in the brush:—Young, the wounded man, was killed a short time afterwards.

Head-Quarters of the Regiment remained at Raytown about one month, during which time the troops were kept constantly on the move; various expedients were resorted to, to entrap the wary enemy, but they had become aware of the dangerous locality; and quietly decamped, until a more favorable opportunity presented itself.

On the 10th of May, Lt. Gooding, with 20 men of Co's H, and G, started from Pleasant Hill, after night had set in—on a scout of three days duration; on the night of the second day out, while scouting 20 miles north east of Pleasant Hill, they drew up to a house, owned by one Webb; upon entering, although past eleven o'clock, the table was found ready "set," and every necessary preparation made, for a meal; upon inquiry, our party was informed that there were no *Bushwhackers* in the country, but—not being inclined to give credence to the smooth tongues, and unqualified assertions of the "war-widows" who were so numerous in that portion of the country, and who could live there unmolested, while depredations were being committed all around them—our boys kept a sharp look-out, and, after leaving the house, and proceeding cautiously along the road some three miles, they were met by a party of four men, who were just emerging from the brush, and could barely be discerned in the darkness of the night: "Who are you?" challenged their leader: "Who are *you*?" demanded Gooding, while every man grasped his revolver with a firmer grip: without deigning to give answer, the four men wheeled about, put spurs to their horses, and fled through the thick under-brush, amid a shower of bullets from the well directed fire of the advance; the next day, the dead bodies of two of the *Bandits,* were found near the scene of the rencountre.

During the campaign, a portion of the troops had been stationed at Camp Smith, some three miles southwest of Independence, and on the morning of the sixth of July, Captain S. Wagoner, of C. Company, and twenty-five of his men, left Camp, and proceeded in a northeasterly direction, until arriving on the Pleasant Hill and Independence road, and about eight miles distant from the latter mentioned place; here, they saw four men, who immediately took to flight, and while pursuing them, our party was charged upon, by nearly one hundred *Bushwhackers,* who were lying in ambush awaiting their approach; unconscious of the presence of so large a body of the foe, until they rushed forth from the dense thicket, with savage yells, and poured a deadly volley into the midst of the scout, who, nothing daunted, firmly stood their ground, and with their brave Captain leading them on, returned the fire, although outnumbered four to one, by the foe, who came rushing on, until the combatants were mingled together, fighting a hand to hand encounter, midst the fallen dead, and dying, until the gallant Wagoner fell, mortally wounded, and dragging himself a few feet to one side, he gave a farewell shot, that sent an enemy reeling to the ground, with his life-blood spirting from the wound—and shouted "give them death boys," and breathed his last: completely overpowered by numbers, our troops were forced to fall back, and surrender the field to the enemy—with the loss of their valiant Captain, and seven brave men killed, and one wounded: the loss of the enemy were nine men killed, and fifteen wounded; they took the arms and what money was on the persons of our boys, and left their bodies lying as they fell, where a strong force of our troops, who were sent out, found them and brought them to Independence, the next morning, and buried them in a body, in the Cemetery, with a brick wall surrounding the entire number; and the Company, assisted by the Officers of the Regiment, erected a fine Marble Monument, to mark their resting place.— The Monument bears the following inscription, from the pen of Mrs. Williams, of Company A:

> "Brave heroes rest beneath this sculptured stone;
> In unfair contest slain by murderous hands:
> They knew no yielding to a cruel foe—
> And thus, this tribute to their memory stands—
> Our country's honor, and a Nation's pride;—
> 'Twas thus they nobly lived, and bravely died."

Captain Wagoner was a brave man, of which his surviving followers can testify, and his loss, and that of the brave men who fell with him, cast a gloom o'er the entire Regiment.

Notwithstanding the increased vigilance of our troops, in scouring the country, in search of these *Brigands*, it was seldom they caught them "napping," for they were cognizant of the danger they were incurring, by remaining in the country, and committing their depredations, and, were cautious of their movements—only making a demonstration, when assured of success, on their part; being intimately acquainted with the entire country, (having resided there for years) and having the advantage of acting on the defensive, when our troops were sent in pursuit of them—they for a long time, succeeded in evading an open collision with them,—feeling uninclined to extend their acquaintance with men who gave them such a rough introduction.

About this time, a desperado by the name of *Thornton*, came into the counties on the North side of the river, and was collecting together all the *Bushwhackers* and other *vagabonds* that would flock to his standard, in order to go into offensive operations against the Union people, on a large scale, and finally escape to the Southern army, as it was getting rather warm for their comfort and safety: through the spies he had employed to watch the movements of the enemy—Col. Ford learned of their place of rendezvous, and about 2 o'clock in the morning of the 13th of July, he quietly embarked on board the Fanny Ogden, and the Emilie, with about 300 men, in the midst of a heavy rainstorm, and proceeded up the river as far as Weston, a town on the North bank of the Missouri river, about seven miles above Leavenworth City:—landing at this point, the troops bivouacked, until 12 o'clock, M, and being reinforced by a portion of the 16th Kansas Cavalry, under Jennison, the column moved towards Camden Point, a town of 150 inhabitants; arriving within 4 miles of the town, our advance encountered the rebel pickets, who hastily fired a volley, and retreated, pursued by the advance, who succeeded in killing two of their number; the others made their escape into the thick brush on the roadside: the Brigade was formed in fours, and the order "gallop" was given, and the column moved forward at a rapid rate over the road. Company F, (Captain West) leading the advance; on arriving at the town, the rebels were found drawn up in line about 350 strong, ready for battle; West also formed his men in line at hailing distance, and demanded— "Who are you?" the question was reiterated by the rebel leader; West replied— "Captain West, of the Second Colorado!" the reply came back, proud and defiant— "We do not *recognize* Captain West, and his party—" and the rebel colors were immediately displayed. Captain West instantly ordered a charge, and the rebel ranks were broken and scattered by the fierce onset of our troops, who bore down on the foe—like an avalanche—sweeping all before them, amid the smoke and din

of battle, and the wild, deafening cheers of our men, that
rang out clear and loud upon the air, and was echoed, and
re-echoed through the surrounding forest: the rebel forces,
after exchanging a few volleys, fled in every direction in the
wildest confusion—in many instances, leaving their horses
and equipments, and quite a number throwing down their
arms, and taking to the brush, pursued closely by our troops,
who, having become exasperated by their former fiendish
transactions—shot them down like so many dogs—without
mercy: the main portion fled on the road leading east of
town, and were hotly pursued, for nearly five miles, but
being mounted on fresh horses, they finally escaped—and our
troops returned, and camped on the same ground occupied
previously, by their forces. Our loss was one man killed,
(private Flannegan) and 1 wounded, (Serg't Crane,) both
of Co. F: that of the rebels was 21 killed; if any were
wounded, they made their escape. In this action, the rebel
colors, which was presented to them, by the ladies of Platte
City, and bore the motto—"Protect Missouri"—was captured
by Company F.

The *Alabama* and the *Kearsarge*

NEXT IN FAME to the fight between the *Monitor* and
the *Merrimac* among naval battles of the Civil War
is the engagement between the Confederate *Alabama*
and the Federal *Kearsarge* fought off Cherbourg on June
19, 1864.

In a career a few weeks short of two years the *Alabama*, commanded by Raphael Semmes, had burned,
sunk, or captured more than sixty Federal ships. Her
very name was anathema to the Union Navy, and the
fear his ship incited seems to have been counted on by
Semmes, who is quoted in this account by Frederick
Milnes Edge as having observed with surprise the efficient conduct of the Federal sailors and to have remarked, "Confound them; they've been fighting twenty
minutes, and they're as cool as posts."

Edge was distinctly Northern in his sympathies. His
is, nevertheless, a careful and considered report of the
fight and is a good antidote for the histrionic sensation-
alism which marks many of the contemporary accounts
of the sea battle.

The loss of the *Alabama* did not end the Confederate Navy, but it left only the cruisers *Florida* and *Shenandoah* as major dangers to Federal shipping. The *Florida* surrendered at Bahia, Brazil, in October, 1864. The *Shenandoah* survived the war and finally gave herself up to British authorities at Liverpool in November, 1865.

By the summer of 1864 the Federal Navy had been built up to controlling strength. Slowly its blockade was throttling commercial activity in Southern ports. Its gunboats were exceedingly efficient in operations in inland waters. It could be used for the transport of troops and for joint operations with the army. From virtually nothing in 1861 it had been made into an effective war force.

Within a few days of the fight, the writer of these pages crossed from London to Cherbourg for the purpose of obtaining by personal examination full and precise information in reference to the engagement. It would seem as though misrepresentation, if not positive falsehood, were inseparable from everything connected with the *Alabama*, for on reaching the French naval station he was positively assured by the people on shore that nobody was permitted to board the *Kearsarge*. Preferring, however, to substantiate the truth of these allegations, from the officers of the vessel themselves, he hired a boat and sailed out to the sloop, receiving on his arrival an immediate and polite reception from Captain Winslow and his gallant subordinates. During the six days he remained at Cherbourg, he found the *Kearsarge* open to the inspection, above and below, of any and everybody who chose to visit her; and he frequently heard surprise expressed by English and French visitors alike that representations on shore were so inconsonant with the truth of the case.

I found the *Kearsarge* lying under the guns of the French ship-of-the-line *Napoleon*, two cables' length from that vessel, and about a mile and a half from the harbour; she had not moved from that anchorage since entering the port of Cherbourg, and no repairs whatever had been effected in her hull since the fight. I had thus full opportunity to examine the extent of her damage, and she certainly did not look at all like a vessel which had just been engaged in one of the hottest conflicts of modern times.

The *Kearsarge*, in size, is by no means the terrible craft represented by those who, for some reason or other, seek to detract from the honour of her victory; she appeared to me a mere yacht in comparison with the shipping around her, and disappointed many of the visitors who came to see her. The relative proportions of the two antagonists were as follows:—

	ALABAMA.	KEARSARGE.
Length over all...........	220 ft.	232 ft.
" of keel	210 "	198½ "
Beam	32 "	33 "
Depth	17 "	16½ "
Horse power, 2 engines of 300 each		400 h.p.
Tonnage	1,040	1,031*

The *Alabama* was a barque-rigged screw propeller, and the heaviness of her rig, and, above all, the greater size and height of her masts would give her the appearance of a much larger vessel than her antagonist. The masts of the

* The *Kearsarge* has a four-bladed screw, diameter 12 ft 9-in. with a pitch of 20-ft.

latter are disproportionately low and small; she has never carried more than top-sail yards, and depends for her speed upon her machinery alone. It is to be questioned whether the *Alabama*, with all her reputation for velocity, could, in her best trim, outsteam her rival. The log book of the *Kearsarge*, which I was courteously permitted to examine, frequently shows a speed of upwards of fourteen knots the hour, and her engineers state that her machinery was never in better working order than at the present time. I have not seen engines more compact in form, nor, apparently, in finer condition; looking in every part as though they were fresh from the workshop, instead of being, as they are, half through the third year of the cruise. . . .

Numerous facts serve to prove that Captain Semmes had made every preparation to engage the *Kearsarge*, and that wide-spread publicity had been given to his intention. As soon as the arrival of the Federal vessel was known at Paris, an American gentleman of high position came down to Cherbourg, with instructions for Captain Winslow; but so desirous were the French authorities to preserve a really honest neutrality, that permission was only granted to him to sail to her after his promise to return to shore immediately on the delivery of his message. Once back in Cherbourg, and about to return to Paris, he was advised to remain over night, *as the Alabama intended to fight the Kearsarge next day* (Sunday). On Sunday morning, an excursion train arrived from the Capital, and the visitors were received at the terminus of the railway by the boatmen of the port, who offered them boats for the purpose of seeing *a genuine naval battle which was to take place during the day.* Turning such a memorable occurrence to practical uses, Monsieur Rondin, a celebrated photographic artist on the *Place d'Armes* at Cherbourg, prepared the necessary chemicals, plates, and *camera,* and placed himself on the summit of the old church tower which the whilom denizens of Cherbourg had very properly built in happy juxtaposition with his establishment. I was only able to see the negative, but that was quite sufficient to show that the artist had obtained a very fine view indeed of the exciting contest. Five days, however, had elapsed since Captain Semmes sent his challenge to Captain Winslow through the Confederate agent, Monsieur Bonfils; surely time sufficient for him to make all the preparations which he considered necessary. Meanwhile the *Kearsarge* was cruising to and fro at sea, outside the breakwater.

The *Kearsarge* reached Cherbourg on the 14th, and her Captain only heard of Captain Semmes' intention to fight him on the following day. Five days, however, elapsed before the *Alabama* put in an appearance, and her exit from the harbour was heralded by the English yacht *Deerhound.* The officer on watch aboard the *Kearsarge* made out a three-masted vessel steaming from the harbour, the movements of which were somewhat mysterious; after remaining a short time only, this steamer, which subsequently proved to be the *Deerhound,* went back into port; only returning to sea a few minutes in advance of the *Alabama,* and the French ironclad *La Couronne.* Mr. Lancaster, her owner, sends a copy of his log to the *Times,* the first two entries being as follows:

"Sunday, June 19, 9 A.M.—Got up steam and proceeded out of Cherbourg harbour.

"10.30.—Observed the 'Alabama' steaming out of the harbour towards the Federal steamer 'Kearsarge.'" *

* The following is the copy of the log of the *Kearsarge* on the day in question:
    "June 19, 1864.   "From 8 to Merid.
        "Moderate breeze from the Wd. weather b. c. At 10 o'clock, inspected crew at quarters. At 10.20, discovered the Alabama steaming out

Mr. Lancaster does not inform us why an English gentleman should choose a Sunday morning, of all days in the week, to cruise about at an early hour with ladies on board, nor does he supply the public with information as to the movements of the *Deerhound* during the hour and a half which elapsed between his exit from the harbour and the appearance of the *Alabama*. The preceding paragraph, however, supplies the omission.

At length the *Alabama* made her appearance in company with the *Couronne,* the latter vessel conveying her outside the limit of French waters. Here let me pay a tribute to the careful neutrality of the French authorities. No sooner was the limit of jurisdiction reached, than the *Couronne* put down her helm, and without any delay, steamed back into port, not even lingering outside the breakwater to witness the fight. Curiosity, if not worse, anchored the English vessel in handy vicinity to the combatants. Her presence proved to

---

from the port of Cherbourg, accompanied by a French iron-clad steamer, and a fore and-aft rigged steamer showing the white English ensign and a yacht flag. Beat to General Quarters, and clear the ship for action. Steamed ahead standing off shore. At 10.50, being distant from the land about two leagues, altered our course and approached the Alabama. At 10.57, the Alabama commenced the action with her starboard broadside at 1,000 yards range. At 11, we returned her fire, and came fairly into action, which we continued until Merid., when observing signs of distress in the enemy, together with a cessation of her fire, our fire was withheld. At 12.10, a boat with an officer from the Alabama came alongside and surrendered his vessel, with the information that she was rapidly sinking, and a request for assistance. Sent the Launch and 2d Cutter, the other boats being disabled by the fire of the enemy. The English yacht before mentioned, coming within hail, was requested by the Captain (W.) to render assistance in saving the lives of the officers and crew of the surrendered vessel. At 2.24, the Alabama went down in forty fathoms of water, leaving most of the crew struggling in the water. Seventy persons were rescued by the boats, two pilot boats and the yacht also assisted. One pilot boat came alongside us, but the other returned to the port. The yacht steamed rapidly away to the Nd. without reporting the number of our prisoners she had picked up.

(Signed) JAMES S. WHEELER, Actg. Master."

be of much utility, for she picked up no less than fourteen of the *Alabama*'s officers, and among them the redoubtable Semmes himself.

So soon as the *Alabama* was made out, the *Kearsarge* immediately headed seaward and steamed off the coast, the object being to get a sufficient distance from the land so as to obviate any possible infringement of French jurisdiction; and, secondly, that in case of the battle going against the *Alabama*, the latter could not retreat into port. When this was accomplished, the *Kearsarge* was turned shortly round and steered immediately for the *Alabama*, Captain Winslow desiring to get within close range, as his guns were shotted with five-seconds shell. The interval between the two vessels being reduced to a mile, or thereabouts, the *Alabama* sheered and discharged a broadside, nearly a raking fire, at the *Kearsarge*. More speed was given to the latter to shorten the distance, and a slight sheer to prevent raking. The *Alabama* fired a second broadside and part of a third while her antagonist was closing; and at the expiration of ten or twelve minutes from the *Alabama*'s opening shot, the *Kearsarge* discharged her first broadside. The action henceforward continued in a circle, the distance between the two vessels being about seven hundred yards; this, at all events, is the opinion of the Federal commander and his officers, for their guns were sighted at that range, and their shell burst in and over the privateer. The speed of the two vessels during the engagement did not exceed eight knots the hour.

At the expiration of one hour and two minutes from the first gun, the *Alabama* hauled down her colours and fired a lee gun (according to the statements of her officers), in token of surrender. Captain Winslow could not, however, believe that the enemy had struck, as his own vessel had received so little damage, and he could not regard his antag-

onist as much more injured than himself; and it was only
when a boat came off from the *Alabama* that her true condition was known. The 11-inch shell from the *Kearsarge*,
thrown with fifteen pounds of powder at seven hundred
yards range, had gone clean through the starboard side of
the privateer, bursting in the port side and tearing great
gaps in her timber and planking. This was plainly obvious
when the *Alabama* settled by the stern and raised the fore-
part of her hull high out of water.

The *Kearsarge* was struck twenty-seven times during the
conflict and fired in all one hundred and seventy-three (173)
shots. These were as follows:

Two 11-inch guns	55 shots.
Rifle in forecastle	48 "
Broadside 32-pdrs.	60 "
12-pdr. boat howitzer	10 "
Total,	173 shots.

The last-named gun performed no part whatever in sinking the *Alabama,* and was only used in the action to create
laughter among the sailors. Two old quartermasters, the two
Dromios of the *Kearsarge,* were put in charge of this gun,
with instructions to fire when they received the order. But
the two old salts, little relishing the idea of having nothing
to do while their messmates were so actively engaged, commenced peppering away with their pea-shooter of a piece,
alternating their discharges with vituperation of each other.
This low-comedy by-play amused the ship's company, and
the officers good-humoredly allowed the farce to continue
until the single box of ammunition was exhausted. . . .

The first accounts received of the action led us to suppose
that Captain Semmes' intention was to lay his vessel along-

side the enemy, and to carry her by boarding. Whether this information came from the Captain himself or was made out of "whole cloth" by some of his admirers, the idea of boarding a vessel under steam—unless her engines, or screw, or rudder be disabled—is manifestly ridiculous. The days of boarding are gone by, except under the contingencies above stated; and any such attempt on the part of the *Alabama* would have been attended with disastrous results to herself and crew. To have boarded the *Kearsarge*, Semmes must have possessed greater speed to enable him to run alongside her; and the moment the pursuer came near her victim, the latter would shut off steam, drop astern in a second of time, sheer off, discharge her whole broadside of grape and canister, and rake her antagonist from stern to stem. Our pro-southern sympathizers really ought not to make their *protegé* appear ridiculous by ascribing to him such an egregious intention.

Andersonville

M OST DREADED of Confederate prisons was Camp Sumter at Anderson Station, Georgia. The prison had been designed with humane motives, to take care of the overload of prisoners at Belle Isle caused by the suspension by the Federals of the cartel for exchange. The site was selected with care to provide a healthy, watered area. But the prison was severely overcrowded almost as soon as it opened, and proper preparations for housing had not been made. The drain by the armies on supplies of food in the Confederacy was responsible for a ration far below any humane or healthy standard. By the summer of 1864 more than thirty thousand prisoners were crowded into twenty-six acres. Exposure, a complete lack of even rudimentary sanitation, lack of decent food and medical care, and overcrowding combined to make the prison pen a veritable pesthouse and to cause more than twelve thousand deaths.

Andersonville was a national outrage in the North. In the summer of 1864 a few of the prisoners were exchanged. Their stories of imprisonment were widely publicized and effectively used as propaganda for the strenuous prosecution of the war. Their testimony was most widely circulated in a pamphlet, *Narrative of the Privations and Sufferings of United States Officers and Privates While Prisoners of War in the Hands of Rebel Authorities,* a portion of which is included here.

Deposition of PRIVATE TRACY:—

I am a private in the 82d New York Regiment of Volunteers, Company G. Was captured with about eight hundred Federal troops, in front of Petersburg, on the 22d of June, 1864. We were kept at Petersburg two days, at Richmond, Belle Isle, three days, then conveyed by rail to Lynchburg. Marched seventy-five miles to Danville, thence by rail to Andersonville, Georgia. At Petersburg we were treated fairly, being under the guard of old soldiers of an Alabama regiment; at Richmond we came under the authority of the notorious and inhuman Major Turner, and the equally notorious Home Guard. Our ration was a pint of beans, four ounces of bread, and three ounces of meat, a day. Another batch of prisoners joining us, we left Richmond sixteen hundred strong.

All blankets, haversacks, canteens, money, valuables of every kind, extra clothing, and in some cases the last shirt and drawers, had been previously taken from us.

At Lynchburg we were placed under the Home Guard, officered by Major and Captain Moffett. The march to Danville was a weary and painful one of five days, under a torrid sun, many of us falling helpless by the way, and soon filling the empty wagons of our train. On the first day we received a little meat, but the *sum* of our rations for the five days was thirteen crackers. During the six days by rail to Anderson-ville, meat was given us twice, and the daily ration was four crackers.

On entering the Stockade Prison, we found it crowded with twenty-eight thousand of our fellow-soldiers. By *crowded,* I mean that it was difficult to move in any direction without jostling and being jostled. This prison is an open space, sloping on both sides, originally seventeen acres, now twenty-five acres, in the shape of a parallelogram, without trees or shelter of any kind. The soil is sand over a bottom of clay. The fence is made of upright trunks of trees, about twenty feet high, near the top of which are small platforms, where the guards are stationed. Twenty feet inside and parallel to the fence is a light railing, forming the "dead line," beyond which the projection of a foot or finger is sure to bring the deadly bullet of the sentinel.

Through the ground, at nearly right-angles with the longer sides, runs or rather creeps a stream through an artificial channel, varying from five to six feet in width, the water about ankle deep, and near the middle of the enclosure, spreading out into a swamp of about six acres, filled with refuse wood, stumps and debris of the camp. Before entering this enclosure, the stream, or more properly sewer, passes through the camp of the guards, receiving from this source, and others farther up, a large amount of the vilest material, even the contents of the sink. The water is of a dark color, and an ordinary glass would collect a thick sediment. This was our only drinking and cooking water. It was our custom to filter it as best we could, through our remnants of haversacks, shirts and blouses. Wells had been dug, but the water either proved so productive of diarrhœa, or so limited in quantity that they were of no general use. The cook-house was situated on the stream just outside the stockade, and its refuse of decaying offal was thrown into the water, a greasy coating covering much of the surface. To these was added the daily large amount of base matter from the camp itself. There was a system of policing, but the means was so limited, and so large a number of the men was rendered irresolute and depressed by imprisonment, that the work was very imperfectly done. One side of the swamp was naturally used as a sink, the men usually going out some distance into the water. Under the summer sun this place early became corruption too vile for description, the men breeding disgusting life, so that the surface of the water moved as with a gentle breeze.

The new-comers, on reaching this, would exclaim: "Is this hell?" yet they soon would become callous, and enter unmoved the horrible rottenness. The rebel authorities never removed any filth. There was seldom any visitation by the officers in charge. Two surgeons were at one time sent by President DAVIS to inspect the camp, but a walk through a small section gave them all the information they desired, and we never saw them again.

The guards usually numbered about sixty-four—eight at each end, and twenty-four on a side. On the outside, within three hundred yards, were fortifications, on high ground, overlooking and perfectly commanding us, mounting twenty-four twelve-pound Napoleon Parrotts. We were never permitted to go outside, except at times, in small squads, to gather our firewood. During the building of the cook-house, a few, who were carpenters, were ordered out to assist.

Our only shelter from the sun and rain and night dews was what we could make by stretching over us our coats or scraps of blankets, which a few had, but generally there was no attempt by day or night to protect ourselves.

The rations consisted of eight ounces of corn bread (the

cob being ground with the kernel), and generally sour, two ounces of condemned pork, offensive in appearance and smell. Occasionally, about twice a week, two tablespoons of rice, and in place of the pork the same amount (two table-spoonfuls) of molasses were given us about twice a month.*
This ration was brought into camp about four o'clock, P. M., and thrown from the wagons to the ground, the men being arranged in divisions of two hundred and seventy, subdi-vided into squads of nineties and thirties. It was the custom to consume the whole ration at once, rather than save any for the next day. The distribution being often unequal some would lose the rations altogether. We were allowed no dish or cooking utensil of any kind. On opening the camp in the winter, the first two thousand prisoners were allowed skillets, one to fifty men, but these were soon taken away. To the best of my knowledge, information and belief, our ration was in quality a starving one, it being either too foul to be touched or too raw to be digested.

The cook-house went into operation about May 10th, prior to which we cooked our own rations. It did not prove at all adequate to the work, (thirty thousand is a large town,) so that a large proportion were still obliged to prepare their own food. In addition to the utter inability of many to do this, through debility and sickness, we never had a supply of wood. I have often seen men with a little bag of meal in

* Our regular army ration is:
¾ lb. Pork or 1¼ lbs. Fresh Beef,
18 ozs. Hard Bread, or 20 ozs. Soft Bread or Flour,
1-10 lb. Coffee,
1-6 lb. Sugar,
1-10 lb. Rice, or
1-10 lb. Beans or Hominy.
Vegetables—Fresh or
    Desiccated,   } Irregularly.
Molasses,
Vinegar.

hand, gathered from several rations, starving to death for want of wood, and in desperation would mix the raw material with water and try to eat it.

The clothing of the men was miserable in the extreme. Very few had shoes of any kind, not two thousand had coats and pants, and those were late comers. More than one-half were indecently exposed, and many were naked.

The usual punishment was to place the men in the stocks, outside, near the Captain's quarters. If a man was missing at roll-call, the squad of ninety to which he belonged was deprived of the ration. The "dead-line" bullet, already referred to, spared no offender. One poor fellow, just from Sherman's army—his name was Roberts—was trying to wash his face near the "dead-line" railing, when he slipped on the clayey bottom, and fell with his head just outside the fatal border. We shouted to him, but it was too late—"another guard would have a furlough," the men said. It was a common belief among our men, arising from statements made by the guard, that General WINDER, in command, issued an order that any one of the guard who should shoot a Yankee outside of the "dead-line" should have a month's furlough, but there probably was no truth in this. About two a day were thus shot, some being cases of suicide, brought on by mental depression or physical misery, the poor fellows throwing themselves, or madly rushing outside the "line."

The mental condition of a large portion of the men was melancholy, beginning in despondency and tending to a kind of stolid and idiotic indifference. Many spent much time in arousing and encouraging their fellows, but hundreds were lying about motionless, or stalking vacantly to and fro, quite beyond any help which could be given them within their prison walls. These cases were frequent among those who had been imprisoned but a short time. There were those who were captured at the first Bull Run, July 1861, and had known Belle Isle from the first, yet had preserved their physical and mental health to a wonderful degree. Many were wise and resolute enough to keep themselves occupied—some in cutting bone and wood ornaments, making their knives out of iron hoops—others in manufacturing ink from the rust from these same hoops, and with rude pens sketching or imitating bank notes, or any sample that would involve long and patient execution.

Letters from home very seldom reached us, and few had any means of writing. In the early summer, a large batch of letters—five thousand we were told—arrived, having been accumulating somewhere for many months. These were brought into camp by an officer, under orders to collect ten cents on each—of course most were returned, and we heard no more of them. One of my companions saw among them three from his parents, but he was unable to pay the charge. According to the rules of transmission of letters over the lines, these letters must have already paid ten cents each to the rebel government.

As far as we saw General Winder and Captain Wirtz [Wirz], the former was kind and considerate in his manners, the latter harsh, though not without kindly feelings.

It is a melancholy and mortifying fact, that some of our trials came from our own men. At Belle Isle and Andersonville there were among us a gang of desperate men, ready to prey on their fellows. Not only thefts and robberies, but even murders were committed. Affairs became so serious at Camp Sumter that an appeal was made to General Winder, who authorized an arrest and trial by a criminal court. Eighty-six were arrested, and six were hung, beside others who were severely punished. These proceedings effected a marked change for the better.

Some few weeks before being released, I was ordered to act as clerk in the hospital. This consists simply of a few scattered trees and fly tents, and is in charge of Dr. White, an excellent and considerate man, with very limited means, but doing all in his power for his patients. He has twenty-five assistants, besides those detailed to examine for admittance to the hospital. This examination was made in a small stockade attached to the main one, to the inside door of which the sick came or were brought by their comrades, the number to be removed being limited. Lately, in consideration of the rapidly increasing sickness, it was extended to one hundred and fifty daily. That this was too small an allowance is shown by the fact that the deaths within our stockade were from thirty to forty a day. I have seen one hundred and fifty bodies waiting passage to the "dead house," to be buried with those who died in hospital. The average of deaths through the earlier months was thirty a day: at the time I left, the average was over one hundred and thirty, and one day the record showed one hundred and forty-six.

The proportion of deaths from *starvation,* not including those consequent on the diseases originating in the character and limited quantity of food, such as diarrhœa, dysentery and scurvy, I cannot state; but to the best of my knowledge, information and belief, there were scores every month. We could, at any time, point out many for whom such a fate was inevitable, as they lay or feebly walked, mere skeletons, whose emaciation exceeded the examples given in Leslie's Illustrated for June 18, 1864. For example: in some cases the inner edges of the two bones of the arms, between the elbow and the wrist, with the intermediate blood vessels, were plainly visible when held toward the light. The ration, in quantity, was perhaps barely sufficient to sustain life, and the cases of starvation were generally those whose stomachs could not retain what had become entirely indigestible.

For a man to find, on waking, that his comrade by his side was dead, was an occurrence too common to be noted. I have seen death in almost all the forms of the hospital and battle-field, but the daily scenes in Camp Sumter exceeded in the extremity of misery all my previous experience.

The work of burial is performed by our own men, under guard and orders, twenty-five bodies being placed in a single pit, without head-boards, and the sad duty performed with indecent haste. Sometimes our men were rewarded for this work with a few sticks of fire-wood, and I have known them to quarrel over a dead body for the *job*.

Dr. White is able to give the patients a diet but little better than the prison rations—a little flour porridge, arrow-root, whiskey and wild or hog tomatoes. In the way of medicine, I saw nothing but camphor, whiskey, and a decoction of some kind of bark—white oak, I think. He often expressed his regret that he had not more medicines. The limitation of military orders, under which the surgeons in charge was placed, is shown by the following occurrence: A supposed private, wounded in the thigh, was under treatment in the hospital, when it was discovered that he was a major of a colored regiment. The assistant-surgeon, under whose immediate charge he was, proceeded at once not only to remove him, but to kick him out, and he was returned to the stockade, to shift for himself as well as he could. Dr. White could not or did not attempt to restore him.

After entering on my duties at the hospital, I was occasionally favored with double rations and some wild tomatoes. A few of our men succeeded, in spite of the closest examination of our clothes, in secreting some green-backs, and with those were able to buy useful articles at exorbitant prices:—a tea-cup of flour at one dollar; eggs, three to six dollars a dozen; salt, four dollars a pound; molasses, thirty dollars a gallon; nigger beans, a small, inferior article, (diet of the slaves and pigs, but highly relished by us,) fifty cents a pint. These figures, multiplied by ten, will give very nearly the price in Confederate currency. Though the country abounded in pine and oak, sticks were sold to us at various prices, according to size.

Our men, especially the mechanics, were tempted with the offer of liberty and large wages to take the oath of allegiance to the Confederacy, but it was very rare that their patriotism, even under such a fiery trial, ever gave way. I carry this message from one of my companions to his mother: "My treatment here is killing me, mother, but I die cheerfully for my country."

Some attempts were made to escape, but wholly in vain, for, if the prison walls and guards were passed and the protecting woods reached, the bloodhounds were sure to find us out.

Tunneling was at once attempted on a large scale, but on the afternoon preceding the night fixed on for escape, an officer rode in and announced to us that the plot was discovered, and from our huge pen we could see on the hill above us the regiments just arriving to strengthen the guard. We had been betrayed. It was our belief that spies were kept in the camp, which could very easily be done.

The number in camp when I left was nearly thirty-five thousand, and daily increasing. The number in hospital was about five thousand. I was exchanged at Port Royal Ferry, August 16th.

PRESCOTT TRACY,
Eighty-second Regiment, N. Y. V.

Sherman

IN VIRGINIA in the summer of 1864 the war had ground slow. Grant had set out on a new campaign in May. Despite heavy losses at the Wilderness, Spotsylvania Court House, Second Cold Harbor, and the Crater before Petersburg, he had kept Richmond under continuous threat and had forestalled any effective counteroffensive against the Federals. The greater manpower and greater war potential of the North was beginning to pay off, though slowly, and the Confederacy found itself faced with a war of attrition it could hardly hope to win.

Grant was the most effective of Lincoln's many choices as commander of the army in Virginia. The President stuck by his general. But a campaign which lost soldiers by the thousand could hardly be a popular one, and Lincoln and his administration were heavily criticized for their conduct of the war.

Lincoln was renominated for the Presidency, on a "National Union" ticket, by a convention which met in Baltimore early in June. The Democrats tried to capitalize on the personal popularity of General McClellan and, meeting at Chicago in late August, named him as their candidate and adopted a "peace platform" (virtually repudiated by their candidate) which called for an immediate end to the war and restoration of the Union by peaceful means.

The military situation at the end of the summer made Democratic victory in the November election a real possibility. Grant had been fighting on the Virginia line all summer, with the real extent of his success still not apparent. Sherman had followed Johnston deep into Georgia, and, though his campaign had been definitely successful, he still had not achieved a decisive victory. Lincoln badly needed a decisive victory by one of his generals, both to assure his re-election and to have a mandate through the vote of the people for thorough and complete prosecution of the war.

William Tecumseh Sherman gave him that victory. On September 1 he telegraphed the President: "Atlanta is ours and fairly won."

Sherman did not plan to garrison the city indefinitely. There would be no profit in bottling himself up there. To prepare for his further campaign he ordered all civilians to evacuate Atlanta. His order was regarded by General John B. Hood and the civilian authorities in Atlanta as one of extreme cruelty. But Sherman knew that war itself was cruelty and that if, for military purposes, the city must be destroyed before he could continue his campaign, it would be far less cruel to remove its inhabitants before the destruction. Here is his exchange of letters with the authorities in Atlanta.

THE AUTHORITIES TO GEN. SHERMAN.

ATLANTA, GA., Sept. 11, 1864.

Major-General W. T. Sherman—*Sir:* The undersigned, Mayor and two members of Council for the city of Atlanta, for the time being the only legal organ of the people of said city to express their wants and wishes, ask leave most earnestly but respectfully to petition you to reconsider the order requiring them to leave Atlanta. At first view, it struck us that the measure would involve extraordinary hardship and loss, but since we have seen the practical execution of it, so far as it has progressed, and the individual condition of many of the people, and heard the statements as to the inconvenience, loss and suffering attending it, we are satisfied that the amount of it will involve in the aggregate consequences appalling and heart-rending.

Many poor women are in an advanced state of pregnancy; others having young children, whose husbands, for the greater part, are either in the army, prisoners, or dead. Some say: "I have such a one sick at my house; who will wait on them when I am gone?" Others say: "what are we to do; we have no houses to go to, and no means to buy, build, or rent any; no parents, relatives or friends to go to." Another says: "I will try and take this or that article of property; but such and such things I must leave behind, though I need them much." We reply to them: "Gen. Sherman will carry your property to Rough and Ready, and then Gen. Hood will take it thence on;" and they will reply to that: "But I want to leave the railroad at such a place, and cannot get conveyance from thence on."

We only refer to a few facts to illustrate, in part, how this measure will operate in practice. As you advanced, the people north of us fell back, and before your arrival here a large portion of the people here had retired south; so that the country south of this is already crowded, and without sufficient houses to accommodate the people, and we are informed that many are now staying in churches and other outbuildings. This being so, how is it possible for the people still here (mostly women and children) to find shelter, and how can they live through the winter in the woods; no shelter or subsistence; in the midst of strangers who know them not, and without the power to assist them much if they were willing to do so?

This is but a feeble picture of the consequences of this measure. You know the woe, the horror, and the suffering cannot be described by words. Imagination can only conceive to it, and we ask you to take these things into consideration. We know your mind and time are continually occupied with the duties of your command, which almost deters us from asking your attention to the matter, but thought it might be that you had not considered the subject in all of its awful consequences, and that, on reflection, you, we hope, would not make this people an exception to all mankind, for we know of no such instance ever having occurred—surely not in the United States. And what has this helpless people done that they should be driven from their homes, to wander as strangers, outcasts and exiles, and to subsist on charity?

We do not know as yet the number of people still here. Of those who are here a respectable number, if allowed to remain at home, could subsist for several months without assistance; and a respectable number for a much longer time, and who might not need assistance at any time.

In conclusion, we most earnestly and solemnly petition you to reconsider this order, or modify it, and suffer this unfortunate people to remain at home and enjoy what little means they have.

Respectfully submitted,

JAMES M. CALHOUN, Mayor
E. E. RAWSON, S. C. WELLS, Councilmen.

GEN. SHERMAN'S REPLY

HDQRS. MILITARY DIVISION OF THE MISSISSIPPI, IN THE FIELD,
ATLANTA, GA., Sept. 12, 1864.

JAMES M. CALHOUN, *Mayor*, E. E. RAWSON and S. C. WELLS, *representing City Council of Atlanta.*

Gentlemen: I have your letter of the 11th, in the nature of a petition to revoke my orders removing all the inhabitants from Atlanta. I have read it carefully, and give full credit to your statements of the distress that will be occasioned by it, and yet shall not revoke my order, simply because my orders are not designed to meet the humanities of the case, but to prepare for the future struggles, in which millions, yea hundreds of millions of good people outside of Atlanta have a deep interest. We must have *Peace*, not only at Atlanta, but in all America. To secure this, we must stop the war that now desolates our once happy and favored country. To stop war we must defeat the Rebel armies that are arrayed against the laws and Constitution which all must respect and obey. To defeat these armies we must prepare the way to reach them in their recesses, provided with the arms and instruments which enable us to accomplish our purpose.

Now, I know the vindictive nature of our enemy, and that we may have many years of military operations from this quarter, and therefore deem it wise and prudent to prepare in time. The use of Atlanta for warlike purposes is inconsistent with its character as a home for families. There will

be no manufactures, commerce or agriculture here for the
maintenance of families, and sooner or later want will compel the inhabitants to go. Why not *go now,* when all the
arrangements are completed for the transfer, instead of
waiting till the plunging shot of contending armies will renew the scene of the past month? Of course I do not apprehend any such thing at this moment, but you do not suppose
that this army will be here till the war is over. I cannot discuss this subject with you fairly, because I cannot impart
to you what I propose to do, but I assert that my military
plans make it necessary for the inhabitants to go away, and
I can only renew my offer of services to make their exodus
in any direction as easy and comfortable as possible. You
cannot qualify war in harsher terms than I will.

War is cruelty, and you cannot refine it; and those who
brought war on the country deserve all the curses and male-
dictions a people can pour out. I know I had no hand in
making this war, and I know I will make more sacrifices
to-day than any of you to secure peace. But you cannot have
peace and a division of our country. If the United States
submits to a division now, it will not stop, but will go on
until we reap the fate of Mexico, which is eternal war. The
United States does and must assert its authority wherever
it has power; if it relaxes one bit to pressure it is gone, and
I know that such is not the national feeling. This feeling
assumes various shapes, but always comes back to that of
Union. Once admit the Union, once more acknowledge the
authority of the National Government, and instead of devoting your houses and streets and roads to the dread uses of
war, I, and this army, become at once your protectors and
supporters, shielding you from danger, let it come from what
quarters it may. I know that a few individuals cannot resist
a torrent of error and passion such as has swept the South

into rebellion; but you can point out, so that we may know those who desire a Government and those who insist on war and its desolation.

You might as well appeal against the thunderstorm as against these terrible hardships of war. They are inevitable, and the only way the people of Atlanta can hope once more to live in peace and quiet at home is to stop this war which can alone be done by admitting that it began in error and is perpetuated in pride. We don't want your negroes or your horses, or your houses or your land, or anything you have; but we do want and will have a just obedience to the laws of the United States. That we will have, and if it involves the destruction of your improvements, we cannot help it. You have heretofore read public sentiment in your news-papers, that live by falsehood and excitement, and the quicker you seek for truth in other quarters the better for you.

I repeat, then, that, by the original compact of the govern-ment, the United States had certain rights in Georgia which have never been relinquished, and never will be; that the South began war by seizing forts, arsenals, mints, custom-houses, etc., etc., long before Mr. Lincoln was installed, and before the South had one jot or tittle of provocation. I my-self have seen in Missouri, Kentucky, Tennessee, and Mis-sissippi, hundreds and thousands of women and children fleeing from your armies and desperadoes, hungry and with bleeding feet. In Memphis, Vicksburg, and Mississippi we fed thousands upon thousands of the families of rebel sol-diers left on our hands, and whom we could not see starve. Now that war comes home to you, you feel very different— you deprecate its horrors, but did not feel them when you sent car-loads of soldiers and ammunition and molded shell and shot to carry war into Kentucky and Tennessee, and desolate the homes of hundreds and thousands of good people, who only asked to live in peace at their old homes, and under the government of their inheritance. But these comparisons are idle. I want peace, and believe it can only be reached through Union and war, and I will ever conduct war purely with a view to perfect and early success.

But, my dear sirs, when that peace does come, you may call on me for anything. Then will I share with you the last cracker, and watch with you to shield your homes and families against danger from every quarter. Now, you must go, and take with you the old and feeble; feed and nurse them, and build for them in more quiet places proper habitations to shield them against the weather, until the mad passions of men cool down, and allow the Union and peace once more to settle on your old homes at Atlanta.

Yours, in haste,

W. T. SHERMAN, Maj.-Gen.

Sheridan at Winchester

B<small>Y THE FALL</small> of 1864 the generals who the North, in
1861, had expected to be the heroes of the war were
gone from the scene. In their stead there had risen a
new breed of generals, a new breed of heroes. Schooled
in the war itself, Grant, Sherman, Phil Sheridan, George
Thomas asked no quarter and gave none. They knew
war was rough and cruel and were willing to accept it
on its own terms.

The next selection describes Sheridan's victory over
Confederate General Jubal A. Early in September, 1864.
This was the second Battle of Winchester, "Stonewall"
Jackson having bested General Banks there in 1862, and
the town had changed hands a number of times during
the course of the war. After his win over Early, Sheridan
proceeded systematically to destroy the supplies and the
potential for supplies in the Valley of Virginia. He defeated Early a second time a month later at Cedar Creek
in the battle made famous by T. Buchanan Read's poem
"Sheridan's Ride."

This description of the September battle is by John
William DeForest, a veteran of the campaigns of the

Army of the Gulf, who was here in his first fighting in Virginia. DeForest later became known as the author of the first truly realistic Civil War novel, *Miss Ravenel's Conversion from Secession to Loyalty.*

SHERIDAN'S BATTLE OF WINCHESTER.

On the morning of the 19th of September, 1864, I was marching at the head of my company along the narrow and wooded gorge through which the Berryville and Winchester pike winds between the Opequan Creek and the town of Winchester. My regiment belonged to the Second Brigade of the First Division of the Nineteenth Army Corps, and formed a fraction of the Army of Major-General Philip Sheridan, which, at two o'clock that morning, had quitted its intrenched position near Berryville.

For a month Sheridan had been watching his opportunity. He had advanced to Front Royal, and retreated to Halltown; he had manoeuvred in face of a superior enemy with curious and happy dexterity; he had guarded himself, where it was necessary to make a stand, with miles of field-fortifications; he had parried Early's threatened second raid upon Washington and Pennsylvania; and now, when his antagonist was weakened by the departure of Kershaw's division, he promptly resumed the offensive.

The army at this moment was engaged in the perilous movement of filing through a narrow gorge and deploying in face of a strongly-posted and veteran enemy. The road was crowded with artillery, ammunition-wagons, and ambulances, all hurrying forward. On each side of it a line of infantry in column of march stumbled over the rocky, guttered ground, and struggled through the underbrush. The multitudes of men who belong to an army, yet who do not fight—the cooks, the musicians, the hospital attendants, the quarter-masters' and commissaries' people, the sick, and the skulkers—sat on every rock and under every bush, watching us pass. Here, too, were jammed the troopers of the cavalry advance, who, for the present, had finished their fighting, having cleared the passage of the Opequan Creek, and opened the way thus far for the infantry and artillery. Presently we met litters loaded with pale sufferers, and passed a hospital-tent, inside of which I saw surgeons surrounding a table, and amputated limbs and pools of blood underneath it. The stern and sad business of the day had evidently begun in front, although the sound of it was not yet audible to us, excepting an occasional boom of cannon, deadened to a dull *pum pum* by the woods and the distance.

The battle of Winchester was fought on this plan: A narrow ravine, winding among hills so steep and thickly wooded as to be impassable for any troops but light infantry, debouches into an irregular, undulating valley, faced on the south by an amphitheatre of stony heights, laid, with regard to each other, like detached fortifications. The object of Sheridan was to pass through this ravine, deploy in the valley, amuse the enemy's right, fight his centre vigorously, turn and force his left. The object of Early was to allow us to deploy up to a certain extent; then to beat in our attacking columns and throw them back in confusion on our line of advance; lastly, to ruin us by pushing his strong left through our right, and reaching the mouth of the gorge so as to cut off our retreat. To effect this final purpose his army was not drawn up at right angles to the pike, but diagonally to it, so as to bring his left nearer to our vital debouching point. And this fatal stroke he attempted early in the day, with a strong column, pushed with remarkable vigor, and for a time with terrible promise of success.

At about ten o'clock the head of the Sixth Corps emerged from the ravine, took ground rapidly to the left, and advanced in two lines, the first of which presently carried a rifle-pit and wood that formed the outwork of the enemy's right. This right being refused, or held aloof, our extreme left had throughout the day, so far as I could learn, no very serious fighting. The opening struggle of supreme importance came in the centre, where it was necessary, firstly, to gain ground enough to bring up our second line: and, secondly, to hold the approaches to the ravine at no matter what cost of slaughter. I beg the reader to remark that if this was not done our striking right could not be deployed, and our retreat could not be secured; that if this was not done there could be no victory, and there must be—if the enemy pushed us with energy—calamitous defeat. Upon the Nineteenth Corps and upon Ricketts' Division of the Sixth Corps devolved this bloody task. They were to sustain the principal burden of the battle during the long hours which would be necessary to let the Eighth Corps sweep around on its more enviable and brilliant mission of turning the hostile position. How the Nineteenth Corps performed its portion of the task is shown by its list of killed and wounded. Swept by musketry and artillery from the front, enfiladed by artillery from the right, pressed violently by the one grand column of attack which Early massed to decide the battle, it bled, but it stood, and, after hours of suffering, advanced.

Closely following the Sixth Corps—lapping its rear, indeed —Grover's Division emerged from the defile at a little before eleven o'clock, and forming in two lines, each consisting of two brigades, moved promptly forward in superb order.

Steep hills and a thick wood, impracticable for artillery until engineered, rendered it necessary for the infantry to open the contest without the support of cannon. In face of a vigorous shelling the column swept over the hills, struggled through the wood, and emerged upon a broad stretch of rolling fields, on the other side of which lay the rebel force, supported by another wood and by a ledge of rocks, which answered the purpose of a fortification, with the semicircular heights of Winchester in the rear, as a final rallying base. As the lines of advance from the gorge were divergent, opening outward like the blades of a fan, General Emory found it necessary, in order to keep up a connection with the Sixth Corps, to hurry Molineux's brigade from the rear to the front. This was done at a double-quick, in face of the hostile musketry, without checking the general advance. And now the division quickened its pace into a charge of unusual and unintended impetuosity, the officers being dragged on by the eagerness of the men, the skirmishers firing as they ran, and the brigades following at a right-shoulder-shift, with deafening yells. Birge's men carried the detached wood with a rush: they were ordered to halt there and lie down, but it was impossible to stop them; they hurried on, pell-mell, and drove the enemy three hundred yards beyond. The rebel General Rhodes [Rodes] was killed while placing a battery in position. Three colonels taken by Sharpe's Brigade were sent back to Emory as prisoners. Early's first line in the centre was every where thrown back in confusion.

But an advance as vehement as this is liable to sudden reverse when the attacked party has a strong second line well in hand, as was the case on the present occasion. It is possible even that Grover's opening success changed the plans of Early, and forced him quicker than he had intended into decisive action. At all events he suddenly developed at this early stage of the battle the greatest mass of troops that he showed at any period of the day. From the position where it had been lying sheltered a force estimated at two divisions of infantry rose up, poured in a stunning volley, followed by a steady file-fire, and moved forward against the ranks of Grover and Ricketts, already disordered by their rapid push. Artillery on a height near Winchester, firing over the heads of the rebel troops, and other artillery on a height far to our right, enfilading our line, supported the movement with shell, grape, and canister. For a while this powerful and well-timed advance was fearfully successful, and threatened Sheridan with repulse, if not with serious disaster. Ricketts' Division was forced, after a bloody though brief struggle, up the Berryville and Winchester pike toward the mouth of that gorge which was so vital to our army. Grover's line fought for a time at close quarters; for instance his extreme left regiment, the One Hundred and Fifty-Sixth New York (Lieutenant-Colonel Neafie), faced a rebel regiment at thirty yards distance; and around the colors of the latter not more than forty men remained, the rest having fled or fallen. But now the One Hundred and Fifty-Sixth, and presently the entire brigade, was exposed to a fatal fire from the left flank as well as from the front. Neafie's loss of one hundred and fifteen men nearly all occurred at this time and within a few minutes. Colonel Sharpe, commanding the brigade, and all the regimental commanders except one, were disabled. To attempt to hold the position longer was to be slaughtered uselessly or to be taken prisoners. The order to retire was given, and passed rapidly down the division line from left to right, being obeyed by each brigade in succession. The bloody but victorious advance was changed into a bloody and ominous retreat.

And here let me beg the reader to conceive the inevitable

circumstances of hopeless, unresisting slaughter which attend the withdrawal of troops from the immediate presence of a powerful enemy. There is no inspiriting return of blow for blow; there is no possibility of quelling the hostile fire by an answering fire; the soldier marches gloomily in his file, imagining that his foe is ever gaining on him; the ranks are rapidly thinned, and the organization of the companies shattered; and thus, from both physical and moral causes, the bravest battalions go to pieces. Rarely does it happen, if ever, that a force is extricated from this fearful trial without breaking. Grover's and Ricketts' commands reached the base from which they had advanced in a state of confusion which threatened wide-spread disaster. Sixth Corps men and Nineteenth Corps men were crowding together up the line of the Berryville pike, while to the right and left of it the fields were dotted with fugitives, great numbers of them wounded, bursting out of the retiring ranks and rushing toward the cover of the forest. Some regiments disappeared for a time as organizations. Early's veterans advanced steadily, with yells of triumph and a constant roll of murderous musketry, threatening to sweep away our centre and render our struggle a defeat almost before it had become a battle. It was the bloodiest, the darkest, the most picturesque, the most dramatic, the only desperate moment of the day. General Emory and General Grover, with every brigade commander and every staff officer present, rode hither and thither through the fire, endeavoring by threats, commands, and entreaties to halt and re-form the panic-stricken stragglers.

"Halt here, men," Emory cried to group after group. "Here is good cover. Halt and form a line here."

"I am looking for my own regiment," was the usual reply.

"Never mind your own regiments. Never mind if you belong to fifty regiments. Make a regiment here."

Pointing out other groups to this and that officer of his staff, he would say, "My God! look at these men; ride over to them, and bring them up here."

Captain Yorke of the staff seized a regimental flag and bore it forward, shouting, "Men, don't desert your colors," when a spent ball struck him in the throat, paralyzing him for a time and causing him to drop his burden. Of the other staff officers Captain Wilkinson had his horse killed under him. Captain Coley had a bullet pass through his coat collar, and Major Walker received a spent shot in his shoulder.

One instance of coolness and discipline, which contrasted curiously with the general panic, was noticed by Captain Bradbury of the First Maine Battery, now Major and Chief of Artillery on General Emory's staff. Through the midst of the confusion came a captain of infantry, Rigby of the Twenty-fourth Iowa, leading a sergeant and twelve men, all marching as composedly as if returning from drill.

"Captain, you are not going to retreat any further, I hope?" said Bradbury.

"Certainly not," was the reply. "Halt; front. Three cheers, men; hip, hip, hurrah!"

The little band cheered lustily. It was the first note of defiance that broke the desperate monotony of the panic; it gave heart to every one who heard it, and made an end of retreat in that part of the field. In a few minutes the platoon swelled to a battalion composed of men from half a dozen regiments.

"Bradbury," said General Grover, "you must push a section into the gap. We *must* show a front there."

Under a heavy fire of musketry and artillery two pieces galloped into the open, under the charge of Bradbury himself, and, unsupported by infantry, commenced a cannonade which assisted greatly in checking the rebel advance and encouraging our men to rally. A Confederate line which attempted to carry these pieces was repulsed in a somewhat singular manner. General Emory had personally aided in rallying the One Hundred and Thirty-first New York, and had posted it in a narrow grove projecting from the wood which now formed Grover's base of resistance. The charging rebels were allowed to pass this point, and then a volley was poured into their backs. As they staggered under the unexpected shock a fire was opened upon their front by another rallied line, and breaking ranks, they fled pell-mell across the fields to cover.

Thus piece by piece our shattered first line was picked up and reunited. The rebel attack was checked, and a large portion of the lost ground recovered. On the left Neafie, now commanding the Third Brigade, made a second charge nearly up to his original position, while on the right Molineux pushed a line to within two hundred yards of the isolated wood which Birge had carried and lost. And now came into action the famous First Division of the Nineteenth Corps—a division that had never been put to shame on any field of battle, the division that under Weitzel had triumphed at Camp Bisland and Port Hudson, that under Emory had prevented defeat at Sabine Cross Roads and Pleasant Hill. From this moment my story of the battle will become to some extent a record of personal observation.

We of the First Division were already out of the defile, and drawn up in two columns behind Grover, when the failure of his attack became evident. The difficulty was, not that we were not in hand, but that, as we had only two brigades present (the Third having been left at Halltown), we were hardly strong enough to face the enemy's left, which far outreached our right, and at the same time make head against the vehement attack which threatened our centre.

It had been intended that we should remain in reserve until the time came for us to join the Eighth Corps, in the grand turning movement of the day. Now we must fill up gaps, run from one imperiled point to another, and, in short, be used as the urgency of circumstances required.

Lying in a hollow across which the rebel shell screamed harmlessly, I saw our First Brigade disappear over the crest of the hill in our front. Then we of the Second Brigade moved in column to the right, and halted on a lofty slope, where we could discover some parts of the field of battle, and where the earth was occasionally furrowed by the shot of hostile artillery. Far away to the left I saw a part of the Sixth Corps mount an aclivity and charge into a wood on its summit from which the smoke of musketry issued. I distinguished their distant cheer, and rejoiced in their gallantry and triumph. We knew nothing all this while of the disaster which had occurred in our front, and did not doubt that we should have our customary success. Presently we advanced into the wood, on the extreme verge of which Grover's men were rallying and resuming the conflict. We did not see them, but we plainly heard the incessant rattle of their musketry, and, not knowing the rolling nature of the ground, wondered that the bullets did not hum more frequently through our ranks. Soon we turned to the right again, and emerged into an opening from which we obtained our first clear view of the fighting. Nearly a quarter of a mile in advance of us we saw our First Brigade in line behind a rail-fence, the men kneeling or lying down and keeping up a violent file-firing. Two hundred yards beyond them was the wood which Early had retaken from Birge, a smoke of rebel musketry now rising from it, although not a rebel was visible. As we looked our men rose up, formed, faced about and came slowly toward us, the officers running hither and thither to check a momentary confusion in the ranks. The report flew along our line that they were ordered back to the fence where we stood, and that we were to relieve them; but while we watched the unaccomplished movement two of our four regiments, the Twelfth Connecticut and Eighth Vermont, were faced to the left and hurried back through the wood which we had just traversed. The last thing that I saw as I re-entered the covert was the One Hundred and Sixteenth New York facing about with a cheer and charging back to the fence. I afterward learned that the whole brigade followed it; that the line was a second time ordered back, and then again resumed its position. Here it was that the One Hundred and Fourteenth New York offered up its glorious sacrifice of one hundred and eighty-eight men and officers, being three-fifths of the number which it took into battle. After the engagement the position of the brigade was distinguishable by a long, straight line of dead and dying, here and there piled one upon another, the prostrate and bloody ranks telling with matchless eloquence how the American soldier can fight.

While the One Hundred and Sixtieth New York and Forty-seventh Pennsylvania remained to support the First Brigade and share its fatal honors my regiment and the Eighth Vermont moved back to the centre. We were apparently wanted in many places at once. Pressing and contradictory orders repeatedly changed our direction and position. It was, "Forward!" and "About face!" "By the right flank!" and "By the left flank!" "Double quick!" and "Halt!" until our heads were half turned by the confusion. At last we came to the outskirt of the wood, and looked out upon Grover's field of battle. No ranks of enemies were visible athwart those undulating fields, but there were long light lines of smoke from musketry and great piles of smoke from batteries, while the rush and crash of shell tore through the forest. Bradbury was putting two of his pieces in position, and we lay down in their rear to support them. General Emory and General Dwight, mounted and surrounded by staff officers, were a little to the front surveying the position. "My God!" remarked the former as he saw men and horses falling around him, "this is a perfect slaughterhouse. It must be held; it is the key of the position. But tell Captain Bradbury to keep his people covered as much as possible."

Here fell one of the best and bravest gentlemen in the service, the only field-officer present with our regiment, Lieutenant-Colonel Peck. He had just given the command, "Officers rectify the alignment," as we were about to move forward, when a shell burst among us, one piece of it shattering his knee and mortally mangling the arteries. A moment afterward the Eighth and Twelfth were ordered to move into the open, wheel to the right, and relieve a portion of Molineux's brigade, which lay about two hundred yards from the isolated wood. At a double quick we went nearly a quarter of a mile over gently-rolling fields, pulling up occasionally from pure lack of breath, and then hurrying on again, until we flung ourselves on the ground among the Fourteenth New Hampshire and One Hundred and Thirty-first New York. As the enemy were firing low we suffered very little in our advance; but we had not been in position five minutes before we felt how coolly and surely Lee's veterans could aim; for, stretched at full length as we all were, and completely concealed by tall grass, the bullets searched out our covert with fatal certainty. A groan here, a shriek of agony there, a dying convulsion, a plunge of some wounded wretch to the rear, showed from instant to instant how rapidly our men were being disabled. We lay on a gentle, very gentle slope, and aimed upward, so that our fire was probably even more fatal than that of our adversaries, an ascending range being more sure of its mark than a descending one. After a quarter of an hour here (what a Frenchman would call a *mauvais quart d'heure*), our commander, Captain Clarke, ordered a volley. With the usual cautionary commands from the officers of "Steady men!" "Wait for the word!" "Aim low!" the regiment rose up, closed its ranks, and poured in a splendid crash of musketry, dropping immediately that it was delivered. For a few minutes our antagonists were silenced. Perhaps we had slaughtered them; perhaps the venomous flight of hissing Miniés had frightened them into taking cover; perhaps they simply saved their powder because they supposed that we were about to charge. But presently the steady file-firing was resumed. On each side the men fired low, fired slowly, fired calmly, knowing full well the hostile position, although able to discover no hostile sign except the light opposing line of musketry smoke. For two or more hours this tranquil, changeless, mortal contest continued. For two or more hours the bullets whizzed through the grass which scarcely concealed us, striking into our prostrate ranks so frequently that every one occasionally searched the branches of the trees in our front to discover the forms of hostile sharp-shooters. It seemed impossible that they could strike so many of us, and yet not see us. Of the seventy men and officers whom our regiment lost during the day, at least sixty must have been hit on this line. But the enemy fired much more rapidly and continuously than we did. The word was repeatedly passed along our ranks to spare the cartridges, for we were a long way from our supports, or from any chance of replenishing ammunition, and it was necessary to save shots enough to repulse the rebels in case they should charge us with the bayonet.

"Fire down to ten cartridges a piece, and then stop," was the order of our commander.

A curious change came over our men during this long trial. At first they were grave and anxious, but this passed away as they became accustomed to the position; at the last they laughed, jested, and recklessly exposed themselves. Corporal Gray, of Company C, dashed to the front, and with his shelter-tent beat out a flame which was kindling in the autumn grass, returning unhurt out of a frightful peril. "Here's one for Corporal Gray!" shouted several men, leaping up and pulling trigger. Then followed, "Here's one for Sheridan!" and "Here's one for Lincoln!" and "Here's one for M'Clellan, who'll pay us off in gold!" and "Here's one for Jeff Davis!" until the grim joke was played out for lack of cartridges.

All this time our dead and wounded lay among us, with the exception of a few of the latter who crawled a little to the rear, and found shelter in a ditch. Among us, too, were the dead and wounded of the regiments which we had relieved; and the ground in front of us was strewn with other sufferers who had fallen there when Birge met his reverse. The position of these last was horrible; the musketry of both sides passed over them in a constant stream; the balls of friend and foe added to their agony, or closed it in death. One of our men, Private Brown, of Company C, was mortally wounded while giving a drink of water to an officer of an Iowa regiment who lay within ten paces of us, pierced by three bullets. We could not carry away these children of suffering, not even our own, until the battle should be over. It was forbidden by orders; it was contrary to the regulations of the United States Army; it would have been simply an act of well-meant folly and cruelty. We could not spare the men who would surely be killed or wounded in the attempt; or who, reaching the shelter of the rear with their dangerous burdens, would not find their way back again.

I have been thus minute in describing this experience of our regiment in close line-fighting, because it was a picture of what passed in every part of the field during the central period of the battle. Along the entire front each side clung to its own positions, too exhausted or too cautious to advance, and too obstinate to recede. The duty of the Sixth and Nineteenth Corps now was to hold the enemy desperately occupied until the Eighth Corps could execute the turning movement with which Sheridan meant to decide the combat.

At three o'clock the hour of defeat for Early struck. To our right, *where* precisely I could not see because of the rolling nature of the ground, but in the direction of the spot where our First Brigade was forming those prostrate and bloody ranks which I have previously mentioned, we heard a mighty battle-yell, which never ceased for ten minutes, telling us that Crook and his men were advancing. To meet this yell there arose from the farthest sweep of the isolated wood, where it rounded away toward the rebel rear, the most terrific, continuous wail of musketry that I ever heard. It was not a volley, nor a succession of volleys, but an uninterrupted explosion without a single break or tremor. As I listened to it I despaired of the success of the attack, for it did not seem to me possible that any troops could endure such a fire. The captain of our right company, who was so placed that he could see the advance, afterward described it to me as magnificent in its steadiness; the division which accomplished it moving across the open fields in a single line without visible supports, the ranks kept well dressed, in spite of the stream of dead and wounded which dropped to the rear, the pace being the ordinary quick-step, and the men firing at will, but coolly and rarely.

At this moment our whole army assumed the offensive. Looking back I saw General Emory's reserves emerging from the wood in our rear. And now occurred one of those happy dashes, almost spontaneous in their character, which so frequently aid in deciding a battle. At the first yell of Crook's charge our men reopened fire violently, exhausting their ammunition in five minutes; and then Colonel Thomas, of the Eighth Vermont, regardless of unloaded muskets and empty cartridge-boxes, led on his command at a double quick with the bayonet. General officers and staff officers, misunderstanding the orders of General Emory, which were to advance, came up at a gallop, telling us that we were to be relieved by the One Hundred and Sixtieth New York, warning us to wait for our supports, and shouting, "Halt! Lie down!" But it was impossible to check the crowd of yelling, running madmen; a few would hesitate, and stare around at their advancing comrades, then they would dash on with renewed speed to make up the lost distance. While the regiment thus wavered between discipline and impulse, a mounted officer belonging, as I afterward heard, to Sheridan's staff—a florid, dashing young fellow, in a gayly-embroidered blue shirt, with trowsers tucked into his long boots —galloped in front of us from the direction of the Eighth Corps, and pointed to the wood with his drawn sabre. It was the most chivalrous, the most picturesque equestrianism of battle that I ever saw. It was as fine as a painting of Horace Vernet or of Wouvermans. As a contrasting picture, let me introduce an infantry officer whom I noticed at the same moment, running breathless, twenty feet in advance of the line, his blanket-roll over his shoulders, and his sword sheathed, but waving his men forward with a large brierwood pipe, for he was smoking when the charge was ordered. From the instant that that American St. George in the embroidered shirt appeared all hope of stopping us vanished. The men sprang out with a yell like wild beasts, and the wood was carried on a full run, while the rebels rushed out of it at the top of their speed, many of them throwing away their guns and accoutrements. As we came in from one side Crook's troops entered from another, the two commands converging, and for a moment mingling together in the tumultuous triumph.

Thus passed the crisis of the battle. Early had used up at least two divisions of infantry in retaking and endeavoring to hold this wood, which was so essential to him; firstly, as covering his centre, and secondly, as being his most favorable base whence to launch an attack against our course of retreat, the Berryville and Winchester Pike. The slaughter in and around the grove proved the importance which each party attached to the possession of it. Looking down the gentle slopes over which our troops had advanced, retreated, and again advanced, we saw piles and lines of dead and wounded which could hardly be estimated at less than fifteen hundred men. In the wood lay the slaughtered skirmishers of Birge's brigade, mingled with the dead and severely wounded of the rebels, who also dotted the fields beyond. I noticed that most of our slain here had been stripped of their clothing, probably to cover the backs of Early's ragged soldiers. Colonel Thomas observed one of our officers propped against a tree with a wounded rebel on each side of him.

"Courage, my friend," said he. "We will take care of you soon; but first we want to finish the enemy."

The sufferer waved his hand feebly, and answered in a low voice, "Colonel, you are doing it gloriously."

Thomas started, for he now recognized in this mortally wounded man his old companion in arms, the brave Lieutenant-Colonel Babcock, of the Seventy-fifth New York, formerly of our brigade.

"Don't trouble yourself about me now," said Babcock. "But when you have done your fighting, will you spare me a couple of men to carry me away?"

Thomas promised, and followed his regiment. Colonel Babcock's watch and money had been taken by a rebel officer, probably with the intention of preserving them for him; but he had also been plundered in cruel earnest by the soldiers, who roughly dragged off his boots although one of his thighs was shattered by a musket-ball.

The Eighth Corps now moved against the heights, where Early made his final stand. The Eighth Vermont and One Hundred and Sixtieth New York, in conjunction with Upton's men of the Sixth Corps, followed the troops who had been forced out of the wood, and, flanking them with a heavy enfilading fire, drove them successively from a rail-fence and a stone-wall, where they attempted to rally. Lieutenant-Colonel Van Petten, of the One Hundred and Sixtieth, already had a bullet through the thigh, but refused to give up the command of his regiment until the fighting was over. As he led off at the head of it General Emory said to him, "Colonel, you are going into a hot fire; you had better dismount."

"Can't walk, Sir," replied Van Petten, pointing to his bandaged thigh, and rode onward.

Our regiment halted in the grove, and waited for ammunition. Twice it wheeled into column of companies to give passage to Birge's and Molineux's brigades of Grover's Division, which were now pushed up as supports to the general advance. I could not see that these commands bore any trace of the repulse of the morning; the ranks moved steadily, and the air of the men was composed and resolute. It must be observed, however, that up to this time I did not know that our line had suffered any disaster. They had just passed when a mounted officer, followed by a single orderly, galloped up to us. As he reined in his horse a rebel shell, one of the many which were now tearing through the wood, burst within a few feet of him, actually seeming to crown his head with its deadly halo of smoke and humming fragments.

"That's all right, boys," he said, with careless laugh. "No matter; we can lick them."

The men laughed; then a whisper ran along the ranks that it was Sheridan; then they burst into a spontaneous cheer.

"What regiment is this?" he asked, and dashed off toward the firing.

Presently we advanced, in support of a battery of artillery, over high ground lately occupied by Early's centre. Our close fighting was over, and for the rest of the day we were spectators. At the distance of half a mile from us, too far away to distinguish the heroism of individuals, but near enough to observe all the grand movements and results, the last scene of the victorious drama was acted out. Crook's column carried the heights and the fort which crowned them. We could see the long, dark lines moving up the stony slopes; we could see and hear the smoke and clatter of musketry on the deadly summit; then we could hear our comrades' cheer of victory. Early's battle was rapidly reduced to a simple struggle to save himself from utter rout. His mounted force had been beaten as usual by Averell, Torbert, and Custer. His infantry, dreadfully weakened by killed, wounded, prisoners, and stragglers, was retreating in confusion, presenting no reliable line of resistance. And now, just in the nick of time, our cavalry formed its connection with the extreme right of our infantry, so that Sheridan was able to use it

promptly to complete his victory. I saw a brigade of these
gallant troopers gallop in a long, straight line along the crest
of the hill, rush upon Early's rear, and break up and sweep
away his disorganized regiments as easily, to all appearance,
as a billow tosses its light burden of sea-weed. Seven hundred prisoners and two guns were the results of this well-
timed and brilliant onslaught. It was, I believe, the most
effective cavalry charge that has been delivered during the
war; and it was certainly one of the most spirit-stirring and
magnificent spectacles conceivable.

The victory was now won, and our infantry quietly bivouacked two miles beyond the field of battle, while the cavalry pushed on picking up materiel and prisoners.

The fruit of the battle, gathered on the spot or during the
pursuit of the next day, were five cannon, fifteen flags, six or
seven thousand small arms, and three thousand prisoners,
besides two thousand wounded who were left on the field, or
in the town of Winchester, or on the road between there and
Strasburg. The entire loss of the enemy in killed, wounded,
and prisoners, and in stragglers who did not again rejoin him,
could not have been less than seven thousand men. But the
results of this bloody and successful combat did not stop
here. It thoroughly demoralized Early's remaining troops,
thus rendering possible, indeed rendering easy, the extraordinary victory of Strasburg, which was but the sequel, the
moral consequence, of that of Winchester.

Of the loss of our own army I can not speak with certainty
for lack of official information. But the heaviest slaughter
must have fallen, I think, upon the Nineteenth Corps, which
had nineteen hundred and forty killed and wounded, besides
losing some prisoners, most of whom, however, were recaptured.

It was the first battle of our corps in Virginia; and I must say that Lee's veterans somewhat disappointed us. They made desperate fighting, but not more desperate than we had been accustomed to see. They were neither better nor worse soldiers than the Texans, Louisianians, Arkansans, and Alabamians, whom we had met, and had beaten too, in the Department of the Gulf.

Victory for Christmas

SHERMAN MOVED SOUTHEAST from Atlanta in mid-November. Hood had marched north in a vain attempt to carry the war to Federal territory. Sherman had no serious opposition to impede his course to Savannah. In Tennessee Hood ran headlong into the well-trained Union veterans under General George H. Thomas. Sherman took Savannah almost without incident. Thomas repulsed Hood in decisive battles at Nashville and Franklin, Tennessee.

Sherman was in Savannah, in contact with Federal navy units, and poised to attack Charleston or to aim a march north toward Virginia. His old foe, the Confederate Army of Tennessee, had been wrecked by Thomas and could no longer give him trouble. With only General Joe Wheeler to harass him on a march or General William J. Hardee to oppose him with an outnumbered and worn-out army at Charleston there was every reason for this to be a happy Christmas in the loyal states.

The "Official Bulletin" released by the War Department and published in the *Army and Navy Official Gazette* reflected the heightened pace with which the war

321

entered its final stages. A high spot in them is General Sherman's Christmas message to President Lincoln.

SAVANNAH, GA., *December* 22, 1864,
Via FORTRESS MONROE, *Dec.* 25.

To His Excellency President LINCOLN:

I beg to present you, as a Christmas gift, the city of Savannah, with one hundred and fifty heavy guns and plenty of ammunition; and also about twenty-five thousand (25,000) bales of cotton. W. T. SHERMAN,
Major General.

1865

Peace Conference

B Y FEBRUARY, 1865, the Confederates were anxious, even desperate, for peace. Confederate Vice-President Alexander H. Stephens, John A. Campbell, and Robert M. T. Hunter met with President Lincoln and Secretary of State Seward in an informal conference at Hampton Roads on February 3 to discuss possible peace terms.

President Lincoln would not accede to any conditions on less than the terms he had already enunciated: "no cessation or suspension of hostilities, except on the basis of the disbandment of the insurgent forces, and the restoration of the national authority throughout all the States in the Union" and no departure "from the positions he had heretofore assumed in the proclamation of emancipation and other documents."

The conference produced no immediate results, but the end grew nearer.

Here is Secretary Seward's letter to Charles Francis Adams in London, written to keep the ambassador apprised of developments at home.

DEPARTMENT OF STATE,
Washington, February, 7, 1865.

SIR: It is a truism, that in times of peace there are always instigators of war. So soon as a war begins there are citizens who impatiently demand negotiations for peace. The advocates of war, after an agitation, longer or shorter, generally gain their fearful end, though the war declared is not unfrequently unnecessary and unwise. So peace agitators in time of war ultimately bring about an abandonment of the conflict, sometimes without securing the advantages which were originally expected from the conflict.

The agitators for war in time of peace, and for peace in time of war, are not necessarily, or perhaps ordinarily, unpatriotic in their purposes or motives. Results alone determine whether they are wise or unwise. The treaty of peace concluded at Guadalupe Hidalgo was secured by an irregular negotiator, under the ban of the government. Some of the efforts which have been made to bring about negotiations with a view to end our civil war are known to the whole world, because they have employed foreign as well as domestic agents. Others, with whom you have had to deal confidentially, are known to yourself, although they have not publicly transpired. Other efforts have occurred here which are known only to the persons actually moving in them and to this government. I am now to give, for your information, an account of an affair, of the same general character, which recently received much attention here, and which, doubtless, will excite inquiry abroad.

A few days ago Francis P. Blair, esq., of Maryland, obtained from the President a simple leave to pass through our military lines, without definite views known to the government. Mr. Blair visited Richmond, and on his return he showed to the President a letter which Jefferson Davis had written to Mr. Blair, in which Davis wrote that Mr. Blair was at liberty to say to President Lincoln that Davis was now, as he always had been, willing to send commissioners, if assured they would be received, or to receive any that should be sent; that he was not disposed to find obstacles in forms. He would send commissioners to confer with the President, with a view to a restoration of peace between the two countries, if he could be assured they would be received. The President thereupon, on the 18th of January, addressed a note to Mr. Blair, in which the President, after acknowledging that he had read the note of Mr. Davis, said that he was, is, and always should be willing to receive any agents that Mr. Davis or any other influential person now actually resisting the authority of the government might send to confer informally with the President, with a view to the restoration of peace to the people of our one common country. Mr. Blair visited Richmond with this letter, and then again came back to Washington. On the 29th instant we were advised from the camp of Lieutenant General Grant that Alexander H. Stephens, R. M. T. Hunter, and John A. Campbell were applying for leave to pass through the lines to Washington, as peace commissioners, to confer with the President. They were permitted by the Lieutenant General to come to his headquarters, to await there the decision of the President. Major Eckert was sent down to meet the party from Richmond at General Grant's headquarters. The major was directed to deliver to them a copy of the President's letter to Mr. Blair, with a note to be addressed to them, and signed by the major, in which they were directly informed that if they should be allowed to pass our lines they would be understood as coming for an informal conference, upon the basis of the aforenamed letter of the 18th of January to Mr. Blair. If they should express their assent to this condition in writing, then Major Eckert was directed to give them safe conduct to Fortress Monroe, where a person coming from the President would meet them. It being thought probable, from a report of their conversation with Lieutenant General Grant, that the Richmond party would, in the manner prescribed, accept the condition mentioned, the Secretary of State was charged by the President with the duty of representing this government in the expected informal conference. The Secretary arrived at Fortress Monroe in the night of the first day of February. Major Eckert met him on the morning of the second of February with the information that the persons who had come from Richmond had not accepted, in writing, the condition upon which he was allowed to give them conduct to Fortress Monroe. The major had given the same information by telegraph to the President, at Washington. On receiving this information, the President prepared a telegram directing the Secretary to return to Washington. The Secretary was preparing, at the same moment, to so return, without waiting for instructions from the President; but at this juncture Lieutenant General Grant telegraphed to the Secretary of War, as well as to the Secretary of State, that the party from Richmond had reconsidered and accepted the conditions tendered them through Major Eckert, and General Grant urgently advised the President to confer in person with the Richmond party. Under these circumstances, the Secretary, by the President's direction, remained at Fortress Monroe, and the President joined him there on the night of the 2d of February. The Richmond party was brought down the James river in a United States steam transport during the day, and the transport was anchored in Hampton Roads.

On the morning of the 3d the President, attended by the Secretary, received Messrs. Stephens, Hunter, and Campbell on board the United States steam transport River Queen, in Hampton Roads. The conference was altogether informal. There was no attendance of secretaries, clerks, or other witnesses. Nothing was written or read. The conversation, although earnest and free, was calm, and courteous, and kind on both sides. The Richmond party approached the discussion rather indirectly, and at no time did they either make categorical demands, or tender formal stipulations, or absolute refusals. Nevertheless, during the conference, which lasted four hours, the several points at issue between the government and the insurgents were distinctly raised, and discussed fully, intelligently, and in an amicable spirit. What the insurgent party seemed chiefly to favor was a postponement of the question of separation, upon which the war is waged, and a mutual direction of efforts of the government, as well as those of the insurgents, to some extrinsic policy or scheme for a season, during which passions might be expected to subside, and the armies be reduced, and trade and intercourse between the people of both sections resumed. It was suggested by them that through such postponement we might now have immediate peace, with some not very certain prospect of an ultimate satisfactory adjustment of political relations between this government and the States, section, or people now engaged in conflict with it.

This suggestion, though deliberately considered, was nevertheless regarded by the President as one of armistice or truce, and he announced that we can agree to no cessation or suspension of hostilities, except on the basis of the disbandment of the insurgent forces, and the restoration of the national authority throughout all the States in the Union. Collaterally, and in subordination to the proposition which was thus announced, the anti-slavery policy of the United States was reviewed in all its bearings, and the President announced that he must not be expected to depart from the positions he had heretofore assumed in his proclamation of emancipation and other documents, as these positions were reiterated in his last annual message. It was further declared by the President that the complete restoration of the national authority everywhere was an indispensable condition of any assent on our part to whatever form of peace might be proposed. The President assured the other party that, while he must adhere to these positions, he would be prepared, so far as power is lodged with the Executive, to exercise liberality. His power, however, is limited by the Constitution; and when peace should be made, Congress must necessarily act in regard to appropriations of money and to the admission of representatives from the insurrectionary States. The Richmond party were then informed that Congress had, on the 31st ultimo, adopted by a constitutional majority a joint resolution submitting to the several States the proposition to abolish slavery throughout the Union, and that there is every reason to expect that it will be soon accepted by three-fourths of the States, so as to become a part of the national organic law.

The conference came to an end by mutual acquiescence, without producing an agreement of views upon the several matters discussed, or any of them. Nevertheless, it is perhaps of some importance that we have been able to submit our opinions and views directly to prominent insurgents, and to hear them in answer in a courteous and not unfriendly manner.

I am, sir, your obedient servant,

WILLIAM H. SEWARD

The Second Inaugural

ABRAHAM LINCOLN'S ADDRESS at his second inauguration
as President ranks with his address at Gettysburg as
an eloquent document. The President himself wrote of
it, in a letter to Thurlow Weed, March 15: "Every one
likes a compliment. Thank you for yours on my little
notification speech, and on the recent Inaugural Address.
I expect the latter to wear as well as—perhaps better
than—anything I have produced; but I believe it is not
immediately popular. Men are not flattered by being
shown that there has been a difference of purpose between the Almighty and them. To deny it, however, in
this case, is to deny that there is a God governing the
world. It is a truth which I thought needed to be told,
and, as whatever of humiliation there is in it, falls most
directly on myself, I thought others might afford for me
to tell it."

INAUGURAL ADDRESS.
MARCH 4, 1865.

FELLOW-COUNTRYMEN: At this second appearing to take the oath of the presidential office, there is less occasion for an extended address than there was at the first. Then, a statement, somewhat in detail, of a course to be pursued, seemed fitting and proper. Now, at the expiration of four years, during which public declarations have been constantly called forth on every point and phase of the great contest which still absorbs the attention and engrosses the energies of the nation, little that is new could be presented. The progress of our arms, upon which all else chiefly depends, is as well known to the public as to myself; and it is, I trust, reasonably satisfactory and encouraging to all. With high hope for the future, no prediction in regard to it is ventured.

On the occasion corresponding to this four years ago, all thoughts were anxiously directed to an impending civil war. All dreaded it—all sought to avert it. While the inaugural address was being delivered from this place, devoted altogether to *saving* the Union without war, insurgent agents were in the city seeking to *destroy* it without war—seeking to dissolve the Union, and divide effects, by negotiation. Both parties deprecated war; but one of them would *make* war rather than let the nation survive; and the other would *accept* war rather than let it perish. And the war came.

One-eighth of the whole population were colored slaves, not distributed generally over the Union, but localized in the southern part of it. These slaves constituted a peculiar and powerful interest. All knew that this interest was, somehow, the cause of the war. To strengthen, perpetuate and extend this interest was the object for which the insurgents would rend the Union, even by war; while the government claimed no right to do more than to restrict the territorial enlargement of it. Neither party expected for the war the magnitude or the duration which it has already attained. Neither anticipated that the *cause* of the conflict might cease with, or even before, the conflict itself should cease. Each looked for an easier triumph, and a result less fundamental and astounding. Both read the same Bible, and pray to the same God; and each invokes His aid against the other. It may seem strange that any men should dare to ask a just God's assistance in wringing their bread from the sweat of other men's faces; but let us judge not, that we be not judged. The prayers of both could not be answered—that of neither has been answered fully. The Almighty has His own purposes. "Woe unto the world because of offences! for it must needs be that offences come; but woe to that man by whom the offence cometh." If we shall suppose that American slavery is one of those offences which, in the providence of God, must needs come, but which, having continued through His appointed time, He now wills to remove, and that He gives to both north and south this terrible war, as the woe due to those by whom the offence came, shall we discern therein any departure from those divine attributes which the believers in a living God always ascribe to Him? Fondly do we hope—fervently do we pray—that this mighty scourge of war may speedily pass away. Yet, if God wills that it continue until all the wealth piled by the bondsman's two hundred and fifty years of unrequited toil shall be sunk, and until every drop of blood drawn with the lash shall be paid by another drawn with the sword, as was said three thousand years ago, so still it must be said, "The judgments of the Lord are true and righteous altogether."

With malice toward none; with charity for all; with firmness in the right, as God gives us to see the right, let us strive on to finish the work we are in; to bind up the nation's wounds; to care for him who shall have borne the battle, and for his widow, and his orphan—to do all which may achieve and cherish a just and a lasting peace among ourselves, and with all nations.

All Going Finely

As spring weather made possible the renewal of active campaigning, the war in Virginia moved swiftly to a close. Grant's generalship met that severest and truest of all tests of military ability—victory.

The Confederate lines at Petersburg broke, and Lee's army retreated to the southwest, hoping to join with Johnston and the remnants of his Army of Tennessee somewhere in North Carolina for at least one more desperate offensive. But destiny, hunger, and Grant's army met together at Appomattox Court House, and the war in Virginia was over.

These bulletins from the *Army and Navy Official Gazette* illustrate the staccato pace with which event succeeded event in the final days of March and the first days of April.

No. 162

WAR DEPARTMENT,

WASHINGTON, *April* 1, 1865, 10 a. m.

Major General J. A. DIX, *New York:*

The following telegram, in relation to military operations now going on at the front, was received this morning.

Nothing later has reached this Department.

EDWIN M. STANTON,

Secretary of War.

CITY POINT, VA., *March* 31, 8.30 p. m.

Hon. EDWIN M. STANTON, *Secretary of War:*

At 12.30 p. m., to-day, General Grant telegraphed me as follows:

"There has been much hard fighting this morning. The enemy drove our left from near Dabney's house back well toward the Boydtown plank road.

"We are now about to take the offensive at that point, and I hope will more than recover the lost ground."

Later he telegraphed again, as follows: "Our troops, after being driven back on to the Boydtown plank road, turned and drove the enemy in turn, and took the White Oak road, which we now have. This gives us the ground occupied by the enemy this morning.

"I will send you a rebel flag captured by our troops in driving the enemy back. There have been four flags captured to-day."

Judging by the two points from which General Grant telegraphs, I infer that he moved his headquarters about one mile since he sent the first of the two dispatches.

A. LINCOLN.

No. 163.

WAR DEPARTMENT,
WASHINGTON CITY, *April* 1, 1865, 11 p. m.

Major General DIX, *New York:*

The following dispatch from the President, received to-night, shows that the desperate struggle between our forces and the enemy continues undecided, although the advantage appears to be on our side.

EDWIN M. STANTON,
Secretary of War.

CITY POINT, VA., *April* 1, 1865, 5.30 p. m.

Hon. EDWIN M. STANTON, *Secretary of War:*

Dispatch just received showing that Sheridan, aided by Warren, had at 2 p. m. pushed the enemy back so as to re-take the five forks and bring his own headquarters up to J. Boisseau's. The five forks were barricaded by the enemy, and carried by Diven's division of cavalry. This part of the enemy seem to now be trying to work along the White Oak road to join the main force in front of Grant, while Sheridan and Warren are pressing them as closely as possible.

A. LINCOLN.

No. 164.

WAR DEPARTMENT, *April* 2, 6 a. m.

Major General J. A. DIX, *New York:*

A dispatch just received from General Grant's Adjutant General at City Point announces the triumphant success of our arms after three days of hard fighting, during which the forces on both sides exhibited unsurpassed valor.

EDWIN M. STANTON,
Secretary of War.

CITY POINT, VA., *April* 2, 1865, 5.30 a. m.

A dispatch from General Grant states that General Sheridan, commanding cavalry and infantry, has carried everything before him. He captured three brigades of infantry, a wagon train, and several batteries of artillery. The prisoners captured will amount to several thousand.

Respectfully,

T. S. BOWERS, *A. A. G.*

No. 165.

WAR DEPARTMENT,

WASHINGTON, *April* 2, 1865, 11 a. m.

Major General DIX, *New York:*

The following telegram from the President, dated at City Point, at half past 8 o'clock this morning, gives the latest intelligence from the front, where a furious battle was raging, with continued success to the Union arms.

EDWIN M. STANTON,

Secretary of War.

CITY POINT, V., *April* 2, 8.30 a. m.

Hon. EDWIN M. STANTON, *Secretary of War:*

Last night General Grant telegraphed that General Sheridan, with his cavalry and the Fifth corps, had captured three brigades of infantry, a train of wagons, and several batteries, prisoners amounting to several thousands. This morning General Grant, having ordered an attack along the whole line, telegraphs as follows:

"Both Wright and Parke got through the enemy's lines.

"The battle now rages furiously. General Sheridan with his cavalry, the Fifth corps, and Miles's division of the Second corps, which was sent to him since 1 o'clock this morning, is now sweeping down from the west. All now looks highly favorable. General Ord is engaged, but I have not yet heard the result in his front."

A. LINCOLN.

No. 166.

WAR DEPARTMENT,
April 2, 1865, 12.30 p. m.

Major General DIX, *New York:*

The President, in the subjoined telegram, gives the latest news from the front.

EDWIN M. STANTON,
Secretary of War.

CITY POINT, VA., *April 2, 1865, 11 a. m.*

Hon. EDWIN M. STANTON, *Secretary of War:*

Dispatches frequently coming in. All going finely. Parke, Wright, and Ord, extending from the Appomattox to Hatcher's run, have all broken through the enemy's intrenched lines, taking some forts, guns, and prisoners.

Sheridan, with his own cavalry, Fifth corps, and part of the Second, is coming in from the west on the enemy's flank, and Wright is already tearing up the Southside railroad.

A. LINCOLN.

No. 167.

WASHINGTON, D. C., *April 2, 11 p. m.*

Major General John A. DIX, *New York:*

The following telegrams report the condition of affairs at half past 4 o'clock this afternoon.

EDWIN M. STANTON,
Secretary of War.

CITY POINT, VA., *April* 2, 1865, 2 p. m.
Hon. EDWIN M. STANTON, *Secretary of War:*

At 10.45 a. m. General Grant telegraphs as follows:

"Everything has been carried from the left of the Ninth corps. The Sixth corps alone captured more than 3,000 prisoners. The Second and Twenty-Fourth corps both captured forts, guns, and prisoners from the enemy, but I cannot tell the numbers. We are now closing around the works of the line immediately enveloping Petersburg. All looks remarkably well. I have not yet heard from Sheridan."

His headquarters have been moved up to T. Banks's house, near the Boydtown road, about three miles southwest of Petersburg.

A. LINCOLN.

CITY POINT, VA., *April* 2, 1865, 8.30 p. m.
Hon. EDWIN M. STANTON, *Secretary of War:*

At 4.30 p. m. to-day General Grant telegraphs as follows:

"We are now up and have a continuous line of troops, and in a few hours will be intrenched from the Appomattox, below Petersburg, to the river above.

"The whole captures since the army started out will not amount to less than 12,000 men and probably 50 pieces of artillery. I do not know the number of men and guns accurately, however. A portion of Foster's division, Twenty-Fourth corps, made a most gallant charge this afternoon and captured a very important fort from the enemy with its entire garrison."

All seems well with us, and everything quiet just now.

A. LINCOLN.

No. 168.

WAR DEPARTMENT,
WASHINGTON CITY, *April* 3, 1863, 10 a. m.

Major General DIX, *New York:*

The following telegram from the President, announcing the evacuation of Petersburg and probably of Richmond, has just been received by this Department.

EDWIN M. STANTON,
Secretary of War.

This morning General Grant reports Petersburg evacuated, and he is confident Richmond also is. He is pushing forward to cut off, if possible, the retreating army.

A. LINCOLN.

No. 169.

WAR DEPARTMENT,
WASHINGTON CITY, *April* 3, 1865, 10.45 a. m.

Major General DIX, *New York:*

It appears from a dispatch of General Weitzel, just received by this Department, that our forces under his command are in Richmond, having taken it at 8.15 this morning.

EDWIN M. STANTON,
Secretary of War.

Raising the Flag at Sumter

EVEN BEFORE THE SURRENDER at Appomattox plans were under way to celebrate on the fourth anniversary of the fall of Fort Sumter the long-term reversal of the immediate outcome of that battle.

The same flag that Major Robert Anderson had ceremoniously lowered on April 14, 1861, would be as ceremoniously raised by that same officer, now a general but broken in health ever since his ordeal of four years before. Formalities would be kept to a minimum in deference to General Anderson's health, but there would be an accomplished speaker to commemorate the occasion, the Rev. Henry Ward Beecher, most famous and most sought-after of the orators of the day. President Lincoln was invited to attend, but the press of duties in Washington would not permit his presence. Instead he would choose the evening of that same day to try to relax from the cares of the Presidency by attending a performance at Ford's Theater.

342

GENERAL ORDERS,}
   No. 50.   }

WAR DEPARTMENT,
ADJUTANT GENERAL'S OFFICE,
Washington, March 27, 1865.

ORDERED—

First. That at the hour of noon, on the 14th day of April, 1865, Brevet Major General ANDERSON will raise and plant upon the ruins of Fort Sumter, in Charleston harbor, the same United States flag which floated over the battlements of that Fort during the rebel assault, and which was lowered and saluted by him and the small force of his command when the works were evacuated on the 14th day of April, 1861.

Second. That the flag, when raised, be saluted by one hundred guns from Fort Sumter, and by a National salute from every fort and rebel battery that fired upon Fort Sumter.

Third. That suitable ceremonies be had upon the occasion, under the direction of Major General WILLIAM T. SHERMAN, whose military operations compelled the rebels to evacuate Charleston, or, in his absence, under the charge of Major General Q. A. GILLMORE, commanding the Department. Among the ceremonies will be the delivery of a public address by the Reverend HENRY WARD BEECHER.

Fourth. That the naval forces at Charleston, and their Commander on that station, be invited to participate in the ceremonies of the occasion.

BY ORDER OF THE PRESIDENT OF THE UNITED STATES:

EDWIN M. STANTON,
Secretary of War.

OFFICIAL:

Assistant Adjutant General.

Rev. Henry Ward Beecher's

FORT SUMTER ORATION.

April 14th, 1865.

On this solemn and joyful day we again lift to the breeze our father's flag, now again the banner of the United States, with the fervent prayer that God would crown it with honor, protect it from treason, and send it down to our children with all the blessings of civilization, liberty, and religion. Terrible in battle, may it be beneficent in peace. Happily no bird or beast of prey has been inscribed upon it. The stars that redeem the night from darkness, and the beams of red light that beautify the morning, have been united upon its folds. As long as the sun endures, or the stars, may it wave over a nation neither enslaved nor enslaving.

Once, and but once, has treason dishonored it. In that insane hour, when the guiltiest and bloodiest rebellion of time hurled its fires upon this fort, you, sir (turning to General Anderson), and a small heroic band stood within these now crumbled walls, and did gallant and just battle for the honor and defence of the nation's banner. In that cope of fire this glorious flag still peacefully waved to the breeze above your head, unconscious of harm as the stars and skies above it. Once it was shot down; a gallant hand, in whose care this day it has been placed, plucked it from the ground, and reared it again, "cast down but not destroyed." After a vain resistance, with trembling hand and sad heart, you withdrew it from its height, closed its wings, and bore it far away, sternly to sleep amid the tumults of rebellion and the thunder of battle.

The first act of war had begun. The long night of four years had set in. While the giddy traitors whirled in a maze of exhilaration, dim horrors were already advancing, that were ere long to fill the land with blood. To-day you are returned again; we devoutly join with you in thanksgiving to Almighty God, that He has spared your honored life, and vouchsafed to you the glory of this day. The heavens over you are the same; the same shores are here. Morning comes and evening as they did. All else how changed! What grim batteries crowd the burdened shores! What scenes have filled this air and disturbed these waters! These shattered heaps of shapeless stones are all that is left of Fort Sumter. Desolation broods in yonder sad city. Solemn retribution hath avenged our dishonored banner.

You have come back with honor who departed hence four years ago, leaving the air sultry with fanaticism. The surging crowds that rolled up their frenzied shouts as the flag came down are dead, or scattered, or silent, and their habitations are desolate. Ruin sits in the cradle of treason, rebellion has perished, but there flies the same flag that was insulted! With starry eyes it looks all over this bay for that banner that supplanted it, and sees it not. You, that then for the day were humbled, are here again to triumph once and forever. In the storm of that assault this glorious ensign was often struck, but, memorable fact, not one of its *stars* was torn out by shot or shell. It was a prophecy. It said, "Not one State shall be struck from this nation by treason." The fulfilment is at hand. Lifted to the air, to-day, it proclaims, that after four years of war, "Not a State is blotted out." Hail to the flag of our fathers and our flag! Glory to the banner that has gone through four years, black with tempests of war, to pilot the nation back to peace without dismemberment! And glory be to God who, above all hosts and banners, hath ordained victory and shall ordain peace!

Wherefore have we come hither, pilgrims from distant

places? Are we come to exult that Northern hands are stronger than Southern? No! but to rejoice that the hands of those who defend a just and beneficent Government are mightier than the hands that assaulted it. Do we exult over fallen cities? We exult that a nation has not fallen! We sorrow with the sorrowful, we sympathize with the desolate, we look upon the shattered fort and yonder dilapidated city with sad eyes, grieved that men should have committed such treason; but glad that God hath set such a mark upon treason, that all ages shall dread and abhor it. We exult, not for a passion gratified, but for a sentiment victorious; not for temper, but conscience; not, as we devoutly believe, that *our* will is done, but that God's will hath been done. We should be unworthy of that liberty intrusted to our care if, on such a day as this, we sullied our hearts by feelings of aimless vengeance, and equally unworthy if we did not devoutly thank Him who hath said, "Vengeance is mine, I will repay, saith the Lord," that He hath set a mark upon arrogant rebellion ineffaceable while time lasts.

Since this flag went down, on that dark day, who shall tell the mighty woes that have made this land a spectacle to angels and men! The soil has drunk blood and is glutted; millions mourn for millions slain, or, envying the dead, pray for oblivion; towns and villages have been razed; fruitful fields have turned back to wilderness. It came to pass, as the prophet said: *The sun was turned to darkness and the moon to blood.* The course of law was ended. The sword sat chief magistrate in half the nation; industry was paralyzed, morals corrupted; the public weal invaded by rapine and anarchy; whole States were ravaged by avenging armies. The world was amazed. The earth reeled. When the flag sunk here, it was as if political night had come, and all beasts of prey had come forth to devour. That long night is ended, and for this returning day we have come from afar to rejoice and give thanks. No more war! No more accursed secession! No more slavery that spawned them both! Let no man misread the meaning of this unfolding flag. It says, Government hath returned hither; it proclaims, in the name of vindicated Government, peace and protection to loyalty; humiliation and pains to traitors. This is the flag of sovereignty. The nation, not the State, is sovereign! Restored to authority, this flag commands, not supplicates. There may be pardon, but no concession. There may be amnesty and oblivion, but no honeyed compromises. The nation to-day has peace for the peaceful, and war for the turbulent. The only condition of submission is to submit. There is the Constitution, there are the laws, there is the Government. They rise up like mountains of strength that shall not be moved. They are the conditions of peace. One nation under one Government, without slavery, has been ordained and shall stand. There can be peace on no other basis. On this basis reconstruction is easy, and needs neither architect nor engineer. Without this basis no engineer or architect shall ever reconstruct these rebellious States.

We do not want your cities or your fields; we do not envy you your prolific soil, nor heavens full of perpetual summer. Let agriculture revel here; let manufactures make every stream twice musical; build fleets in every port; inspire the arts of peace with genius second only to that of Athens, and we shall be glad in your gladness and rich in your wealth. All that we ask is unswerving loyalty and universal liberty; and that, in the name of this *high sovereignty of the United States of America,* we demand, and that, with the blessing of Almighty God, *we will have!*

We raise our fathers' banner, that it may bring back better blessings than those of old, that it may cast out the devil of discord; that it may restore lawful government and a prosperity purer and more enduring than that which it protected before; that it may win parted friends from their alienation; that it may inspire hope and inaugurate universal liberty; that it may say to the sword, *Return to thy sheath,* and to the plough and sickle, *Go forth;* that it may heal all jealousies, unite all policies, inspire a new national life, compact our strength, purify our principles, ennoble our national ambitions, and make this people great and strong; not for aggression and quarrelsomeness, but for *the peace of the world;* giving to us the glorious prerogative of leading all nations to juster laws, to more humane policies; to sincerer friendship, to rational instituted civil liberty, and to universal Christian brotherhood. Reverently, piously, in hopeful patriotism, we spread this banner on the sky, as of old the bow was planted on the cloud, and with solemn fervor, beseech God to look upon it, and make it the memorial of an everlasting covenant and decree, that never again on this fair land shall a deluge of blood prevail.

Why need any eye turn from this spectacle? Are there not associations which, overleaping the recent past, carry us back to times when, over North and South, this flag was honored alike by all! In all our colonial days we were one; in the long Revolutionary struggle, and in the scores of prosperous years succeeding we were united. When the passage of the Stamp Act, in 1765, aroused the colonies, it was Gadsden, of South Carolina, that cried with prescient enthusiasm: *"We stand on the broad common ground of those natural rights that we all feel and know as men.* There ought to be no New England man, no New Yorker known on this continent, but all of us," said he, "Americans." That *was* the voice of South Carolina, that *shall be* again the voice of South Carolina!

Faint is the echo; but it is coming; we now hear it sighing sadly through the pines, but it shall yet break in thunder upon the shore—no North, no West, no South, but the United States of America! There is scarcely a man born in the South who has lifted his hand against this banner, but had a father who would have died for it. Is memory dead? Is there no historic pride? Has a fatal fury struck blindness or hate into eyes that used to look kindly toward each other, that read the same Bible, that hung over the historic pages of our national glory, that studied the same Constitution?

Let this uplifting bring back all of the past that was good, but leave in darkness all that was bad. The flag was never before so wholly unspotted, so clear of all wrong, so purely and simply the sign of justice and liberty. Did I say that we brought back the same banner that you bore away, noble and heroic sir? It is not the same—it is more and better than it was.

The land is free from slavery since that banner fell. When God would prepare Moses for emancipation, he overthrew his first steps, and drove him for forty years to brood in the wilderness. When our flag came down, four years it lay brooding in darkness; it cried to the Lord, Wherefore am I deposed? Then arose before it a vision of its sin. It had strengthened the strong and forgotten the weak. It proclaimed Liberty, but trod upon slaves. In that seclusion it dedicated itself to liberty. Behold, to-day it fulfils its vows. When it went down, four millions of people had no flag; to-day it rises, and four million people cry out, Behold *our* flag! Hark, they murmur; it is the Gospel that they recite in sacred words: "It is a Gospel to the poor, it heals our broken hearts; it preaches deliverance to captives; it gives sight to the blind; it sets at liberty them that are bruised." Rise up, then, glorious Gospel banner, and roll out these messages of God! Tell the air that not a spot now sullies thy whiteness. Thy red is not the blush of shame, but the flush of joy. Tell the dews that wash thee that thou art pure as they. Say to the night that thy stars lead toward the morning, and to the morning, that a brighter day arises with healing in its wings. And then, oh glowing flag, bid the sun pour light on all thy folds with double brightness, while thou art bearing round and round the world, the solemn joy—a race set free! a nation redeemed!

The mighty hand of Government made strong in war by the favor of the God of battles, spreads wide to-day the Banner of Liberty, that went down in darkness, that arose in light; and there it streams like the sun above it, neither parcelled out nor monopolized, but flooding the air with light for all mankind. Ye scattered and broken, ye wounded and dying, bitten by the fiery serpents of oppression, everywhere, in all the world, look upon this sign lifted up, and live! Ye homeless and houseless slaves, look, and ye are free. At length *you*, too, have put part and lot in this glorious ensign, that broods with impartial love over small and great, over the poor and the strong, the bond and the free.

In this solemn hour let us pray for the quick coming of reconciliation and happiness under this common flag. But we must build again from the foundations in all these now free Southern States. No cheap exhortations to forgetfulness of the past, to restore all things as they were, will do. God does not stretch out His hand as He has for four dreadful years, that men may easily forget the might of His terrible acts. Restore things as they were? What, the alienations and jealousies, the discords and contentions, and the causes of them? No! In that solemn sacrifice on which a nation has offered up for its sins so many precious victims loved and lamented, let our sins and mistakes be consumed utterly and

forever. No! Never again shall things be restored as before
the war!

It is written in God's decree of events fulfilled, "Old things
have passed away." That new earth in which dwelleth righteousness draws near. Things as they were? Who has an
omnipotent hand to restore a million dead, slain in battle,
or wasted by sickness, or dying of grief, broken-hearted?
Who has omniscience to search for the scattered ones? Who
shall restore the lost to broken families? Who shall bring
back the squandered treasure, the years of industry wasted,
and convince you that four years of guilty rebellion and
cruel war are no more than dirt upon the hand which a moment's washing removes, and leaves the hand clean as before? Such a war reaches down to the very vitals of society.
Emerging from such a prolonged rebellion, he is blind who
tells you that the State, by a mere amnesty and benevolence
of government, can be put again, by a mere decree, in its
old place. It would not be honest—it would not be kind or
fraternal for me to pretend that Southern revolution against
the Union has not reacted and wrought revolution in the
Southern States themselves, and inaugurated a new dispensation. Society here is like a broken loom, and the piece
which rebellion put in and was weaving has been cut, and
every thread broken. You must put in new warp, and new
woof, and weaving anew, as the fabric slowly unwinds, we
shall see in it no gorgon figures, no hideous grotesques of the
old barbarism, but the figures of liberty,—vines, and golden
grains, framing in the heads of justice, love, and liberty. The
august convention of 1787 framed the Constitution with this
memorable preamble: "We the people of the United States,
in order to form a more perfect union and establish justice,
insure domestic tranquillity, provide for the common defence, promote the general welfare, and secure the blessings

of liberty to ourselves and our posterity, do ordain this Constitution for the United States of America."

Again, in an awful convention of war, the people of the United States, for the very ends just recited, have debated, settled, and ordained certain fundamental truths which must henceforth be accepted and obeyed; nor is any State or any individual wise who shall disregard them. They are to civil affairs what the natural laws are to health—indispensable conditions of peace and happiness. What are the ordinances given by the people speaking out of fire and darkness of war, with authority inspired by that same God who gave the law from Sinai amid thunders of trumpet voices?

1. That these United States shall be one and indivisible.

2. That States have not absolute sovereignty, and have no right to dismember the Republic.

3. That universal liberty is indispensable to Republican Government, and that slavery shall be utterly and forever abolished.

Such are the results of war; these are the best fruits of the war. They are worth all they have cost. They are foundations of peace. They will secure benefits to all nations as well as to ours. Our highest wisdom and duty is to accept the facts as the decrees of God. We are exhorted to forget all that has happened. Yes, the wrath, the conflict, the cruelty, but not those overruling decrees of God which this war has pronounced as solemnly as on Mount Sinai. God says: "Remember—*remember*,"—hear it to-day. Under this sun, under that bright child of the sun, our banner, with the eyes of this nation and of the world upon us, we repeat the syllables of God's providence, and recite the solemn decrees—

No MORE DISUNION!

No MORE SECESSION!

No MORE SLAVERY! . . .

We have shown by all that we have suffered in war how great is our estimate of the importance of the Southern States to this Union, and we will honor that estimate now in peace by still greater exertions for their rebuilding. Will reflecting men not perceive, then, the wisdom of accepting established facts, and with alacrity of enterprise begin to retrieve the past? Slavery cannot come back. It is the interest, therefore, of every man to hasten its end. Do you want more war? Are you not yet weary of contest? Will you gather up the unexploded fragments of this prodigious magazine of all mischief, and heap them up for continued explosions? Does not the South need peace? And since free labor is inevitable, will you have it in its worst forms or its best? Shall it be ignorant, impertinent, indolent, or shall it be educated, self-respecting, moral, and self-supporting? Will you have men as drudges, or will you have them as citizens? Since they have vindicated the Government and cemented its foundation stones with their blood, may they not offer the tribute of their support to maintain its laws and its policy? It is better for religion, it is better for political integrity, it is better for industry, it is better for *money*, if you will have that ground-motive, that you should educate the black man, and by education make him a citizen. They who refuse education to the black man would turn the South into a vast poorhouse, and labor into a pendulum incessantly vibrating between poverty and indolence.

From this pulpit of broken stone, we speak forth our earnest greeting to all our land. We offer to the President of these United States our solemn congratulations that God has sustained his life and health under the unparalleled burdens and sufferings of four bloody years, and permitted him to behold this auspicious consummation of that national unity for which he has waited with so much patience and fortitude, and for which he has labored with such disinterested wisdom. To the members of the Government associated with him in the administration of perilous affairs in critical times; to the Senators and Representatives of the United States, who have eagerly fashioned the instruments by which the popular will might express and enforce itself, we tender our grateful thanks.

To the officers and men of the army and navy, who have so faithfully, skilfully, and gloriously upheld their country's authority by suffering, labor, and sublime courage, we offer a heart-tribute beyond the compass of words. Upon those true and faithful citizens, men and women, who have borne up with unflinching hope in the darkest hour, and covered the land with their labors of love and charity, we invoke the the divinest blessing of Him whom they have so truly imitated.

But chiefly to Thee, God of our fathers! we render thanksgiving and praise for that wondrous providence that has brought forth from such a harvest of war the seed of so much liberty and peace. We invoke peace upon the North; peace be to the West; peace be upon the South. In the name of God, we lift up our banner, and dedicate it to Peace, Union, and Liberty, now and forevermore. Amen!

Index

355

The Confederate
Reader

Copyright © 1957 by Longmans, Green and Co., Inc.

Reprinted with permission by William S. Konecky Associates, Inc. and
Richard B. Harwell.

Published by The Blue and Grey Press, a division of Book Sales, Inc.,
110 Enterprise Avenue, Secaucus, N.J. 07094.

85 86 87   9 8 7 6 5 4 3 2

ISBN 0-89009-847-6

Printed and bound in the United States of America.

For
THOMAS H. ENGLISH
and
ROSS H. McLEAN
gentlemen scholars

Acknowledgment

Years of investigation into the printed records of the Confederacy have multiplied the thanks due to helpful scholars, librarians, and collectors in the compilation of *The Confederate Reader*. Several thousand Confederate publications have been closely examined and many, many of them read in their entirety. As some of these publications are rare (located perhaps in a single known copy), many libraries have been used to build the book. Chief among them are the Emory University Library, the Henry E. Huntington Library, the Boston Athenaeum, the Confederate Museum, and the Alderman Library of the University of Virginia.

The first tangible work on *The Confederate Reader* was made possible by a grant from the Huntington Library to work in its fine collection of Confederate material and by a corollary leave of absence from Emory University. My gratitude to both of these institutions is deep and sincere.

Individuals as well as institutions demonstrate the cooperative spirit of the scholarly world. My particular thanks are due Miss Margaret Jemison of Talladega, Alabama; Mr. Harold Mason of New Rochelle, New York; Miss Eleanor Brockenbrough, Miss India Thomas, Mr. McDonald Wellford, Mr. Louis Rubin, and Mr. Clifford Dowdey of Richmond; Miss Mary Isabel Fry, Miss Gertrude Ruhnka, and

v

Mr. Carey S. Bliss of San Marino, California; Mr. John Cook Wyllie of Charlottesville, Virginia; Mr. John L. B. Williams and Mr. Earl S. Miers of New York; Mr. Floyd M. Cammack and Mr. Ralph G. Newman of Chicago; Mr. Robert H. Woody of Durham, North Carolina; and Miss Marjorie Lyle Crandall and Mr. Walter Muir Whitehill of Boston: all these and many more.

RICHARD BARKSDALE HARWELL

September 2, 1957

Contents

1860

1861

1862

1864

Illustrations

Introduction

THIS is *The Confederate Reader*. This is the story of
the Confederacy as the Confederates themselves
(and a few foreign sympathizers with the Confederates)
wrote it for one another. It is a roughly chronological
selection from the writings of the times, the writings that
were, theoretically at least, available to the Confederate
reading public. It does not exhaust the aspects of Confederate life, but it touches on most of them. It does not
attempt to give an over-all military history of the war,
but there is a generous sampling of battle reports and
general orders. Rather, it fills in the picture of Confederate life from a variety of sources (sources which were
nearly always heavily influenced by the military, though
not directly military)—from sermons, songs, humorous
sketches, novels, prison narratives, travel observations.
These are the living artifacts of the life of a Southerner
of the sixties, as important to the historian as the treasured guns of Confederates and Federals are important to
the student of ordnance. Ink and paper survive with a
peculiar freshness, and the words of the Confederates
re-create their own era with an immediacy and truth that

bring new understanding of the period to the reader of nearly a century later.

The South is a state of mind. And the state of mind that was the South of the Confederacy is interwoven into the heritage and traditions of the modern South. Much of the continuing mental pattern of the South was established by the generation that preceded the Civil War. Its social pattern was solidified by the generation that followed the war. Its geographic pattern was established by the war itself. The war is the center of reference in the South's past. The thinking of the South, as opposed to that of the North, was set in the days of Calhoun. The modern social behavior of the South found its form when the Bourbons of the Reconstruction era succeeded in continuing, within a growing democracy, many of the features of the older plantation way of life. And the temporary geographic solidarity that united the South into the Confederate States of America is preserved in politics and in memory, so that Virginia's Northern Neck and the Texan Border have a common heritage which marks their citizens, in their own minds at least, as compatriots.

The heritage of a special past, or of a past that the romanticist likes to regard as special, needs understanding. The South is justly proud—and sometimes unjustly prideful—of its past. It loves to tell its history. Perhaps the best understanding of the present comes through understanding its relation to the past. The South's past can best be understood as the South explained its present of that day to itself.

The South is self-conscious. Now and historically, it is

self-conscious. The Nullification controversy between the forces of Jacksonism and Calhounism imposed upon the South a compulsion to explain itself. This compulsion has never been thrown off and has, at times, been almost a sectional monomania. It found its first region-wide expression in the slavery controversy. As tons of Northern paper were filled with abolitionist sentiments, equal amounts of Southern paper attempted to demonstrate ethnographic, economic, and religious advantages of the "peculiar institution." Concurrent with the expressions on slavery was a growing propaganda for Southern nationalism that culminated in South Carolina's Ordinance of Secession. After the war, the earlier memoirs of the participants in the Confederacy are a treasury of Southern self-examination, but the generation of historians that followed left, through their apologies for the South, a stigma which has only recently been eliminated from Southern writing. The Southerner is still self-conscious, but the introspective examination of the region by Wilbur J. Cash, Will Percy, and Ben Robertson; the perceptive reporting of Jonathan Daniels, Ralph McGill, and Hodding Carter; the distinguished historiography of Douglas Southall Freeman, Charles S. Sydnor, Clement Eaton, E. Merton Coulter, T. Harry Williams, and C. Vann Woodward attest that the South can look fairly and squarely at itself.

The history of the Civil War is the common heritage of all Americans. No period in our history has been more written about. The bibliography of those four years is enough to fill volumes, the books themselves enough to fill whole libraries. And here, more than about any other period, the South has felt it necessary to explain itself. Hardly was the ink dry on General Lee's farewell at Appomattox before the South began its attempts to vindicate in print its course during the war.

The flow of Confederate history has never ceased. First it was motivated by desire for vindication. Soon nearly every Confederate general was easily convinced that it would be a dereliction of his duty should he deny the public his memoirs. Unpretending reminiscences of private soldiers gradually filled in another side of the story. Regimental histories were published to gratify the pride of special units. Books about the war found a ready and continuing market. Women deprived of wealth and station by defeat could write and still preserve their social dignity. Personal diaries were given to the public. Material "written solely for the eyes of the author" found its way into print when tempted by the lure of financial gain. Publication of the official records of both armies by the United States government gave impetus to more and more serious histories. Over a generation had elapsed since the end of the war, but the game was not over when the course had been once run. A re-evaluation was due. Continued interest in the war has justified continued examination of it. Continued examination has turned up more and more of the facts of history, has presented more and more pictures of what the life of the South in the Confederacy was like, and has made the American Civil War the best documented of all wars.

It is a convenient war. It has a beginning and an end.

Its causes stretch back to the beginnings of our national life and its influences are still with us, but 1861–1865 is a tangible period. It was a war in which the same language was spoken on both sides and which, therefore, can be studied by one not trained in languages. It was a war in which the participants understood the ideology of one another (perhaps better than it has been understood since). By contrast to America's twentieth-century conflicts, it was a small war. It was a modern war in that in its theaters were developed many of the tactics which have since become standard military practice, in that it used modern weapons, and in that its armies were recruited and organized along lines similar to those of later American wars. Beyond all this, it was a romantic, sentimental, exciting war. Little wonder that the veterans of the Grand Army of the Republic loved to tell of the War of the Rebellion or that unreconstructed Confederates should recount again and again the glories of Southern Independence in the War for Separation.

The materials of the history of the Civil War have been worked over and over again—with one signal exception, the publications of the Confederates themselves. The Confederates were as self-conscious as any Southerners before or since. They were constrained to explain, not only to themselves but also to any other readers they could reach, the reasons for secession, their ambitions as an independent nation, and the glories of their heroic armies. The South was fighting for full independence—social, economic, and literary as well as political.

"Paper," wrote one Southerner in prefacing his narrative as a prisoner of the Yankees, "among other things, is scarce in the South, and paper may be turned into excellent account in the composition of cartridges, while metal that might be moulded into bullets is run into type. Yet newspapers and books are printed, and most of them eagerly read, especially any that have the most remote bearing upon the present contest." The Confederates realized the value of propaganda. It was important that paper be put to account to give a semblance of normalcy to existence in a nation fighting for its life, to bolster the morale of the people of the Confederacy, and to record for posterity a living record of the South's brief experiment in independence. The record left by these printed evidences of Confederate life is the truest record of the war. Prejudiced and incomplete as it is, it is nevertheless an accurate picture of the Confederacy.

Here, in their own words, written for their own people, is the story of the war as the Confederates knew, not remembered, it. Here is *The Confederate Reader*.

1860

To Dissolve the Union

THE FOCUS of growing tension throughout 1860 was Charleston. The question of secession had been close to the surface of political thinking in the Palmetto State since the Nullification controversy of President Andrew Jackson's administration. It had reached the boiling point in 1852, only to subside after the passage of an ordinance affirming the state's right to secede. Now it was ready to boil over. Continued affronts to the advocates of state rights had caused South Carolina in 1859 to forewarn Washington of secessive intentions by an invitation to her sister slaveholding states to consider measures for concerted action.

Positive action was deferred pending the results of the political canvass of 1860. The election of Abraham Lincoln was the signal for secession—and separation—and war to come.

The South Carolina Convention, originally convened in Columbia, adjourned to Charleston to escape a threatened epidemic of smallpox and proceeded to bring upon the state and upon the South the greater scourge of war. The proud little city, arrogantly conscious that she was

3

for the moment the center of national attention, awaited the passage of the Ordinance of Secession. After sober deliberation, feeling the responsibility of setting an example of dignity and reason, the delegates to the convention approved the ordinance early in the afternoon of December 20. Beneath the banner "The South Alone Should Govern the South" that stretched across Broad Street from the propaganda headquarters of the 1860 Association, crowds of citizens and militiamen streamed to the office of the *Mercury*, the fire-eating newspaper of secessionist Robert Barnwell Rhett, to confirm the news. And in scarcely fifteen minutes after its passage at St. Andrew's Hall copies of the Ordinance were rolling from the presses as a *Mercury* extra.

AN ORDINANCE

TO DISSOLVE THE UNION BETWEEN THE STATE
OF SOUTH CAROLINA AND OTHER STATES UNITED
WITH HER UNDER THE COMPACT ENTITLED "THE
CONSTITUTION OF THE UNITED STATES OF AMER-
ICA."

*We, the People of the State of South Carolina, in Convention
assembled, do declare and ordain, and it is hereby declared
and ordained,*

That the Ordinance adopted by us in Convention, on the
twenty-third day of May, in the year of our Lord one thousand seven hundred and eighty-eight, whereby the Constitution of the United States of America was ratified, and also, all
Acts and parts of Acts of the General Assembly of this State,
ratifying amendments of the said Constitution, are hereby
repealed; and that the union now subsisting between South
Carolina and other States, under the name of "The United
States of America," is hereby dissolved.

D. F. JAMISON, *Del. from Barnwell, and Pres't Convention.*

5

1861

Fort Sumter

SENTIMENT in the lower South was overwhelmingly in favor of secession and separation. From the beginning the extremists in South Carolina counted on the early accession of Georgia, Florida, Alabama, Louisiana, Mississippi, and Texas to their ranks. In each of these states cool heads warned against the consequences of secession, but enthusiasm and emotion overrode wise admonition. The wisdom and love for the old Union of such as Alexander H. Stephens in Georgia, Benjamin F. Perry in South Carolina, and old Sam Houston in Texas could not prevail against the ambition-fired confidence and irresponsible claims of the fire-eaters. It mattered little that the South was not materially prepared for war. It was far too well prepared psychologically. What matter if there were not enough arms for a long war? What matter if there was no Southern navy? The war would be over in three months. Any Southerner could whip a dozen Yankees. Secession fever swept from Charleston to Montgomery, Jackson, Milledgeville, and Tallahassee. By February Louisiana had cast its lot with the secessionists, and the decision of Texas was a foregone conclusion.

"Hurrah, hurrah! for Southern Rights Hurrah," soon sang comedian Harry Macarthy as he plugged his own song "The Bonnie Blue Flag":

> First, gallant South Carolina nobly made the stand;
> Then came Alabama, who took her by the hand;
> Next, quickly Mississippi, Georgia and Florida,
> All raised on high the Bonnie Blue Flag that bears
>   a Single Star.

The secession of Texas was brought about after a bitter Unionist stand by her old patriot and governor, Sam Houston. But Houston could not hold back the hard-riding enthusiasm of the Texans for secession. The decision of the mammoth state, which remembered its own independence of less than a generation before, brought all the states of the great cotton belt into the new Confederacy and extended its territory from the Atlantic to ill-defined lines in the Western Territories.

The South moved in orderly and parliamentary fashion toward the formation of a new government. The *Star of the West* was fired on as she attempted to bring supplies to Major Robert Anderson's garrison at Fort Sumter in January, but the threat of immediate war subsided. Delegates were elected to a convention to be assembled in Montgomery. The Southern senators and representatives withdrew from the United States Congress. Secessionists in the army and navy resigned to place their services with their native states.

On February 4 the Montgomery convention began its sessions, and four days later a provisional government

had been established. The convention at first looked to
Georgia for the president of the new nation. But Bob
Toombs, on hearing that some of the delegations had decided to vote for Jefferson Davis of Mississippi, asked
that his name not be presented. The vote for Davis was
unanimous. The ex-senator received the news with apparent surprise. His ambition lay in military, not administra-
tive, duties. His first fame had come from his career in
the war with Mexico, and he had served a distinguished
term as President Franklin Pierce's Secretary of War.
But Davis resigned the appointment the new Republic of
Mississippi had given him as major general of its army
and left his plantation "Brierfield" for Montgomery.

William Lowndes Yancey, eloquent champion of secession in Alabama, introduced Davis to an assembled crowd
on the evening of February 17: "The man and the hour
have met." The next day, before an audience thoroughly
conscious of the historic importance, if not of the historic
implications, of the occasion they witnessed, Jefferson
Davis become the President of the Provisional Government of the Confederate States of America in a simple
and impressive ceremony. He delivered a short, dignified,
and well-reasoned statement of his position as head of a
new government. "We have changed the constituent
parts, but not the system of our government," he declared. "Sustained by the consciousness that the transition
from the former Union to the present Confederacy has
not proceeded from a disregard on our part of just obligations, or any failure to perform any constitutional duty—
moved by no interest or passion to invade the rights of

others—anxious to cultivate peace and commerce with all nations, if we may not hope to avoid war, we may at least expect that posterity will acquit us of having needlessly engaged in it. Doubly justified by the absence of wrong on our part, and by wanton aggression on the part of others, there can be no doubt that the courage and patriotism of the people of the Confederate States will be found equal to any measures of defence which honor and security may require."

Herman Arnold led his Montgomery Theatre band through the catchy strains of "Dixie," and the government of the Confederate States set about the task of establishing a new nation in fact as well as in name.

While the government in Montgomery burgeoned with red tape, appointments and bureaus, the military situation in Charleston Harbor was one of growing tension. Major Anderson had moved his garrison from Fort Moultrie to the unfinished, but more easily defended, harbor stronghold of Fort Sumter the day after Christmas. His position was an anomalous one, as both North and South were aware of the advantage to be gained by not striking the first blow.

The continued occupation by the Federals of a fort in sight of the birthplace of secession was particularly galling to Southern pride and patriotism, so it was here, on April 12, 1861, that war really began. It began in the fashion of a much-heralded theatrical event. All the niceties were complied with. Until the last, Major Anderson continued to exchange friendly notes with his acquaintances in Charleston. (The belief still existed that the

problems of the day could be solved without violent interference with the personal lives of the participants.) The
venerable Edmund Ruffin and the vigorous Roger Pryor
came down from Virginia to share the honors of commencing hostilities. The people of Charleston lined the
famous Battery to witness the spectacle of war. And, despite heavy artillery bombardment, not a single human
life was lost during the battle for the fort. The only casu-
alty occurred during Anderson's salute to the old flag at
his surrender.

                              Friday, April 12, 1861.
The bombardment of Fort Sumter, so long and anxiously
expected, has at last become a fact accomplished.

At about two o'clock, on the afternoon of Thursday, Gen-
eral Beauregard, through his Aides, Col. James Chesnut, Jr.,
Col. Chisolm and Capt. Lee, made a demand on Major Ander-
son for the immediate surrender of Fort Sumter. Major
Anderson replied that such a course would be inconsistent
with the duty he was required by his Government to perform.
The answer was communicated by the General-in-Chief to
President Davis.

This visit, and the refusal of the commandant of Fort
Sumter to accede to the demand made by General Beauregard, passed from tongue to tongue, and soon the whole city
was in possession of the startling intelligence. Rumor, as she
is wont to do, shaped the facts to suit her purposes, enlarged
their dimensions, and gave them a complexion which they
had not worn when fresh from the pure and artless hands of
truth.

A half an hour after the return of the orderlies it was confidently believed that the batteries would open fire at eight o'clock, and in expectation of seeing the beginning of the conflict, hundreds congregated upon the Battery and the wharves, looking out on the bay. There they stood, straining their eyes over the dark expanse of water, waiting to see the flash and hear the boom of the first gun. The clock told the hour of eleven, and still they gazed and listened, but the eyelids grew weary, and at the noon of the night the larger portion of the disappointed spectators were plodding their way homeward. At about nine o'clock, General Beauregard received a reply from President Davis, to the telegram in relation to the surrender of Sumter, by which he was instructed to inform Major Anderson that if he would evacuate the fort he held when his present supply of provisions was exhausted, there would be no appeal to arms. This proposition was borne to Major Anderson by the Aids who had delivered the first message, and he refused to accept the condition. The General-in-Chief forthwith gave the order that the batteries be opened at half-past four o'clock on Friday morning. Major Anderson's reply was decisive of the momentous question, and General Beauregard determined to apply the last argument. The stout soldier had resolved to make a desperate defence, and the bloody trial of strength must be essayed. The sword must cut asunder the last tie that bound us to a people, whom, in spite of wrongs and injustice wantonly inflicted through a long series of years, we had not yet utterly hated and despised. The last expiring spark of affection must be quenched in blood. Some of the most splendid pages in our glorious history must be blurred. A blow must be struck that would make the ears of every Republican fanatic tingle, and whose dreadful effects will be felt by generations yet to come. We must transmit a heritage of rankling and undying hate to our children.

The restless activity of Thursday night was gradually worn down; the citizens who had thronged the battery through the night, anxious and weary, had sought their homes, the Mounted Guard which had kept watch and ward over the city, with the first grey streak of morning were preparing to retire, when two guns in quick succession from Fort Johnson announced the opening of the drama. Upon that signal, at twenty-five minutes past four o'clock, A.M., the circle of batteries with which the grim fortress of Fort Sumter is beleaguered opened fire. The outline of this great volcanic crater was illuminated with a line of twinkling lights; the clustering shells illuminated the sky above it; the balls clattered thick as hail upon its sides; our citizens, aroused to a forgetfulness of their fatigue through many weary hours, rushed again to the points of observation; and so, at the break of day, amidst the bursting of bombs, and the roaring of ordnance, and before thousands of spectators, whose homes, and liberties, and lives were at stake, was enacted this first great scene in the opening drama of this most momentous military history. . . .

Steadily alternating, our batteries spit forth their wrath at the grim fortress rising so defiantly out of the sea. Major Anderson received the shot and shell in silence. And some excited lookers on, ignorant of the character of the foe, were fluent with conjectures and predictions, that revived the hope fast dying out of their hopeful and tender hearts. But the short-lived hope was utterly extinguished when the deepening twilight revealed the Stars and Stripes floating defiantly in the breeze. The batteries continued at regular intervals to belch iron vengeance, and still no answer was returned by the foe. About an hour after the booming began, two balls rushed hissing through the air, and glanced harmless from the stuccoed bricks of Fort Moultrie. The embrasures of the hostile fortress gave forth no sound again till between six and seven o'clock, when, as if wrathful from enforced delay, from casemate and parapet the United States officer poured a storm of iron hail upon Fort Moultrie, Stevens' Iron Battery and the Floating Battery. The broadside was returned with spirit by the gallant gunners at these important posts. The firing now began in good earnest. The curling white smoke hung above the angry pieces of friend and foe, and the jarring boom rolled at regular intervals on the anxious ear. The atmosphere was charged with the smell of villainous salt-petre, and as if in sympathy with the melancholy scene, the sky was covered with heavy clouds, and everything wore a sombre aspect.

About half past nine o'clock, Capt. R. S. Parker reported from Sullivan's Island to Mount Pleasant that everything was in fine condition at Fort Moultrie, and that the soldiers had escaped unhurt. The same dispatch stated that the embrasures of the Floating Battery were undamaged by the shock of the shot, and though the formidable structure had been struck eleven times, the balls had not started a single bolt. Anderson, after finding his fire against the Iron Battery ineffectual, had concentrated his fire upon the Floating Battery, and the Dahlgren Battery, both under command of Capt. Hamilton. A number of shells had dropped into Fort Sumter, and one gun *en barbette* had been dismounted. . . .

The venerable Edmund Ruffin, who, so soon as it was known a battle was inevitable, hastened over to Morris' Island and was elected a member of the Palmetto Guard, fired the first gun from Stevens' Iron Battery. Another son of the Old Dominion was appointed on General Beauregard's Staff on Thursday, bore dispatches to the General in com-

mand, from Brigadier-General James Simons, in command
of Morris' Island, during the thickest of the fight, and in the
face of a murderous fire from Fort Sumter. Col. Roger A.
Pryor, in the execution of that dangerous commission, passed
within speaking distance of the hostile fortress.

Fort Moultrie has fully sustained the prestige of its glorious name. Here, Col. Ripley, who was commandant of all the
artillery of Sullivan's Island and Mount Pleasant, made his
headquarters. The battery bearing on Sumter consisted of
nine guns, in command of Lieut. Alfred Rhett, with a detachment of seventy men, Company B. It fired very nearly gun
for gun with Fort Sumter. We counted the guns from eleven
to twelve o'clock, and found them to be forty-two to forty-six,
while the advantage was unquestionably upon the side of
Fort Moultrie. In that fort not a gun was dismounted, not a
wound received, not the slightest permanent injury sustained
by any of its defences, while every ball from Fort Moultrie
left its mark upon Fort Sumter. Those aimed at the barbette
guns swept with a deadly fire the parapet of the battery bearing on Cummings' Point, and also that against Sullivan's
Island, clearing the ramparts of men, striking the guns, or
falling with terrible effect upon the walls and roofing of the
quarters on the opposite side of the fortress. Many of its
shells were dropped into that fort, and Lieut. John Mitchell,
the worthy son of that patriot sire, who has so nobly vindicated the cause of the South, has the honor of dismounting
two of its parapet guns by a single shot from one of the
Columbiads, which at the time he had the office of directing.
During the morning, Major Anderson had paid his respects
to all, and had tested the Floating Battery and the Iron Battery, and made nothing for the trouble. The last two or three
hours before dark, he devoted himself exclusively to Fort
Moultrie, and the two fortresses had a grand duello. Game to

the last, though much more exposed, Fort Moultrie held her own, and, it is believed, a little more than her own. Towards night, several rounds of red-hot shot were thrown into the barracks of the enemy. This battery has received universal applause and admiration.

A brisk fire was kept up by all the batteries until about seven o'clock in the evening, after which hour the guns boomed, throughout the night of Friday, at regular intervals of twenty minutes. The schooner Petrel, J. L. Jones, commanding, while lying off the mouth of Hog Island Channel, was fired into from Fort Sumter, about half-past eight o'clock. One shot took effect in the bow of the schooner, and several passed over her.

It were vain to attempt an exhibition of the enthusiasm and fearless intrepidity of our citizens in every department of this eventful day. Boats passed from post to post without the slightest hesitation, under the guns of Fort Sumter, and, with high and low, old and young, rich and poor, in uniform or without, the common wish and constant effort was to reach the posts of action; and amid a bombardment resisted with the most consummate skill and perseverance, and with the most efficient appliances of military art and science, it is a most remarkable circumstance, and one which exhibits the infinite goodness of an overruling Providence, that, so far as we have been able to learn from the most careful inquiry, not the slightest injury has been sustained by the defenders of their country.

It may be added, as an incident that contributed no little interest to the action of the day, that from early in the forenoon three vessels of war, two of them supposed to be the Harriet Lane and Pawnee, lay just beyond the bar, inactive spectators of the contest.

———

CLOSE OF THE BOMBARDMENT.

Second Day, Saturday, April 13, 1861.

We closed the account of the grand military diorama in progress on our Bay amidst the clouds and gloom and threatening perils of Friday night. The firing, abated in the early evening, as though for the concentration of its special energies, commenced again at ten o'clock, and amid gusts of rain, and clouds that swept the heavens, the red-hot shot and lighted shells, again streamed from the girt of batteries around, and concentrated in fearful import over Fort Sumter. Of the effects little was visible, of course, and anxious citizens, who from battery, spire and housetop, had bided the peltings of the storm, mute spectators of the splendid scene, could only wait the opening of the coming day for confirmation of the hopes and fears with which the changes in the scene successively inspired them. As dawn approached, the firing again abated, and when the rising sun threw its flood of light over the sparkling waters from a cloudless sky, it was but by random shots from outlying batteries, with scarce an answer from Fort Sumter, that spectators were assured the contest still continued, and that human feeling was not in harmony with the grace and glory of the scene. It was but a little while, however, before the energy of action was restored, and as the work of destruction still went on, it was feared that still another day of expectation and uncertainty was before us. A light issue of thin smoke was early seen at Sumter. At seven o'clock, a vigorous and steady fire was opened from Fort Moultrie, and a heavy cannonade ensued. But at eight o'clock the cry arose from the wharves, and rolled in one continuous wave over the city, "FORT SUMTER IS ON FIRE!" The watchers of the night before, who had retired for a few moments, were aroused, occupations were instantly suspended, and old and young, either mounted to their points of observation, or rolled in crowds upon the Battery, to look upon the last and most imposing act in this great drama. The barracks to the south had been three times set on fire during the bombardment of the day before, but each time the flames were immediately extinguished. Subsequently, however, a red-hot shot from Fort Moultrie, or a shell from elsewhere, found a lodgment, when the fact was not apparent, and the fire, smouldering for a time, at length broke forth, and flames and smoke rose in volumes from the crater of Fort Sumter. The wind was blowing from the west, driving the smoke across the fort and into the embrasures, where the gunners were at work, and pouring its volumes through the port-holes; the firing of Fort Sumter appeared to be renewed with vigor. The fire of the Fort, long fierce and rapid, however, was gradually abated, and although at distant intervals a gun was fired, the necessity of preserving their magazines and of avoiding the flames, left the tenants little leisure for resistance. But the firing from without was continued with redoubled vigor. Every battery poured in its ceaseless round of shot and shell. The enthusiasm of success inspired their courage and gave precision to their action; and thus, as in the opening, so in the closing scene, under the beaming sunlight, in view of thousands crowded upon the wharves and house-tops, and amid the booming of ordnance, and in view of the five immense ships sent by the enemy with reinforcements, lying idly just out of gun shot on the Bar, this first fortress of despotic power fell prostrate to the cause of Southern Independence.

About eight o'clock, Fort Moultrie had commenced to pour in hot shot, to prevent the extinguishment of the spreading flames, and to kindle new fires in all the quarters. The fight between the two forts was terrific. At this time, Sumter fired

fifty-four shots at Moultrie in one hour, tearing the barracks
to pieces. But the work was vain. Moultrie was too much for
Sumter. In five minutes, she returned eleven shots. At about
nine o'clock the flames appeared to be abating, and it was
apprehended that no irreparable injury had been sustained;
but near ten o'clock, a column of white smoke rose high
above the battlements, followed by an explosion which was
felt upon the wharves, and gave the assurance that if the
magazines were not exploded, at least their temporary ammunition were exposed to the element still raging. Soon after
the barracks to the east and west were in flames, the smoke
rose in redoubled volume from the whole circle of the fort,
and rolling from the embrasures, it seemed scarcely possible
that life could be sustained. Soon after another column of
smoke arose as fearful as the first. The guns had been completely silenced, and the only option left to the tenants of
the fortress seemed to be whether they would perish or
surrender. At a quarter to one o'clock, the staff, from which
the flag still waved, was shot away, and it was long in doubt
whether, if there were the purpose, there was the ability to
re-erect it. But at the expiration of about twenty minutes, it
again appeared upon the eastern rampart, and announced that
resistance was not ended. In the meantime, however, a small
boat started from the city wharf, bearing Colonels Lee,
Pryor and Miles, Aides to Gen. Beauregard, with offers of
assistance, if, perchance, the garrison should be unable to
escape the flames. As they approached the fort, the United
States' flag re-appeared; and shortly afterwards a shout from
the whole circle of spectators on the islands and the main,
announced that the white flag of truce was waving from the
ramparts. A small boat had already been seen to shoot out
from Cummings' Point, in the direction of the fort, in which
stood an officer with a white flag upon the point of his sword.

This officer proved to be Col. Wigfall, Aid to the Commanding General, who, entering through a port-hole, demanded the surrender. Major Anderson replied, that "they were still firing on him." "Then take your flag down," said Col. Wigfall: "they will continue to fire upon you so long as that is up."

After some further explanations in the course of which it appeared, that Major Anderson's men were fast suffocating in the casemates, the brave commander of Sumter agreed that he would, unconditionally, surrender—subject to the terms of Gen. Beauregard, who, as was said by Col. Wigfall, "is a soldier and a gentleman, and knows how to treat a brave enemy." When this parley had been terminated, another boat from the city containing Major Jones, Cols. Chesnut and Manning, with other officers and the Chief of the Fire Department and the Palmetto Fire Company came up to the Fort. All firing had meantime ceased. The agreement to unconditional surrender was reiterated in the presence of new arrivals, and Messrs. Chesnut and Manning immediately came back to the city to bring the news, when it was also positively stated afterwards, that no one was killed on either side. It may seem strange, but it is nevertheless true. The only way to account for the fact is in the excellent protection offered by the unparalleled good works behind which the engagement was fought. The long range of shooting must also be taken into account. In addition to this, on each side, the men, seeing a discharge in their direction, learned to dodge the balls and to throw themselves under cover. A horse on Sullivan's Island was the only living creature deprived of life during the bombardment.

General Beauregard decided upon the following terms of Anderson's capitulation:

That is—First affording all proper facilities for removing

him and his command, together with company arms and property and all private property.

Secondly—That the Federal flag he had so long and so bravely defended should be saluted by the vanquished on taking it down.

Thirdly—That Anderson should be allowed to fix the time of surrender; to take place, however, some time during the ensuing day (Sunday).

These terms were the same as those offered before the contest. In pursuance of this programme, Major Anderson indicated Sunday morning as the time for his formal surrender.

The Tune of Dixie

THE AFFAIR at Sumter set off a chain of events that was to lead, irresistibly, to Appomattox. The first reaction was Lincoln's call for volunteers. This was immediately followed by the accession of Virginia to the Southern Confederacy and only a little later by the addition of Arkansas, Tennessee, and North Carolina to the group of seceding states.

It was apparent that Virginia would be the first great battlefield, and young Southerners nurtured in the righteousness of state rights and the belief in their military superiority to the Yankee foe were quick to volunteer—to join the army in time to participate in the glorious three months of warfare that would turn back the Northern invader. In the years immediately preceding the war volunteer companies had been formed in most of the Southern cities. As often as not essentially social organizations, these companies were little prepared for the kind of war that lay ahead. But the future of bloody battles and years of hardship did not worry them so long as the dangers were unforeseen, and the best of young Southern manhood marched defiantly, almost gaily, to Virginia.

24

One such company was the Mobile Cadets. They left Alabama in April, 1861, and proceeded to Virginia to be stationed in the vicinity of Norfolk for more than a year. In the summer of 1861 they felt keenly that they had not participated in the great battle of Manassas, but, before the war was over, they had taken part in nearly every other major engagement in Virginia and had amassed one of the bloodiest of regimental records.

Here, in a lighthearted excerpt from the contemporary account of one of its members, is a description of part of the journey of the Mobile Cadets to their post in Virginia and an account of the amazing rapidity with which "Dixie" was becoming the tuneful symbol of Southern nationalism. Its author, Henry Hotze, was a member of the Mobile Cadets at this time but was later detached and sent to London as commercial agent of the Confederacy. There he established and edited the remarkable propaganda organ of the Confederacy, *The Index*. It was in the columns of this paper that the following account appeared in the spring of 1862.

THE TUNE OF DIXIE

Norfolk, May 5, 1861.

We arrived here at daylight this morning in two special trains, after nearly twenty hours' continued but slow travelling. Our conveyances were again, as for the greater part of our many days' journey, cattle-cars, or box-cars, as they are termed; but these had been well aired and cleaned, a sort of rough benches fitted into them, and the sliding side-doors kept open, so that our situation, if not comfortable, was at least endurable. One passenger car was attached to each train for the officers and sick, of which latter we have already a goodly number, owing to the sudden change of climate, and of water and food, though no serious cases. The officers, for the most part, remained in the box-cars among the men, sharing their discomforts, and assisting in turning them into subjects of merriment.

The scenes on the way were a repetition of those we had witnessed in Georgia and Tennessee. Bevies of girls to greet us wherever the train stopped for wood and water, and gifts of flowers, cakes, and early fruit by the enthusiastic fair. Our "boys" have composed a set of doggerel rhymes to the tune of "Dixie," commemorative of the recent accession of Virginia and Tennessee to the Confederacy, and especially complimentary to the former. This they sing on every appropriate occasion, with marked effect upon the hearts of the Virginian beauties. Such was the popularity of the song at Norfolk, where it originated, that some considerate persons bethought themselves of having it printed on little slips of paper, as "The Song of Dixie, sung by the 3rd Regiment of Alabama Volunteers, on their passage through Virginia." These slips have been plentifully distributed on the road, and, I doubt not, will be preserved as historical relics, when the pretty girls who welcomed us shall have become grandmothers, and relate to the wondering little ones about the times when the first troops of Confederate volunteers came from the far South to fight the Yankees on Virginian soil.

> Oh, have you heard the joyful news?
> Virginia does old Abe refuse,
>   Hurrah! hurrah! hurrah!

And Tennessee and brave Kentuck
Will show the North their Southern pluck,
   Hurrah! hurrah!

and so on, through a dozen stanzas, each of which ends with
the patriotic refrain—

"We'ill die for old Virginia."

It is marvellous with what wild-fire rapidity this tune of
"Dixie" has spread over the whole South. Considered as an
intolerable nuisance when first the streets re-echoed it from
the repertoire of wandering minstrels, it now bids fair to become the musical symbol of a new nationality, and we shall
be fortunate if it does not impose its very name on our country. Whether by a coincidence simply accidental, or from
some of those mysterious causes which escape our limited
intelligence, its appearance in its present form was the knell
of the American Republic, and as such it seems to have been
instantaneously received by the masses in the South everywhere. What magic potency is there in those rude, incoherent
words, which lend themselves to so many parodies, of which
the poorest is an improvement on the original? What spell is
there in the wild strain that it should be made to betoken the
stern determination of a nation resolved to achieve its independence? I cannot tell.

Most persons believe it to be of recent origin, first introduced during the last Presidential contest by an "Ethiopian
minstrels'" troop performing in New Orleans. This is only
partially true; its real origin is of much older date. Those who
have travelled much on Western rivers must often have heard
it, in various forms, among the firemen and deck-hands of
the river steamers. For years the free negroes of the North,

especially those employed on board the steamers on the Western rivers making periodical voyages South, have cheered their labours with this favorite song:—

"I WISH I WAS IN DIXIE!"

Plaintive Air—Sung nightly in Washington by that Celebrated Delineator, Abraham Lincoln.

I wish I was in Dixie;
    In Dixie's land
    I'll take my stand,
And live and die in Dixie.
    Away, away,
Away down South in Dixie—

expressed the negro's preference for his more genial and sunny native clime, the land which is the negro's true home, and the only land where he is happy and contented, despite the morbid imaginings of ill-informed or misguided philanthropists.

The word "Dixie" is an abbreviation of "Mason and Dixon's line," as the line separating Maryland and Pennsylvania is called, and which both geographically and rhetorically, has expressed the Northern frontier of the South ever since the line was drawn by the surveyors whose names it immortalizes. Years before I heard the tune I have heard negroes in the North use the word "Dixie" in that sense, as familiarly as we do the more lengthy phrase from which it is derived.

A Visit to the Capitol at Montgomery

WILLIAM HOWARD RUSSELL, correspondent of the London *Times*, came to America in 1861 with an unsurpassed journalistic reputation gained as a reporter of the Crimean War. He was welcomed in both North and South and shown courtesies which allowed him to give a relatively full picture of the American scene. But generally scornful of American institutions, be they Northern or Southern, he soon managed to arouse the enmity of Confederate and Yankee partisans alike and was denied permission to accompany McClellan's army in its march on Richmond in 1862. He shortly returned to London and published his remarkably illuminating account of the first year of the war.

Although his letters were written as dispatches to the London *Times*, they were widely reprinted in both the United States and the Confederacy. His letter from Montgomery, for example, appeared in the Mobile *Advertiser & Register* for June 23, 1861.

Monday, May 6.—To-day I visited the capitol, where the Provisional Congress is sitting. On leaving the hotel, which is like a small Willard's, so far as the crowd in the hall is concerned, my attention was attracted to a group of people to whom a man was holding forth in energetic sentences. The day was hot, but I pushed near to the spot, for I like to hear a stump-speech, or to pick up a stray morsel of divinity in the *via sacra* of strange cities, and it appeared as though the speaker was delivering an oration or a sermon. The crowd was small. Three or four idle men in rough, homespun, make-shift uniforms, leaned against the iron rails enclosing a small pond of foul, green-looking water, surrounded by brick-work, which decorates the space in front of the Exchange hotel. The speaker stood on an empty deal packing case. A man in a cart was listening with a lacklustre eye to the address. Some three or four others, in a sort of vehicle which might either be a hearse or a piano van, had also drawn up for the benefit of the address. Five or six other men, in long black coats and high hats, some whittling sticks, and chewing tobacco, and discharging streams of discolored saliva, completed the group. "N-i-n-e h'hun'nerd and fifty dollars offered for him!" exclaimed the man, in the tone of injured dignity, remonstrance and surprise, which can be insinuated by all true auctioneers into the dryest numerical statements. "Will *no one* make any advance on nine hundred and fifty dollars?" A man near me opened his mouth, spat, and said, "twenty-five." "Only nine hundred and seventy-five dollars offered for him. Why, at's radaklous—only nine hundred and seventy-five dollars! Will no one," &c. Beside the orator auctioneer stood a stout young man of five-and-twenty years of age, with a bundle in his hand. He was a muscular fellow, broad-shoul-dered, narrow flanked, but rather small in stature; he had on a broad greasy, old wide-awake, a blue jacket, a coarse cotton shirt, loose and rather ragged trowsers, and broken shoes. The expression of his face was heavy and sad, but it was by no means disagreeable, in spite of his thick lips, broad nostrils, and high cheek-bones. On his head was wool instead of hair. I am neither sentimentalist nor black republican, nor negro-worshipper, but I confess the sight caused a strange thrill through my heart. I tried in vain to make myself familiar with the fact that I could, for the sum of $975, become as absolutely the owner of that mass of blood, bones, sinew, flesh, and brains, as of the horse which stood by my side. There was no sophistry which could persuade me the man was not a man—he was, indeed, by no means my brother, but assuredly he was a fellow-creature. I have seen slave markets in the East, but somehow or other the Orientalism of the scene cast a coloring over the nature of the sales there which deprived them of the disagreeable harshness and matter-of-fact character of the transaction before me. For Turk, or Smyrniote, or Egyptian to buy and sell slaves seemed rather suited to the eternal fitness of things than otherwise. The turbaned, shawled, loose-trowsered, pipe-smoking merchants speaking an unknown tongue looked as if they were engaged in a legitimate business. One knew that their slaves would not be condemned to any very hard labor, and that they would be in some sort the inmates of the family, and members of it. Here it grated on my ear to listen to the familiar tones of the English tongue as the medium by which the transfer was effected, and it was painful to see decent-looking men in European garb engaged in the work before me. Perchance these impressions may wear off, for I meet many English people who are the most strenuous advocates of the slave system, although it is true that their perceptions may be quickened to recognize its beauties by their participation in the profits. The negro was sold to one of the bystanders, and walked off with his bundle, God knows where. "Niggers is cheap," was the only remark of the bystanders. I continued my walk up a long, wide, straight street, or more properly, an unpaved sandy road, lined with wooden houses on each side, and with trees by the side of the footpath. The lower of the two stories is generally used as a shop, mostly of the miscellaneous store kind, in which all sorts of articles are to be had if there is any money to pay for them; and, in the present case, if any faith is to be attached to the conspicuous notices in the windows, credit is of no credit, and the only thing that can be accepted in exchange for the goods is "cash." At the end of this long street, on a moderate eminence, stands a whitewashed or painted edifice, with a gaunt lean portico, supported on lofty lanky pillars, and surmounted by a subdued and dejected-looking little cupola. Passing an unkempt lawn, through a very shabby little gateway in a brick frame, and we ascend a flight of steps into a hall, from which a double starcase conducts us to the vestibule of the chamber. Any thing much more offensive to the eye cannot well be imagined than the floor and stairs. They are stained deeply by tobacco juice, which has left its marks on the white stone steps and on the base of the pillars outside. In the hall which we have entered there are two tables, covered with hams, oranges, bread and fruits, for the refreshment of members and visitors, over which two sable goddesses, in portentous crinoline, preside. The door of the chamber is open and we are introduced into a lofty, well-lighted and commodious apartment, in which the Congress of the Confederate States holds its deliberations. A gallery runs half round the room, and is half filled with visitors—country cousins, and farmers of cotton and maize, and, haply, seekers of places great or small. A light and low semicircular screen separates the body of the house, where the members sit, from the space under the gallery, which is appropriated to ladies and visitors. The clerk sits at a desk above this table, and on a platform behind him are the desk and chair of the presiding officer or Speaker of the Congress. Over his head hangs the unfailing portrait of Washington, and a small engraving, in a black frame, of a gentleman unknown to me. Seated in the midst of them, at a senator's desk, I was permitted to "assist," in the French sense, at the deliberations of the Congress. Mr. Howell Cobb took the chair, and a white-headed clergyman was called upon to say prayers, which he did, upstanding, with out-stretched hands and closed eyes, by the side of the speaker. The prayer was long and sulphureous. One more pregnant with gunpowder I never heard, nor could aught like it have been heard since.

> "Pulpit, drum ecclesiastic,
> Was beat with fist instead of stick."

The reverend gentleman prayed that the Almighty might be pleased to inflict on the arms of the United States such a defeat that it might be the example of signal punishment forever—that this president might be blessed, and the other president might be the other thing—that the gallant, devoted young soldiers who were fighting for their country might not suffer from exposure to the weather or from the bullets of their enemies; and that the base mercenaries who were fight-ing on the other side might come to sure and swift destruc-tion, and so on.

Are right and wrong mere geographical expressions? The prayer was over at last, and the house proceeded to business. Although each state has several delegates in Congress, it is only entitled to one vote on a strict division. In this way some curious decisions may be arrived at, as the smallest state is equal to the largest, and a majority of the Florida

representatives may neutralize a vote of all the Georgia representatives. For example, Georgia has ten delegates; Florida
has only three. The vote of Florida, however, is determined
by the action of any two of its three representatives, and
these two may, on a division, throw the one state vote into
the scale against that of Georgia, for which ten members are
agreed. The Congress transacts all its business in secret session, and finds it a very agreeable and commendable way of
doing it. Thus, to-day, for example, after the presentation of
a few unimportant motions and papers, the speaker rapped
his desk, and announced that the house would go into secret
session, and that all who were not members should leave.

As I was returning to the hotel there was another small
crowd at the fountain. Another auctioneer, a fat, flabby,
perspiring, puffy man, was trying to sell a negro girl, who
stood on the deal box beside him. She was dressed pretty
much like a London servant-girl of the lower order out of
place, except that her shoes were mere shreds of leather
patches, and her bonnet would have scarce passed muster in
the New Cut. She, too, had a little bundle in her hand, and
looked out at the buyers from a pair of large sad eyes. "Nig-
gers were cheap;" still here was this young woman going for
an upset price of $610, but no one would bid, and the
auctioneer, after vain attempts to raise the price and excite
competition, said, "Not sold to-day, Sally; you may get
down."

Tuesday, May 7.—The newspapers contain the text of the
declaration of a state of war on the part of President Davis,
and of the issue of letters of marque and reprisal, &c. But it
may be asked, who will take these letters of marque? Where
is the government of Montgomery to find ships? The answer
is to be found in the fact that already numerous applications
have been received from the shipowners of New England,

from the whalers of New Bedford, and from others in the
Northern States, for these very letters of marque, accompanied by the highest securities and guaranties! This statement I make on the very highest authority. I leave it to you
to deal with the facts.

To-day I proceeded to the Montgomery Downing street
and Whitehall, to present myself to the members of the cabinet, and to be introduced to the President of the Confederate
States of America. There is no sentry at the doors, and access
is free to all, but there are notices on the doors warning visitors that they can only be received during certain hours. The
President was engaged with some gentlemen when I was
presented to him, but he received me with much kindliness
of manner, and, when they had left, entered into conversation
with me for some time on general matters. Mr. Davis is a man
of slight, sinewy figure, rather over the middle height, and of
erect, soldierlike bearing. He is about fifty-five years of age;
his features are regular and well-defined, but the face is
thin and marked on cheek and brow with many wrinkles, and
is rather careworn and haggard. One eye is apparently blind,
the other is dark, piercing, and intelligent. He was dressed
very plainly, in a light-gray summer suit. In the course of
conversation, he gave an order for the Secretary of War to
furnish me with a letter as a kind of passport, in case of my
falling in with the soldiers of any military posts who might
be indisposed to let me pass freely, merely observing that I
had been enough within the lines of camps to know what
was my duty on such occasions. I subsequently was presented
to Mr. Walker, the Secretary of War, who promised to furnish me with the needful documents before I left Montgomery. In his room were General Beauregard and several
officers, engaged over plans and maps, apparently in a little
council of war, which was, perhaps, not without reference to

the intelligence that the United States troops were marching on Norfolk Navy-Yard, and had actually occupied Alexandria. On leaving the Secretary, I proceeded to the room of the Attorney-General, Mr. Benjamin, a very intelligent and able man, whom I found busied in preparations connected with the issue of letters of marque. Everything in the offices looked like earnest work and business.

On my way back from the State Department, I saw a very fine company of infantry and three field-pieces, with about one hundred and twenty artillerymen, on their march to the railway station for Virginia. The men were all well equipped, but there were no ammunition wagons for the guns, and the transport consisted solely of a few country carts, drawn by poor horses, out of condition. There is no lack of muscle and will among the men. The troops which I see here are quite fit to march and fight as far as their personnel is concerned, and there is no people in the world so crazy with military madness. The very children in the streets ape the air of soldiers, carry little flags, and wear cockades as they strut in the highways, and mothers and fathers feed the fever by dressing them up as Zouaves or Chausseurs.

Mrs. Davis had a small levee to-day in right of her position as wife of the President. Several ladies there probably looked forward to the time when their states might secede from the new Confederation, and afford them the pleasure of holding a reception. Why not Presidents of the State of Georgia, or Alabama? Why not King of South Carolina, or Emperor of Florida? Soldiers of fortune, make your game! Gentlemen politicians, the ball is rolling. There is, to be sure, a storm gathering at the North, but it cannot hurt you, and already there are condottieri from all parts of the world flocking to your aid, who will eat your Southern beeves the last of all.

One word more as to a fleet. The English owners of several large steamers are already in correspondence with the government here for the purchase of their vessels. The intelligence which had reached the government that their commissioners have gone on to Paris is regarded as unfavorable to their claims, and as a proof that as yet England is not disposed to recognize them. It is amusing to hear the tone used on both sides toward Great Britain. Both are most anxious for her countenance and support, although the North blusters rather more about its independence than the South, which professes a warm regard for the mother country. "But," say the North, "if Great Britain recognizes the South, we shall certainly look on it as a declaration of war." "And," say the South, "if Great Britain does not recognize our privateers' flag, we shall regard it as proof of hostility and of alliance with the enemy." The government at Washington seeks to obtain promises from Lord Lyons that our government will not recognize the Southern Confederacy, but at the same time refuses any guaranties in reference to the rights of neutrals. The blockade of the Southern ports would not occasion us any great inconvenience at present, because the cotton-loading season is over; but if it be enforced in October, there is a prospect of very serious and embarrassing questions arising in reference to the rights of neutrals, treaty obligations with the United States government, the trade and commerce of England, and the law of blockade in reference to the distinctions to be drawn between measures of war and means of annoyance.

As I write, the guns in front of the State Department are firing a salute, and each report marks a state of the Confederacy. They are now ten, as Arkansas and Tennessee are now out of the Union.

"Glorious, Triumphant and Complete Victory"

THE SPRING of 1861 was a readying time. The new government at Montgomery worked vigorously to put itself on a working basis, and finally removed to Richmond. Efforts were made to procure arms from Northern and foreign sources. In the South itself new manufactories were established to provide goods for home consumption and to create a military potential. The South was determined to assert industrial and commercial as well as political and military independence.

The first big military test did not occur until late July, when the Confederates met the Federal forces in the great amphitheater ringed by the hills near Manassas Junction, Virginia. Neither army was properly seasoned for a full-scale battle, and the fight at Bull Run had comic-opera as well as tragic aspects. What at first looked like a Northern victory was turned into a heavy defeat as reinforcements under Joseph E. Johnston joined the troops of Gustave Toutant Beauregard and routed the Yankees under McDowell.

Manassas was a memorable victory. Perhaps it created an overconfidence that eventually hurt the Confederacy. But it gave the South a hero in Thomas Jonathan Jackson. ("There stands Jackson like a stone wall," cried General Bee, and the name was evermore "Stonewall" Jackson.) It gave the South a martyr. ("They have killed me, but never give up the field" were the dying words of Francis Bartow.) And it gave the South a minor spoil, for if "Dixie" had not become Southern property by that time, the defeat of McDowell's troops, who had marched from Washington singing it as they crossed Long Bridge, made it Confederate and Southern forever.

Here is President Davis' telegram to General Samuel Cooper, Richmond's first word of the victory at Manassas. Following it is the address published by Generals Johnston and Beauregard to thank the soldiers for a "glorious, triumphant and complete victory." Though signed by both generals, the neo-Napoleonic rhetoric stamps it as actually written by the glamorous Creole. Frank Potts, a Virginia infantryman, recorded in his diary after the address was read to the troops: "It shows that our Beauregard not only wields the sword of Washington but the pen of Hamilton."

President Davis' telegram from the field of battle at Manasses[!], dated "July 21, at night," will become an important historical document. It is guarded in its statement, and thus falls far short of the facts as they afterward came out:

To General S. Cooper:

Night has closed on a hard-fought field. Our forces have won a glorious victory. The enemy was routed and fled precipitately, abandoning a very large amount of arms, munitions, knapsacks and baggage. The ground was strewn with their killed for miles and the farm houses and grounds around were filled with their wounded. The pursuit was continued along several routes toward Leesburg and Centreville until darkness covered the fugitives. We have captured several field batteries and regimental standards, and one United States flag. Many prisoners have been taken. Too high praise cannot be bestowed, whether for the skill of the principal officers, or for the gallantry of all the troops. The battle was mainly fought on our left several miles from our field works— our force engaged there not exceeding fifteen thousand; that of the enemy estimated at thirty-five thousand.

(Signed)   Jeff. Davis.

Soldiers of the Confederate States:

One week ago, a countless host of men, organized into an army, with all the appointments which modern art and practiced skill could devise, invaded the soil of Virginia. Their people sounded their approach with triumphant displays of anticipated victory. Their Generals came in almost royal state; their great Ministers, Senators and women came to witness the immolation of our army and subjugation of our people, and to celebrate the result with wild revelry.

It is with the profoundest emotions of gratitude to an overruling God, whose hand is manifest in protecting our homes and liberties, that we, your Generals commanding, are enabled, in the name of our whole country, to thank you for that patriotic courage, that heroic gallantry, that devoted daring, exhibited by you in the actions of the 18th and 21st, by which the hosts of the enemy were scattered, and a signal and glorious victory obtained.

The two affairs of the 18th and 21st were but the sustained and continued effort of your patriotism against the constantly recurring columns of an enemy, fully treble your numbers; and these efforts were crowned, on the evening of the 21st, with a victory so complete, that the invaders are driven disgracefully from the field, and made to fly in disorderly rout back to their entrenchments—a distance of over thirty miles.

They left upon the field nearly every piece of their artillery, a large portion of their arms, equipments, baggage, stores, etc., etc., and amost every one of their wounded and dead, amounting, together with the prisoners, to many thousands. And thus the Northern hosts were driven from Virginia.

Soldiers! we congratulate you on an event which ensures the liberty of our country. We congratulate every man of you, whose glorious privilege it was to participate in this triumph of courage and of truth—to fight in the battle of Manassas. You have created an epoch in the history of liberty and unborn nations will rise up and call you "blessed."

Continue this noble devotion, looking always to the protection of a just God, and before time grows much older, we will be hailed as the deliverers of a nation of ten millions of people.

Comrades! our brothers who have fallen have earned undying renown upon earth, and their blood shed in our holy cause is a precious and acceptable sacrifice to the Father of Truth and Right.

Their graves are beside the tomb of Washington; their spirits have joined with his in eternal communion.

We will hold fast to the soil in which the dust of Washington is thus mingled with the dust of our brothers. We will transmit this land free to our children, or we will fall into the fresh graves of our brothers in arms. We drop one tear on their laurels and move forward to avenge them.

Soldiers! we congratulate you on a glorious, triumphant and complete victory, and we thank you for doing your *whole duty* in the service of your country.

(Signed)   J. E. JOHNSTON,
General C. S. A.

(Signed)   G. T. BEAUREGARD,
General C. S. A.

The Texans Leave for War

WHEN HE VISITED Texas in 1863, Englishman Sir Arthur James Lyon Fremantle commented: "At the outbreak of the war it was found very difficult to raise infantry in Texas, as no Texan walks a yard if he can help it. Many mounted regiments were therefore organized, and afterwards dismounted." The Texans were probably wise in their prejudice against infantry service; perhaps they knew the hardships that would await them on a long march to Virginia. But they were no less patriotic, no less eager to join the Southern armies, than troops in other states.

Out of Texas came the famous Hood's Texas Brigade. Chaplain of Hood's Texans was Nicholas A. Davis, a devout Presbyterian and a determined advocate of the glory of his soldier charges. In 1863 he had printed in Richmond a small volume that was one of the first of Confederate regimental histories. In this little book he recounts the difficulties which beset the Texans on their march to the Virginian theater of war, experiences in strong contrast to the journey of Henry Hotze's Cadets from Mobile to Norfolk.

44

Hundreds of Texans flocked to the Camps of Instruction set up by the state government in April, 1861, but only four companies could be formed when the Confederate government announced that it would accept their enlistments only as Confederate, not Texas state, troops. After weeks spent in the miasmic camps of a Texas summer the troops were finally dispatched toward Richmond by General Earl Van Dorn. Here is Chaplain Davis' story of the start of that long journey.

The hour of departure was hailed with rejoicing by the men, and all countenances were beaming with animation; all hearts were high with hope and confidence, and every bosom seemed warmed by enthusiasm;—the last greetings among friends were interchanged, the last good-byes were said, and away we sped over the flowery prairies, with colors fluttering in the breeze, each hoarse whistle of the locomotive placing distance between us and our loves at home . . .

The men of whom we are now writing had come together from the hills and valleys of Texas, at the first sound of the tocsin of war. The first harsh blast of the bugle found them at their home, in the quiet employment of the arts and avocations of peace. It is a singular fact, but no less singular than true, that those men who, at home, were distinguished among their fellows as peculiarly endowed to adorn and enrich society by their lives and conversation, who were first in the paths of social communion, whose places when they left were unfilled, and until they return again must be deserted shrines, should be the first to leap from their sequestered seats, the first to flash the rusty steel from its scabbard, and to flash it in the first shock of battle. But so it is, and we venture to assert, that of all those whom this war has drawn to the field, and torn away from the domestic fireside, there will be none so much missed at home as those who left with the first troops for Virginia. They were representative men from all portions of the State—young, impetuous and fresh, full of energy, enterprise, and fire—men of action—men who, when they first heard the shrill shriek of battle, as it came from the far-off coast of South Carolina, at once ceased to argue with themselves, or with their neighbors, as to the why-fores or the where-fores—it was enough to know that the struggle had commenced, and that they were Southrons.

Where companies had not been formed in their own counties, they hastened to adjoining counties, and there joined in with strangers. Some came in from the far-off frontier. Some came down from the hills of the North, and some came up from the savannahs of the South—all imbued with one self-same purpose, to fight for "Dixie."

Among them could be found men of all trades and professions—attorneys, doctors, merchants, farmers, mechanics, editors, scholastics, &c., &c.—all animated and actuated by the self-same spirit of patriotism, and all for the time being willing to lay aside their plans of personal ambition, and to place themselves on the altar of their country, and to put themselves under the leveling discipline of the army.

On the evening of the 17th, we were embarked at Beaumont on the steamer Florilda, a large and comfortable steamer, upon which we glided off from the landing, and set sail for the Bluff, the terminus of navigation, and from whence our journey had to be made by land. The trip was unattended by any feature of particular interest, and all arrived at Nibletts Bluff, on the morning of the 18th, at an early hour, and after debarking and getting all the baggage ashore, the men went into camp in the edge of the town.

Here we had the first realization of the fact, that we were *actual soldiers*, and had the first lesson illustrated to us, that a soldier must be patient under wrong, and that he is remediless under injustice—that he, although the self constituted and acknowledged champion of liberty, has, nevertheless, for the time being, parted with that boon, and, that he is but the victim of all official miscreants who choose to subject him to imposition.

The poor soldier receives many such lessons, and his fortitude and patriotism is often taxed to bear them without open rebellion, but as this was the first instance in which we had an opportunity of seeing and feeling such lessons experimentally, we here chronicle the circumstances for the benefit of all concerned. Gen. Van Dorn had entered into a contract with one J. T. Ward to transport these troops from Texas across to Louisiana, and Ward had undertaken as per agreement to furnish transportation in wagons across the country. He had been going back and forth for weeks, looking at the different roads, preparing the means of transportation; had delayed us getting off from Texas until all his vast arrangements were systematized, and until all his immense resources could be deployed into proper order, and concentrated at Niblett's Bluff for this grand exodus of two thousand soldiers, who were but awaiting his movements to begin their own pilgrimage to the great Mecca of their hopes, the "Old Dominion." To hear this man, Ward, spout and splutter among the streets of Houston about his teams and his teamsters, his wagons and his mules, one would have thought that the weight of the whole Quartermaster's Department of the Confederate Army rested upon his shoulders, and that his overburdened head was taxed with the superintendence of trains from California to the Potomac. Be this as it may, on arriving at the Bluff, whatever may have been the resources of our quartermaster, Ward, on this special occasion he fell short of an approximation of our necessities. We had started on the trip with clothing, camp-equipage, medical stores, and commissary supplies, all complete. The citizens of Texas had left nothing undone on their part to send their sons into the field well supplied with everything essential for their comfort, and, in addition, many things that had just been drawn from the agent of the Government, at Houston, which it was important should be carried with us. The troops were new to service, and unaccustomed to marching. It could not be expected that they could make the tedious trip through the swamps of Louisiana, unaided by liberal transportation. Van Dorn had unwisely and unjustly kept them in the sickly miasma of Buffalo Bayou until disease had already fallen in the veins of many, and all of them were suffering more or less from the enervating effects of that confinement. Such was the condition of the men now thrown into a thin and sparsely settled region of Louisiana, dependent alone upon others for every necessity to their new condition.

Under this state of affairs we found *seven wagons*, with indifferent teams, which Ward had procured for the purpose of transporting five hundred men, with the equipments and outfit mentioned. Ward had come to the Bluff with us on the steamer, but had gone immediately back, after leaving assurances that his preparations for our conveyance were ample. It is said that the wagons that he did furnish, were gathered up in that immediate vicinity, and that he engaged some of them even at so late an hour as our arrival at the Bluff.

The consequences were, that the officers in command had to rely upon themselves for the means of prosecuting the march. Tents, cooking utensils, clothing, medical stores, &c.,

to a large amount, were stowed away with whosoever would promise to take care of them for us until they could be sent on. Our sick men were left behind, and our journey commenced with what few things could be carried in these wagons.

Such an inauspicious introduction to the service, was far from being encouraging to the patriotic ardor, and many vented their curses against Ward, Van Dorn, and all concerned; but so earnest were the men in their devotion to the cause in which they had engaged, and so deep the confidence that all things would work right when we once got fairly along under the protecting aegis of our new Government; that soon all mutinous mutterings or complainings were suppressed, and the men set about relieving themselves of their difficulties as soon as possible.

A Skirmish of the Horse Artillery

THE TEXANS did not reach Virginia in time for the battle at Manassas, but their force was to be felt many times later in the war.

As the summer of 1861 wore into fall there were no more decisive battles. The Federals withdrew toward Washington to reorganize the "On to Richmond" march. General Beauregard went into camp at Centreville, where he undertook to train further his relatively raw Confederate soldiers. It was here that he received a visit from the famous Baltimore belles Hetty and Jennie Cary and their magnetic cousin Constance, the future wife of Jefferson Davis' private aide, Burton Harrison. The Misses Cary inspected the recent battlefield at Manassas and enlivened camp life generally. But they will be remembered for their introduction to the Confederate troops gathered at Centreville of "My Maryland," the stirring song written by James Ryder Randall and set to the tune of "Lauriger Horatius" by Jennie Cary. In a mock ceremony at Beauregard's headquarters Constance, Hetty, and Jennie were made, respectively, "captain-general," "lieutenant-colonel," and "first lieutenant" of the "Cary Invincibles." The South was still enjoying its war.

A few weeks later the three girls were called upon by a committee of the Confederate Congress to execute the design for the new battle flag. (The "Stars and Bars" had been difficult to distinguish from the "Stars and Stripes" in battle.) The young ladies soon dispatched their flags of the new design—"The Southern Cross," as this battle flag came to be known—to their heroes along the battle front in Northern Virginia, Generals Beauregard, Johnston, and Van Dorn.

But all was not socializing and playing at war. There were constant skirmishes as Yank met Rebel. Out of the skirmishes and small battles was emerging a new Southern hero, the dashing J. E. B. Stuart. In a family of torn loyalties, Jeb Stuart had no doubt on which side his duty lay. A trained soldier, and a good one, he entered the Confederate Army determined to inflict disaster on the enemy.

Here is his report of a small but typical engagement in the fall of 1861—the skirmish at Lewinsville, Virginia, September 11.

REPORT OF THE ENGAGEMENT AT LEWINSVILLE, VIRGINIA, J. E. B. STUART, COL. COMMANDING.

> Headquarters Munson's Hill,
> September 11th, 1861.

General:

I started about 12 o'clock, with the 13th Virginia Volunteers, commanded by Maj. Terrill, 305 men, one section of

Rosser's Battery, Washington Artillery, and a detachment of First Cavalry, under Captain Patrick, for Lewinsville, where I learned from my cavalry pickets, the enemy were posted with some force. My intention was to surprise them, and I succeeded entirely. Approaching Lewinsville by the enemy's left and rear, taking care to keep my small force an entire secret from their observation, I, at the same time, *carefully provided* against the disaster to myself which I was striving to inflict upon the enemy, and felt sure, that if necessary, I could fall back successfully before any force the enemy might have, for the country was favorable to retreat and ambuscade. At a point, nicely screened by the woods from Lewinsville, and a few hundred yards from the place, I sent forward, under Maj. Terrill, a portion of his command, stealthily to reach the woods at a turn of the road and reconnoitre beyond; this was admirably done, and the Major soon reported to me that the enemy had a piece of artillery in position, in the road just at Lewinsville, commanding our road. I directed him immediately to post his riflemen so as to render it impossible for the cannoniers to serve the piece, and if possible, capture it. During subsequent operations, the cannoniers tried ineffectually to serve the piece, and finally, after one was shot through the head, the piece was taken off. While this was going on, a few shots from Rosser's section, at a cluster of the enemy, a quarter of a mile off, put the entire force of the enemy in full retreat, exposing their entire column to flank fire from our pieces. Some wagons and a large body of cavalry first passed in hasty flight, the rifle piece and howitzer firing as they passed; then came flying a battery, eight pieces of artillery, (Griffin's,) which soon took position about six hundred yards to our front and right, and rained shot and shell upon us during the entire engagement, but with harmless effect, although striking very near. Then passed three regiments of infantry, at double quick, receiving in succession as they passed, Rosser's unerring salutation—his shells bursting directly over their heads and creating the greatest havoc and confusion in their ranks. The last infantry regiment was followed by a column of cavalry, which at one time, rode over the rear of the infantry in great confusion. The Field, General and Staff-Officers were seen exerting every effort to restore order in their broken ranks, and my cavalry videttes, observing their flight, reported that they finally rallied a mile and-a-half below, and took position there, firing round after round of artillery from that position up the road, where they supposed our columns would be pursuing them. Capt. Rosser having no enemy left to contend with, at his own request, was permitted to view the ground of the enemy's flight, and found the road plowed up by his solid shot, and strewn with fragments of shells—two men left dead in the road, one mortally wounded, and one not hurt, taken prisoner. The prisoners said the havoc in their ranks was fearful, justifying what I saw myself of the confusion.

Major Terrill's sharp-shooters were by no means idle, firing wherever a straggling Yankee showed his head, and capturing a Lieutenant, (captured by Maj. T., himself,) one Sergeant and one private, all belonging to the Nineteenth Indiana, (Col. Merideth's).

The prisoners reported to me that General McClellan himself was present, and the enemy gave it out publicly that the occupancy of Lewinsville was to be permanent. Alas for human expectations!

The officers and men behaved in a manner worthy of the General's highest commendations, and the firing done by the section, under direction of Capt. Rosser and Lieut. Slocumb, all the time under fire from the enemy's battery, certainly, for accuracy and effect, challenges comparison with any ever made.

Valuable assistance was rendered me by Chaplain Ball, as usual, and Messrs. Hairston and Burke, citizens attached to my staff, were conspicuous in daring. Corp'l Hagan, and Bugler Freed, are entitled to special mention for good conduct and valuable service.

Our loss was not a scratch to man or horse. We have no means of knowing the enemy's, except it must have been heavy from the effects of the shots. We found in all four dead and mortally wounded, and captured four. Of course they carried off all they could. . . .

Please forward this report to General Johnston, Gen. J. Longstreet.

Most respectfully,
Your obed't serv't.
(Signed.)   J. E. B. Stuart.
Colonel Commanding.
(Official.)   R. H. Chilton, A. A. General.

A Prayer for Our Armies

THE PRAYERS of the people, as well as their material support, were with the armies of the Confederacy. Here is "A Prayer for Our Armies" written for the use of the Confederate soldiers in 1861 by Bishop William Green of Mississippi.

Almighty God, whose Providence watcheth over all things, and in whose hands is the disposal of all events, we look up to Thee for Thy protection and blessing amidst the apparent and great dangers with which we are encompassed. Thou hast, in Thy wisdom, permitted the many evils of an unnatural and destructive war to come upon us. Save us, we beseech Thee, from the hands of our enemies. Watch over our fathers, and brothers, and sons, who, trusting in Thy defence and in the righteousness of our cause, have gone forth to the service of their country. May their lives be precious in Thy sight. Preserve them from all the dangers to which they may be exposed. Enable them successfully to perform their duty to Thee and to their country, and do Thou, in Thine infinite wisdom and power, so overrule events, and so dispose the

55

hearts of all engaged in this painful struggle, that it may soon end in peace and brotherly love, and lead not only to the safety, honor and welfare of our *Confederate States,* but to the good of Thy people, and the glory of Thy great name, through Jesus Christ our Lord. Amen.

Winter in Virginia

A s soldiers of fortune, unofficial observers, or reporters a number of foreigners fought with the Confederate Army. Their accounts of the war are sometimes
particularly illuminating as they wrote from a vantage
point conditioned by neither Yankee nor Confederate
prejudices and preconceptions. Though most of their accounts were printed only in England or on the Continent,
copies of them (particularly of the English books) found
their way back to the Confederacy, for the Southerners
were intensely interested in what impression they made
on such outsiders.

A brief glimpse of winter in a Confederate Army camp
in northern Virginia and a short description of the bustle
that had descended on Richmond as the capital of the
Confederacy are contained in the following account ex-
cerpted from the anonymous *Battle-fields of the South.*

For the next two weeks scarcely any sound was heard but
that of axe-men engaged in felling trees; and within a very

short time we were all well housed in log-huts, covered with layers of straw and mud. The fire-places being large, admitted 'sticks' of wood four feet long; and sometimes ten logs of this length constituted a fire. Some bought stoves to cook on, and built additional dwellings for their servants; but within the fortnight all were comfortably provided for. Our commanders occupied some princely residences owned by Union men in Maryland, who had been large lottery dealers, and possessed of immense wealth. The various regiments were placed on the east side of the forts, ready to occupy them within five minutes' notice.

Amusements of all kinds were soon introduced, but chiefly cock-fighting, as in summer. Men were sent out in all directions to buy up game fowl; and shortly there rose up a young generation of "trainers," versed in every point of the game, and of undisputed authority in the settlement of a quarrel. These, for the most part, were gentlemen from the Emerald Isle, not a few of whom were in every regiment in the service. In the matches, regiment fought against regiment, and company against company, for stakes varying from 5 dols. to 2,000 dols. a side; and such was the mania for "roosters" that the camps sounded like a poultry show, or a mammoth farmyard. "Snow-balling" was also a favourite pastime with the Southerners, and, together with skating and sledging, much delighted them; the majority had never seen snow or ice, except when the latter was used with "sherry-cobblers," "whisky-skins," "cocktails," &c.

I was loth to leave the brigade; but service called me to Richmond. So, having partaken of all the enjoyments of "singing clubs," "negro minstrels," "debating clubs," and the like, I departed for Manassas by a quartermaster's waggon, and soon arrived at Centreville. The outposts and guards at the latter place were extremely vigilant—annoyingly so, I thought

—and for the slightest irregularity in our 'passes' and papers would have sent us back to Leesburg. Fortifications of immense strength and extent arose on every hand, and were all well mounted. Though I could not comprehend the half of what fell under my notice, I felt strongly impressed that no army in the world could capture the place by an assault in front or flank. For miles these earthworks could be seen stretching through the country; and I counted not less than five hundred heavy pieces, without numbering them all.

The troops were comfortably quartered in well-built frame-houses, placed in lines of streets, with parade grounds in front; sinks, gutters, and other sanitary arrangements seemed complete. The care and forethought displayed by our generals for the comfort, health, and convenience of the men surprised and delighted me: large bakeries, wash-houses, infirmaries, blacksmiths' shops, numerous sutlers' establishments (where no liquors were sold), chapels, parade and drill grounds, head-quarters, chiefs of departments, immense stables, warehouses and State depots—even a railroad connecting the place with Centreville to facilitate communication and send supplies.

The only drawback here—and this was sufficient to mar the whole—was the incredible quantity and tenacity of the mud. Locomotion in rainy or damp weather baffles all description; and to say that I have seen whole waggon trains fast in the road, with mud up to the axles, would afford but a faint idea of the reality. If timber had been plentiful, the roads might have been "corduroyed," according to the Yankee plan, viz., of piling logs across the road, filling the interstices with small limbs, and covering with mud; but timber was not to be procured for such a purpose; what little there might be was economically served out for fuel.

On arriving at Richmond a wonderful contrast to the well-disciplined order of Manassas presented itself. The Government offices were quiet and business-like, but no other part of the capital was so. The hotels were crowded to excess, as they always are; and great numbers of officers in expensive uniforms strutted about on "sick leave," many of whom had never been in the army at all, and after running up bills with all classes of tradesmen would suddenly depart for parts unknown. The marvel was, that people could be so deceived, for it is no exaggeration to say that every third man was dignified with shoulder-straps, and collectively they far out-numbered all the officers at Manassas! In theatres, bar-rooms, and shops, on horseback or on foot, all wore the insignia of office. Not one was to be found of less rank than captain, and as for colonels—their name was legion! I was measured by a youth for a pair of boots, and bought some dry-goods of another, one morning: in the evening I saw both of them playing at billiards at the "Spottswood," dressed out in bran-new uniforms, with insignia belonging to the rank of major! This was sufficient explanation; and it did not at all surprise me afterwards to hear that nearly all the thousand and one gambling hells were kept by captains, majors, and colonels. General Winder, the provost-marshal, subsequently made it a punishable offence for any to assume uniforms except soldiers. The change was sudden and ludicrous in effect.

The floating population of Richmond was made up of the strangest elements. Some came to see friends, others with wonderful inventions or suggestions for Government. Not a few were impressed with an idea that the Cabinet needed their advice and counsel; but the majority of these strangers came with the modest determination to offer their services at large salaries, pretending that if they were not accepted for this or that office, some State or other would feel humbled,

perhaps secede from the Confederacy, and I know not what.
It was laughable indeed to hear the self-sacrificing Solons
holding forth in bar-rooms or in private. Their ideas of all
things military were decidedly rich, and would have astonished poor Johnston or Beauregard, who were put down as
mere schoolboys beside them. General Washington Dobbs,
who had been engaged all his life in the leather business
somewhere in Georgia, had come up to proffer his valuable
services as brigadier; but being unsuccessful, his patriotism
and indignation electrified the whole private family where
he boarded. Colonel Madison Warren, some poor relation of
the English blacking-maker, had lived in some out-of-the-
way swamp in the Carolinas; he came to Richmond to have
a private talk with the President, to let him know what *he*
thought about General M'Clellan and old Scott. Not getting
an audience, he offered himself for the vacancy of quartermaster-general, and not being accepted was sure that Jefferson Davis was a despot, and that the Southern Confederacy
was fast going to the devil.

Smith had a self-loading, self-priming field-piece, that
would fire a hundred times a minute, and never miss. Each
gun would only weigh twenty tons, and cost 10,000 dols. He
had asked a commission to make a thousand of them only,
was willing to give Government the patent right gratis; and
they would not listen to him! How *could* the South succeed
when neglecting such men as Smith? Jones was another type
of a numerous class of patriots. Tracts were necessary food
for the soldiers. He (Jones) "only" wanted the Government
to start a large Bible and Tract house, give him the control of
it, and he would guarantee to print as many as were needed,
and sell them as cheaply as anybody else, considering the
high price of everything. Jones, like a thousand others, did
not succeed with any of the departments, and after being

jammed and pushed about in the various lobbies and stair-
cases for a whole month, arrived at the conclusion that the
Confederate Government was not "sound" on the Bible
question, and, therefore, ought not to be trusted in this
enlightened and Gospel-preaching age!

When the high price of every necessary is considered, it
appears strange that the city should be so crowded. Boarding
averaged from 2 dols. to 5 dols. per day at the hotels, and
not less than 10 dols. per week in any family. Boots were 35
dols. per pair; a suit of clothes (civil), 175 dols.; military,
200 dols., or more; whisky (very inferior), 5 dols. per quart;
other liquors and wines in proportion; smoking tobacco, 1.50
dols. per pound; socks, 1 dol. per pair; shoes, 18 dols. to 25
dols.; haircutting and shaving, 1 dol.; bath, 50c.; cigars
(inferior) four for 1 dol., &c. The city, however, knew no
interruption to the stream of its floating population, and
balls, parties, and theatres, made a merry world of it; and
Frenchmen say, it was Paris in miniature. Four in the afternoon was grand promenade hour; and, in fine weather, the
small park and principal streets were crowded. Military and
naval officers would sun themselves on balconies, or stretch
their limbs elegantly at hotel doors.

1862

Naval Victory in Hampton Roads

THE CONFEDERACY had virtually no navy when the war began in 1861. President Davis wasted no time in issuing letters of marque to ships which would request them, but more effective methods were needed to build an adequate navy. Congress authorized the building of ships abroad, and enterprising men undertook the construction and outfitting of vessels at Selma, Alabama; Columbus, Georgia; and New Orleans. The capture of the Yankee warships in the Gosport Navy Yard at Norfolk eased the situation, but the Confederacy was never able to keep pace with the Union in adding ships to its fleet. Though the blockade was, indeed, often hardly more than a paper blockade, the Confederate Navy was just as often hardly more than a paper navy.

One of the Confederate prizes at Gosport was the USS *Merrimac*, a relatively new cruiser. She was repaired and re-outfitted for the Confederates as the CSS *Virginia*. Her duel with the USS *Monitor* was one of the turning points of naval history. Their battle spelled the end of wooden navies. Before she met her doom against the revolutionary *Monitor*, the *Virginia* threw terror into the hearts of

the Federal Navy by her audacious and victorious foray
against the frigates *Cumberland* and *Congress*.

Here is Flag Officer Franklin Buchanan's official account of the Battle of Hampton Roads, March 8 and 9,
1862. It is worthy of note that the Lieutenant Parker
mentioned was William Harwar Parker who had previously made a long Pacific voyage as an officer of the
U.S. Navy aboard the *Merrimac*. Although he comes off
none too well in Buchanan's report, he subsequently had
a distinguished career in the Confederate Navy and
served as commandant of the Confederate States School-
Ship *Patrick Henry*, the Confederate naval academy
which conducted its courses on board ship in the James
River.

Naval Hospital }
Norfolk, March 27th, 1862 }

Sir: Having been confined to my bed in this building since
the 9th inst., in consequence of a wound received in the
action of the previous day, I have not had it in my power at
an earlier date to prepare the official report, which I now
have the honor to submit, of the proceedings on the 8th and
9th insts., of the James River Squadron under my command,
composed of the following named vessels: Steamer Virginia,
Flag Ship, ten guns; steamer Patrick Henry, twelve guns,
Commander John R. Tucker; steamer Jamestown, Lieut.
Commanding J. N. Barney, two guns, and gunboats Teazer,
Lieut. Commanding W. A. Webb; Beaufort, Lieut. Commanding W. H. Parker, and Raleigh, Lieut. Commanding
J. W. Alexander, each one gun. Total 27 guns.

On the 8th inst., at 11, A. M., the Virginia left the Navy-Yard, Norfolk, accompanied by the Raleigh and Beaufort, and proceeded to Newport News to engage the enemy's frigates Cumberland and Congress, gunboats and shore batteries. When within less than a mile of the Cumberland, the Virginia commenced the engagement with that ship with her bow gun, and the action soon became general, the Cumberland, Congress, gunboats and shore batteries concentrating upon us their heavy fire, which was returned with great spirit and determination. The Virginia stood rapidly on towards the Cumberland, which ship I had determined to sink with our prow, if possible. In about fifteen minutes after the action commenced we ran into her on her starboard bow; the crash below the water was distinctly heard, and she commenced sinking, gallantly fighting her guns as long as they were above water. She went down with her colors flying. During this time the shore batteries, Congress, and gunboats kept up their heavy concentrated fire upon us, doing us some injury. Our guns, however, were not idle; their fire was very destructive to the shore batteries and vessels, and we were gallantly sustained by the rest of the squadron.

Just after the Cumberland sunk, that gallant officer, Commander John R. Tucker, was seen standing down the James River under full steam, accompanied by the Jamestown and Teazer. They all came nobly into action and were soon exposed to the heavy fire of shore batteries. Their escape was miraculous, as they were under a galling fire of solid shot, shell, grape and canister, a number of which passed through the vessels without doing any serious injury, except to the Patrick Henry, through whose boiler a shot passed, scalding to death four persons, and wounding others. Lieut. Commanding Barney promptly obeyed a signal to tow her out of the action. As soon as damages were repaired, the Patrick

Henry returned to her station and continued to perform good service during the remainder of that day and the following.

Having sunk the Cumberland, I turned our attention to the Congress. We were some time in getting our proper position, in consequence of the shoalness of the water, and the great difficulty of managing the ship when in or near the mud. To succeed in my object, I was obliged to run the ship a short distance above the batteries on James River, in order to wind her. During all the time her keel was in the mud; of course she moved but slowly. Thus we were subjected twice to the heavy guns of all the batteries in passing up and down the river, but it could not be avoided. We silenced several of the batteries, and did much injury on shore. A large transport steamer alongside the wharf was blown up, one schooner sunk, and another captured and sent to Norfolk. The loss of life on shore we have no means of ascertaining.

While the Virginia was thus engaged in getting her position for attacking the Congress, the prisoners state it was believed on board that ship that we had hauled off; the men left their guns and gave three cheers. They were soon sadly undeceived, for a few minutes after we opened upon her again, she having run on shore in shoal water. The carnage, havoc and dismay caused by our fire compelled them to haul down their colors, and to hoist a white flag at their gaff, and half mast another at the main. The crew instantly took to their boats and landed. Our fire immediately ceased, and a signal was made for the Beaufort to come within hail. I then ordered Lieut. Commanding Parker to take possession of the Congress, secure the officers as prisoners, allow the crew to land, and burn the ship. He ran alongside, received her flag and surrender from Commander Wm. Smith and Lieut.

Pendergrast, with the side-arms of those officers. They delivered themselves as prisoners of war on board the Beaufort, and afterwards were permitted, at their own request, to return to the Congress, to assist in removing the wounded to the Beaufort. They never returned, and I submit to the decision of the Department whether they are not our prisoners. While the Beaufort and Raleigh were alongside the Congress, and the surrender of that vessel had been received from the commander, she having two white flags flying, hoisted by her own people, a heavy fire was opened upon them from the shore and from the Congress, killing some valuable officers and men. Under this fire the steamers left the Congress; but as I was not informed that any injury had been sustained by those vessels at that time, Lieut. Commanding Parker having failed to report to me, I took for granted that my order to him to burn her had been executed, and waited some minutes to see the smoke ascending from her hatches. During this delay we were still subjected to the heavy fire from the batteries, which was always promptly returned.

The steam frigates Minnesota and Roanoke, and the sailing frigate St. Lawrence, had previously been reported as coming from Old Point, but as I was determined that the Congress should not again fall into the hands of the enemy, I remarked to that gallant young officer, Flag Lieut. Minor, "that ship must be burned." He promptly volunteered to take a boat and burn her, and the Teazer, Lieut. Commanding Webb, was ordered to cover the boat. Lieut. Minor had scarcely reached within fifty yards of the Congress, when a deadly fire was opened upon him, wounding him severely and several of his men. On witnessing this vile treachery, I instantly recalled the boat and ordered the Congress destroyed by hot shot and incendiary shell. About this period

I was disabled and transferred the command of the ship to that gallant, intelligent officer, Lieut. Catesby Jones, with orders to fight her as long as the men could stand to their guns.

The ships from Old Point opened their fire upon us. The Minnesota grounded in the north channel, where unfortunately the shoalness of the channel prevented our near approach. We continued, however, to fire upon her until the pilots declared that it was no longer safe to remain in that position, and we accordingly returned by the south channel, (the middle ground being necessarily between the Virginia and Minnesota, and St. Lawrence and the Roanoke having retreated under the guns of Old Point,) and again had an opportunity of opening upon the Minnesota, receiving her heavy fire in return; and shortly afterwards upon the St. Lawrence, from which vessel we also received several broadsides. It had by this time become dark and we soon after anchored off Sewell's Point. The rest of the squadron followed our movements, with the exception of the Beaufort, Lieut. Commanding Parker, who proceeded to Norfolk with the wounded and prisoners, as soon as he had left the Congress, without reporting to me. The Congress having been set on fire by our hot shot and incendiary shell, continued to burn, her loaded guns being successively discharged as the flames reached them, until a few minutes past midnight when her magazine exploded with a tremendous report. . . .

While in the act of closing this report, I received the communication of the Department, dated 22d inst., relieving me temporarily of the command of the squadron for the naval defences of James River. I feel honored in being relieved by the gallant Flag Officer, Tattnall.

I much regret that I am not now in a condition to resume

my command, but trust that I shall soon be restored to health, when I shall be ready for any duty that may be assigned to me.

Very respectfully,
FRANKLIN BUCHANAN,
Flag Officer.

Hon. S. R. Mallory,
    Secretary of the Navy.

The Texans Invade New Mexico

THE BATTLE OF GLORIETTA, or Pigeon's Ranch, was a small but important battle in the course of the war in the West. Texan troops under Brigadier General H. H. Sibley moved into New Mexico Territory during January and February, 1862, with signal success. The Federals retired from the principal settlements at Albuquerque and Sante Fe, and the Confederates were victorious in a series of minor engagements. The Battle of Glorietta was fought the last of March in a canyon twenty-three miles east of Santa Fe. Both Confederates and Federals reported it as a victory. Actually the Confederates won the field, but the loss of their supply train (which occurred as a corollary of the battle) was fatal to their New Mexican campaign.

The two Confederate reports here printed are typical of the hyperbole of which the Confederates were often guilty in their official claims. In his informal report to the President, Tom Ochiltree, aide to General Sibley, called accurately the losses on his own side but exaggerated by many score the Yankee losses. His "met, attacked, whipped and routed" is Texan for *"Veni, vidi, vici."* In his address to his soldiers Colonel Scurry is dramatic enough, yet he surpassed himself in his official report of the battle in which he declares: "The intrepid Ragnet, and the cool, calm, courageous Pyron, had pushed forward among the rocks, until the muzzle[s] of the opposing forces guns passed each other."

San Antonio, Texas, April 27th, 1862

His Excellency President Davis:

I have the honor to inform your Excellency of another glorious victory achieved by the Confederate army of New Mexico.

On the 27th March, Lt. Col. Scurry, with 1,000 men from 2nd, 4th, 5th and 7th Texas volunteers, met, attacked, whipped and routed 2,000 Federals, 23 miles east of Santa Fe.

Our loss was 33 killed and 35 wounded—among the killed was Major Ragnet, and Capt. Buckholtz, of the 4th, and Major Shropshire of the 5th Texas mounted volunteers, Lt. Col. Scurry, commanding was twice slightly wounded, and Major Pyron, commanding battalion T. M. R., had his horse blown from under him by a shell.

The enemy's loss was over seven hundred killed and wounded—five hundred being left on the field. Their rout was complete, and they were scattered from the battle field to Fort Union.

The Confederate flag flies over Santa Fe and Albuquerque. At the latter place, the flag was made of a captured United States flag, raised upon a United States flag-staff—the salute fired by a captured United States battery, and Dixie played by a captured United States band.

The Federal force defeated at Glorietta, consisted of 1,600 Pike's Peak volunteers and 600 regulars, under command of Col. Slough. I have the honor to inform your excellency, that I will wait upon you with important despatches in a few days.

Very respectfully,
Tom P. Ochiltree.
Assistant Adjutant General,
Army of New Mexico

HEAD-QUARTERS ADVANCE DIVISION ARMY OF NEW MEXICO

Canon Glorietta, March 29, 1862.

GENERAL ORDER
No. 4.

Soldiers— You have added another victory to the long list of triumphs won by the Confederate *armies*. By your conduct you have given another evidence of the daring courage and heroic endurance which actuate you in this great struggle for the independence of your country. You have proven your right to stand by the side of those who fought and conquered on the red field of San Jacinto. The battle of Glorietta—where for six long hours you steadily drove before you a foe of twice your numbers—over a field chosen by themselves, and deemed impregnable, will take its place upon the rolls of your country's triumphs, and serve to excite your children to imitate the brave deeds of their fathers, in every hour of that country's peril.

Soldiers— I am proud of you. Go on as you have commenced, and it will not be long until not a single soldier of the United States will be left upon the soil of New Mexico. The Territory, relieved of the burden imposed on it by its late oppressors, will once more, throughout its beautiful valleys, "blossom as the rose," beneath the plastic hand of peaceful industry.

By order of

   Lieut. Col. WM. R. SCURRY, Commanding.

ELLSBERRY R. LANE, Adjutant.

The Drummer Boy of Shiloh

DURING EARLY 1862 the Federal forces moved steadily into Tennessee. Confederate fortunes reached their lowest ebb since the war began. The key point of the campaign was the Battle of Shiloh, one of the bloodiest fights of all time. The Confederates won an initial victory but failed to follow it up, and the net result to the South was a crushing defeat and the loss of one of their ablest general officers, Albert Sidney Johnston.

Out of the Battle of Shiloh came a folk hero for all America. The drummer boy of Shiloh was a Yankee drummer who is supposed to have met his death in the battle. His story was put in rhyme and set to music by Will Shakespeare Hays, who wrote music for a publishing firm in Louisville. The sentimentality of the piece brought it immediate popularity in a period of the war when the folks at home wanted just such outlets for their emotions. As the words of the song avoided identifying its hero as either Yankee or Confederate, it was easy for it to cross the battle lines, and it enjoyed wide popularity in the South as well as in the North.

THE DRUMMER BOY OF SHILOH

On Shiloh's dark and bloody ground, the dead and wounded
    lay.
Amongst them was a drummer boy, that beat the drum that
    day.
A wounded soldier raised him up, His drum was by his side.
He clasped his hands and raised his eyes and prayed before
    he died:
Look down upon the battle field, Oh Thou, our Heav'nly
    friend,
Have mercy on our sinful souls. The soldiers cried, "Amen."
For gather'd round a little group, Each brave man knelt and
    cried.
They listen'd to the drummer boy who prayed before he
    died.

"Oh, Mother!" said the dying boy, "Look down from Heav'n
    on me,
Receive me to thy fond embrace, Oh take me home to thee.
I've loved my country as my God, To serve them both I've
    tried."
He smiled, shook hands. Death seized the boy who prayed
    before he died.

Each soldier wept then like a child, Stout hearts were they
    and brave.
The flag his winding sheet, God's book the key unto his
    grave.
They wrote upon a simple board these words "This is a guide
To those who mourn the drummer boy who prayed before
    he died."

Stealing the Telegraph

DURING THE SUMMER of 1862 Confederates read with glee of the daring raids of John Hunt Morgan and his men into Kentucky. On Morgan's staff was an efficient and resourceful young telegrapher called George Ellsworth. His report of how he tapped the Union telegraph lines to send spurious messages and generally confound the Federal forces chasing Morgan was widely printed in the newspapers of the South and stands as one of the most amusing spots in the often laborious official records of the war.

Morgan's dashing raids and his much-publicized romance with a "secesh lady" of Kentucky captured the imagination of the South. Mrs. Sally Rochester Ford wove the story of Morgan and his men (as far as it had gone) into a novel published by Sigmund H. Goetzel in Mobile in the spring of 1863. Here is her adaptation of Ellsworth's account of his manipulations of the Union telegraph as told in her chapter "Paris, Richmond, Crab Orchard, Somerset."

The alarm and uncertainty which pervaded the Federal forces in Central Kentucky at the brilliant exploits of Colonel Morgan, and the rapidity of his movements, can scarcely be conceived. Lexington and Paris both threatened, Cynthiana taken, no one could decide which would be the next point of attack. Lexington called upon Paris for reinforcements—Paris in reply demanded succor of Lexington. But the condition of the latter city became so hazardous, menaced as it was from the direction of Georgetown and Richmond, that it was finally decided to concentrate the troops within its limits for its defence. Accordingly, the forces were ordered from Paris to Lexington, leaving the former town wholly at the mercy of the advancing foe.

On the 19th of July, the day following the capture of Cynthiana, Colonel Morgan moved upon Paris, now entirely undefended. When within a few miles of the city, he met a flag of truce, tendering him the peaceful and quiet possession of the place, and when he entered the streets, cheers and welcomes rang out on the air. Remaining here through the night, Colonel Morgan understood through his scouts that very nearly the entire force from Lexington was being moved upon Paris, for the purpose of attacking him. Not desiring an engagement, when it could be avoided, Colonel Morgan determined to fall back upon Richmond, preparatory to leaving the State. Accordingly, orders were issued to the men to be ready to march early the following morning. Meanwhile, pickets kept watch, lest at any time they should be surprised.

As the Confederates were setting out the next day towards Richmond, they discovered the Federals moving towards the town from Lexington. Colonel Morgan called a halt, and by a little manœuvering so scared the Yankees, who supposed he intended to flank them, that they wheeled about and made a quick retreat. Thus relieved of their presence, Colonel Morgan was enabled to bring off all his guns and stores without molestation or detriment. The only loss sustained was that of one picket, who, it was supposed, was surprised and captured by the enemy in their advance.

From Paris the Confederate force moved to Richmond. Here the warmest enthusiasm greeted them on all sides. Their passage through the town to their encampment beyond was a grand ovation, each individual vieing with his neighbor in his endeavors to manifest his delight and approbation. Ladies showered bouquets and waved handkerchiefs —children waved handkerchiefs and smiled—men, old and young, smiled, and bowed, and hurraed. Ample provision was made for a luxurious repast for the whole command, who partook of the kindly cheer with right good zest, their appeties being well developed by their long and weary ride. Several recruits joined them here, who were furnished with arms and mounted.

It had been Colonel Morgan's intention to remain in Richmond several days, thereby giving an opportunity for the enrollment of many who were desirous to enlist under his standard, but being informed that a large cavalry force had been sent out by way of Danville to intercept and cut off his retreat, he determined to thwart their plans by pushing forward to Crab Orchard, which point he reached the 22d of July, at day-break.

There he found about one hundred and twenty wagons and one million dollars' worth of stores, all of which was given into the hands of his men to be destroyed, as it was impossible to remove anything over that rugged, broken country. The boys gave themselves to the work of burning and breaking with great zest, and soon the gigantic task was accomplished and the whole column again on the adcance towards Somerset, which was reached at sun-down of the same day. This point was the depot of the Federal army at Cumberland Gap, and contained large stores. Colonel Morgan feeling entire safety, took possession of the telegraph office, and countermanded every order of Gen. Boyle with regard to the movement of the troops still in pursuit of him. There another million dollars' worth of Federal property was destroyed, and a thousand stand of arms recaptured that had been taken from Gen. Zollicoffer's forces at the memorable and disastrous engagement of Fishing Creek.

Having here rested his troops, Col. Morgan moved forward to Sparta, which point he reached July 24th, having been absent on his expedition just twenty days, during which time he "captured (and parolled) over twelve hundred prisoners, seven thousand stand of arms, one gun and destroyed, at lowest computation, seven and a half million dollars' worth of stores, arms and subsistence, besides hospital buildings, bridges and other property. Besides this, with the loss of only ninety men, he dispersed over seventeen hundred Home Guards, captured seventeen towns, in which he destroyed war material, and marched above one thousand miles, and recruited his force of eight hundred and seventy men, to twelve hundred."

After Col. Morgan's return from Kentucky into Tennessee, the latter part of July, he removed his headquarters to Hartsville, a small town on the north bank of the Cumberland, some twelve or fifteen miles from Gallatin, in a direct line, but much farther than this by the river.

There was a Federal force, mostly Kentuckians, in possession of Gallatin, commanded by Col. Boone. Col. Morgan determined to capture the town, Yankees and all, and to this end sent a force under Capt. Desha to execute his purpose. This was on the morning of the 12th of August. The

detachment was accompanied by George A. Ellsworth, telegraph operator, who had, on so many occasions, rendered
Col. Morgan valuable assistance while in Kentucky. The
morning was beautifully bright; the sun had scarcely risen
when the party found themselves within two miles of the
town. Dashing forward so as to catch the Federal Colonel
unawares, the Confederates were demanding the surrender
of the place before the Yankees knew aught of their unwelcome presence in their vicinity. The movement was *comme il
faut*. The Federals were completely surprised. No resistance
whatever was offered, but surrender came as if it had been a
premeditated thing. The men, with their Colonel was parolled by Captain Desha. When, however, the parolled Colonel and his men reached Louisville, a few days afterwards,
they were arrested on a charge of cowardice, and sent forward to Camp Chase for imprisonment.

Col. Boone was severely reprimanded for yielding his
command into the hands of the enemy without a struggle;
but he argued that resistance under the circumstances, was
wholly useless. They were surrounded by the Confederates
without a moment's warning. His men were not under arms,
there was no organization, nor could any be effected before
the rebels were upon them.

While Captain Desha, assisted by Captain McCann of
the Cheatham Rifles, was scaring the Yankee Kentuckians
out of all sense of propriety by marching upon them *sans
cérémonie*, and claiming them as prisoners, Mr. Ellsworth
was playing his part of the game by annoying the enemy
with despatches. Dashing into Gallatin, on his fine chestnut
sorrel steed, booted and spurred like any other brave knight
of the Southern cross, he rode quickly up to the principal
hotel and inquired in quite a peremptory tone, for the telegraph office.

"At the depot, sir," replied the waiter of the public house looking at him in blank astonishment.

Ellsworth hesitated no longer. Spurring his horse he galloped off at full dash to the depot. Alighting, hurriedly, and throwing the rein over his horse's head, he burst open the door, and sprung up stairs to the bed-room of the sleeping operator, who, aroused by the dreadful noise, looked up from his bed to see—oh horror!—a "rebel" standing over him with a six-shooter presented to his head.

Pale with affright at this most fearful apparition, he sat stark upright in the bed. Could it be so? He rubbed his eyes and gazed wildly up. There it stood. Was it ghost or de'il, or what was tenfold worse than either—an avenging rebel? His hair stood on end. His eyes stared fearfully from their sockets; his lips were pale and motionless; he trembled from head to foot, like one suddenly seized with a strong ague.

"Why are you so scared, man?" said Ellsworth to him. "I do not want your life—behave yourself, and you have nothing to fear. Resist, and you are a dead man. Dress yourself and come with me; Colonel Morgan needs your services in the room below."

The poor affrighted operator, somewhat reassured, sprung from his bed at the word of command and hastily donned his apparel. As he gave the last of a few hurried strokes to his hair, Ellsworth, impatient of waiting, turned upon him and said:

"Now, follow me, sir, to the room below."

The man seized his hat and obeyed the command with alacrity.

"Now, show me all your signals. Mind, no cheat. I will not be imposed on," said Ellsworth, sternly, as the two reached the room and stood beside the desk.

Had the operator thought for a moment of deception, the

blood-thirsty look of the huge revolver which Ellsworth still held in his hand, would have dissipated any such intention.

"Now, let me test the line to Nashville and Louisville."

The Yankee, with a gracious smile, stepped aside.

"O. K.," said Ellsworth; "what is your earliest office hour?"

"Seven thirty minutes, sir," responded the operator, bowing obsequiously.

"And it is now just five," said Ellsworth, taking out his watch and looking at the time; "two hours and a half before I can begin my work."

Ellsworth ordered breakfast for himself and prisoner, and the two sat down side by side to the steaming coffee and smoking rolls as if they had always been the veriest cronies.

"Seven o'clock! we must to our work, sir!" and Ellsworth escorted his new-found friend from the breakfast table back to the office.

Placing Mr. Brooks outside the office under guard, Ellsworth entered and took possession, feeling that he sufficiently understood matters to communicate with any point.

The signal was given at seven and ten minutes. It was from the depot office in Nashville.

"Train left here for Louisville on time."

Another signal, and the operator at Franklin, Kentucky, informed Gallatin that the train had left *on time* for the South.

Ellsworth stepped to the door.

"Tell Captain McCann I wish to see him at this place immediately," he said to a Confederate soldier, who was standing near.

In a few minutes the Captain rushed into the room.

"Any trouble, Ellsworth?"

"The train from Franklin will be due, Captain, in a very

little while. Had you not as well prepare to take charge of her?"

"Certainly, certainly, Ellsworth. I will do so with pleasure"; and the Captain dashed out, called together his men and posted them in proper position for the proposed business.

Soon the train came steaming on, all unconscious of danger. She had scarcely reached the water tank, just outside the town, when the Confederates very politely made known their desire to take her in charge.

This was readily assented to by the engineer and conductor, who saw that resistance or escape was not for a moment to be thought of.

The train from Nashville was due, but there was no indication yet of her arrival.

Ellsworth seating himself, asked of the Nashville operator: "Train No. 6 not yet arrived. What can be the trouble with her?"

The reply soon came. "Guess Morgan's got her; she left on time with twenty-four cars, six loaded."

Bowling Green called Gallatin. "Where is the Nashville train? Heard anything from her?"

"Not yet arrived," responded Ellsworth.

Bowling Green then called Nashville. "Gallatin says No. 6 not yet arrived; have you heard from it?"

Nashville, in reply, said: "No; they left on time."

Bowling Green, quite perturbed and beginning to suspect foul play, called to Nashville: "Any rumors of the enemy between Nashville and Gallatin?"

"Nary rumor!" was the laconic answer.

Gallatin was then informed by Nashville that the passenger train had left on time, bound north.

Inquiry after inquiry was made of Gallatin with regard to

the two trains, both by Nashville and Bowling Green. The invariable response of Gallatin was, "Not yet arrived."

Eleven o'clock came. Nashville, as if aroused by some sudden fury, began to call on Gallatin with great earnestness.

Ellsworth suspected the cause. The cars, having obtained information of the occupancy of Gallatin by the Confederates, had suddenly put back to Nashville and given the alarm. Questions were asked which Ellsworth did not dare to answer, for fear of betrayal.

He stepped to the door and invited in the Federal operator, Mr. Brooks.

"Now, sir," said Ellsworth to him, "I want you to answer Nashville in the most satisfactory manner. I shall listen to your replies, and if there is anything wrong, it will have to be atoned for by a life during the war in a Dixie prison."

"All shall be right, sir," responded the accomodating operator, glad to be at his old work again.

Nashville, with suspicions highly aroused, called to Gallatin: "What was the name of that young lady you accompanied to Major Foster's?"

"Be careful," enjoined Ellsworth, leaning over the shoulder of the operator. "Give a correct reply!"

"I don't remember of going to Major Foster's with any young lady," was the response.

"What about that nitric acid I sent you the other day?" asked Nashville.

"You sent me no nitric acid."

"Is that correct?" and Ellsworth eyed the operator sternly.

"Correct, sir."

Nashville, yet suspicious: "Mr. Marshall, the Superintendent of Railroads, is not yet satisfied that you are not Morgan's operator, and wished you to tell him who you desired to take your place while you were gone on leave of absence, how long you wished to be gone, and where did you wish to go?"

Gallatin responded: "Tell Mr. Marshall that I wished Mr. Clayton to take my place, while I got a week's leave to go to Cincinnati."

Nashville was convinced, and soon there came over the wires the following order:

"*To Murphy, Conductor, Gallatin:*

"You will run to Edgefield Junction to meet and pass trains Nos. 4 and 6, and pass them both at that point. Answer how you understand.

B. MARSHALL."

The answer was promptly returned, that the instructions would be obeyed.

Nashville informed Ellsworth that "trains Nos. 4 and 6 had left again at eleven fifteen minutes."

About 4 o'clock in the afternoon, Nashville again called lustily on Gallatin: "Trains Nos. 4 and 6 are back again, the second time. We have positive information that the enemy is in possession of Gallatin. Where is Murphy?"

It was unnecessary to practice the deception farther. The cars would not come.

At five o'clock Ellsworth sent the following to George D. Prentice:

"GALLATIN, August 12, 1862.

"*George D. Prentice, Louisville, Ky.:*

"Your prediction, in yesterday's paper, regarding my whereabouts, is like most of the items from your pen. You had better go to Jeffersonville to sleep to-night.

"JOHN H. MORGAN,
"Commanding Brigade."

A lady, beautiful and sprightly, accompanied by Capt. McCann, and two other ladies, made her appearance in the office, and was introduced to Mr. Ellsworth.

"Will you, Mr. Ellsworth, send a message to Prentice for me?" she said, laughing.

"Assuredly I will, with pleasure."

She turned to the desk, and hurriedly write her dispatch:

"GALLATIN, August 12, 1862.

"*George D. Prentice, Louisville, Ky.:*

"Your friend, Colonel John H. Morgan, and his brave followers, are enjoying the hospitalities of this town, to-day.

"Wouldn't you like to be here? The Colonel has seen your $100,000 reward for his head, and offers $100,000 better for yours, at short range.

"Wash. Morgan, whom you published in your paper some time ago, when he was in Knoxville, accompanies his cousin John, with four hundred Indians. He seeks no scalp but yours.

"A SECESH LADY."

Mr. Brooks, who was now released from his military position, as prisoner, joined in the conversation of the merry party, with as much zest as any one. He seemed to enjoy highly the whole day's proceedings, and even jested over his morning's fright.

The party repaired to the house of the lady, where, with the assembled fair of the good town of Gallatin, the heroes of the day passed the evening with song and dance, and the graphic recital of thrilling adventure. Every manifestation of joy that the citizens of Gallatin could give at their release from Yankee thraldom, was displayed by all classes.

Captains Desha and McCann, and their men, were welcomed to the best cheer the town could offer—were feted and toasted—and smiled upon by bright eyes, until they were made to appreciate, in some degree, at least, the great favor they had bestowed on the grateful inhabitants.

A Scout for Stuart

About this time another new hero was becoming known to the Army of Northern Virginia. The fabulous character of William D. Farley became a living legend in the camps of Jeb Stuart. His activities were greatest in the campaigns of 1862, and he fell in the Battle of Fleetwood, June 9, 1863. But the impress of his bravery and ability had been felt by his companion-in-arms John Esten Cooke, and the Virginian novelist wrote an article about him for a later issue of *The Southern Illustrated News* that gave his memory of Farley to the whole South.

In the old "Army of the Potomac," and then in the "Army of Northern Virginia," there was a man so notable for daring, skill and efficiency as a partisan, that all who valued those great qualities honored him as their chiefest exemplar. He was known among the soldiers as "Farley, the Scout," but that term did not express him fully. He was not only a scout, but a partisan leader; an officer of excellent judgment and magnificent dash; a soldier born, who took to the work with all the skill and readiness of one who engages in that occupation for which, by Providence, he is especially designed.

He served from the beginning of the war to the hard battle of Fleetwood, in Culpeper, fought on the 9th of June, 1863. There he fell, his leg shattered by a fragment of shell, and the brave true soul went to rejoin its Maker.

One of the "chiefest spites of fate," says an elder poet, "is that oblivion which not seldom submerges the greatest names and events." The design of this brief paper is to put upon record some particulars of the career of one of these men— so that, in "the aftertime," which sums up the work and glory of the men of this epoch, his name shall not be lost to memory.

Captain William Downs Farley was born at Laurens village, South Carolina, on the 19th of December, 1835. He was descended, in a direct line, from the "Douglas" of Scotland, and his father, who was born on the Roanoke river, in Charlotte county, Virginia, was one of the handsomest and most accomplished gentlemen of his time. He emigrated to South Carolina at the age of twenty-one, married, and commenced there the practice of law. To the son, the issue of this marriage, he gave the name of William Downs Farley, after his father-in-law, Colonel William F. Downs, a distinguished lawyer, member of the Legislature, and an officer of the War of 1812. The father of this Colonel Downs was Major Jonathan Downs, a patriot of the times of '76; his mother, a daughter of Captain Louis Saxon, also distinguished in our first great struggle; thus our young partisan of 1863 had fighting blood in his veins, and, in plunging into the present contest, only followed the traditions of his race.

From earliest childhood he betrayed the instincts of the man of genius. Those who recollect him, then, declare that his nature seemed composed of two mingled elements—the one gentle and reflective, the other ardent and enthusiastic. Passionately fond of Shakespeare and the elder poets, he loved to wander away into the woods, and, stretched beneath some great oak, pass hour after hour in dreamy musing—but if, at such times, he heard the cry of the hounds and the shouts of his companions, his dreams were dissipated, and, throwing aside his volume, he would join in the chase with headlong ardor.

At the age of seventeen, he made, in company with a friend, the tour of the Northern States, and then was sent to the University of Virginia, where his education was completed. The summer vacation gave him an opportunity of making a pedestrian excursion through Virginia; and thus, having enlarged his mind by study and travel through the North and a portion of the South, he returned to South Carolina. Here he occupied himself in rendering assistance to his father, who had become an invalid, and, we believe, commenced the practice of the law. His love of roving, however, did not desert him, and his father's business required repeated journeys into the interior of the State. The scenery of the mountains proved a deep and lasting source of joy to him, and, standing on the summits of the great ranges, he has been seen to remain in such rapt contemplation of the landscape, that he could scarcely be aroused and brought back to the real world. These expeditions undoubtedly fostered in the youthful South Carolinian that ardent love of every thing connected with his native State, which, with his love of wild adventure, constituted the controlling elements of his being.

"He had now attained," a friend writes, "the pride and maturity of manhood. There were few handsomer or more prepossessing men. As a young man, after the battle of Culpeper, in speaking of the loss of Farley and Hampton, said, 'two of the handsomest men in our State have fallen.' His figure was of medium height, elegantly formed, graceful, well knit, and, from habitual exercise on the gymnasium, possessing a remarkable degree of strength and activity. His hair was dark brown, his eyebrows and lashes were so dark, and so shaded the dark grey eyes beneath, as to give them the appearance of blackness. His manner was, generally, quiet, polished and elegant; but let him be aroused by some topic which awoke his enthusiasm (Secession and the Yankees, for instance), and he suddenly stood transformed before you; and in the flashing eye and changing cheek you beheld the dashing 'Hero of the Potomac!' "

The same authority says:

"His moral character was pure and noble—'Sans peur et sans reproche.' It is a well-known fact among his friends and associates, that ardent spirits of any kind never passed his lips until the first battle of Manassas, being sick with measles, he fought until almost fainting, and accepted a draught from the canteen of a friend. This was the *first* and *last* drink he ever took.

"His father, whose last hours he watched with untiring care and attention, died just before the opening of the war. Captain Farley had, from an early age, taken great interest in the political affairs of the country; he was a warm advocate of State Rights, and now entered into the spirit of Secession with eagerness and enthusiasm. He was very instrumental in bringing about a unanimity of opinion on this subject in his own district.

"He made frequent visits to Charleston, with the hope of being in the scene of action should an attack be made on the city, and was greatly chagrined that the battle of Sumter was fought during a short absence, and he only reached the city on the day following. He was the first man in his district to fly to the defence of Virginia, whose sacred soil he loved with a devotion only inferior to that which he bore his own State. He joined Gregg's regiment, in which he served three months, and on the disbanding of which he became an independent fighter."

From this time commences that career of personal adventure and romantic exploits which made him so famous. Shouldering his rifle—now riding, then on foot—he proceeded to the far outposts nearest to the enemy, and was indefatigable in penetrating their lines, harassing detached parties, and gaining information for Generals Bonham and Beauregard. Falling back with the army from Fairfax, he fought—though so sick that he could scarcely stand—in the first battle of Manassas, and then pursuing the flying enemy, he entered permanently upon the life of the scout, speedily attracting to himself the unconcealed admiration of the whole army. To note the outlines even of his performances at this time, would require thrice the space we have at our disposal. He seemed omnipresent on every portion of our lines; and if any daring deed was undertaken—any expedition which was to puzzle, harass or surprise the enemy, Farley was sure to be there. With three men he took and held Upton's Hill, directly in face of the enemy; on numberless occasions he surprised and shot the enemy's pickets, and with three others, waylaid and attacked a column of several hundred cavalry led by Colonel (afterwards General) Bayard, whose horse he killed, slightly wounding the rider.—This audacious attack was made some ten or fifteen miles beyond our lines, and nothing but a passionate love of the most desperate adventure could have led to it. Farley ambushed the enemy, concealing his little band of three men in some pines; and although they might easily have remained *perdus* until the column passed, and so escaped, Farley determined to attack, and did attack—firing first upon Bayard, and nearly stampeding his whole regiment.

After a desperate encounter he and his little party were all captured or killed, and Farley was taken to the Old Capitol in Washington, where he remained some time in captivity. General Bayard mentioned this affair afterwards in an interview with General Stuart, and spoke in exalted terms of the courage which led Farley to undertake so desperate an adventure.

Released from prison, Farley hastened back to his old "stamping ground" around Centreville, reaching that place in the winter of 1861. He speedily received the most flattering proposals from some eminent officers who were going to the South-West, but chancing to meet General J. E. B. Stuart, that officer took violent possession of him, and thenceforth kept him near his person, as volunteer aid-de-camp. With this arrangement Farley soon became greatly pleased. He had already seen Gen. Stuart at work, and that love of adventure and contempt of danger—the coolness, self-possession and mastery of the situation, however perilous—which characterized both, proved a lasting bond of union between them.

Thenceforth, Farley was satisfied. His position was one which suited his peculiar views and habits admirably. Untrammeled by special duties—never tied down to the routine of command, or the commonplace round of camp duty—free as the wind to go or come whenever and wheresoever he pleased, all the instincts of his peculiar organization had "ample room and verge enough" for their development; and his splendid native traits had the fullest swing and opportunity of display. It was in vain that Gen. Stuart, estimating at their full value his capacities for command, repeatedly offered him position. He did not want any commission; he said his place suited him perfectly, and he believed he could do more service to the cause as scout and partisan, than as a regular line-officer. He had not entered the army, he has often declared to me, for place or position; promotion was not his object; to do as much injury as possible to the hated foe was his sole, controlling sentiment, and he was satisfied to be where he was.

His devotion to the cause was indeed profound and almost passionate. He never rested in his exertions, and seemed to feel as if the success of the struggle depended entirely on his own exertions. A friend once said to him: "If, as in ancient Roman days, an immense gulf should miraculously open, and an oracle should declare that the honor and peace of the country could only be maintained by one of her youths throwing himself into it, do you believe you could do it?" He looked seriously, and answered earnestly and with emphasis, "*I believe I could.*"

This devotion he proved by his tireless energy, his wonderful adventures, his contempt for danger, and the concentration of every faculty of his soul and being upon the pursuit of the enemy. He seemed to hunt Yankees as he had formerly done wild animals in the mountains of South Carolina, and more than once told me that he did not feel as if they were human beings; they were *wolves* that had come to attack our homes, and ought to be dealt with as such, hunted down and destroyed on all occasions. "My principle is," he said one day, "to kill a Yankee wherever I find him. If they don't like that, let them stay at home." He had probably killed a hundred with his own hand.

Thus permanently attached as volunteer aid to Gen. Stuart, Farley thereafter took part in all the movements of the cavalry. He was with them in that hot falling back from Centreville, in March, 1862; in the combats of the Peninsula, where, at Williamsburg, he led a regiment of infantry in the assault; in the battles of Cold Harbour and Malvern Hill, at the second Manassas, Sharpsburg, Fredericksburg, and the scores of minor engagements which marked almost every day upon the outposts. He missed the battle of Chancellorsville, greatly to his regret, having gone home, after an absence of two years, to witness the bombardment of Charleston, and see his family.

It was soon after his return in May, that the fatal moment came which deprived the service of this eminent partisan. At the desperately contested battle of Fleetwood, in Culpeper county, on the 9th of June, 1863, he was sent by Gen. Stuart to carry a message to Col. Butler, of the 2d South Carolina cavalry. He had just delivered his message, and was sitting upon his horse by the Colonel, when a shell, which also wounded Col. Butler, struck him upon the right knee and tore his leg in two at the joint. He fell from the saddle, and was borne to an ambulance, where surgical assistance was promptly rendered. His wound was, however, mortal, and all saw that he was dying.

At his own request the torn and bleeding member, with the cavalier's boot still on, was put in the ambulance, and he was borne from the field. His strength slowly declined, but his consciousness remained. Meeting one whom he knew, he called him by name, and murmured "I am almost gone." He lingered but a few hours, and at twilight of that day, the writer of these lines looked on him in his shroud; the pale, cold features calm and tranquil in their final sleep.

He was clad in his new uniform coat, and looked every inch the soldier, taking his last rest. He had delivered this coat to a lady of Culpeper, and said, *"If anything befalls me, wrap me in this and send me to my mother."*

Such was the end of the famous partisan. His death has left a void which can scarcely be filled. I believe that this is the sentiment of thousands who never saw him, but who feel acutely the loss which we have experienced in his death. His extraordinary career had become fully known, and a writer some months before his death gave utterance to the sentiment of everyone when he wrote: "The story—the plain, unvarnished story of his career since the war began, is like a tale of old romance. Such abnegation of self! Office and money both spurned, because they seemed to stand in the way of his duty. What thrilling incidents! What strength and courage! and what wonderful escapes! No wonder, as he rides by, we so often hear it exclaimed, 'There goes the famous scout, Farley! The army has no braver man, no purer patriot!'"

We put on record here the following passage from the letter of a lady in Culpeper to his mother, giving, as it does, an outline of the man, and bearing testimony in its simple words, warm from a woman's heart, to the affection which was felt for him:

"My dear madam, I want you to know how we in Virginia admired, appreciated and loved your son. Had he been *her own*, Virginia could not have loved him more; certainly she could not *owe* him more—and so long and so bravely had he fought upon her soil. He was particularly well known in this unfortunate part of the State, which has been, sometimes for months, overrun by our foes. Many families will miss his coming, so daring was he, and so much depended on by General Stuart. He scouted a great deal alone in the enemy's lines, and was often the bearer of letters and messages from loved ones, long unheard from. Often, when we have been cut off from all communication from our own people, he has been the first to come as the enemy were leaving, often galloping up when they were scarcely out of sight—always inspiring us with fresh hope and courage, his cheerful presence itself seeming to us a prophecy of good.

"On Tuesday night, just one week before the battle in

which he fell, he came here, about one o'clock at night. We were surprised and alarmed to see him, as a large party of the enemy had passed our very doors only a few hours before. When my aunt opened the door she found him sitting on the steps, his head resting on his hands, as if tired and sleepy. We asked him if he did not know the Yankees were near. 'O yes,' he replied; 'they have been chasing me, and compelled me to lengthen my ride considerably.' He came in, but said, 'I cannot rest with you long, as I must be riding all night.' We gave him some bread, honey and milk, which we knew he loved (he said he had been fasting since morning.) —'Ah,' said he, 'this is just what I want.' He buckled on his pistols again before sitting down, and said laughingly to me, 'Lock the doors and listen well, for I'll never surrender.' We stood in the porch when he left, and watched him walk off briskly (he had come on foot, having left his horse in the woods). We hated to see him go out in the dark and rainy night time, but *he* went cheerfully, so willing was he to encounter danger, to endure hardships, 'to spend and be spent' in his country's service."

To "spend and be spent" in the great cause of the South, was truly this brave spirit's chief delight. These are not idle words, but the truth in relation to him. The writer of this piece was long and intimately associated with him, and so far from presenting an exaggerated picture of him, the incidents and extracts above given do him only partial justice. I never saw a braver man, nor one more modest. He had a peculiar refinement of feeling and bearing which stamped him a *gentleman* to the inmost fibre of his being. This delicacy of temperament was most notable; and it would be difficult to describe the remarkable union of the most daring courage and the sweetest simplicity of demeanor in the young partisan. Greater simplicity and modesty was never seen in human bearing—and so endearing were these traits of his character that children and ladies—those infallible critics— were uniformly charmed with him. One of the latter wrote:

"His death has been a great sorrow to us. He was with us frequently the week before the battle, and won our entire hearts by his many noble qualities, and his superiority to all around him. He talked much about his family; he loved them with entire devotion. He read to us some of your poems and repeated one of his own. I close my eyes and memory brings back to me the thrilling tones of that dear voice, which though heard no more on earth, has added to the melody of heaven."

His manner was the perfection of good breeding, and you saw that the famous partisan, whose exploits were the theme of every tongue, had not been raised, like others of his class, amid rude associates and scenes, but with gently nurtured women, and surrounded by the sweet amenities of home. His voice was a peculiar one—very low and distinct in its tones; and these subdued inflections often produced upon the listener the impression that it was a habit acquired in scout- ing, when to speak above a murmur is dangerous. The low, clear words were habitually accompanied by a bright smile, and the young man was a favorite with all—so cordial was his bearing, so unassuming his whole demeanor. His personal appearance has already been described, but it may interest some of his friends in the far South to know how he appeared when "at work." He dressed uniformly in a plain suit of gray, wearing a jacket, and over this a dark blue overcoat, with a belt, holding his pistol, tightly drawn around the waist. In his hat he wore the black cavalry feather, and his boots were of that handsome pattern which are worn by Federal officers, with patent leather tops and ornamental thread work. Boots, saddles, sabres, pistols—none of these things cost him or the Confederate States a single dollar. They were all captured—either from sutlers' wagons or the enemies he had slain with his own hand. I never knew him to purchase any portion of his own or his horse's equipment —saddle, bridle, halter, sabre, pistols, belt, carbine, spurs, were all captured from the enemy. His horses were in the same category, and he rarely kept the same riding horse long. They were with great regularity shot under him; and he mounted the first he found running riderless, or from which his pistol hurled one of the enemy.

I have spoken of his modest, almost shy demeanor. All this disappeared in action. His coolness remained unaffected, but he evidently felt himself in his proper element, and entitled to direct others. At such moments his suggestions were boldly made, and not seldom resulted in the rout of the enemy. The cavalry once in motion, the quiet, modest gentleman was metamorphosed into the fiery partisan. He would lead a charge with the reckless daring of Murat, and cheer on the men, with contagious ardor, amid the most furious storm of balls. The thought that there was danger at such moments evidently never crossed his mind. His disregard of personal exposure was supreme, and the idea that he was surrounded by peril never occurred to him. He has repeatedly told the present writer, with that simplicity and sincerity which produce conviction, that in action he was scarcely conscious of the balls and shells flying and bursting around him—that his interest in the general result was so strong as to cause him to lose sight of the danger from them. Those who knew him did not venture to doubt the assertion.

He delighted in the wild charge, the clash of meeting squadrons, and the roar of artillery. All these martial sights and sounds ministered to the passionate ardor of that temperament which made him most at home where balls were whistling and the air oppressive with the odor of battle. But, I think, he even preferred the life of the scout—the long and noiseless hunt for his foe—the exercise of those faculties by means of which an enemy is surprised and destroyed—the single combat with sabre and pistol, often far off in the silence of the woods, where a dead body half concealed amid the grass is all that remains to tell the tale of some desperate hand-to-hand encounter. The number of such contests through which Farley had passed would seem incredible to those who did not know him, and thus comprehend how the naked truth of his career beggared romance. He rarely spoke of these affairs, and never unless to certain persons and under peculiar circumstances. He had a great horror of appearing to boast of his own exploits, and so greatly feared securing the reputation of coloring his adventures that he would rarely speak of them. Fortunately for his memory, many persons witnessed his most desperate encounters, and still live to testify to the reckless daring of the young partisan. With these his eventful career will long remain the subject of fire-side tales; and in the coming days of peace, when years have silvered the hair of his contemporaries, old men will tell their grand-children of his strange adventures and those noble traits which made his name so famous.

To the world at large, he will always thus appear—as the daring partisan and high-souled lover of his country—as one who risked his life in a hundred desperate encounters, and in all those bloody scenes never quailed or shrunk before a foe, however powerful or dangerous. But to those who lived with him—heard his low, friendly voice, and saw every day his bright, kindly smile—he appears in a different character. To such the loss we have sustained is deeper—it seems irreparable. It was the good fortune of the writer of these lines to thus see the brave young man—to be beside him in the field, and, at home, to share his confidence and friendship. Riding through the summer forests, or wandering on across the fields of broom-straw, near Fredericksburg, last autumn—better still, beside the good log fire of winter—we talked of a thousand things, and I saw what a wealth of kindness, chivalry and honor he possessed—how beautifully the "elements were mixed" in his character. Brave and true—simple and kind— he has passed away; and among those eminent natures which the writer has encountered in this struggle, few are remembered with such admiration and affection as this noble son of Carolina.

The best conclusion of this brief and inadequate sketch will be the mention of the brave partisan in General Stuart's report of the battle of Fleetwood. It is as follows:

"Captain W. D. Farley, of South Carolina, a volunteer aid on my staff, was mortally wounded by the same shell which wounded Colonel Butler, and displayed, even in death, the same loftiness of bearing and fortitude which has characterized him through life. He had served, without emolument, long, faithfully and always with distinction. No nobler champion has fallen. May his spirit abide with us."

What nobler epitaph!

"God Save the South,"
words by George H. Miles,
music by C. T. DeCoëniél,
engraving by Ernest Crehen,
Richmond, 1863

GENERAL P. G. T. BEAUREGARD

From the frontispiece to the sheet music,
"Gen'l Beauregard's Grande Polka Militaire!"
New Orleans, 1861

Beauregard Answers Butler

UNION GENERAL BEN F. BUTLER had earned the unsavory nickname of "Bethel Failure" at the battle of Big Bethel, Virginia, in the spring of 1861. In success at New Orleans the next year he earned an even more unsavory reputation as a tyrannical ruler of conquered territory.

Butler's General Orders were anathema to the people of New Orleans, who felt that the bounds of civilized warfare had been passed in the stringency and vindictiveness of his regulations. Most reprehensible of a series of reprehensible edicts was his famous "Women of the Streets" order of May 15, which aroused public opinion of the whole world against him. In issuing such an order Butler served well the propaganda mills of the Confederacy.

Here is General Beauregard's answer to it.

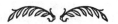

YOUNG LADIES WANTED
IN THE
ENGINEER CORPS

A Few Places Yet Left!

GREAT INDUCEMENTS!

Are offered YOUNG LADIES in the Engineers.

TRY IT!

COME INTO THE ENGINEERS & BE HAPPY!

NO HUMBUG!

The ENGINEER CORPS are stationed exclusively on the SEABOARD! Young ladies fond of *Oysters! Crabs! Eels! Turtles! Catfish! or Clam Soup!* may enjoy this diet all the year round by securing a husband in the ENGINEERS!! **LARGE FORTUNES** considered *no objection* in the Engineer Corps! Consumptive and **delicate** YOUNG LADIES of large means, *try the Engineer Corps and the Sea Air!* YOUNG LADIES mourning the loss of wealthy and indulgent parents, and with no sympathising brothers and sisters, *seek consolation in the Engineer Corps.* A hearty welcome is offered; the pleasures of a home by the sounding sea are secured; sympathising hearts are found, and true happiness is warranted only in the ENGINEER CORPS! **TRY IT! TRY IT!**

APPLY EARLY. Offers received for a few days only.

N B *Grass and California Widows need not apply.*

104

Head Quarters Western Department,
Corinth, Mississippi, May 19th, 1862.

GENERAL ORDERS,⎱
    No. 44.   ⎰

For the information of this army, the following General Orders No. 28, of the Federal Officer, Major General Butler, ("the Haynau of the North,") commanding at New Orleans, will be read on dress parade:

NOTICE.

HEADQUARTERS DEPARTMENT OF THE GULF, NEW ORLEANS, May 15, 1862.

General Orders, No. 28.

As the officers and soldiers of the United States have been subject to repeated insults from the women (calling themselves ladies) of New Orleans, in return for the most scrupulous non-interference and courtesy on our part, it is ordered that hereafter when any female shall, by word, gesture or movement, insult or show contempt for any officer or soldier of the United States, she shall be regarded and held liable to be treated as a woman of the town plying her avocation.

By command of

MAJOR GENERAL BUTLER.

GEO. C. STRONG, A. A. G., Chief of Staff.

Men of the South! shall our mothers, our wives, our daughters and our sisters, be thus outraged by the ruffianly soldiers of the North, to whom is given the right to treat, at their pleasure, the ladies of the South as common harlots? Arouse friends, and drive back from our soil, those infamous invaders of our homes and disturbers of our family ties.

(Signed,)   G. T. BEAUREGARD,
                        General Commanding.

Behind the Lines in Carolina

WILLIAM WYNDHAM MALET was an interested and interesting visitor to the South in the summer of 1862. He left his vicarage at Ardeley, Hertfordshire, England, to go to South Carolina and break to his sister the news of a death in their family. He spent the summer there at the plantations of patrician Plowden C. J. Weston and visited most of the rest of South Carolina as well as Richmond and the mountain country of western North Carolina. His comments on the South are colored with the impressions of an enjoyable visit, but he presents an interesting picture of life behind the lines in an area not yet too much disturbed by the progress of the war.

Perhaps the Southerners were on their best behavior for the Rev. Mr. Malet. Mary Boykin Chesnut in her charming *Diary from Dixie* commented that "everybody has his best foot foremost at McMahon's because the stray Englishman there is supposed to be writing a book." Mrs. McMahon's was the choicest boardinghouse of Columbia and it was there that Malet met Mrs. Chesnut, the poet Paul Hamilton Hayne, Governor Francis Pickens, and others of the most prominent citizens of South

Carolina. He had little reason to form any but a favorable opinion of what he saw.

In the first of the following passages the Englishman describes his arrival at Conwayboro and gives some details about plantation life. Here is a picture of slavery at its paternalistic best. His references to the making of saltpeter is reminiscent of the famous vulgar poem which was later circulated from Selma, Alabama, concerning the making of saltpeter for use in manufacturing gunpowder from the "chamber-lye" from Selma homes. Columbia is described in the next excerpt from Malet's *An Errand to the South in the Summer of 1862.* Here the reference to the bells is to the church bells which had been collected to melt into Confederate cannons. The idea was the subject of a Confederate poem and of an etching by Adalbert J. Volck, but the donation of the bells was more of a patriotic gesture than the fulfillment of a real military need.

On Friday the 13th of June I arrived at the place of refuge. Here was an English lady with her little maid, both from the peaceful vale of Taunton, "dwelling among her own people," the sable descendants of Canaan, as safely as if in their native land, protected by county police—yea, safer; for they slept with their doors and windows unbolted, and did not feel afraid.

The county is called Horry (after some colonial governor), in the north-east corner of the State of South Carolina, which is 500 by 450 miles. Conwayboro' is the county town,

having the county courthouse and gaol, with its sheriff and
mayor, &c.; the population about 350. There are two churches
—one Presbyterian, one Methodist; the houses are never more
than two stories high—most of them only one—all built of
wood, with brick chimneys; raised on brick or wooden piers
two feet or more high. Every negro hut is built in this way,
keeping the floors very dry, and free from snakes, which
rather abound at Conwayboro': from the earth under every
house, saltpetre is obtainable. A contractor told me he found
fifteen pounds under a negro's house built ten years; and a
house of that size—say thirty feet square—would yield one
pound and a-half per annum. About three inches of earth
is scraped up, and water percolated in casks, evaporation
developing the saltpetre: by this means, and by sulphur
from the north-west part of South Carolina, and charcoal
which the endless woods supply, the army is provided with
abundance of gunpowder. The houses are far apart, placed
in their own gardens—like the compounds of our Indian
bungalows—with their negro huts nearly all surrounded by
neat fences. Thus Conwayboro', though of small population,
is of considerable extent, fields lying between some of the
houses. The court-house and gaol are of brick, the former
having the usual façade of Doric pillars. Evergreen oaks cast
their welcome shade in all directions; fig-trees and vines cool
the houses; peach orchards yield their delicious fruit. The
treatment for these peach-trees is very simple; viz., baring
the roots in winter, and just before spring covering them
with a coat of ashes and then with earth: with this they
beat any wall-fruit I ever saw in England. The gardens produce abundance of tomatos, okras, egg-plants, &c. Tomatos
in soup and stewed are the standard dish; and they are also
eaten as salads.

Every house was full; many refugees from the coast about

George-Town, fifty miles distant, having obtained lodgings. The house I came to is on a bluff, looking over a "branch" of the Wakamaw river: the negroes' huts formed quite a little hamlet of itself, the number of souls being forty; these buildings being ready, besides stabling, &c. for four horses, and about fifty acres of land, made it convenient for Mrs. W——'s purpose, whose plantation too was within a drive, about forty-two miles down the river, where 350 negroes used to be employed; but a fresh estate of 800 acres was just bought about 300 miles inland, to which 150 were removed by rail. Never did I see a happier set than these negroes. For six months had this lady been left with them alone. Her husband's regiment had been ordered to the Mississippi, about 1000 miles west. In this army the officers are all elected; the men of each company choose the lieutenants and captains, and the captains choose the field-officers from themselves, the colonel appointing his adjutant. This gentleman had procured Enfield rifles from England for 120 men of his regiment, the 10th South Carolina, before the Queen's proclamation came out, and cloth for their clothing, but he himself served for several months as a private: he has since refused promotion beyond captain. All his ambition is with his company, which is said to be a pattern of discipline and dash—indeed the whole regiment commanded by Lieutenant-Colonel Manigault is General Bragg's "pet regiment." The negro servants watched for tidings from their master by the tri-weekly mails as anxiously as their mistress. This gentleman, and some other masters, deemed it the best policy to be open with their negroes, and let them know the real cause of the war; and that probably the Abolitionists would try and induce them to desert. On the 30th December this Mr. W—— appointed a special prayer and fast-day at his plantation church, and after service addressed the negroes, previous to his leaving for the House of Representatives, of which he was a member (elected for George-Town). Not only women, but the men wept: they said they would never leave him—they loved their "massa and missis:" and not one of them has left. Lately two Southern gentlemen, on their way to George-Town, met one of them, and pretending to be Yankees, to try the man, asked him if he would go with them to the United States fleet, and be free. He asked, how he could leave his master and mistress?—"No! he would never do that!" Fifteen negroes were bringing up a "flat" (i.e., a river barge) load of rice to Conwayboro'; en route they heard of the approach of some Yankee gunboats, when they ran the flat up a creek till they were clear away, and then continued their course. They declared they would have swamped the flat and its cargo, if the Yankees had discovered it, and would themselves have taken to the swamps, where no white man could follow them: 300 barrels of rice were thus brought up and sold by Mrs. W——, at the Boro', for eleven and a-half dollars a barrel (the half-dollar going for commission) retail to the inhabitants; the usual price before the war being sixteen to eighteen dollars, and from four to six dollars a cwt.; for this boon the neighborhood was most grateful.

Now I hear the sounds peculiar to this region, the land of sand, of woods, of "branches," of creeks, and swamps:—the hollow bark of the crocodile; the bellowing of the bull-frog, all night long—the note of summer, just as the cuckoo's is in England; also, breaking the silence of the night, the mournful cry of the "whip-poor-will." I had feared, from this latitude being about that of Morocco, it would be too hot for singing-birds; but, on the contrary, the mocking-bird, plain to eye but charming to ear, sent forth its varied song by night and by day; the nightingale's notes at night, and the

thrush and the blackbird's warble by day. Some told me
they imitate caterwauling, but I was glad not to hear that
phase of their song. It is a plain bird, having black, brown,
and white feathers, about the size of our thrush; it is heard
everywhere in North and South Carolina and Virginia, and
all through the spring and summer. On the 19th June the
thermometer at Conwayboro' was 80° at eleven A.M., and
76° at nine P.M.: during the day a heavy thunderstorm
echoed through the forests; the wind here blowing over lofty
pines, sounds like the wind at sea.

There are seven negro cottages around the bungalow. Mrs.
W—— gives out supplies of food weekly, viz., corn flour, rice
and bacon, and salt;—molasses, of which they are very fond, is
now scarcely to be had; but they have a little, and plenty
of honey and milk, and they are well clothed. In all the
houses of negroes the boys and girls have separate bed-
rooms. After dark the court-yard in front of the cottages
is illuminated with pine-wood bonfires, which destroy the
mosquitoes, and the children dance round the blaze; never
a company of negroes, but some one plays a fiddle, and often
tambourine or banjo to accompany. Here the coachman,
"Prince," is a capital fiddler; his favourite tunes are "Dixie
Land" and country dances. Just before bed-time more solemn
sounds are heard: the negro is demonstrative in his religion,
and loud and musical were heard every evening the hymns,
many of them meeting in one of the houses. Remarkable for
correctness are their songs, and both men and women's
voices mingled in soft though far-sounding harmony. Some
old church tunes I recognised. Sometimes they sent forth
regular "fugues;" then, after a pause, would come the prayer,
offered up by "Jemmy," or some "gifted" man. I could over-
hear some of the words; e. g. "O Lord, in whose palm of his
hand be the waters of the ocean—who can remove moun-

tains—who weighs the earth in a balance—who can still the
waves of the storm—who can break the pines of the forest
—who givest us a land of rivers of waters—O Jesus! who died
on the cross for us—O forgive us our sins; O help us in this
time of trial and need. Protect our massa far away; protect
our brothers 'Hector' and 'Caesar' with him; defend us now
we are away from home; defend our friends and relatives
at home, &c." All the 350 negroes (except old Pemba, about
70 years of age, who had been brought from Africa, when a
little girl) were born on the estate: like Abraham's servants,
"born in his own house." The smile and voice of the negroes
are most agreeable, and their manners very polite. The
names are curious: "Prince," the capital coachman, a regular
Jehu, not afraid of any horse, drove me out; his assistant-
groom is "Agrippa." Prince always has a book with him on
the box, which he reads directly he stops at a visit; his favourite book is "Pilgrim's Progress." Prince has a son, "Napoleon.". . .

On 3rd July I started for Columbia and Winsboro'. The
train from Wilmington arrived at Fairbluff at 12.30 night;
cars full of wounded men from Richmond, reached Kingsville, 100 miles, at 7. A.M. Near this place the Wateree River
and its tributaries and swamps are traversed by a viaduct
raised on timber tressel-work for five miles. Kingsville is the
junction of the branches to Augusta and Columbia; therefore many of the poor wounded soldiers got out. It was sad
to see them. The station hotel, by no means adequate to
the demand now put upon it by the war, did not meet their
wants; the hot fries and beefsteaks of the American breakfast
they could not taste. I asked "mine host" if there was nothing
else. "No—only pay 75 cents, and sit down." Several of them
said, "We only want a little milk and water and a biscuit,"—
which were not to be had; water was indeed scarce! They

covered the station, some on stretchers, some on crutches—
no one to attend to them. It was twenty miles to Columbia,
which we did in the luggage-car of a freight train. On 4th
July I arrived at Columbia, capital of South Carolina, a very
pretty city, called the "Garden City." Every street has an
avenue of trees and one long street, a double one. I was
provided with a letter to the Governor, Mr. Pickens, by the
kindness of Mr. Mason; and I lost no time in making use
of it. Found him at his office, and, luckily, the general of
the district with him. I reported the state of things at Kingsville, and orders were issued then and there for an assistant
surgeon to be stationed there, and a wayside hospital erected,
with all the needments for the sick and wounded. I avoided
the crowded hotels, and put up at Mrs. McMahon's boarding-house. These houses are to be found in every town, and
very nice they are, having the table-d'hote system well
carried out; the drawing-room, pianoforte, &c. Never was
there a cleaner house than Mrs. McMahon's; and most agreeable society. She had Colonel Hayne, aide-de-camp to the
general, a poet and a friend of poets; Mrs. Bartow, the widow
of one of the brave men who fell at the battle of Bull Run,
1861; and Colonel Chesnut (one of the State Council), with
his lady, and several others. Our good hostess gave us a
great treat in real tea and coffee; but her supply was nearly
out.

On the 5th of July, Governor Pickens took me a drive
round and through the city. It stands high, looking down
South on the Congeree River, which runs from west to east;
the Congeree and Wateree meeting a few miles off make the
Santee. The country is pretty, healthy, and undulating; they
call it a "rolling" country. The soil is good; substratum rocky.
The gardens and fields are very productive. The water is
excellent.

The Governor was for three years United States Minister at St. Petersburg. He showed his determination to stand up for the state rights in the affair of Fort Sumter in April, 1861. Of course we talked about that. . . .

The hanging gardens and public park of Columbia, with fountains playing among beautiful shrubberies, slope down towards the rapid and winding Congeree. Every evening they were crowded with the promenaders and beautiful children, enjoying the cool vesper breeze. Many are the gardens here, but for elegance and beauty, and sweetness of flowers, I suppose Colonel Preston's is equal to any in the world. It is a land redolent with fruit and flowers, and milk and honey abound.

In the evening, at a veritable tea, I was introduced to Mrs. Pickens, one of the fairest of the fair daughters of Louisiana. Great was the luxury of high-flavoured tea from Russia, and coffee from Mocha, after weeks of burnt rye for coffee, and water bewitched with short supply of tea; and, while travelling, only sassafras, or holly tea at the best. In these warm latitudes the custom of paying visits in the evening is most agreeable, and this is the thing to do. Dinner is done from two to four; then I daresay many a siesta is taken, to string the bow for the soiree quivers of conversation. . . .

I was rejoiced to hear, that of the hundreds of bells which had been sent to the Columbian depot from churches and plantations, to be made into cannon, not one had been melted. "How so?" said I. The answer was, "We are foundering our own cannon from our own iron mines, and we have taken a great many from the enemy."

General Robert Edward Lee

THE CONFEDERACY produced two undying heroes. And the first of these was Robert E. Lee. Posterity has made of him truly a knight beyond compare. But Lee's fame is no myth. At the beginning of the war his services were as eagerly sought by the Union as by the Confederacy. How he followed his state into the war as his conception of his highest patriotic duty and led the Confederate armies to their greatest glories is an oft-told tale, but it resumes a new freshness in the words with which it was freshly told in Richmond in 1864 in a booklet called *The War and Its Heroes.*

The achievements of this distinguished officer form the most remarkable chapter, not only in the history of the present gigantic war, but, in some respects, in the entire annals of war. To detail them minutely would fill a volume even larger than this, and we, therefore, leave this agreeable task to the future historian. In the halcyon days, which we opine are not far distant, the student of history will delight to dwell upon them, even as we delight to find rescued from

115

oblivion any little circumstance of early youth in which Napoleon or Washington was concerned.

Robert Edward Lee is a member of the old historical family of Westmoreland Lees. He is the youngest son, by a second marriage of General Henry Lee, better known to history by his *soubriquet* of "Light Horse Harry," the friend and confidant of Washington, and the author of one of the most pleasant histories ever written by a Virginian. He was born at Stratford, in Westmoreland county, in 1806 [*sic*], in the same house and in the same chamber in which Richard Henry Lee and Francis Lightfoot Lee, two signers of the Declaration of Independence, were born.

He entered West Point, as a cadet from his native State, in 1825. On the first day of his entrance he took the head of his class, and kept it until he graduated in 1829, having never been marked with a demerit, or been subjected to a reprimand, or received any other species of punishment whatever, during the whole time of his residence. Having graduated at the head of his class, he was, of course, selected for service in the corps of topographical engineers, which was always filled from the ranks of the highest graduates. He entered upon his new field of duty in July, 1829, with the brevet rank of second lieutenant. We hear no more of him until 1835, when he was appointed assistant astronomer for fixing the boundary line between Ohio and Michigan. He became first lieutenant in September, 1836, and captain in July, 1838. In 1845, he was chief engineer in the army of General Wool, in Mexico. In 1847, he was brevetted major, for "gallant and meritorious conduct" in the battle of Cerro Gordo, fought April 18th, 1847. He received a second brevet for "gallant and meritorious conduct" in the battles of Contreras and Cherubusco, and was now lieutenant-colonel by brevet. For gallant and meritorious conduct in the battle of Chapultepec, where he was wounded, on the 1st September, 1852, he was appointed superintendent of the Military Academy. How long he continued in that post we do not know; but we find him, in 1858, lieutenant-colonel of the famous regiment of cavalry of which Albert Sydney Johnston was colonel, and as such highly distinguishing himself in the desperate fight with the Indians on the prairies of Texas, which created so much excitement at the time. Nor do we know how he came to be at Washington at the time of John Brown's attempt at insurrection; but we *do* know that he was sent by President Buchanan, with a body of marines, to capture the outlaw, and that he did it.

Such is a brief outline of the services rendered to the old United States by Robert E. Lee during the long period of thirty years.

In the old army he was believed by all officers, almost without exception to be, by many degrees, the most accomplished soldier in the whole army. His superiority, indeed, was so incontestable, that it excited no jealousy whatever in any quarter. When his reputation had been somewhat impaired for the time, by his campaign in Western Virginia, a distinguished officer, now in the service of Virginia, but heretofore for many years an officer in the old army of the United States, observed that injustice was done to General Lee—that in the old army, each officer perfectly understood the calibre of every other—that Lee was, by the acknowledgment of all, the first man in the service—and that, if an opportunity were afforded him, he would prove what he was, in a way that would silence scepticism forever. The opinion entertained of him by General Scott is well known. "Lee," said that vain and self-sufficient old coxcomb, "is the greatest military genius in America, myself not excepted." He might very well say so, if it be true, as has often been said, that to the genius of Lee he owed the laurels he had reaped in Mexico. Whether this anecdote, however, be true or false, it is well known that he regretted the loss of Lee more than that of all the other officers, when Lee determined to stand by the land that gave him birth, and that he made the most strenuous efforts to retain him. He might as well have attempted to roll back the earth in its daily revolution upon its axis. General Lee is the most thorough of all Virginians. Virginian in sentiment and feeling, his father's son could scarcely avoid being; but he is more thoroughly Virginian than could be expected even from a person born and connected like himself. So intense is this feeling, that he has been heard to say, even since his wonderful successes have placed him at the very head of his age, that he had but one ambition, and that was to be Governor of Virginia. It was, therefore, as certain as any future event could be, that as soon as Vriginia seceded, he would go along with her. She did secede in April, 1861, and a few days after, her Convention appointed him Commander-in-Chief of her forces. He arrived in Richmond about the 25th of April, having sent in his resignation of his commission in the old army some time before.

General Lee immediately entered upon the duties of his office. It may be presumed that they were of the most arduous character; but difficulties disappeared beneath his fingers, as though they had been dissolved by magic. He had an army to organize and drill, the materials of war to create almost out of nothing, the troops to arm, clothe and feed, after they had been collected, and all the duties of a minister of war to discharge, in addition to his more immediate duties of General-in-Chief. It is impossible, for the want of materials, to furnish an account of his administration between the time of entering upon his office and that of turning the army of Virginia over to the Confederacy. When the difficulties with which he was surrounded are taken into consideration, we feel convinced that his services will bear a comparison with those of Carnot, or any other war minister that ever existed. When President Davis made his appointments of generals, he was the third on the list; General Cooper being first and General Sydney Johnston second. The appointments were made with reference to the rank held by each officer in the old army.

After the defeat and death of General Garnett, General Lee was appointed by President Davis to take command of our forces in Western Virginia. In the early part of August he repaired to his command, carrying with him reinforcements enough to swell his force to 16,000 men. On the short campaign which ensued it is not our purpose to dwell. It is well known to have failed, whether through any fault of the General it is impossible, among conflicting statements, to decide. The hopes of the people were very high when he took command, and their confidence in his skill unbounded. When, therefore, the campaign resulted in a failure, there was no measure to the indignation of the country. President Davis, however, who is himself a military man, and had the whole facts in his possession, formed a very different opinion of the case from any that had been formed by those who knew nothing but what had been gathered from the newspapers. He acquitted General Lee thoroughly, and that acquittal must be considered decisive. It was not so considered at the time, however, by the people. General Lee's military reputation fell immeasurably, and from one of the most popular generals in the service he became decidedly unpopular. His case presents one of the strongest examples on record of the folly and injustice of judging any man by the standard of popular appreciation. Had he not had an opportunity afforded him of proving what he really was, he would have gone down to posterity as an inefficient officer, entirely unequal to the command of even a brigade.

Immediately on his return from this unsuccessful campaign, General Lee was appointed to command in the military district of which Charleston is the centre. His skill as an engineer had never been doubted, notwithstanding his ill success as Commander-in-Chief; and he was expected to put it in practice in fortifying the city and harbor of Charleston. He succeeded completely. Having accomplished this object, General Lee returned to Richmond. It was soon after this that our disasters in Kentucky and Tennessee began to occur. Their effect upon the country was depressing in the extreme. Congress, at that time in session, passed a joint resolution appointing General Lee Commander-in-Chief. Whether this act was vetoed by the President we do not know, but he seems of his own accord to have placed General Lee in a position almost equivalent; in one which gave him, in fact, the largest share in the control and direction of the war, It was probably owing to his advice that the policy of concentration was adopted as the only one that could enable our inferior forces to contend successfully with the huge levies of the Yankees.

We now come to the *real* commencement of General Lee's career, a career so brilliant as to establish his claim to be reckoned among the greatest captains that have risen in the world. The army of McClellan was around Richmond. It had been, at the commencement of the Peninsula campaign, 168,000 strong. It had suffered severely in battle, and more severely still from disease. Still it numbered, according to the best estimate we have been able to make, at least 130,000 men. General Johnston had gained a great victory at Seven Pines, but the country was deprived of his services at this critical juncture by the severe wound which he had received in that battle. President Davis believed that nobody could so well supply his place as General Lee, and he was accordingly ordered to take the command. He did so on the 1st of June. He saw, at a glance, that the seige of Richmond could not be raised without beating the enemy out of the formidable works in which they had entrenched themselves, and he immediately set about devising the means to accomplish it. How it was done we leave to the future historian to describe. It suffices our purpose to chronicle the result. In the course of one week, General Lee, by a series of combinations unsurpassed in the history of war, had succeeded in beating the enemy out of a succession of fortifications of the most formidable character, had driven him from around Richmond, to a place thirty miles below, and had relieved all fears for the safety of the capital. That he did not completely destroy the enemy was no fault of his.

General Lee is the most successful general of the age. His exploits are brilliant almost beyond example. When we say this of a man who commands an immense army, it is supererogatory to say anything of his talents. Nothing but genius of the highest order can conceive the combinations necessary to insure the uninterrupted success of so large a host, over an enemy greatly superior in force. In all departments of science his acquirements are great, and has besides an uncommon stock of general information. His judgment is as quick as his military glance, and it rarely deceives. Withal he is one of the most unpretending men in the world —a thorough gentleman in his manner—very affable to all who approach him—and extremely amiable in private life. He is about five feet ten inches high, was eminently handsome in his youth, is still one of the finest looking men in the army, rides like a knight of the old crusading days, is indefatigable in business, and bears fatigue like a man of iron.

Morgan in Kentucky

THE RAIDS of the romantic Morgan thrilled Southerners throughout the Confederacy. What matter the numerical superiority of the North, what matter the blockade, what matter the output of thousands of Yankee factories if a small body of partisans could outwit and outfight the enemy?

Here is Morgan's own proclamation to his men praising them for their actions in late August, 1862.

Proclamation.

Headquarters Morgan's Brigade,
Hartsville, Tenn., *August 22, 1862.*

Soldiers: Your gallant bearing during the last two days will not only be inscribed in the history of the country and the annals of this war, but is engraven deeply in my heart.

Your zeal and devotion on the 20th, at the attack of the trestle-work at Saundersville, and of the Springfield Junction Stockade—your heroism during the two hard fights of yester-

day, have placed you high on the list of those patriots who
are now in arms for our Southern rights.

All communication cut off betwixt Gallatin and Nashville
—a body of 300 infantry totally cut up or taken prisoners—
the liberation of those kind friends arrested by our revengeful foes—for no other reason than their compassionate care
of our sick and wounded, would have been laurels sufficient
for your brows. But, soldiers, the utter annihilation of Gen.
Johnson's brigade—composed of twenty-four picked companies of regulars, and sent on purpose to take us, raises
your reputations as soldiers, and strikes fear into the craven
hearts of your enemies. General Johnson and his staff, with
200 men taken prisoners, sixty-four killed and 100 wounded,
attests the resistance made, and bears testimony to your
valor.

But our victories have not been achieved without loss.
We have to mourn some brave and dear comrades. Their
names will remain in our breasts, their fame outlives them.
They died in defence of a good cause. They died like gallant
soldiers—with their front to the foe.

Officers and men! Your conduct makes me proud to command you! Fight always as you fought yesterday, and you
are invincible.

> John H. Morgan,
> Colonel Commanding Cavalry

A Hit at Everybody

Bᴜᴛ ɴᴏ ᴀʀᴍʏ has ever been all heroes and heroics. Like all other large bodies of men, the Confederate Army had its shirkers, its malcontents, its cowards, and its criminals. Officers, especially during the first years of the war when company grade officers were generally elected, were not always of the highest caliber. It speaks well, however, of the army as a whole that there was so little of misconduct that the Confederates could freely poke fun at it.

The following piece was intended for a soldier paper, *The Army Argus*, but reached first the editors of the Mobile *Register* and was published in that paper. It appears here as later reprinted, for a wider audience, in the columns of *The Southern Literary Messenger*.

The following document, intended for the "Army Argus," while that paper was published at Corinth, having lost its way, has fallen into our hands. If its generalities hit anybody in particular, it is their fault, and those who are not hurt by it, who, we are sure, must constitute the great majority in the different classes enumerated, cannot fail to be amused by it, and perhaps instructed as to the errors into which they may be in danger of falling unsuspiciously.

<*Mobile Register*.

MILITARY CATECHISM.

By Col. T. C. J****

Scene—School-room—Class in Military Affairs stand up.

Question. What is the first duty of a Brigadier General?

Answer. To swear by note.

Q.—What is the second duty?

A.—To drink every day a large quantity of bad whiskey.

Q.—What is the third duty?

A.—To be constantly astonished that these and other feats do not bring him a Major General's commission.

Q.—What is the first duty of a Colonel?

A.—To put three stars on his collar.

Q.—What is the second duty?

A.—To see that his regiment is never put to such useless work as drilling in the School of the Battalion.

Q.—What is the third duty?

A.—To imitate the Brigadier Generals in a small way, especially in the fine arts of swearing and drinking.

Q.—What is the first duty of a Captain?

A.—To forget all the promises he made to the boys when he was elected, and put on dignified airs in the presence of his old associates.

Q.—What is the second duty?

A.—To get a finer uniform than his Colonel.

Q.—What the third duty?

A.—To become the best poker-player in the army.

Q.—What is the first duty of an Adjutant General?

A.—To become so huffish that every one will dislike to do business with him.

Q.—What is the second duty?

A.—To fill his office with young squirts, as clerks and assistants, to look fiercely at visiters.

Q.—What is the third duty?

A.—To perpetually intrigue for a higher position in the line, provided it is not attended with personal danger.

Q.—What is the duty of a regular aid?

A.—To make himself important.

Q.—What is the second duty?

A.—To make himself very important.

Q.—What is the third duty?

A.—To look upon those gentlemen who, through patriotic motives, or admiration of his chief, volunteer to serve the country without compensation, in the capacity of an aid, as a sort of interloper that interferes with his importance.

Q.—What is the first duty of a Quartermaster?

A.—A great Captain has laid down the three great duties of this officer. He says the first duty is to make himself comfortable.

Q.—What does he say is the second duty?

A.—To make himself damned comfortable.

Q.—What does he lay down as his third duty?

A.—To make everybody else damned uncomfortable.

Q.—What is the first duty of a Commissary?

A.—To take all the delicacies provided in the army for his own use.

Q.—What is the second duty?

A.—To share sparingly said delicacies with his friends, and never let them go into such vulgar places as the mouths of sick soldiers.

Q.—What is the third duty?

A.—To be very particular to see that the requisitions for rations are in proper form—all the t's crossed and i's dotted —when presented by soldiers who are sick or who have had nothing to eat for three or four days.

Q.—What is the first duty of a Medical Director?

A.—To permit the sick and wounded to take care of themselves.

Q.—What is the second duty?

A.—To learn the sick and wounded to be of little trouble to the medical department, and to this end to constantly ship those mortally wounded, or *in extremis*, to distant points, without attendants, and without any thing to eat or drink.

Q.—What is the third duty?

A.—To employ a good part of his time in cursing the physician, in charge of those distant hospitals, for letting so many of the sick and wounded die.

Q.—What is the first duty of a surgeon?

A.—Under the names of drugs and medicines, to purchase a full supply of good liquors.

Q.—What is the second duty?

A.—To cause all private cellars to be searched, and all the good brandies found there to be confiscated, lest the owners should smuggle them to the soldiers, give them away and make the whole army drunk.

Q.—What is the third duty?

A.—To see that he and his assistants drink up all of said liquors.

Q.—What is the fourth duty?

A.—To wear the largest amount of gold lace, and be always absent from the post of danger and of duty.

Q.—What is the first duty of a Chaplain?

A.—Never to mention the subject of religion to the soldiers.

Q.—What is the second duty?

A.—To preach to the regiment only once a year, and not that unless specially requested by the Colonel.

Q.—What is the third duty?

A.—To grumble all the time about the smallness of his pay.

Q.—What is the first duty of pickets?

A.—To go to sleep on their posts.

Q.—What is the second duty?

A.—To wake up when the enemy's pickets invite them to come over and take a drink.

Q.—What is the third duty?

A.—To be "driven in" upon the explosion of the first shell.

Q.—What is the first duty of an army?

A.—To destroy as much private property as possible, particularly that belonging to its friends.

Q.—What is the second duty?

A.—To parole all prisoners taken from the enemy who are known to have burned houses, stolen negroes or murdered women.

Q.—What is the third duty?

A.—Always to act on the defensive and never to invade the enemy's territory however good may be the opportunity, although he may be ravaging yours all the time.

Q.—What is the first duty of the Government?

A.—To fill all its important posts with Yankees and foreigners.

Q.—What is the second duty?

A.—To deliver its chief cities without striking a blow.

Q.—What is the third duty?

A.—Never to learn from experience.

Q.—What is the first duty of the Southern people?

A.—To keep out of the army.

Q.—What is the second duty?

A.—To make all the money they can out of the Government and the soldiers, as wars come seldom.

Q.—What is the third duty?

A.—To surrender the entire trade in shoes and clothing—on which trade the army is dependent—to that patriotic class of men known as Jews, who are too conscientious to charge the government or the army a profit exceeding two thousand per cent.

Q.—What is the fourth duty?

A.—To let success cause a relaxation of their exertions, and see in every little reverse the ruin of our cause.

That will do—take your seats.

Richmond Views of the News

T
HE SOUTH was conscious that not only its political independence, but its independence in every type of endeavor, must be won to give the Confederacy a truly national existence. "The South must not only fight her own battles," admonished a Mobile music publisher on sheets of his music, "but sing her own songs & dance to music composed by her own children." She must make her own ordnance, build her own ships, and publish her own books and papers.

The Southern Illustrated News was established in Richmond in the late summer of 1862. Frankly patterned after *The Illustrated News* of London, this new weekly was designed to fill the void left by the inaccessibility of papers formerly received from the North and to provide reading matter more acceptable than the Yankee publications in both quality and point of view. Despite the lack of professional authors, trained engravers, and adequate supplies of paper, *The Southern Illustrated News* was a resounding success and was soon the leading weekly in the South. Here are four excerpts from the columns of its early issues: an editorial comment on the invasion of Maryland, an explanation of British failure to recognize the Confederacy, a report of President Lincoln's Emancipation Proclamation, and a sketch of Belle Boyd, the most famous of Confederate women spies.

THE INVASION OF MARYLAND

The movement which has placed our troops upon the soil of Maryland has electrified the country, already exulting in the glory achieved by the unrivalled couraged of our noble army and the high skill of its great commander. The loftiest hopes are entertained, and not a shadow of doubt seems to obtrude itself for a moment upon the enlivening prospect. Criticism, abashed by the brilliant successes that have cleared Virginia of the Yankees in a space of time so brief that we can hardly recognize its existence, is silent for the time, and no voice is heard but that of approbation. The public, indeed, has, all along, been ahead of the government in regard to this particular matter. It eagerly desired to march into Maryland immediately after the battle of Manassas in July of last year. Its wishes were not gratified then for reasons which, no doubt, appeared sufficient to the government, but it is has never abandoneed that favorite project, or ceased to hope that the day might come when it would be gratified. It has come at last, and the advance has been made under the most favorable circumstances that it is possible to imagine. The veteran forces of the enemy have been either destroyed or demoralized by the battles of July and August. To meet our troops in Maryland, they have little else than raw recruits, many of them averse to the service and all of them cowed and over-awed by the ill-success of the last three months and the high reputation of the enemy they are brought to oppose. Be the numbers of these recruits as large as they may, they will still be no match for our veterans. Indeed, the larger the force, the greater the confusion and the more certain and more fatal the defeat. But our Generals have it in their power, by breaking up the railways, to prevent a very great accumulation even of raw recruits.

It is evident that this movement has either taken the enemy entirely by surprise, or that if he anticipated it, he was utterly unable to prevent it. As late as the 6th of September, when our troops were already, if not in actual possession of Fredericktown, at least within a few miles of it, a Philadelphia paper assured its readers that all the passages of the Potomac were securely guarded, and that it would be impossible for the "Rebels" to cross that river. A day or two before, the Washington Star expressed the most scornful incredulity upon the same subject, declaring that it wished nothing better than for them to make the attempt. It hoped General McClellan would not interrupt them, but suffer them to pass over without molestation, that he might cut off their retreat and capture the whole of them. We were inclined, at first, to believe that this was mere empty braggadocio—mere whistling to keep up courage—but from the entire absence of all precautions to delay our passage, we are induced to think that it was spoken in earnest, and that it was not believed at Washington any more than at Philadelphia, that the attempt would be made. The inhabitants, thus far, have shown themselves highly favorable to our cause, which is, indeed, their own. It is reported—with what degree of truth we know not—that the county of Frederick has already furnished a brigade of infantry and 150 cavalry. As it has been generally believed that the Western portion of Maryland was that which was least disposed to join with the South, this fact, if it be a fact, is of the greatest significance. The Eastern counties and the city of Baltimore have long been known to be unanimous, or nearly so, in our favor, and the sign thus given in Frederick indicates a very feeble party in favor of the Yankee rule.

Mighty events—mightier than any that have yet occurred —are evidently on the wing. Before another issue of this paper, a great battle may have been fought, and the fate of Washington, possibly of the war, have been determined. We wait with anxiety, yet without the smallest fear, for the result. Our brave boys are not to be beaten by any force the Yankees can bring against them.

THE REASONS WHY WE HAVE NOT YET BEEN ACKNOWLEDGED BY GREAT BRITAIN

A great deal of indignation has been felt and expressed in certain quarters because we have not been acknowledged as an independent nation by Great Britain, and not a little astonishment. For indignation, we cannot but think there is great reason. The old Government of the United States, taking warning from the events of the Revolution, established a rule from which it never departed with respect to such matters. It was to acknowledge the Government *de facto* of every country with which it had political relations. This was a wise rule, instituted by the great Southern Presidents who ruled the destinies of the country for so many years, and made for it all of its history which is not absolutely contemptible. Of late years this has also been the policy of Great

Britain, borrowed, no doubt, from the practice of the United States, and founded on the plainest dictates of justice and common sense. Great Britain had suffered awfully from having pursued the opposite course, and she seemed to have taken warning from the past. She had entered into a war of five years' standing with France for acknowledging the independence of the thirteen colonies, and had come out of it with a beggared exchequer, a defeated army, and an empire sundered in twain. She had refused to acknowledge the independence of the French Republic, and the bloodiest and most dangerous war she had ever been engaged in to that time was the consequence. She refused to recognise the French Empire, and a war more bloody and dangerous still had been the consequence. The practice which she borrowed from the United States was a wise and a safe practice. It committed her to no discussion of the right of the government she recognised to rule the country which it professed to rule, and to no interference with the internal affairs of such country. It disclaimed, indeed, all pretension to knowledge upon that head. It merely addressed itself to the Government which it found in power, without asking any questions whatever. Thus, when Louis Philippe established the throne of July upon the ruins of the throne of the elder Bourbon dynasty, Great Britain at once recognised the new Government. When the Orleans dynasty was overthrown, she made haste to acknowledge the Republic. When Louis Napoleon established his Presidency, she did the same thing, as she did likewise when he made himself Emperor. She recognised all the Republics of South America, and the Empire of Iturbide in Mexico, though, to the best of our belief, Spain has never acknowledged their independence to this day. She recognised and assisted to set up Greece. She not only recognised Belgium, but contributed to get Prince Leopold made

King. But two years ago, when the King of Naples was driven from his throne, she immediately recognised his successor, Victor Emmanuel. The Confederate States are the only new power she has refused to recognise, and yet they have manifested a degree of strength greater than all those we have enumerated put together. We have, under these circumstances, we think, some right to be indignant. We have not the smallest right to be astonished.

Great Britain has been trying to bring about the very state of things now existing here ever since the United States became a recognised power of the earth. She never could find it in her heart to forgive the successful revolt of the colonies. During Mr. Madison's first term, disclosures were made by the celebrated John Henry, which, although attempts of the most strenuous kind were made to discredit the witness, proved, beyond a doubt, that a deeply laid plot had been concocted by the Government of Canada and certain traitors in New England to separate that part of the country from the Union and annex it to the British Empire. In the war which followed shortly after, the people and press of New England were almost unanimous in favor of Great Britain, and opposed to those whom they ought to have regarded as their countrymen. In latter days England has been jealous of the growing power of the United States to an inordinate degree. She has clearly foreseen that, if they continue united, they must become, before the close of this century, the first nation of the world, with an invincible army, a navy that must assume the empire of the seas, and a commerce that must swallow up all the commerce of the Old World. Thus, in addition to the old grudge, she has been stimulated by the fear of losing her position among the powers of the earth. Cost what it might, she has felt that for her the greatest of all objects has been to destroy the Union.

She has succeeded at last, and it is not wonderful that she
should desire to see the war carried on as long as both parties
may have the strength to maintain themselves. She feels that
intervention would follow recognition, and this she is by no
means disposed to undertake, because it might have the
effect of shortening the war.

The war in question, besides removing a powerful rival
from her path, is useful to her in another respect. If it should
last long enough, it may be the means of getting her cotton
from India into demand, and it may stimulate the production
in Australia. When we consider that cotton constitutes the
very basis upon which her enormous power is built, we shall
see at once the importance of having it all under her own
control. This she hopes to accomplish by destroying the cul-
ture in this country, which can only be done by destroying
the labor which produces it. The abolition of slavery in her
West Indian possessions was but the preliminary step to the
abolition of slavery in this country. . . . She cares nothing
for the slave in Brazil, where his condition is infinitely worse
than it is here, or in Cuba, where it is worse even than it is in
Brazil. All her sympathy is reserved for the slave in the
Southern States of this Confederacy, who cultivates the products of which she wishes to preserve a monopoly.

In addition to these causes, it may be that the British Government feels itself in no condition to intervene, because of
the present condition in Europe. Affairs are far from satisfactory in Italy, and any moment may witness the outbreak of a
general war. As we have already observed, recognition might
bring on intervention as a necessary consequence, and intervention would be sure to bring on war. This the British Government will avoid if it can. It already has a most exaggerated
opinion of the strength of the Yankee Government, and is
evidently very unwilling—we might almost say afraid—to

come into collision with it. A late debate in Parliament plainly revealed an extraordinary degree of alarm on the subject of Canada. Entangled as it already is in a war which it supports with difficulty, the Ministry apparently think Yankeedom yet strong enough to tear that noble province from their grasp.

These, we think, are the reasons why Great Britain—meaning the British Government—is averse to recognise us. That the majority of the people sympathise with us, while they detest the Yankees, we do not doubt.

A NOTE ON THE EMANCIPATION PROCLAMATION

Lincoln seems to be in a state of desperation. He has issued a proclamation, declaring all negroes belonging to rebels free. As his armies have freed the negroes wherever they have been, this proclamation does not at all alter the character of the war. He has issued another, in which he proclaims martial law all over the United States. As he has no authority in the Southern States, of course it is altogether inoperative there. But it does operate in the Yankee States, and was no doubt designed for them. The Democratic party has of late begun to show itself very formidable in those States, and there was fair prospect of their beating the Abolitionists proper, at the next elections. This proclamation is intended to keep them quiet, or to dispose of them in the most summary manner, if they should succeed in their ticket. Opposition is not tolerated north of the Potomac, and any man who attempts it will be dealt with as a traitor. The government there is a military despotism, as absolute as that of Russia. The old Constitution of the United States has sunk into absolute contempt. Those who express a wish to see it respected, are forthwith clapped into jail on a charge of treason.

MISS BELLE BOYD

This young lady, who has, by her devotion to the Southern cause, called down upon her head the anathemas of the entire Yankee press, was in our city last week. Through the politeness of Mr. Cowel[l], the artist at Minnis's gallery, we are enabled, in this issue of our paper, to present her picture.

Miss Belle is the daughter of Benjamin B. Boyd of Martinsburg, at which place he was for a long time prominently engaged in the mercantile profession. He afterwards removed to Knoxville, Tennessee, where he lived about three years, but returned to Martinsburg about two years previous to the breaking out of the present war. Her mother was the daughter of Captain Glenn of Jefferson county. Miss Belle is the oldest child of her parents, and is about 23 years of age. An uncle of Miss Belle, James W. Glenn, of Jefferson county, commanded a company during the present war, known as the "Virginia Rangers," until recently, the captaincy of which he resigned on account of ill-health. James E. Stuart, a prominent politician of the Valley, and who was a member of the Virginia Convention of 1850, married a sister of Miss Belle's mother.

During her early years Miss Belle was distinguished for her sprightliness and the vivacity of her temper.

That our readers may have an opportunity of seeing what the Yankee correspondents say about this young lady, we extract the following article from the columns of the Philadelphia "Inquirer," which was written by the army correspondent of that sheet:

"These women are the most accomplished in Southern circles. They are introduced under assumed names to our officers, so as to avoid detection or recognition from those to whom their names are known, but their persons unknown. By such means they are enabled to frequently meet combinedly, but at separate times, the officers of every regiment in a whole column, and by simple compilation and comparison of notes, they achieve a full knowledge of the strength of our entire force. Has modern warfare a parallel to the use of such accomplishments for such a purpose? The chief of these spies is the celebrated Belle Boyd. Her acknowledged superiority for machination and intrigue has given her the leadership and control of the female spies in the valley of Virginia. She is a resident of Martinsburg, when at home, and has a pious, good old mother, who regrets as much as any one can the violent and eccentric course of her daughter since this rebellion has broken out. Belle has passed the freshness of youth. She is a sharp-featured, black-eyed woman of 25, or care and intrigue have given her that appearance. Last summer, whilst Patterson's army lay at Martinsburg, she wore a revolver in her belt, and was courted and flattered by every Lieutenant and Captain in the service who ever saw her. There was a kind of Di Vernon dash about her, a smart pertness, a quickness of retort, and utter abandonment of manner and bearing which were attractive from the very romantic unwontedness.

"The father of this resolute black-eyed vixen is a paymaster in the Southern army, and formerly held a place at Washington under our Government. She has undergone all that society, position and education can confer upon a mind suited to the days of Charles the Second, or Louis the Fourteenth— a mind such as Mazarin or Richelieu would have delighted to employ from its kindred affinities.

"Well, this woman I saw practicing her arts upon our young lieutenants and inexperienced captains, and in each case I uniformly felt it my duty to call them aside and warn them of whom she was. To one she had been introduced as Miss Anderson, to another as Miss Faulkner, and so to the end of the chapter. She is so well known now that she can only practice her blandishments upon new raw levies and their officers. But from them she obtains the number of their regiments and force. She has, however, a trained band of coadjutors, who report to her daily—girls aged from 16 upward—women who have the common sense not to make themselves as conspicuous as she, and who remain unknown, save to her, and are therefore effective. The reports that she is personally impure are as unjust as they are undeserved. She has a blind devotion to an idea, and passes far the boundary of her sex's modesty to promote its success.

"During the past campaign in the Valley this woman has been of immense service to the enemy. She will be now if she can."

The Battle of Fredericksburg

T HE BATTLE OF FREDERICKSBURG on December 12, 1862, was one of the great victories of the Confederacy and one of the first great winter battles of the war. Here is the account of it which appeared in the weekly review of military events in *The Southern Illustrated News.*

We have had stirring times since our last issue—important movements, resulting in a great pitched battle and a glorious victory. — On Thursday, the 11th, the Yankees opened a tremendous fire of shot and shell upon the devoted town of Fredericksburg. No less than 173 pieces of the heaviest artillery were in action at once, from the hills of Stafford, which completely overlook and command the place. Under cover of this fire, the Yankees attempted to construct two pontoon bridges opposite the city, but were repeatedly driven off by our sharpshooters in the rifle pits along the shore and in the houses. About 4 o'clock, however, they succeeded in crossing. Instantly the event was announced by the telegraph to all

141

Yankeedom as a glorious victory, the New York Herald next morning proclaiming the movement to have been "decisive and victorious." At nearly the same moment, two bridges were thrown over below, and the Yankees crossed there also. Our men fell back, and the Yankees became certain of victory. The Baltimore American's correspondent said next morning, "A battle is predicted to day, but we think it doubtful whether the Rebels design to fight us in their present position." It is evident that they had not the remotest conception of what was in store for them. All day Friday, the enemy were engaged in passing over their troops. There was some skirmishing along the line, but nothing of serious moment occurred. On Saturday, at an early hour, Gen. Lee drew up his forces on the heights beyond Fredericksburg. Gen. Jackson, on the right, farthest down the river, and Gen. Longstreet on the left. The Confederate army then drawn up presented the appearance of a huge crescent, concave to the front. Its line was five miles long, and its artillery was posted in such a manner as to command all the approaches with a cross fire.

About 9 o'clock, under cover of a dense fog, a heavy body of the enemy advanced against the right of our line, where Gen. Jackson commanded. Gen. Stuart, who was stationed on the extreme right with two brigades of cavalry, immediately moved up two sections of his horse artillery and opened a heavy fire on his flank. The enemy, in advancing, was met by the division of Gen. A. P. Hill of Jackson's corps, and assailed with such fury that he was compelled to fall back after an obstinate resistance. During this combat, two of Hill's brigades, overwhelmed by numbers were compelled to fall back. Gen. Lee ordered Gen. Early to support Gen. Hill. The enemy had already seized a wood which lies in that part of the field. Furiously assailed by Early, he was compelled to relinquish his prize, and fled pursued by Early until he came under fire of his batteries. So large was the force of the enemy at this point, that his right overlapped the left of Hill, and came opposite to Hood's division, the extreme right of Longstreet's corps. He took possession of a wood in front of Hood, but was speedily dislodged.

While this battle was going on upon the right of our line, the enemy were engaged in passing over large bodies of troops from the Stafford shore, for the purpose of attacking our left under Longstreet. After he had already been repulsed on our right, he commenced a furious assault upon our left with the view of getting possession of the heights which command the town of Fredericksburg. He was repulsed with great slaughter, only to renew the attempt. On this part of the line, the destruction of the enemy was fearfully great. He behaved with great resolution, and repeatedly renewed his efforts, only to be continually driven back with increased slaughter. Gen. Longstreet had placed a division in certain stone enclosures used as farm fences, and from behind these the men shot down the Yankees at their leisure and in comparative security. The ground was literally piled up with dead men. The Washington Artillery—as they always do—distinguished themselves on this part of the field. Having exhausted all their ammunition, they were withdrawn about night from the spot which they had rendered immortal, and their place was filled by a portion of McLaws' division, which also highly distinguished itself. All their attacks upon Longstreet were seconded by the fire of the enemy's heavy batteries on the Stafford heights. But they were of no avail against the steady courage and immovable pertinacity of our troops. By sunset the enemy was hopelessly beaten at all points, and although he made another assault after dark, upon Longstreet, it was designed only to aid him in drawing off his troops. This he did under cover of the night, leaving his dead and wounded and the field of battle in our possession. A few more hours of daylight would have witnessed the utter destruction of the Yankee army.

Persons in Fredericksburg at the time, who have since come away, assert that the scenes of Saturday night were terrific beyond description. The Yankees had become completely demoralized by their defeat. Their officers were utterly unable to restrain them.— They pillaged every house that had been left. The whole army seemed to be a drunken mob. This frightful scene continued until Monday night, when, under cover of the darkness, Burnside withdrew his whole force to the Northern bank of the Rappahannock.— When our troops re-entered the town they began for the first time to have some idea of the greatness of their victory. Piles of Yankee dead, which they had not had time to bury, (in such alarm were they,) were found lying about in all directions. About 300 wounded and sick had been left behind in their haste. The field of battle presented a horrible spectacle. At least six, some say eight, Yankees were found dead for one Confederate. At one place an officer saw what he supposed to be a regiment lying in ambush in a small enclosure. It proved to be dead Yankees. It is computed, so we learn from a city paper, in official quarters, that the Yankee loss in killed, wounded and prisoners, amounts to at least 18,000 men.— The prisoners were very few. Our own loss in killed, wounded and missing, is over 2,000. The cause of the difference is plain. Our forces were stationed on commanding eminences, and our fire swept the vast plain through which the Yankees approached to attack us. They could do us little injury, while every shot of ours told.

Burnside has disappeared, but whither he is gone, seems not to be known. One account, and that the most probable, is, that he has gone to Acquia Creek, to get on board his fleet. Gen. Lee, it seems, has made him take water; but where next, it is hard to say.

1863

The Alabama Versus the Hatteras

HARDLY as large as a modern destroyer, the Confederate cruiser *Alabama* earned a fame all out of proportion to her size. Her record of fifty-seven ships burned and many others boarded and examined brought a glory to a Confederate Navy that had little enough of success. She was the chief of a trio of raiding cruisers built in England for the Confederacy. The *Alabama* and the *Shenandoah* did damage to Federal shipping amounting to more than six million dollars each, and the *Florida* added another three millions. Under her gallant and vigorous captain, Commander Raphael Semmes, the *Alabama* sailed more than seventy-five thousand miles—from as far as the China Sea to her doom off the coast of France.

In this unidentified officer's account of her engagement with the *Hatteras* in January, 1863, the *Alabama* is presented in her prime—fresh from her successful sortie from Liverpool and outfitting in the Azores and a victorious maiden cruise in the Atlantic and the Caribbean.

Sunday, 11th.— Fine moderate breeze from the eastward. Read Articles of War. Noon: Eighteen miles from Galveston. As I write this some are discussing the probability of a fight before morning. 2.25 P.M.: Light breeze; sail discovered by the look-out on the bow. Shortly after, three, and at last five, vessels were seen; two of which were reported to be steamers. Every one delighted at the prospect of a fight, no doubt whatever existing as to their being war-vessels—blockaders we supposed. The watch below came on deck, and of their own accord began preparing the guns, &c., for action. Those whose watch it was on deck were engaged in getting the propeller ready for lowering; others were bending a cable to a kedge and putting it over the bow—the engineers firing up for steam, officers looking to their side-arms, &c., and discussing the size of their expected adversary or adversaries. At 2.30 shortened sail and tacked to the southward. 4 P.M.: A steamer reported standing out from the fleet towards us. Backed main-topsail and lowered propeller. 4.50: Everything reported ready for action. Chase bearing N.N.E., distant ten miles. Twilight set in about 5.45. Took in all sail. At 6.20 beat up to quarters, manned the starboard battery, and loaded with fine second shell; turned round, stood for the steamer, having previously made her out to be a two-masted side-wheel, of apparent 1200 tons, though at the distance she was before dark we could not form any correct estimate of her size, &c.

At 6.30 the strange steamer hailed and asked: "What steamer is that?" We replied (in order to be certain who he was), "Her Majesty's ship Petrel! What steamer is that?" Two or three times we asked the question, until we heard, "This is the United States steamer———," not hearing the name. However, United States steamer was sufficient. As no doubt existed as to her character, we said, at 6.35, that this was the "Confederate States steamer, Alabama," accompanying the last syllable of our name with a shell fired over him. The signal being given, the other guns took up the refrain, and a tremendous volley from our whole broadside given to him, every shell striking his side, the shot striking being distinctly heard on board our vessel, and thus found that she was iron.

The enemy replied, and the action became general. A most sharp spirited firing was kept up on both sides, our fellows peppering away as though the action depended on each individual. And so it did. Pistols and rifles were continually pouring from our quarter-deck messengers most deadly, the distance during the hottest of the fight not being more than forty yards! It was a grand, though fearful sight, to see the guns belching forth, in the darkness of the night, sheets of living flame, the deadly missiles striking the enemy with a force that we could *feel*. Then, when the shells struck her side, and especially the percussion ones, her whole side was lit up, and showing rents of five or six feet in length. One shot had just struck our smoke-stack, and wounding one man in the cheek, when the enemy ceased his firing, and fired a lee gun; then a second, and a third. The order was given to "Cease firing." This was at 6.52. A tremendous cheering commenced, and it was not till everybody had cleared his throat to his own satisfaction, that silence could be obtained. We then hailed him, and in reply he stated that he had surrendered, was on fire, and also that he was in a sinking condition. He then sent a boat on board, and surrendered the U. S. gun-boat, Hatteras, nine guns, Lieutenant-Commander Blake, 140 men. Boats were immediately lowered and sent to his assistance, when an alarm was given that another steamer was bearing down for us. The boats were recalled and hoisted up, when it was found to be a false alarm. The order was given, and the boatswain and his mates piped "All hands out boats to save life;" and soon the prisoners were transferred to our ship—the officers under guard on the quarter-deck, and the men in single irons. The boats were then hoisted up, the battery run in and secured, and the main brace spliced. All hands piped down, the enemy's vessel sunk, and we steaming quietly away by 8.30, all having been done in less than two hours. In fact, had it not been for our having the prisoners on board, we would have sworn nothing unusual had taken place—the watch below quietly sleeping in their hammocks. The conduct of our men was truly commendable. No flurry, no noise—all calm and determined. The coolness displayed by them could not be surpassed by any old veterans—our chief boatswain's mate apparently in his glory. "Sponge!" "Load with cartridge!" — "Shell-fire seconds!" — "Run out!" — "Well, down compressors!" — "Left, traverse!" — "Well!" — "Ready!" — "Fire!" — "That's into you!" — "Damn you! that kills your pig!" — "That stops your wind!" &c., &c., was uttered as each shot was heard to strike with a crash that nearly deafened you. The other boatswain's mate seeming equally to enjoy the affair. As he got his gun to bear upon the enemy, he would take aim, and banging away, would plug her, exclaiming, as each shot told — "That's from the scum of England!" — "That's a British pill for you to swallow!" the New York papers having once stated that our men were the "scum of England." All other guns were served with equal precision. We were struck seven times; only one man being hurt during the engagement, and he only receiving a flesh wound in the cheek. One shot struck under the counter, penetrating as far as a timber, then glancing off; a second struck the funnel; a third going through the side, across the berth-deck, and into the opposite side; another raising the deuce in the lamp-room; the others lodging in the coal-bunkers. Taking a shell up and examining it, we found it filled with sand instead of powder. The enemy's fire was directed chiefly towards our stern, the shots flying pretty quick over the quarter-deck, near to where our Captain was standing. As they came whizzing over him, he, with his usual coolness, would exclaim — "Give it to the rascals!" — "Aim low, men!" — "Don't be all night sinking that fellow!" when, for all or anything we knew, she might have been an iron-clad or a ram.

On Commander Blake surrendering his sword, he said that "it was with deep regret he did it." Captain Semmes smacked his lips and invited him down to his cabin. On Blake giving his rank to Captain Semmes, he gave up his state-room for Blake's special use, the rest of the officers being accommodated according to their rank in the ward-room and steerages, all having previously been paroled, the crew being placed on the berth-deck, our men sleeping any-where, so that the prisoners might take their places. Of the enemy's loss we could obtain no correct accounts, a differ-ence of seventeen being in their number of killed, the Hat-teras having on board men she was going to transfer to other ships. Their acknowledged loss was only two killed and seven wounded. A boat had been lowered just before the action to board us; as we anticipated, and learnt afterwards, it pulled in for the fleet and reached Galveston. From con-versation with her First-Lieutenant, I learnt that as soon as we gave our name and our first broadsides, the whole after division on board her left the guns, apparently para-lyzed; it was some time before they recovered themselves. The conduct of one of her officers was cowardly and dis-graceful in the extreme. Some of our shells went completely through her before exploding, others burst inside her, and set her on fire in three places. One went through her engines, completely disabling her; another exploding in her steam chest, scalding all within reach. Thus was fought, twenty-eight miles from Galveston, a battle, though small, yet the first yard arm action between two steamers at sea. She was only inferior in weight of metal—her guns being nine in number, viz, four thirty-two pounders, two rifled thirty pounders, carrying 60lb. shot (conical), one rifled twenty pounder, and a couple of small twelve pounders. On account of the conflicting statements made by her officers, we could never arrive at a correct estimate of her crew. Our prisoners numbered seventeen officers, one hundred and one seamen. We further learnt that the Hatteras was one of seven vessels sent to recapture Galveston, it being (although unknown to us) in the possession of our troops. We also found that the flag-ship Brooklyn, twenty-two guns, and the Oneida, nine guns sailed in search of us. By their account of the course they steered they could not fail to have seen us.

The New Richmond Theatre

THE ROLE of a major capital was new to Richmond and bore heavily on her shoulders. Along with the generals and Cabinet members who flocked to the new capital came a horde of hangers-on—charlatans, profiteers, prostitutes, and gamblers. The activities of these members of society were repeatedly deplored by the more responsible citizens. But Richmond was a gayer and more bustling city than she had ever been before. Business was good. The hotels were full to overflowing. The offices were jammed with workers for the mushrooming bureaus of a new government. The saloons and theaters entered an era of unprecedented prosperity. Soldiers on leave as well as the myriad strangers in the city sought public entertainment as never before.

On January 2, 1862, the Richmond Theatre burned. No time was lost in replacing it, first with a company called the Richmond Varieties acting in a converted church building, and then with an entirely new building constructed for the New Richmond Theatre. The opening of the new theater was long heralded in the press. Here are pieces which reflect divergent points of view concerning it.

The first is a sermon by John Lansing Burrows, a prominent Baptist minister, decrying the opening of the theater with its "twenty *gentlemen* for the chorus and the ballet" who might better be in the army. Burrows' complaint is not against the theater as such but against the immorality which seemed to find a home in the theaters of wartime Richmond. His view of the theatrical profession in Richmond was shared by John Hill Hewitt, Confederate poetaster and musician who had briefly managed the old Richmond Theatre. In his manuscript autobiography Hewitt described the difficulties of getting together a company: "How to gather a company was the question. On the breaking out of the war, the best of the profession had fled North, thinking it the safest ground to stand upon—for actors are cosmopolites and claim citizenship no where. I however managed in a short time to collect enough of the *fag-ends* of dismantled companies to open the theatre with a passable exhibition of novelty, if not of talent. . . . The thing took well, and money flowed into the treasury but often had I cause to upbraid myself for having fallen so low in my own estimation, for, I had always considered myself a gentleman, and I found that, in taking the control of this theatre and its vagabond company I had forfeited my claim to a respectable stand in the ranks of Society—with one or two exceptions, the company I had engaged was composed of harlots and 'artful dodgers.' "

Following the extracts from Burrows' sermon is the account of the theater's opening by the drama critic of

The Southern Illustrated News. The account was made memorable by the incorporation into it of Henry Timrod's "Inaugural Poem." Timrod submitted this poem in the competition inspired by manager Richard D'Orsey Ogden's offer of a prize of three hundred dollars for the best such production.

To-morrow night the New Richmond Theatre is to be opened. I deem it fitting, in addition to the notices so liberally given through the daily press, to give this public notice from the pulpit. With surprising energy, and regardless of cost, in these pinching times of war, a splendid building, with most costly decorations, has been reared from the ashes of the old. Builders, artists, workmen, have devoted themselves with an enterprise and industry that would be praiseworthy, if, in any sense, their work were useful in these pressing times of war. Enough able-bodied men have escaped from the conscription, have, perhaps, purchased the right to keep away from the camp and the battle in order to accomplish this magnificent work, for a consideration. The work is completed; the decorations are finished, and to-morrow night the New Richmond Theatre is to be opened. A strong corps of actors, male and female, have been secured, and, in addition to them, "twenty *gentlemen* for the chorus and the ballet." No cripples from the battle-fields are these—they can sing and dance; they can mimic fighting on the stage. For the serious work of repelling a real enemy they have neither taste nor heart. But they can sing while the country groans, and dance while the cars are bringing, in sad funeral procession, the dead to their very doors, and the dismal ambulance bears the sick and the wounded under the very glare of their lights, and within the sound of their music. They keep themselves out of the war for the noble duty of amusing the populace. Should they not, in these times, be especially encouraged, particularly by those whose own brave sons are in the camp or in the hospital, or whose mangled bodies are mouldering in uncoffined graves? Does it not seem a peculiarly happy time for theatrical amusements? Shall we all go and laugh and clap to the music and the dance, while the grasp of relentless foes is tightening upon the throats of our sons, and the armed heels of trampling hosts are bruising the bosom of our beloved mother land? What fitter time for opening a theatre in the capital of our bleeding country, unless it could have been on the evening of the battle of Malvern Hill or of Fredericksburg? But enterprise and industry could not secure the completion of the building in time for those bloody days, or we should, doubtless, have had the theatre open every night, while the battle raged by day, around the very suburbs of Richmond. "A strong stock company," and "twenty gentlemen for the chorus and the ballet," besides artists, musicians, etc., etc. Men enough, perhaps, to form an effective artillery company, deny themselves the patriotic desire to aid in defending the country against assailing foes, in order that they may devote themselves, fellow citizens, to your amusement. And you, doubtless, in your general liberality, will pay them enough to purchase substitutes, that they may abide in safety, and with these "twenty gentlemen of the chorus and the ballet," minister to your amusement.

I find, in my heart, no sympathy with that austere and morose idea of religion, which forbids a laugh, and prohibits recreation and amusement. I find no pleasure in tracing the wrinkles of seventy upon the brow of seventeen. It is contrary to nature and piety to curb and cramp, perpetually, the cheerful impulses of the young heart, and force it into the unnatural faith that gloom is godliness, and that innocent mirth is but the outburst of depravity. If God had not meant we should laugh, He would not have created the risible nerves and muscles. From the severer duties and struggles of life there may be and there ought to be relaxations and mere pleasures in every family and in every community. Sincere and intelligent piety is always cheerful, and Christians are enjoined in the Word to rejoice and to "rejoice evermore." I am not disposed, therefore, to insist upon any captious or churlish denunciation of the theatre, merely because it is a place of amusement. If there were no graver objections to it than this, you would not be troubled with utterances against it from this desk. Nor is it against the ideal theatre of some pure and poetic minds that I protest. . . . When we hear of a theatre which is not the favorite gathering place of the vicious, where the Gospel of Jesus is preached, or even where a pure and chaste morality is inculcated, where we are not compelled to countenance and mingle with vice in its most odious forms, we shall recommend the place. But the question is not, might not the good visit the theatre if the representations and associations were pure and respectable, but may they do so as it exists? Some talk of the possibility of reforming the theatre and making it reputable. When this is done it will be time to invite the good and the pure within its walls.

Pollock has well said of the theatre,

> "It was, from the very first,
> "The favorite haunt of sin, though honest men,
> "Some very honest, wise and worthy men,

"Maintained it might be turned to good account,
"And so, perhaps, it might, *but never was.*"

"From first to last it was an evil place.
"And now—such things were acted there as made
"The devils blush; and from the neighborhood
"Angels and holy men, trembling, retired."

I would not be understood as denouncing indiscriminately dramatic writings. Shakespeare, and Milton, and Young, and Coleridge, and Sheridan Knowles, and numerous others have written plays that may be profitably read and studied. The dramatic literature is rich in gems. At the same time it cannot be denied that much that assumes the name is rotten and pestiferous, and can scarcely be read even in solitude without polluting the soul. These preliminary remarks will be deemed sufficient to show that I am not, in my views of this subject, ascetical or austerely pietistic . . .

And now, I ask, in all seriousness, is a theatre so conducted, as this New Richmond Theatre is evidently to be, worthy the patronage and presence of reputable people? That there will be crowds nightly gathered within its walls is very probable. There are, alas! in our community enough of the vile, the unprincipled, and the mere pleasure loving to support such an institution liberally. There are also many very respectable people who will seek for amusement without regard to the influence of their example upon others. It may be that some very decent fathers and mothers will take their sons and even their daughters to a place, a portion of which they know is set apart for vilest assignations, where libertines parade their shameless profligacy, where the infamous wait for the vicious.

None of this congregation shall do this without honest and faithful warning; without an exposure of the influences to which they choose to subject themselves and their children.

I am not morose or puritanic. My religion is not of the gloomy type. God has made men to be cheerful and happy. The ringing laugh of innocent enjoyment I love to hear. I am no enemy to pleasure. I take delight in witnessing the sports of childhood and youth. I strive to cultivate and exhibit a cheerful, joyous spirit. But life has its stern, grave duties, and whatever unfits the mind and heart for these; whatever creates a distaste for their earnest fulfilment; whatever sullies the innocency of the heart, or perverts and distorts the nobler faculties of the soul; whatever ministers to the development of a prurient imagination, at the expense of the more practicable and serviceable powers of the mind, is injury to the individual and a mischief to society. All this, and more than this, I believe to be the influence of the stage in its best aspects, and even without the infamous associations to which I have alluded. You cannot visit the theatre and love it and remain innocent and pure.

✻   ✻   ✻   ✻

THE OPENING OF THE NEW RICHMOND THEATRE

According to announcement the New Richmond Theatre was opened on Monday night last. Glowing descriptions of the magnificence of the building, and the lengthy announcements in all the Richmond papers of the opening by the manager, had raised public expectation to its very highest pitch. The old man who had not crossed the portals of a hall of amusement since his hair had become tinged with gray—the young cavalier who had read, seen or heard of nothing but "wars and rumors of wars," since the vandal horde had invaded our land—the gay-hearted maiden, with sweet and ruby lips—the politician or man of office, with care-worn look, as if great matters of State still weighed heavily upon his heart—all Monday night, quietly wending their way to the new and gorgeous temple of Thespis. Through the courtesy of the manager, we, in company with several other members of the press, were *"undeservedly"* shown through a private entrance to a box (thus saving ourselves the necessity of elbowing through the crowd).

At half-past seven a full head of gas is turned on—the interior of the building is brilliantly illuminated—the dress circle is lined with a bevy of handsome and bright faces— some with that beautiful rosy tinge upon the cheeks and lips which nature alone gives, while others appear fresh from the artist's hand, the superfluous *rouge* not yet brushed away —the soldier with his immense circular-saw spurs, jingling like so many sleigh bells—the gay gambler, with his flash apparel, and magnificent diamonds dazzling the eye as the soft lambent light falls upon them, while he saunters to and fro with a *nonchalant* air, and seemingly wondering if the whole audience is not gazing admiringly upon him—the quiet observer commanding the beautiful Arabesque, and pointing out the failures of the artists in their attempts at Figures—all rise involuntarily and gaze in wonder and ad- miration. At quarter to eight the door in the Orchestra box opens the members of the Orchestra singly appear and take their respective seats—Prof. Loebman nods his head and the members join in one grand "concord of sweet sounds."

The strains of the music had scarcely died away, when Mr. Keeble entered from the door under the private box and delivered the following

INAUGURAL POEM,

By Harry Timrod.

A fairy ring
Drawn in the crimson of a battle plain,—
From whose weird cricle every loathsome thing
And sight and sound of pain
Are banished, while about in the air,
And from the ground and from the low-hung skies,
Throng in a vision fair
As ever lit a prophet's dying eyes,
Gleams of that unseen world
That lies about us, rainbow-tinted shapes
With starry wings unfurled,
Poised for a moment on such airy capes
As pierce the golden foam
Not on themselves, but on some outstretched hand,
That once a single mind suffice to quell
The malice of a tyrant; let them know
That each may crowd in every well-aimed blow,
Not the poor strength alone of arm and brand,
But the whole spirit of a mighty land!

Bid Liberty rejoice! Aye, though its day
Be far or near, these clouds shall yet be red
With the large promise of the coming ray.
Meanwhile, with that calm courage which can smile

Amid the terrors of the wildest fray,
Let us among the charms of Art awhile
    Fleet the deep gloom away;
Nor yet forget that on each hand and head
Rest the dear rights for which we fight and pray.

The reading of the Poem was followed by the singing of the "Marseillaise," by Mr. Chas. Morton, aided by a full chorus. The group which surrounded the gentleman during the singing of the Hymn presented a picture which an artist would not fail to gaze admiringly on. There stood the maiden of "sweet sixteen," blushing and laughing—the "lambs of many summers" with the pristine smile yet hanging upon their lips—and towering head and shoulders above them all, in theatrical knowledge, stood the Queen of all the party, Mrs. DeBar—all joining in the chorus with a hearty good will. The singing was succeeded by a tableau representing the Virginia coat of arms.

Then came the play—Shakespeare's "As You Like It," but not as *we like it*. . . .

We are glad to announce that the audience evinced a disposition at once to stop all rowdyism. When the "call boy" appeared in front of the curtain, for the purpose of fastening down the carpet some ill-bred persons commenced to yell "Soup, Soup," which was promptly hushed by the audience. Another marked alteration was the ignoring of the rapturous, boisterous manner of applauding, so much in vogue of late years. The clapping of hands was the loudest manifestations of applause evinced during the night.

Thus was our new Richmond Theatre dedicated. We trust it will ever continue a place of amusement, where all may be able to enjoy themselves in a rational manner, without fear of having the blush brought to their cheeks by the imprudence of jack-plane actors, who have no ambition above that of making the unwashed laugh, stamp their feet, and yell in an uncouth and demi-savage style—that it may prove a temple where the wife, the mother, the sister and the sweetheart may pass some of their leisure hours pleasantly, in defiance of the sickly sentimentality and hypocrisy of the present day is the desire of all lovers of the legitimate drama.

Mosby Makes a Night Raid

IN MAJOR JOHN SINGLETON MOSBY Confederates found a hero almost equal to his commanding general, Jeb Stuart. Here is the commendatory general order published by Stuart to announce to the army Mosby's brilliant capture of Yankee General E. H. Stoughton. Following Stuart's order is the sketch of Mosby published in *The War and Its Heroes*. Much of this sketch was drawn from an article written for *The Southern Illustrated News* in the spring of 1863 by John Esten Cooke.

HEADQUARTERS CAVALRY DIVISION,⎫
ARMY OF N. VA., March 12, 1863.   ⎬

General Orders,⎫
   No. —— ⎬

Captain JOHN S. MOSBY has for a long time attracted the attention of his Generals by his boldness, skill and success, so signally displayed in his numerous forays upon the invaders of his native State.

None know his daring enterprise and dashing heroism, better than those foul invaders, though strangers themselves to such noble traits.

His late brilliant exploit—the capture of Brig. Gen. STOUGHTON, U. S. A., two Captains, thirty other prisoners, together with their arms, equipments and fifty-eight horses— justifies this recognition in General Orders.

This feat, unparalleled in the war, was performed in the midst of the enemy's troops, at Fairfax C. H., without loss or injury.

The gallant band of Capt. Mosby share the glory, as they did the danger of this enterprise, and are worthy of such a leader.

J. E. B. Stuart,
Major General Commanding.

MAJOR JOHN SINGLETON MOSBY

Among the daring partisans of the present war, few have rendered such valuable services to the cause as Major John S. Mosby.

John Singleton Mosby is the son of Alfred D. Mosby formerly of Albemarle county, Va., but now residing in the vicinity of Lynchburg. He is the maternal grandson of Mr. James McLaurine, Sr., late of Powhatan county, Virginia. His mother was Miss Virginia J. McLaurine.

The subject of our sketch was born in Powhatan county, Va., on the 6th of December, 1833, and was educated at the University of Virginia. When quite a young man he was married to the daughter of the Hon. Beverly Clarke, late United States minister to Central America.

At the commencement of hostilities between the North and South, Mosby resided at Bristol, Washington county,

Va., where he was successfully engaged in the practice of law. He immediately gave up his profession, and entered the army as a private, becoming a member of a company raised in Washington county, and commanded by Captain Jones—now General Jones—in which position he served for twelve months. Upon the promotion of Captain Jones to the colonelcy of the 1st Virginia Cavalry, Mosby was chosen as adjutant.

He continued in this position but a short time, for upon the re-organization of the regiment, from some cause the colonel was thrown out, and consequently his adjutant relieved of duty. Mosby was then chosen by General J. E. B. Stuart as a sort of independent scout.

He first attracted public attention when General Joseph E. Johnston, then in command of the Army of the Potomac, fell back from Manassas. On this occasion, desiring to ascertain whether the movement of McClellan was a feint, or if he really intended to march his army to the Peninsula, General Johnston despatched Mosby to gain the desired information. Taking five men with him. Mosby went in the rear of McClellan's army, where he remained some days, spending his time in converse with the Yankee soldiers, from whom he gained all necessary information, and then made his way safely back to General Johnston's headquarters.

During the summer of 1862, Major Mosby was sent from Hanover Courthouse on a mission to General Jackson, who was then on the upper Rapidan. He was the bearer of an oral communication, and as the route was dangerous, had no papers about him except a brief note to serve as a voucher of his identity and reliability. With this note the major proceeded on his journey, and stopping at Beaver Dam station, on the Virginia Central Railroad, to rest and feed his horse, was, while quietly sitting on the platform at the depot, surprised and bagged by a detachment of the enemy's cavalry.

Now, to be caught thus napping, in an unguarded moment, was gall and wormwood to the brave major. He had deceived and outwitted the enemy so often, had escaped from their clutches so regularly up to that time, that to find himself surprised thus, filled him with internal rage. From that moment his sentiments toward the enemy increased in intensity. They had been all along decidedly unfriendly— they were now bitter. They took him away with them, searched him, and filched his credentials, and published them as an item of interest in the Northern papers, and immured the partisan in the Old Capitol.

In due course of time he was exchanged. He returned with a handsome new satchel and an increased affection for the Yankees. He laughed at his misfortunes, but set down the account to the credit of the enemy, to be settled at a more convenient opportunity.

One of the most daring exploits of this gallant partisan is thus graphically described by the army correspondent of the "Illustrated News:"

Previous to the 8th of March, Major Mosby had put himself to much trouble to discover the strength and positions of the enemy in Fairfax county, with the design of making a raid in that direction, if circumstances permitted. The information brought to him was as follows: On the Little River turnpike, at Germantown, a mile or two distant from Fairfax, were three regiments of the enemy's cavalry, commanded by Colonel Wyndham, acting brigadier-general, with his headquarters at the court-house. Within a few hundred yards of the town were two infantry regiments. In the vicinity of Fairfax station, about two miles off, an infantry brigade was encamped. And at Centreville there was another infantry brigade, with cavalry and artillery.

Thus the way to Fairfax Court-house, the point which the major desired to reach, seemed completely blocked up with troops of all arms—infantry, artillery and cavalry. If he attempted to approach by the Little River turnpike, Colonel Wyndham's troopers would meet him full in front. If he tried the route by the Warrenton turnpike, a brigade of infantry, with cavalry to pursue and artillery to thunder at him, was first to be defeated. If he glided in along the railroad, the brigade at Fairfax station was in his track.

The "situation" would have appeared desperate to almost any one, however adventurous, but danger and adventure had attractions for Major Mosby. If the peril was great and the probability of success slender, all the greater would be the glory if he succeeded. And the temptation was great. At Fairfax Court-house, the general headquarters of that portion of the army, Brigadier-General Stoughton and other officers of high rank were there known to be, and if these could be captured, great would be his triumph, and horrible the consequent gnashing of teeth among the enemy.

In spite of the enormous obstacles which presented themselves in his path, Major Mosby determined to undertake no less an enterprise than entering the town, seizing the officers in their beds, destroying the huge quantities of public stores, and bearing off his prisoners in triumph.

The night of Sunday, March 8th, was chosen as favorable to the expedition. The weather was infamous, the night as dark as pitch, and it was raining steadily. With a detachment of twenty-nine men, Major Mosby set out on his raid.

He made his approach from the direction of Aldie. Proceeding down the Little River turnpike, the main route from the court-house to the mountains, he reached a point within about three miles of Chantilly. Here, turning to the right, he crossed the Frying Pan road, about half-way between Centreville and the turnpike, keeping in the woods, and leaving Centreville well to the right. He was now advancing in the triangle which is made by the Little River and Warrenton turnpikes and the Frying Pan road. Those who are familiar with the country there will easily understand the object of this proceeding. By thus cutting through the triangle, Major Mosby avoided all pickets, scouting parties, and the enemy generally, who would only keep a look out for intruders on the main roads.

Advancing in this manner through the woods, pierced with devious and uncertain paths only, which the dense darkness scarcely enabled them to follow, the partisan and his little band finally struck into the Warrenton road, between Centreville and Fairfax, at a point about mid-way between the two places. One danger had thus been successfully avoided— a challenge from parties of cavalry on the Little River road, or discovery by the force posted at Centreville. That place was now in their rear; they had "snaked" around it and its warders; but the perils of the enterprise had scarcely commenced. Fairfax Court-house was still about four miles distant, and it was girdled with cavalry and infantry. Every approach was guarded, and the attempt to enter the place seemed desperate, but the major determined to essay it.

Advancing resolutely, he came within a mile and a half of the place, when he found the way barred by a heavy force. Directly in his path were the infantry camps, of which he had been notified, and all advance was checked in that direction. The major did not waver in his purpose, however. Making a detour to the right, and leaving the enemy's camps far to his left, he struck into the road leading from Fairfax southward to the railroad.

This avenue was guarded like the rest, but by a picket only; and Mosby knew thoroughly how to deal with pickets. Before the sleepy and unsuspicious Yankees were aware of their danger, they found pistols presented at their heads, with the option of surrender or death presented to them. They surrendered immediately, were taken in charge, and, without further ceremony, Major Mosby and his band entered the town.

From that moment the utmost silence, energy and rapidity of action were requisite. The Major had designed reaching the court-house at midnight, but had been delayed two hours by mistaking the road in the pitch darkness. It was now two o'clock in the morning, and an hour and a half, at the very utmost, was left him to finish his business and escape before daylight. If morning found him anywhere in that vicinity, he knew that his retreat would be cut off, and the whole party killed or captured, and this would have spoiled the whole fun of the affair. He accordingly made his dispositions rapidly, enjoined complete silence, and set to work in earnest. The small band was divided into detachments, with special duties assigned to each. Two or three of these detachments were sent to the public stables where the fine horses of the general and his staff officers occupied, with instructions to carry them off without noise. Another party was sent to Colonel Wyndham's headquarters to take him prisoner. Another to Colonel Johnson's, with similar orders.

Taking six men with him, Major Mosby, who proceeded upon sure information, went straight to the headquarters of Brigadier-General Stoughton. This worthy was a Vermonter, and a terrific son of Mars; a graduate of West Point, and a suppress-the-rebellion-in-ninety-days man. He had just been assigned to the command of the post, and much was expected from a brigadier of such ardor and zeal in the service.

Alas! how little control have we over our own fates—a moral observation which the present narrative powerfully enforces:

> " 'Twas midnight, in his guarded tent
>   The Turk was dreaming of the hour
> When Greece, her knee in suppliance bent,
>   Should tremble at his power."

And, lo! the brigadier was even then in the power of that Marco Bozzaris, Major Mosby. "Stoughton's Bitters" came in the shape of a Confederate partisan!

The major entered his chamber without much ceremony, and found him reposing in all the dignity and grandeur of a brigadier-general commanding, whose person and slumbers are sacred. Making his way toward the bed, in the dark, the partisan shook him suddenly by the shoulder.

"Who is that?" growled the sleepy brigadier.

"Get up quick, I want you," responded the major.

"Do you know who I am," cried the brigadier, sitting up in bed, with a scowl. "I will have you arrested, sir."

"Do you know who *I* am?" retorted the major, shortly.

"Who are you?"

"Did you ever hear of Mosby?"

"Yes! Tell me, have you caught the —— rascal!"

"No; but he has caught you!" And the major chuckled.

"What does all this mean, sir?" cried the furious brigadier.

"It means, sir," the major replied, very coolly, "that Stuart's cavalry are in possession of this place, and you are my prisoner. Get up and come along, or you are a dead man!"

The brigadier groaned in anguish of soul, but was compelled to obey, and the partisan mounted, and placed him under guard. His staff and escort were captured without difficulty, but two of the former, owing to the darkness and confusion, subsequently made their escape.

Meanwhile the other detachments were at work. They entered the stables, and led out fifty-eight horses, with their accoutrements, all belonging to officers, and took a number of prisoners. Hundreds of horses were left, for fear of encumbering the retreat.

The other parties were less successful. Colonel Wyndham had gone to Washington on the preceding day; but his acting adjutant-general and aide-de-camp were made prisoners. Colonel Johnson, having received notice of the presence of the party, succeeded in making his escape.

It was now about half-past three in the morning, and it behooved Major Mosby, unless he relished being killed or captured, to effect his retreat. Time was barely left him to get out of the lines of the enemy before daylight, and none was to be lost.

He had intended to destroy the valuable quartermaster, commissary and sutler's stores in the place, but these were found to be in the houses which it would have been necessary to burn; and, even had the proceeding been advisable, time was wanting. The band was encumbered by three times as many horses and prisoners as it numbered men, and day was approaching. The major accordingly made his dispositions rapidly for retiring.

The prisoners, thirty-five in number, were as follows: Brigadier-General E. H. Stoughton; Baron R. Wordener, an Austrian, aide-de-camp to Colonel Wyndham; Captain A. Barker, 5th New York Cavalry; Colonel Wyndham's acting adjutant-general; thirty prisoners, chiefly of the 18th Pennsylvania and 1st Ohio Cavalry, and the telegraph operator at the place. These were placed upon the captured horses, and the band set out in silence on their return.

Major Mosby took the same road which had conducted him into the court-house—that which led to Fairfax station. But this was only to deceive the enemy as to his line of retreat, if they attempted pursuit. He soon turned off, and pursued the same road which he had followed in advancing, coming out on the Warrenton turnpike, about a mile and a half from the town. This time, finding no guards on the main road, he continued to follow the turnpike until he came to the belt of woods, which crosses the road, about half a mile from Centreville. At this point of the march, one of the prisoners, Captain Barker, no doubt counting on aid from the garrison, made a desperate effort to effect his escape. He broke from the guards, dashed out of the ranks, and tried hard to reach the fort. He was stopped, however, by a shot from one of the party, which came so near him that he thought it advisable not to risk a repetition of it. He accordingly came back and gave himself up again to his enemies.

Again turning to the right, the major proceeded on his way, passing directly beneath the frowning fortifications. He passed so near them that he distinctly saw the bristling muzzles of the cannon in the embrazures, and was challenged by the sentinel on the redoubt. Making no reply, he pushed on rapidly—for the day was dawning and no time was to be lost—passed within a hundred yards of the infantry pickets without molestation, swam Cub Run, and again came out on the Warrenton turnpike at Groveton. He had passed through all his enemies, flanked Centreville, was on the open road to the South; he was safe! He had penetrated to the very heart of the enemy's position; glided through their camps; captured their pickets; seized their officers in bed; borne off their horses; laughed at, and befooled, and outwitted them completely; and had not lost a man in the enterprise!

The exploits of Major Mosby would furnish material for a volume which would resemble rather a romance than a true statement of actual occurrences. He has been the chief actor in so many raids, encounters and adventures, that his memoirs, if he committed them to paper, would be regarded as the efforts of his fancy.

The same correspondent gives the annexed pen-and-ink sketch of the gallant major: His figure is slight, muscular, supple and vigorous; his eye is keen, penetrating, ever on the alert; he wears his sabre and pistol with the air of a man who sleeps with them buckled around his waist, and handles them habitually, almost unconsciously. The major is a determined man in a charge, dangerous on a scout, hard to outwit, and prone to "turn up" suddenly where he is least expected, and bang away with pistol and carbine.

A Journey across Texas

A N INTERESTED and acute observer was Sir Arthur James Lyon Fremantle. An officer of the venerable and elite Coldstream Guards, he had a strong curiosity about the war in America. Pro-Union at first, his sympathies shifted toward the Confederacy, and after meeting Commander Raphael Semmes at Gibraltar he determined to visit the scene of the great conflict on his next leave. Entering the Confederacy at Brownsville, Texas, in the spring of 1863, Colonel Fremantle made his way across the breadth of the South and ended his trip as the guest of General James Longstreet and his staff at the Battle of Gettysburg.

Fremantle returned to England and wrote an account of his travels that was admittedly pro-Confederate, but dignified and restrained. A copy of his book was sent by diplomatic courier to President Davis, and other copies soon found their way into the South. In 1864 *Three Months in the Southern States* was republished in a Confederate edition by S. H. Goetzel of Mobile—bound in wallpaper because of the shortage of proper binding materials.

177

This is Fremantle's account of a part of his journey across Texas.

30th April (Thursday).—I have to-day acquired my first experience of Texan railroads.

In this country, where every white man is as good as another (by theory), and every white female is by courtesy a lady, there is only one class. The train from Alleyton consisted of two long cars, each holding about fifty persons. Their interior is like the aisle of a church, twelve seats on either side, each for two persons. The seats are comfortably stuffed, and seemed luxurious after the stage.

Before starting, the engine gives two preliminary snorts, which, with a yell from the official of *"all aboard,"* warn the passengers to hold on; for they are closely followed by a tremendous jerk, which sets the cars in motion.

Every passenger is allowed to use his own discretion about breaking his arm, neck, or leg, without interference by the railway officials.

People are continually jumping on and off whilst the train is in motion, and larking from one car to the other. There is no sort of fence or other obstacle to prevent "humans" or cattle from getting on the line.

We left Alleyton at 8 A. M., and got a miserable meal at Richmond at 12.30. At this little town I was introduced to a seedy-looking man, in rusty black clothes and a broken-down "stove-pipe" hat. This was Judge Stockdale, who will probably be the next governor of Texas. He is an agreeable man, and his conversation is far superior to his clothing. The rival candidate is General Chambers (I think), who has become very popular by the following sentence in his manifesto:— "I am of opinion that married soldiers should be given the opportunity of embracing their families at least once a year, their places in the ranks being taken by unmarried men. The population must not be allowed to suffer."

Richmond is on the Brazos river, which is crossed in a peculiar manner. A steep inclined plane leads to a low, rickety, trestle bridge, and a similar inclined plane is cut in the opposite bank. The engine cracks on all steam, and gets sufficient impetus in going down the first incline to shoot across the bridge and up the second incline. But even in Texas this method of crossing a river is considered rather unsafe.

After crossing the river in this manner, the rail traverses some very fertile land, part of which forms the estate of the late Colonel Terry. There are more than two hundred negroes on the plantation. Some of the fields were planted with cotton and Indian corn mixed, three rows of the former between two of the latter. I saw also fields of cotton and sugar mixed.

We changed carriages at Harrisburg, and I completed my journey to Houston on a cotton truck.

The country near Houston is very pretty, and is studded with white wooden villas, which are raised off the ground on blocks like haystacks. I reached Houston at 4.30 P. M., and drove to the Fannin House hotel.

Houston is a much better place than I expected. The main street can boast of many well-built brick and iron houses. It was very full, as it now contained all the refugees from the deserted town of Galveston.

After an extremely mild supper, I was introduced to Lieutenant Lee, a wounded hero, who lost his leg at Shiloh, also to Colonel Pyron, a distinguished officer, who commands the regiment named after him.

The fat German, Mr. Lee, and myself, went to the theatre afterwards.

As a great favor, my British prejudices were respected, and I was allowed a bed to myself; but the four other beds in the room had two occupants each. A captain, whose acquaintance I had made in the cars, slept in the next bed to me. Directly after we had got into bed a negro came in, who, squatting down between our beds, began to clean our boots. The Southerner pointed at the slave, and thus held forth:—"Well, Kernel, I reckon you've got servants in your country, but not of that color. Now, sir, this is a real genuine African. He's as happy as the day's long; and if he was on a sugar plantation he'd be dancing half the night; but if you was to collect a thousand of them together, and fire one bomb in amongst them, they'd all run like hell." The negro grinned, and seemed quite flattered.

1st May (Friday).—I called on General Scurry, and found him suffering from severe ophthalmia. When I presented General Magruder's letter, he insisted that I should come and live with him so long as I remained here. He also telegraphed to Galveston for a steamer to take me there and back.

We dined at 4 P. M.: the party consisted of Colonel and Judge Terrill (a clever and agreeable man), Colonel Pyron, Captain Wharton, quartermaster-general, Major Watkins (a handsome fellow, and hero of the Sabine Pass affair), and Colonel Cook, commanding the artillery at Galveston (late of the U. S. navy, who enjoys the reputation of being a zealous Methodist preacher and a daring officer). The latter told me he could hardly understand how I could be an Englishman, as I pronounced my h's all right. General Scurry himself is very amusing, and is an admirable mimic. His numerous anecdotes of the war were very interesting. In peace times he is a lawyer. He was a volunteer major in the Mexican war, and distinguished himself very much in the late campaigns in New Mexico and Arizona, and at the recapture of Galveston.

After dinner, the Queen's health was proposed; and the party expressed the greatest admiration for Her Majesty, and respect for the British Constitution. They all said that universal suffrage did not produce such deplorable results in the South as in the North; because the population in the South is so very scattered, and the whites being the superior race, they form a sort of aristocracy.

They all wanted me to put off going to Galveston till Monday, in order that some ladies might go; but I was inexorable, as it must now be my object to cross the Mississippi without delay. All these officers despised sabres, and considered double-barrelled shot-guns and revolvers the best arms for cavalry.

2nd May (Saturday).—As the steamer had not arrived in the morning, I left by railroad for Galveston. General Scurry insisted upon sending his servant to wait upon me, in order that I might become acquainted with "an aristocratic negro." "John" was a very smart fellow, and at first sight nearly as white as myself.

In the cars I was introduced to General Samuel Houston, the founder of Texan independence. He told me he was born in Virginia seventy years ago, that he was United States senator at thirty, and governor of Tennessee at thirty-six. He emigrated into Texas in 1832; headed the revolt of Texas, and defeated the Mexicans at San Jacinto in 1836. He then became President of the Republic of Texas, which he annexed to the United States in 1845. As Governor of the State in 1860, he had opposed the secession movement, and was *deposed*. Though evidently a remarkable and clever man, he is extremely egotistical and vain, and much disappointed at having to subside from his former grandeur. The town of Houston is named after him. In appearance he is a tall, handsome old man, much given to chewing tobacco, and blowing his nose with his fingers. *

I was also introduced to another "character," Capt. Chubb, who told me he was a Yankee by birth, and served as coxswain to the United States ship Java in 1827. He was afterwards imprisoned at Boston on suspicion of being engaged in the slave trade; but he escaped. At the beginning of this war he was captured by the Yankees, when he was in command of the Confederate States steamer Royal Yacht, and taken to New York in chains, where he was condemned to be hung as a pirate; but he was eventually exchanged. I was afterwards told that the slave-trading escapade of which he was accused consisted in his having hired a colored crew at Boston, and then coolly *selling* them at Galveston.

At 1 P. M., we arrived at Virginia Point, a *tête-de-pont* at the extremity of the mainland. Here Bates's battalion was encamped—called also the "swamp angels," on account of the marshy nature of their quarters, and of their predatory and irregular habits.

The railroad then traverses a shallow lagoon (called Galveston Bay) on a trestle-bridge two miles long; this leads to another *tête-de-pont* on Galveston island, and in a few minutes the city is reached.

In the train I had received the following message by tele-

* He is reported to have died in August, 1863.

graph from Colonel Debray, who commands at Galveston: "Will Col. Fremantle sleep to-night at the house of a block- aded rebel?" I answered:—"Delighted;" and was received at the terminus by Capt. Foster of the Staff, who conducted me in an ambulance to headquarters, which were at the house of the Roman Catholic bishop. I was received there by Colonel Debray and two very gentlemanlike French priests.

We sat down to dinner at 2 P. M., but were soon inter- rupted by an indignant drayman, who came to complain of a military outrage. It appeared that immediately after I had left the cars, a semi-drunken Texan of Pyron's regiment had desired this drayman to stop, and upon the latter declining to do so, the Texan fired five shots at him from his "six-shooter," and the last shot killed the drayman's horse. Captain Foster (who is a Louisianian, and very sarcastic about Texas) said that the regiment would probably hang the soldier for being such a *disgraceful bad shot.*

After dinner Colonel Debray took me into the observatory, which commands a good view of the city, bay, and gulf.

Galveston is situated near the eastern end of an island thirty miles long by three and a half wide. Its houses are well built; its streets are long, straight, and shaded with trees; but the city was now desolate, blockaded, and under military law. Most of the houses were empty, and bore many marks of the ill-directed fire of the Federal ships during the night of the 1st of January last.

The whole of Galveston Bay is very shallow, except a nar- row channel of about one hundred yards immediately in front of the now deserted wharves. The entrance to this channel is at the northeastern extremity of the island, and is defended by the new works which are now in progress there. It is also blocked up with piles, torpedoes, and other obstacles.

The blockaders were plainly visible about four miles from land; they consisted of three gunboats and an ugly paddle steamer, also two supply vessels.

The wreck of the Confederate cotton-steamer Neptune (destroyed in her attack on the Harriet Lane), was close off one of the wharves. That of the Westfield (blown up by the Yankee Commodore), was off Pelican Island.

In the night of the 1st January, General Magruder suddenly entered Galveston, placed his field-pieces along the line of wharves, and unexpectedly opened fire in the dark upon the Yankee war vessels at a range of about one hundred yards; but so heavy (though badly directed) was the reply from the ships, that the field-pieces had to be withdrawn. The attack by Colonel Cook upon a Massachusetts regiment fortified at the end of a wharf, also failed, and the Confederates thought themselves "badly whipped." But after daylight the fortunate surrender of the Harriet Lane to the cotton-boat Bayou City, and the extraordinary conduct of Commodore Renshaw, converted a Confederate disaster into the recapture of Galveston. General Magruder certainly deserves immense credit for his boldness in attacking a heavily armed naval squadron with a few field-pieces and two river steamers protected with cotton bales and manned with Texan cavalry soldiers.

I rode with Colonel Debray to examine Forts Scurry, Magruder, Bankhead, and Point. These works have been ingeniously designed by Colonel Sulokowski (formerly in the Austrian army), and they were being very well constructed by one hundred and fifty whites and six hundred blacks under that officer's superintendence, the blacks being lent by the neighboring planters.

Although the blockaders can easily approach to within three miles of the works, and although one shell will always "stampede" the negroes, yet they have not thrown any for a long time.*

Colonel Debray is a broad-shouldered Frenchman, and is a very good fellow. He told me that he emigrated to America in 1848; he raised a company in 1861, in which he was only a private; he was next appointed aide-de-camp to the governor of Texas, with the rank of brigadier-general; he then descended to a major of infantry, afterwards rose to a lieutenant-colonel of cavalry, and is now colonel.

Captain Foster is properly on Magruder's Staff, and is very good company. His property at New Orleans had been destroyed by the Yankees.

In the evening we went to a dance given by Colonel Manly, which was great fun. I danced an American cotillion with Mrs. Manly; it was very violent exercise, and not the least like any thing I had seen before. A gentleman stands by shouting out the different figures to be performed, and every one obeys his orders with much gravity and energy. Colonel Manly is a very gentlemanlike Carolinian; the ladies were pretty, and, considering the blockade, they were very well dressed. Six deserters from Banks' army arrived here to-day. Banks seems to be advancing steadily, and overcoming the opposition offered by the handful of Confederates in the Teche country.

Banks himself is much despised as a soldier, and is always called by the Confederates Mr. Commissary Banks, on account of the efficient manner in which he performed the

* Such a stampede did occur when the blockaders threw two or three shells. All the negroes ran, showing every sign of great dismay, and two of them, in their terror, ran into the sea, and were unfortunately drowned. It is now, however, too late for the ships to try this experiment, as some heavy guns are in position. A description of the different works is of course omitted here.

duties of that office for "Stonewall" Jackson in Virginia. The officer who is supposed *really* to command the advancing Federals, is Weitzel; and he is acknowledged by all here to be an able man, a good soldier, and well acquainted with the country in which he is manœuvring.

3d May (Sunday).—I paid a long visit this morning to Mr. Lynn the British Consul, who told me that he had great difficulty in communicating with the outer world, and had seen no British man-of-war since the Immortalité.

At 1.30 I saw Pyron's regiment embark for Niblitt's Bluff to meet Banks. This corps is now dismounted cavalry, and the procession was a droll one. First came eight or ten instruments braying discordantly, then an enormous Confederate flag, followed by about four hundred men moving by fours—dressed in every variety of costume, and armed with every variety of weapon; about sixty had Enfield rifles; the remainder carried shot-guns (fowling-pieces), carbines, or long rifles of a peculiar and antiquated manufacture. None had swords or bayonets—all had six-shooters and bowie-knives. The men were a fine, determined-looking lot; and I saw among them a short stout boy of fourteen, who had served through the Arizona campaign. I saw many of the soldiers take off their hats to the French priests, who seemed much respected in Galveston. This regiment is considered down here to be a very good one, and its colonel is spoken as one of the bravest officers in the army. The regiment was to be harangued by Old Houston before it embarked.*

In getting into the cars to return to Houston, I was nearly forced to step over the dead body of the horse shot by the

* At the outbreak of the war it was found very difficult to raise infantry in Texas, as no Texan walks a yard if he can help it. Many mounted regiments were therefore organized, and afterwards dismounted.

soldier yesterday, and which the authorities had not thought necessary to remove.

I got back to General Scurry's house at Houston at 4.30 P. M. The general took me out for a drive in his ambulance, and I saw innumerable negroes and negresses parading about the streets in the most outrageously grand costumes—silks, satins, crinolines, hats with feathers, lace mantles, &c., forming an absurd contrast to the simple dresses of their mistresses. Many were driving about in their master's carriages, or riding on horses which are often lent to them on Sunday afternoons; all seemed intensely happy and satisfied with themselves.

—— told me that old Sam Houston lived for several years amongst the Cherokee Indians, who used to call him "the Raven" or the "Big Drunk." He married an Indian squaw when he was with them.

The South Mourns Jackson

IN THE INDOMITABLE WILL of "Stonewall" Jackson was exemplified the strength and the ambition of the Confederacy. His death after the Battle of Chancellorsville, where he was accidentally shot by his own troops, was, in effect, the spiritual climax of the Confederacy. Never again would the tides of Confederate hopes and Confederate victories rise as high as they had at the news of Jackson's successes in the Valley of Virginia, at second Manassas, and at Fredericksburg.

This obituary tribute from *The Southern Illustrated News* is indicative of the grief which swept the South at the news of Jackson's death.

THE ILLUSTRIOUS DEAD

Day before yesterday, at Lexington, in the very heart of Virginia, there was committed to the earth the inanimate remains of one of the most remarkable men of his time. Many beautiful and affecting tributes have been rendered to his lofty character and his immeasurable services, which are yet but a most inadequate expression of the public grief; and we might well hesitate, when the pens of ready writers have failed to set forth the genius and worth of the hero and the love and sorrow which followed him to the tomb, to write one line upon an event at once so august and so appalling as that single death. But we can write of nothing else. The wailing music of the funeral dirge is still sounding in our ears; we still see the ghastly plumes nodding above the bier; and when we endeavor to direct our thoughts to subjects such as ordinarily engage us in these columns, the mournful calamity, in all its weight of woe, rushes back upon us, and excludes every other consideration.

It were unwise, perhaps immodest, in us, all unlearned in the science of war, to attempt a characterization of THOMAS JONATHAN JACKSON as a military man. But we do not hesitate to say that he appears to us to belong to that little family of inspired conquerors who, in the march of the centuries, have seemed to lure Victory to their standards as her own proper perch, and who have made all the difficulties and dangers that stood in their way subservient to their imperial will and auxiliary to their further progress. They are but a small band, indeed, these Makers of Destiny and Masters of War, not enough to form a company, far less a regiment, in Hades—Alexander, Hannibal, Cæsar, Frederick, Napoleon—and others of less shining note, whose path of conquest we trace across the Bosphorus and over the Alps, through Russian snows and under Syrian suns, and to whose career no lapse of time can make the world indifferent, from whose wonderful achievements no physical changes of the earth's surface, no shiftings of empire from East to West, can ever withdraw the attention of mankind. Among these heroes JACKSON will take his place when the Plutarch of the future shall chronicle the Lives of this Nineteenth Century. His military life was short, as compared with that of any one of them. Two years (for we cannot properly include his service in the war with Mexico, distinguished as it was, in the estimate,) comprise all that he did in the eyes of the world. Nor were the results of his astonishing labors comparable with those which attended the long campaigns of the warriors of history. Yet when we place in effective contrast *what he did* with the means at his command to do it; when we consider how he went on from victory to victory, despite every drawback and discouragement, cleaving down the masses of men that opposed him with his irresistible arm, making the little body of troops which he could neither clothe nor feed more than equal to twice their numbers; when we remember that he fought always in a subordinate position, in which his plans were liable at any moment to be overruled, and that he never, indeed, had the theatre and the opportunity for the full exhibition of his genius, we are confirmed in the belief that the common verdict of his contemporaries, which assigns him the first rank in warfare, will not hereafter be set aside.

But if JACKSON achieved less than the great Captains of ancient or modern times, (though it may be doubted if the campaign in the Valley of Virginia in the summer of 1862 has ever been surpassed,) he rises immeasurably above them in contemplation of the motive which impelled him to action. He followed no star, he sought no throne, he asked no earthly guerdon, was guided by no selfish consideration, and lured by no vulgar ambition. Duty, and duty alone, was the principle of his conduct. He recognized a call to fight for Virginia in her hour of agony, and he obeyed it. He felt within him the mastery of the occasion, and he exerted it. Otherwise the world had not heard of JACKSON. But for this diabolical war, the modest Professor would have gone on lecturing to the class of Natural Philosophy at the Military Institute, with less *éclat* than Mr. Faraday across the water; the "Blue Light Elder" might have run his obscure round of serving God in the village where the war found him, until he was called to the Congregation of the Saints above.— Such was the simple, earnest moral of his life. What a record, it is! How bright, how clear, how complete! May we not say, in the language which Clarendon employs in lamenting the death of Lucius Carey, Lord Falkland, that "if there were no other brand upon this odious and accursed civil war, than that single loss, it must be most infamous and execrable to all posterity"?

After all, perhaps, grateful for the services which this illustrious man rendered Virginia in her time of sorest need, and sorrowing over his fall in utter desolation of heart, we may see the greatest good of JACKSON'S life in the example he bequeathes to those who are to come after us. As the images on the friezes of the Parthenon follow one another in one continuous succession of noble and majestic forms, each a hero or a god, so is the long line of the worthies of the Ancient Commonwealth and Dominion of Virginia perpetuated in the lofty figures that move before men in this second age of Greatness and Virtue; and among them none shall more certainly wear the antique cast of heroism, none shall appear worthier of the better, earlier days of the Republic, than the tall, stern effigy of STONEWALL JACKSON. And if the lives of the great and good are the most precious heritage that one generation can hand down to another, the age in which we live, in the story of this one life, shall transmit to its successor an incomputable wealth.

The literature of the future will be rich with the inspiration of his career. Poets will sing of him, and romanticists will

ORDER OF THE PROCESSION
AT THE FUNERAL OF
LIEUT. GEN. T. J. JACKSON.

1st. Military

2d. Pall Bearers. }BODY.{ Pall Bearers.

3d. Family of the deceased.

4th. Faculty of the Va. Military Institute.
Officers " " " " "
Members of the Quartermaster Dep't.
" " " Subsistence "
Servants of the Va. Military Institute.

5th. Elders of the Lex'n. Presbyterian Church.

6th. Deacons of the Lexington Pres. Church.

7th. Reverend Clergy.

8th. Trustees, Professors and Students of Washington College.

9th. Franklin Society.

10th. Town Council.

11th. County Magistrates.

12th. Members of the Bar and Medical Profession.

13th. Officers and Soldiers of the Confederate Army.

14th. Bible Society.

15th. Sabbath Schools.

16th. Citizens.

The Procession will be formed at the V. M. I. at 10 o'clock, A. M., on Saturday, the 16th inst.

The body will lie in state at the V. M. I. during Friday.   FRANCIS H. SMITH,

V. M. I., May 10th, 1863.   Superintendent.

weave his deeds into the warp and woof of fiction. The beautiful region of the Shenandoah will be classic ground as associated with his memory, and the cottages of the Valley will long preserve traditions of his less familiar traits. "Tell us of JACKSON," shall the children cry around the fireside, as Béranger says the idle villagers of France call upon the old women for stories of Napoleon—

> "Parlez nous de lui, grandmère,
> Parlez nous de lui!"

Of the sweet, sad incidents that attended his last illness and death, of his affecting serenity of mind, and humble submission to the will of God, of the general outburst of sorrow all over the land when he was taken from us, of his obsequies here in Richmond, and the consecration of the new flag of the Republic, in its having been first used as his pall—we need not speak, for these are yet too fresh in the hearts of all. "Beautiful! What we might call a classic, sacred death; if it were not rather an Elijah-translation,—in a chariot, not of fire and terror, but of hope and soft vernal sun-beams!"

And here we say farewell to STONEWALL JACKSON. We lay our little wreath upon his coffin, fragrant with lilies deposited by soft white hands, wet with tears rained from bright eyes, and turn sorrowfully away—

> Ashes to ashes, dust to dust;
> He is gone who seem'd so great.
> Gone; but nothing can bereave him
> Of the force he made his own
> Being here, and we believe him
> Something far advanced in state,
> And that he wears a truer crown
> Than any wreath that man can weave him.

But speak no more of his renown,
Lay your earthly fancies down,
And in earth's embraces leave him:
God accept him, Christ receive him.

Defeat at Vicksburg

HAVING successfully repelled the invader throughout one summer, Vicksburg confidently settled down for another long siege in the late spring of 1863. But the Yankees were throwing new and stronger forces at the little city. After a siege of forty-seven days, the Confederates fell before the soldiers of General U. S. Grant. Notwithstanding an unprecedented artillery bombardment and equally heavy hardship caused by the lack of food within the Confederate lines, many Confederates felt bitterly that the siege should have been longer resisted and that General Pemberton had not performed his full duty in relinquishing the city. Pemberton, however, had directed a gallant fight, and the failure of Confederate troops under General Joseph E. Johnston to reach him in time left him no choice but surrender.

Among the Confederates in the besieged city was Alexander St. Clair Abrams. Abrams had served through the siege of 1862, been wounded, and released from the army. In September, 1862, he had resumed his old occupation as a newspaperman in a place on the staff of the Vicksburg *Whig*. After the capture of Vicksburg he was paroled as a prisoner and moved first to Mobile and then to Atlanta, where he published, later in 1863, his account of what had happened. "By the middle of June," he wrote, "Vicksburg was in a deplorable condition. There was scarcely a building but what had been struck by the enemy's shells, while many of them were entirely demolished. The city had the appearance of a half-ruined pile of buildings, and on every street unmistakable signs of the fearful bombardment it had undergone, presented themselves to the observer."

The following passage is Abrams' account of the Confederate surrender.

At about three o'clock in the afternoon of the third of July, Lieutenant General Pemberton, accompanied by Major General Bowen, left our lines and proceeded to the neutral ground, previously designated, and had an interview with General Grant. . . . After an absence of about two hours' duration, Lieutenant General Pemberton and Major General Bowen returned into our lines. As an armistice had been declared until ten o'clock that evening, the firing ceased, and the shades of night descended upon the two opposing armies in quietude, unbroken, save by the voices of the soldiers in low but angry and indignant conversation, at what they deemed a disgrace upon their country in surrendering the city they had so long and nobly fought, and endured the pangs of hunger to defend.

At dark, on the evening of this day, a council of all the Generals was held at General Pemberton's headquarters, which lasted for several hours. Although we could not learn what transpired in an official way, we received information, from good authority, that it was decided, by a majority of the general officers, that the troops were entirely too weak from the want of food to cut their way through, and that if the position had to be yielded, it was useless to sacrifice the lives of the men in a fruitless endeavor; so that the only course left was to surrender the garrison on General Grant's terms of capitulation. Of the Major Generals present, we understand that Major General M. L. Smith was the only one who absolutely opposed surrendering on any condition, preferring to remain behind the breastworks and starve rather than give up the city. A majority of the council, being of a contrary opinion, however, he was, of course, necessitated to abide by their decision, and about three o'clock a messenger was sent into General Grant's lines with dispatches from Lieutenant General Pemberton.

On Saturday morning, a circular was issued from headquarters, announcing the surrender of Vicksburg and garrison, and stating the terms of capitulation to be as follows:

1st. The entire garrison of Confederate troops was to be surrendered to Major General Grant, commanding the United States forces.

2d. The prisoners of war to be paroled and sent out of the city as soon as blank paroles were printed.

3d. All mounted officers to have the privilege of retaining their horses.

4th. All officers of every grade and rank were to retain their side arms, &c.

5th. All citizens desiring to leave the city with the Confederate forces, could do so on being paroled.

6th. All ammunition, stores, field artillery and siege guns, were to be surrendered to the United States forces, as also all small arms in our possession.

These are about the substance of the terms of capitulation. Although we made no copy of Lieutenant General Pemberton's circular, this will be found as correct a statement as could be desired.

When it was officially announced to our men that Vicksburg was surrendered to the enemy, their indignation knew no bounds. Having been among the troops, we can truthfully speak what we heard and saw of the expressions of sentiment on their part relative to the surrender. With almost an unanimous voice the soldiers declared that General Pemberton had yielded the city without their will, and against any desire on their part. All expressed a determination never to serve under him again, many stating, that rather than be under the command of such a man, they would desert from the army, if they were afterwards shot for it. It is not to be denied that the feeling among the men amounted almost to a mutinous one—to such a degree, indeed, was it, that many threats were made, which only the argument and supplication of the officers prevented the men from putting into execution. . . .

On Saturday morning, the fourth of July, and the anniversary of American Independence, the troops composing the army of Lieutenant General Pemberton marched from the line of intrenchments they had defended and held for nearly two months, amid hardships and privations unsurpassed in the annals of modern warfare, and after stacking the arms they had so well and nobly used, and lowering the standards which had proudly floated on many a bloody battle-field, returned inside the works, prisoners of war to their bitterest foe.

On Saturday, at twelve o'clock, M., Logan's division of McPherson's corps, of the Federal army, commenced entering the city, and in a quarter of an hour Vicksburg was crammed with them. Their first act was to take possession of the court house, on the spire of which they hoisted the United States flag, amid the exultant shouts of their comrades, and a deep feeling of humiliation on the part of the Confederate soldiers who witnessed the hauling up of the flag which they had hoped never to see floating over the city they had so long and proudly boasted impregnable, and never to be taken by the enemy of the South.

After the enemy's forces had stacked their arms, they scattered over the city, and then commenced a scene of pillage and destruction which beggars all description. Houses and stores were broken open, and their contents appropriated by the plunderers. The amount of money and property stolen in this way was enormous, and the Yankee soldiers appeared to glory in their vandalism. One merchant, by the name of G. C. Kress, had his safe broken open, and twenty thousand dollars in money, with a large supply of clothing, taken away. Another merchant, and well-known citizen of Mississippi, by the name of W. H. Stephens, had his store broken open and nearly all the contents taken away. In fact, every place that they could possibly enter without fear of resistance, was broken open and robbed of what was contained in them. The enemy appeared to glory in their course, and on one occasion, in reply to a remonstrance on the part of a gentleman whose residence they had broken open, they said, "we have fought hard enough to capture Vicksburg, and now we have got it, we intend to plunder every house in the d——d rebel city." . . .

With that enterprise and greed for gain which characterizes the universal Yankee nation, on the same day that the Federal army entered Vicksburg, several places of business were opened, and signs informing the public that metallic coffins were on hand to remove the dead bodies of friends, and that express offices, book and fruit stores were "within," were to be seen upon several establishments on Washington street.

Soon after the enemy entered the city, Mr. William Lunn, a well-known citizen of Vicksburg, took the oath of allegiance, and General Grant made his headquarters at the residence of this gentleman. The Jewish portion of the population, composed principally of Germans, with but one honorable exception, went forward and received the oath of allegiance to the United States. The one honorable exception sacrificed a store of goods, which cost him between thirty-five and forty thousand dollars, rather than remain under the control of the enemy.

The conduct of the negroes, after the entrance of their "liberators," was beyond all expression. While the Yankee army was marching through the streets, crowds of them congregated on the sidewalks, with a broad grin of satisfaction on their ebony countenances. The next day, which was Sunday, witnessed a sight, which would have been ludicrous had it not galled our soldiers by the reflection that they were compelled to submit to it. There was a great turn out of the "contrabands," dressed up in the most extravagant style imaginable, promenading through the streets, as if Vicksburg had been confiscated and turned over [to] them. In familiar conversation with the negro wenches, the soldiers of the Federal army were seen, arm-in-arm, marching through the streets, while the "bucks" congregated on the corners and discussed the happy event that had brought them freedom.

So arrogant did the negroes become after the entrance of the Federal forces, that no white Confederate citizen or soldier dared to speak to them, for fear of being called a rebel,

or some other abusive epithet. One of the Confederate soldiers, happening to enter the garden of the house that the
author of this work resided in, for the purpose of picking a
peach, a negro, belonging to a gentleman of Vicksburg, who
had charge of the garden, brought out a gun, and, taking deliberate aim at the soldier, was about to fire. We immediately
threw up the gun, and, drawing a knife, threatened the
negro if he fired at the man; no sooner was the threat made,
than the negro, with an oath, levelled the gun at us and drew
the trigger; luckily the cap snapped without exploding, and
we succeeded in getting the gun away and discharging it.

While making these observations about the negroes, we
would say that it was confined to the city negroes alone.
The slaves brought in by planters, and servants of soldiers
and officers, did not appear the least gratified at their freedom. The majority of those connected with our army were
very desirous of leaving with their masters, and General
Grant at first consented that those who desired it should
leave; but as soon as a few passes were made out, he revoked
the order, and compelled the balance to remain. These differences in the conduct of city and country negroes, should
not be a matter of surprise, when we consider the privileges
given to the negroes in the cities of the South, and demands
a change of policy on the part of slaveowners residing in
densely populated places. Many of the negroes, who were
compelled to remain in Vicksburg, when their masters in the
army left, afterwards made their escape, and returned to the
Confederate lines.

The loss of the Confederate forces during the siege, is estimated by good judges at a number not exceeding 4,000 in
killed and wounded. A number of our casualties resulted
from the indiscretion of the soldiers in exposing themselves

to the enemy's sharpshooters. The loss of the enemy we would estimate as follows:

Attack on Shoup's line, 19th
    of May .... 600 killed and wounded
General assault on the 22d May 9,000   "   "
Attack on Hebert's line, 25th
    June 600   "   "
Prisoners captured 500
Other casualties during the
    siege 2,000
Making a total of 12,700

This estimate we believe to be much beneath what it really was, as in our opinion the enemy lost nearly as much as the total, on the twenty-second of May, for, taking the ratio of six men wounded for one killed, we find that as many as two thousand bodies were buried by the enemy on the Monday following. This would make their loss on the day alone 14,000, or more than the grand total we give above. The assertion of Grant, in his official report, that he lost only 8,000 men during the campaign, is a glaring falsehood, as we feel certain that on the day mentioned above he lost more than he states his casualties to be from the landing at Bruinsburg to the surrender of the city.

The total amount of prisoners captured at Vicksburg by the enemy did not exceed twenty-four thousand, of which, nearly six thousand were either sick or wounded. The following general officers were captured. Lieutenant General Pemberton; Major Generals M. L. Smith, J. H. Forney, J. Bowen, and C. L. Stephenson. The names of the Brigadier Generals captured were: Hebert, Moore, Barton, Lee, Buford, Shoup, Baldwin, Vaughn and Taylor, the latter being Inspector General of the army.

Our loss in small arms and artillery was about as follow:

Small Arms	35,000
Siege Guns	27
Field Artillery	70

A great many pieces of the artillery were unfit for use, and could have been of no use to the enemy.

The amount of ammunition delivered over to the Yankee officers was large, and as near as we could find out, was as follows:

Musket Cartridges	600,000	rounds
Field Artillery Cartridges	15,000	"
Heavy Artillery Cartridges	15,000	"
Percussion caps	350,000	"

This estimate we believe very moderate, as it only gives for each man thirty-five rounds of musket cartridges, and about twenty percussion caps each. We are quite certain that a considerably larger amount of ammunition was surrendered to the enemy. This estimate, however, is made to avoid all charges of exaggeration.

Our line of works was pronounced by the enemy's engineer officers to be the most contemptible they had seen erected during the war. All expressed great astonishment that, with fifteen months of time before us, we had not converted Vicksburg into an impregnable fortress. They expressed themselves very much deceived in the strength of our works, as the representations of the Northern press, and our own boasting, had made them believe that Vicksburg was defended by well-made works, and had between two and three hundred guns mounted.

Our works were, indeed, the most outrageous ever made during the war. The supervisors of their construction could

have known no more about erecting fortifications than we
do; in fact, there was not one engineer in the army of Vicks-
who understood his profession thoroughly—they existed but
in name, and in the position they held in the Confederate
service. The ground on which the works were erected was
naturally a strong one, and to that advantage alone were we
enabled to hold the city for so long a time, otherwise they
would have offered but little or no impediment to the overwhelming numbers of the enemy which were thrown on the
line in their attack on the twenty-second of May.

After the enemy had taken possession of Vicksburg, Major
General McPherson rode over the entire line, and was so
impressed with the defective manner in which they were
constructed, that he is reported to have exclaimed: "Good
Heavens! are these the long-boasted fortifications of Vicksburg? It was the rebels, and not their works, that kept us out
of the city." While this was a great compliment to the valor
of the "rebels," it certainly expressed the greatest contempt
possible for the fortifications surrounding Vicksburg.

The Federal officers candidly gave the Confederate garrison the credit of being as brave troops as they ever saw,
and more than one compliment to the heroism of our soldiers
was paid, coupled with a regret on the part of the officers
of rank, that such men should be in arms against the United
States. Not a word was said by the Yankees claiming superiority in fighting qualities; they all acknowledged that starvation had conquered us, and not the prowess of their arms,
and during the stay of the garrison in Vicksburg, the greatest
courtesy and consideration was shown to our soldiers by the
Federal officers; their privates alone manifesting any desire
to gloat over our reverse.

The Confederate army remained in Vicksburg, as prisoners
of war, for one week after the surrender, that time being

taken to prepare the rolls of the different commands, and parole the men. During this period many severe street fights took place between the Federal and Confederate soldiers, in consequence of the taunts and abuse of the victorious army. Several of the Federal soldiers were severely beaten, and one or two killed. In one of these street brawls, a young man, a citizen of Vicksburg, and volunteer aid on Gen. Baldwin's staff, shot a Federal soldier dead for using insulting language. He was taken to General Grant's headquarters, and after a hearing released.

During the week spent in the enemy's lines, we had several opportunities of hearing the sentiments of both the officers and soldiers of the Federal army. Among the officers, it was the same everlasting cant about the Union, and their determination that it should be restored; but among the privates the greed for gain, and the object with which they fight was not concealed in the slightest degree. They spoke in raptures of the capacity of Mississippi's soil for white labor, and declared their intention to get a grant of land from the United States and settle there after the war is over. This unblushing declaration was accompanied by the assertion that, as the South had rebelled against their government, it was only just that the property of the people be divided among their troops. Such remarks were the principal cause of the street fights between the two armies, as the spirit of our soldiers could ill brook this style of apportioning their homes and property by the enemy.

By Friday, the 10th of July, the prisoners having been paroled, the Confederate soldiers took up their line of march. It was a mournful and harrowing sight. The soldiers felt their disgrace, and there was not one gallant heart in the mass of men, that did not feel half bursting with sorrow and humiliation at being compelled to march through the enemy's guards who were stationed on both sides of the road to some distance beyond the entrenchments. But nothing could avert the degradation; so with downcast looks, and countenances on which a knowledge of the bitterness of their defeat could be seen plainly stamped, they filed past the enemy, who gathered in large number to witness their departure.

It was a day never to be forgotten by those who assisted in the defense of Vicksburg. So filled with emotion were many of our men, that large tear drops could be seen on their weather-beaten countenances, and ever and anon they would pause in their march, and, turning back, take one last sad look at the city they had fought and bled for. All felt that, serious as the disaster was to the Confederate cause, it was nothing to their humiliation. Amid the storm of shot and shell that poured upon them, they had remained cheerful and confident; but at this moment their hopefulness had departed; the yell of defiance that had so often struck terror in the hearts of their foe, was not to be heard; their willing hands no longer grasped the weapons of a good cause; their standards trailed in the dust, and they were prisoners of war. Silently and sadly they marched on, and in a few minutes Vicksburg was lost to their view.

Thus fell the city of Vicksburg after a defense of over twelve months, and a siege which lasted for forty-seven days, forty-two of which a garrison of not more than twenty-five thousand effective men had subsisted on less than one-quarter rations. The Confederate army fought with a valor that not even the defenders of Saragossa and Mantua ever surpassed. Subject to a bombardment of a nature so terrific that its equal has never been known in civilized warfare; through rain and sunshine, storm and calm, writhing under the pangs of starvation, these gallant Southern troops, whose deeds will form one of history's brightest pages when the annals of this siege shall become known, stood up to their post, and, with almost superhuman valor, repulsed every attack made by their enemy, and inflicting tremendous loss on him, until surrendered by the General whose want of ability and confidence in himself had entailed these sufferings and hardships on them.

It is estimated that the number of missiles thrown in the entrenchments, exceeded thirty thousand daily; and by the official report of General Grant's Chief of Artillery, it would appear that twenty millions three hundred and seventy thousand one hundred and twenty-two missiles of all kinds were thrown in the works, which would make it, by calculation, over four hundred thousand missiles, including small arms ammunition, daily thrown. This, however, must be an exaggeration, unless Grant's Chief of Artillery included the number of rounds of small arms used in the different battles prior to the investment of Vicksburg, which lasted only forty-seven days. He, however, gives the number as having been fired *into the city*, which, if correct, would only show the gigantic nature of the bombardment. . . .

We cannot close this chapter without passing a just compliment to the Surgeons attached to the garrison at Vicksburg. Although they were from morning to night engaged in their duties to the soldiers, they were always found administering to the sick and wounded non-combatants of the city. Among the many, we must mention Dr. E. McD. Coffey, Chief Surgeon of Bowen's division, who was unremitting in his attention to this class of sufferers, and always had several sick and wounded women and children under his charge. To this gentleman we were indebted for an introduction to Major General McPherson, who is, without doubt, the only real gentleman among the Federal Generals to whom we were introduced. He was very polite, never using the epithet "rebel" in the presence of our officers or soldiers, and avoided, as much as possible, any expression of exultation at the fall of Vicksburg when in our company.

Before bringing this chapter to a close, we would endeavor to remove the false idea among our people, that Vicksburg was surrendered after a feeble defense. The city was defended as desperately as could be required. The only thing to be said is, that had proper generalship been displayed, there would have been no necessity to use the works surrounding Vicksburg. *After* we were invested, the defense of Vicksburg *commenced*, and though the city is now in the hands of the enemy, it has brought him no honor in its capture, nor added a single laurel to his wreath of victory. *Starvation* succeeded in doing what the prowess of their arms could never have performed. The result was a reverse to the Confederate arms; but when future generations shall speak of this war, the deeds of the gallant men who defended the city, will be extolled among the most heroic feats of the war, and the descendants of those who fought behind the entrenchments of Vicksburg, will be proud of the knowledge that their fathers aided in its defense. All honor to these unswerving patriots! Nobly did they sustain the honor of their country, and the glory of their past deeds; and, falling as they did, the historian of this war will declare that, in their fall as much honor was gained as if they had triumphed in their defense.

Mule Meat at the Hotel de Vicksburg

AFTER THE SURRENDER of Vicksburg Northern news-papers published as an amusing tidbit the "Bill of Fare" said to have been found in one of the Confederate Army camps. If authentic, it is the work of a Confederate who had not lost his sense of humor amid almost un-endurable hardship. If the work of a Yankee prankster, it was written by one familiar with conditions behind the Confederate lines.

Reporter Alexander St. Clair Abrams confirms the basis of such a menu in his description of conditions at Vicks-burg in the weeks before the surrender: "Many families of wealth had eaten the last mouthful of food in their pos-session, and the poor class of non-combatants were on the verge of starvation. . . . Starvation, in its worst forms, now confronted the inhabitants, and, had the siege lasted two weeks longer, the consequences would have been terrible. All the beef in the city was exhausted by this time, and mules were soon brought in requisition, and their meat sold readily at one dollar per pound, the citi-zens being as anxious to get it, as they were before the investment to purchase the delicacies of the season. It was also distributed among the soldiers, to those who

209

desired it, although it was not given out under the name
of rations. A great many of them, however, accepted it in
preference to doing without any meat, and the flesh of
the mules was found equal to the best venison. The
author of this work partook of mule meat for three or
four days, and found the flesh tender and nutritious, and,
under the *peculiar circumstances*, a most desirable description of food."

Southern Punch copied the "Bill of Fare" from the
Chicago *Tribune* so that all Confederates might read it.

The Chicago Tribune publishes the following bill of fare
found in one of the camps at Vicksburg. It is surrounded by
an engraving of a mule's head, behind which is a hand bran-
dishing what may be a bowie, or may be a carving knife.
The Tribune thinks it is a melancholy burlesque. The most
melancholy thing about it is the reflection which it must
suggest to a thoughtful Yankee—if there be such an animal—
on the prospect of conquering the men who can live and
jest on such fare:

HOTEL DE VICKSBURG

———

Bill of Fare for July, 1863.

SOUP.

Mule Tail.

BOILED.

Mule bacon with poke greens.
Mule ham canvassed.

ROAST.

Mule sirloin.
Mule rump stuffed with rice.

VEGETABLES.

Peas and Rice.

ENTREES.

Mule head stuffed a-la-Mode.
Mule beef jerked a-la-Mexicana.
Mule ears fricassed a-la-gotch.
Mule side stewed, new style, hair on.
Mule spare ribs plain.
Mule liver, hashed.

SIDE DISHES.

Mule salad.
Mule hoof soused.
Mule brains a-la-omelette.
Mule kidney stuffed with peas.
Mule tripe fried in pea meal batter.
Mule tongue cold a-la-Bray.

JELLIES.

Mule foot.

PASTRY.

Pea meal pudding, blackberry sauce.
Cotton-wood berry pies
China berry tart.

DES[S]ERT.

White-oak acorns.
Beech nuts.
Blackberry leaf tea.
Genuine Confederate Coffee.

LIQUORS.

Mississippi Water, vintage of 1498, superior, $3.00.
Limestone Water, late importation, very fine, $2.75.
Spring Water, Vicksburg brand, $1.50.

Meals at all hours. Gentlemen to wait upon themselves. Any inattention on the part of servants will be promptly reported at the office.

JEFF. DAVIS & CO., Proprietors.

CARD.—The proprietors of the justly celebrated Hotel are now prepared to accommodate all who may favor them with a call. Parties arriving by the river, or Grant's inland route, will find Grape, Canister, & Co's., carriages at the landing, or any depot on the line of intrenchments. Buck, Ball & Co., take charge of all baggage. No effort will be spared to make the visit of all as interesting as possible.

Gettysburg

Atwin with the surrender at Vicksburg was the Confederate failure at Gettysburg. Hailed at the time as a victory by both sides, Gettysburg was in reality a turning point of the war and a far-reaching defeat for the Confederacy. Though Lee had achieved a measure of success on the battlefield, it was a success which left him unable to follow through the advantage gained. His retreat across the Potomac ended the Confederacy's last great thrust into the territory of the enemy, and the campaign upon which the hopes of the South had been banked had amounted to no gain.

Here is *The Southern Illustrated News* account of the blows at Gettysburg and Vicksburg from its fortnightly summary of war news.

On Wednesday, Thursday and Friday, (1st, 2d and 3d of July,) was fought the great battle of Gettysburg, in Pennsylvania, between the forces of Gen. Lee and the Yankee army under the command of Gen. Meade, who succeeds Hooker,

MASTER ABRAHAM LINCOLN GETS A NEW TOY.

superseded for incompetency. This was probably the most obstinate battle of the war. For the first two days our troops drove those of the enemy before them, and captured 4,000 prisoners, who were paroled through the enemy's lines. The Yankee General, taking advantage of the late Washington decision, refused to acknowledge their parole, and ordered the men back into the ranks. On Friday Gen. Lee renewed the attack on the enemy, and drove him to some strong entrenchments which he had on high ground. These entrenchments were stormed after severe fighting, and the victory remained with us. But Gen. Lee, perceiving that they were commanded by entrenchments still higher up the mountains, after holding the works for twelve hours, fell slowly back. He had taken a large number of prisoners, and to secure them he fell back to Hagerstown. The Yankees had already retreated before he did, but he was not aware of the fact. Had he been so, we might have pressed them, in all probability, until they had become entirely demoralized. As it was, finding that *he* also had begun to fall back, the Yankees returned to the field and raised a shout of victory. The most astounding lies were telegraphed to the cities, and spread over the country by means of the press. Lee's army, according to them, had been completely routed and disorganized. Thousands of prisoners and acres of cannon had been taken. The terrible Yankee cavalry were in pursuit, Couch was interposing between Lee and the Potomac, and the death or capture of the whole army was certain. In the meantime, a telegram announcing a great victory and the capture of 40,000 Yankees, had been received in Richmond, and the people were jubilant. Suddenly their joy was cut short by the arrival of the flag of truce boat with the Yankee papers. Something very like a panic succeeded. The people seemed to take the Yankee lies for gospel; and when news arrived of the surrender of Pemberton at Vicksburg, the public pulse ebbed lower than we have ever known it. Before the end of the week, the truth with regard to Lee began to come out. He had gained a great victory, and captured thousands of prisoners. He had fallen back to Hagerstown at his leisure, and in the most perfect order. The Yankees had not dared to pursue him, and he held at the last dates a strong position, with an army in fine condition and eager to renew the trial of strength. The operations of Gen. Stuart, in the meantime, had been eminently successful. He had captured fifteen miles of wagons, and they are believed to be secure on this side of the river.

During the early part of the present week the greatest anxiety was felt by the public in regard to the situation of affairs. This uneasiness, however, was relieved on Thursday evening, by the reception of a despatch from Gen. Lee, announcing that he had re-crossed the Potomac with his army in good condition.— What necessitated this movement on the part of Gen. Lee is, of course, a matter of conjecture. Be the cause what it may, our people repose the utmost confidence in the skill and judgement of the great commander.

Vicksburg capitulated on the 4th, compelled by the presence of absolute famine. This blow was harder on our citizens, even, than the reported repulse of Lee.

All-Out War

T HE HARDEST THING of all for the Confederates to learn
was that this was a new kind of war, not at all like
the battles they had read about in books of ancient history and the romances of Walter Scott. This was a war
brought home to the people. But the Confederates forgot
that all is fair in war and sometimes acted as if they were
still fighting a tournament of sportsmen.

There were atrocities, of course. There are atrocities in
all wars. War itself is an atrocity. But the atrocities were
not all on the part of the Yankees. Both sides attempted
to make propagandistic point of the worst acts of the
other, but the Confederates were far behind the Yankees
in realizing that war is war and that, to win, there must
be no quarter given.

In the following selection the Rev. Joseph Cross cites
how Union troops carried the war home to the people of
the South. It is a chapter from his *Camp and Field*, there
sarcastically titled "Civilized Warfare."

O that Mr. Lincoln could see himself as others see him! Here is an excerpt from an Irish paper, the Belfast News Letter, which is earnestly commended to his perusal. Let it be borne in mind that this voice comes from a country whose sympathies are all against slavery:

"If Mr. Lincoln were a Brahmin we could understand him, for the religion of the Brahmin teaches him that his sins and shortcomings are not to be regarded as those of common men. The law promulgated by Mr. Lincoln is like that of Menu, which declares that the Brahmin is entitled to all that exists in the universe by his primogeniture and eminence of birth. This eminent Yankee claims sovereign sway from Staten island to the Rocky mountains. He can not bring his mind to the contemplation of the indisputable fact that he is a very humble person after all, and that, in all human probability, he will return to his native obscurity in a few short months, and leave behind him nothing but a name infamous for all time.

"His Emancipation proclamation is nothing more nor less than a premium for murdering men and outraging women. It is the most odious and atrocious outburst of brutal and cowardly vindictiveness that ever emanated from a pagan or 'christian' tyrant. The author of it, and the 'christian' people who approve it, are more debased than the besotted savages of the Feejee islands; and, if the great powers of Europe do not step in to prevent it, they will deserve, as assuredly they will incur, the execration of posterity. Heretofore the patriots of the South have scorned to avail themselves of servile defenders. The last and foulest crime just perpetrated by the Lincoln administration will, however, justify any use to which they may now convert the enormous and undeveloped power within their hands.

"Another feature in this cruel and most unnatural war,

which appears to have escaped the attention it deserves, is
the fact that the people of the Confederate States have imposed upon themselves burdens and taxes without a prece-
dent in the history of the world. What would be said in the
United Kingdom of such sacrifices? Yet this sacrifice has been
voluntarily made by this heroic people, who will perish to a
man before they will consent to the hateful yoke of the
detested Yankees."

The London Times speaks of the war waged against the
South by the North as disclosing "a cruelty and ferocity far
surpassing all that is recorded of the wickedness and bar-
barity of men in former wars," and affirms that though men
may wrangle and dispute about the causes, the rights and
wrongs of this great quarrel, yet as to the measures employed by our enemies "posterity can have but one verdict
to pronounce—a verdict of horror and execration." The editor finds it difficult to express the abhorrence inspired in the
British mind by "acts so wanton and ferocious as that of letting loose the waters of the Mississippi over the plantations
of the South, and overwhelming with the waves that which
they found it impossible to subdue." From a long article, in
which he animadverts with just severity upon this most diabolical deed, I copy a few sentences:

"Not satisfied with all the destruction which modern science has enabled mankind to wreak upon each other, the
North has called to its aid the mighty agencies of nature,
and seeks to ruin and mutilate half a continent in the vain
hope to overthrow or intimidate its inhabitants. It is calculated that, by the action of the Federals in cutting the levees,
or dams, which keep the Mississippi in its course as it runs
through the level land toward the sea, a district as large as
Scotland has been drowned in the State of Mississippi, and
five thousand square miles in the State of Louisiana.

"Had some enormous strategical advantage been obtainable by this proceeding, mankind must have deplored the harsh and dreadful necessity which, in a continent of which so small a portion has as yet been reclaimed for the use of civilized man, drove the Federals to lay waste and devastate so considerable a portion of its surface. But there is no reason to suppose that any advantage in the least degree commensurate with the amount of wanton and cruel destruction which has been perpetrated, could anyhow have obtained. Most certainly no such advantage has been gained. The expedition from Yazoo Pass, so far from reaching its destined point near Vicksburg, has been encountered and defeated by Confederate batteries, and driven to take refuge in another river to avoid further injuries. The act, therefore, stands out in all its naked deformity. Those who have called the mighty Mississippi to their aid have proved themselves unworthy of their potent ally, and, powerful only for mischief, have been singularly discomfited in the endeavor to profit by that new and singular enterprise.

"At the beginning of the war the North went forth to battle in all the presumption of overweening strength and numbers. Their notions of success were thoroughly Oriental. They had the largest number of men under arms, and doubted not of victory, especially as they had the largest resources to feed, arm, and recruit them. Received in the field by troops far less numerous than their own, they found to their astonishment how little the leaders of the South had to dread from them in the open field. From that time the whole aspect of the war has entirely changed. In proportion as success has become more difficult, the means employed for its attainment have been more odious and cruel. Every effort has been made to light the torch of servile insurrection, and, as if this was not dreadful enough, water has been called in to supplement the tardy vengeance of that fire which, kindled by the hands of slaves, would, if the pious and decorous North could have had their will, wrap in one mighty conflagration the labors of a hundred years. Men may wrangle and dispute about the causes, the rights and wrongs of this great quarrel, but as to these measures posterity will have but one verdict to pronounce—a verdict of horror and execration.

"It is difficult to say what time—what interest may not effect. Nations have shed each other's blood like water on fields of battle. They have covered the ocean with the wrecks of their naval engagements and the bodies of their seamen. These things may be expiated, may be forgiven, may at last be forgotten; but deeds like those by which the Northern States are making their present war with the South singular and execrable among the worst and bloodiest annals of mankind, can never be forgiven or forgotten. The moment any idea of reconciliation is entertained, these dreadful memories will rise up like a spectre between the two parties, and forbid every attempt at reconciliation.

"No one can presume to say what are the reverses and vicissitudes which fortune, not yet satisfied with the sufferings of the American people, has in store for either party. But the information which has just reached us makes it abundantly evident, if it were not so before, that the choice henceforth for the South is between victory and extermination, for the North between peace and ruin—ruin certain if the war is protracted, as it easily may be, to a point which will leave the President without a revenue and without an army—ruin still more certain and complete if the wicked aspirations of fanatical hate be accomplished, and the central government,

already triumphant over the liberties of the North, shall obtain, as the price of success, the unenviable duty of holding
down, under the heel of military despotism, the struggling
and palpitating remains of what were once the Southern
States."

A Prayer by General Lee

THE FREQUENT DAYS of prayer appointed by President Davis were days of self-examining sermons by the clergy of the Confederate States and of formal addresses to the troops in armies not occupied by sterner duties. As the tide of war went against the South in the summer of 1863, a day of "fasting, humiliation and prayer" was appointed by the President for August 13.

In the second paragraph of his General Order directing observance of this day General Lee wrote a sincere prayer beseeching the eventual success of Confederate arms on a foundation of national rectitude.

HEAD QRS. ARMY NORTHERN VA.
August 13, 1863.

GENERAL ORDERS,⎱
    No. 83.   ⎰

The President of the Confederate States has, in the name of the people, appointed the 21st day of August as a day of fasting, humiliation and prayer. A strict observance of the

223

day is enjoined upon the officers and soldiers of this army. All military duties, except such as are absolutely necessary, will be suspended. The commanding officers of brigades and regiments are requested to cause divine services, suitable to the occasion, to be performed in their respective commands.

Soldiers! we have sinned against Almighty God. We have forgotten his signal mercies, and have cultivated a revengeful, haughty and boastful spirit. We have not remembered that the defenders of a just cause should be pure in his eyes; that "our times are in his hand"—and we have relied too much on our own arms for the achievement of our independence. God is our only refuge and our strength. Let us humble ourselves before him. Let us confess our many sins, and beseech him to give us a higher courage, a purer patriotism and more determined will: that he will convert the hearts of our enemies: that he will hasten the time when war, with its sorrows and sufferings, shall cease, and that he will give us a name and place among the nations of the earth.

R. E. Lee,
General.

In Camp near Chickamauga

LIKE COLONEL FREMANTLE, Captain Fitzgerald Ross was
an observer at the Battle of Gettysburg. Ross was an
officer of hussars in the Imperial Austrian Army. Unlike
Fremantle, Ross could not sit calmly in a tree and watch
a battle, but succumbed to the temptation to pick up a
rifle and join in the fight. For him Gettysburg was the first
stop, not the last, on a tour of Confederate camps, battle-
fields, and cities, and he went on from Gettysburg to visit
Richmond and the lower South.

In the following excerpt he describes his visit to the
Confederate camp near Chickamauga, where the Confederates had shortly before gained a considerable victory.

After a few sunshiny days we had some pouring wet ones;
it was found that our camp was on too low ground to be
comfortable, and we removed some distance to the rear.

By this time Dr. Cullen had arrived from Richmond, and
with him came [Francis] L[awley]; and as Dr. Cullen had

—besides his own tent and those of the other staff doctors who had not yet arrived—a large hospital tent, large enough to accommodate twenty people, I thought I had crowded my friends long enough, and accepted his kind invitation to move over and take up my old quarters again with him.

Old Jeff, the cook, was rather in a grumbling mood. "This is not like old Virginy, sir; I shall find it very hard to keep up my dignity here, sir;" his dignity consisting in providing us good breakfasts and dinners. And, indeed, provisions are scarce and not very good. Beef is tough, bacon is indifferent, and mutton is rarely to be had; chickens and eggs are almost unheard-of delicacies, and we have to ride ten miles to get a pat of butter.

During anything like a long stay in one camp all energies very soon tend to the point of how to improve the diet, and many long rides are taken with that sole object in view, and with very various success.

If any one can boast of a leg of mutton, he considers it quite a company dish, to which friends must be invited. One of the most successful caterers is General Preston, and another is his adjutant-general, Major Owens, an old friend, who in Virginia was aide to Colonel Walton. Owens is believed to have a flock of sheep hidden away somewhere. The General gave us a splendid supper one evening, with a profusion of delicate viands, and more than one bowl of hot punch made of some capital peach-brandy.

Our own little camp was particularly well off, as Cullen came pretty well provided, and L. brought a box of good things with him from Richmond. No schoolboys can hail a hamper of prog with more gratification than a hungry lot of campaigners do, especially if they have been teetotalling rather more than they like.

After a victory in Virginia there had always been a profusion of delicacies in the Confederate camp for a long time, but from these Western people nothing had been captured but guns and empty waggons, at which there was great disappointment; and many were quite indignant, thinking themselves cheated. "Why, these Yankees are not worth killing," said General ———; "they are not a bit better off than ourselves."

L., after having one horse stolen at Richmond, had purchased another at Atlanta, and as mine had arrived with Cullen we had many a ride together. The camp was pretty extensive, and it was a three or four miles' ride to visit many of our friends.

There was a grand bombardment of Chattanooga one day, of which we had a splendid view from the top of Lookout Mountain. Not much harm was done, but it was a grand sight to see the guns blazing away far below us. On the top of the mountain is a large hotel, besides several villas and cottages. This used to be a favourite gathering-place in summer, but now every dwelling-place was deserted.

We made our way into the hotel, and purchased half-a-dozen chairs from an old woman, who said they were not hers and that she had nothing to do with them; but she took our money and made our consciences easy. And the chairs were very useful.

About this time the President came to pay a visit to the camp, and there was a general expectation that a change would take place; but none came, except in the weather, which had been dry and sunshiny, with a storm or a shower now and then, but now settled down to be wet and cold and nasty.

The President remained two days, and on the second day went with a large suite to Lookout Mountain. Homewards he rode with General Longstreet, a hundred yards in ad-

vance of the rest of the party, and they had a long confabu-
lation, and, I believe, not a very satisfactory one. I rode with
General Breckenridge, with whom, and General Custis Lee,
I dined afterwards at General Gracie's. After dinner we had
some capital singing by some young fellows in Gracie's brigade.

Going home, I fell in with a courier who was riding in the
same direction. He was a Louisianian, and we had a long
chat together. Amongst other things, he told me that if he
met a negro in a fight, he should give him no quarter—that
they had always treated the negroes well, and if they fought
against them now, they deserved no quarter, and he, for
one, should give them none. I remonstrated, saying, it was
no fault of the negro that he was forced to fight by the
Yankees, and that he never would fight if he could help it,
&c. To all which my friend assented, with a "That's so," and
I thought that I had made a convert; but when I had exhausted my arguments, although he again repeated his
"That's so," he added, "For all that, I shan't give them any
quarter."

Our black cook, Jeff, confided to me the other day his
idea as to how the war should be carried on.

"Why, sir, why don't they do now as they used formerly
to do? The generals used to dine together, and take their
wine, and then one would say, 'General, I'll fight you to-morrow at such and such a place,' and then they would shake
hands, and the next day they would fight their battle. That's
what Napoleon used to do," Jeff concluded, "and why don't
they do so now?"

A month after the battle of Chicamauga, we rode over the
field of battle, which is seven or eight miles to the rear of our
camp. The Yankee dead are still unburied, which is a great
shame.

Perhaps General Thomas thinks it beneath his dignity to ask permission to bury them; or perhaps he thinks General Bragg will do it for him, This, however, he has no right to expect, as he is little more than a mile further from the battle-field than Bragg, who, if he sent large details of men eight miles to the rear whilst active operations are going on, would just as much have to demand a truce for the purpose as General Thomas, whose business it is. Besides, these poor fellows' friends will be very anxious that they should be identified, that they may know where to find their graves. If there be one good feeling to be found in the North, it is the respect they show to their dead; and doubtless, if these poor fellows had been identified and properly buried, very many of them would have been brought to their homes after the war, and their bones laid amongst their own kindred. Now the pigs are fattening on them—a disgusting sight to behold.

The rains had become continuous now, and the roads were nearly impassable for waggons, and no movements of importance could therefore be anticipated. The army was in a bad way. Insufficiently sheltered, and continually drenched with rain, the men were seldom able to dry their clothes; and a great deal of sickness was the natural consequence. Few constitutions can stand being wet through for a week together; and, moreover, the nights were bitterly cold, and the blankets were almost as scarce as tents. There was a great deal of discontent, which was increased by its being well known that General Bragg was on very bad terms with many of his generals.

The weather made it disagreeable to move about, and L., [Frank] V[izetelly], and I resolved to leave the army, and on the 22d of October we bade farewell to our friends, and rode over to Chicamauga station, some eight miles off.

General Joseph E. Johnston

DEFENDING the Confederacy from the thrust aimed at cutting through her mid-section was General Joseph E. Johnston. Johnston had had a distinguished career in the United States Army and much was expected of him as a Confederate general. His reputation suffered both during and after the war because of his repeated failure to meet the enemy in a decisive battle. But he was a master of holding and withdrawing. To borrow a word made fashionable in more recent wars, he was a master of containment.

This biographical sketch of him was written by Chaplain Cross in December, 1863, just about the time that the general was settling into winter quarters at Dalton, Georgia.

GENERAL JOSEPH E. JOHNSTON

December, 1863.

"The brave man is not he who feels no fear,
For that were stupid and irrational;

But he whose noble soul its fear subdues,
And bravely dares the danger nature shrinks from.
As for your youth whom blood and blows delight,
Away! with them there is not in their crew
One valiant spirit."—*Shakspeare.*

This illustrious officer is the youngest son of the late distinguished Judge Peter Johnston, of Virginia. He was born in Prince Edward county, but received the rudiments of his education at Abingdon, where his father exercised his judicial functions. In 1825 he became a cadet at the West Point military academy, then at the very acme of its prosperity. In 1829 he graduated in the same class with General Robert E. Lee, and was immediately assigned to the Fourth artillery, with the rank of second lieutenant by brevet. Seven years after this he was appointed assistant commissary of subsistence; and, the year following, first lieutenant of topographical engineers.

In 1838 commenced the Indian war in Florida, in which his gallant conduct gave interesting presage of his future heroism. Being sent, with an escort of infantry, across a lake to make an important reconnoissance, immediately upon landing the party came upon an ambuscade of Indians. At the first fire every officer fell, and the men fled in confusion. Johnston, with great self-possession, assumed command, and rallied the affrighted fugitives. Seizing a tree, amid a perfect storm of bullets, he maintained his position till the men returned to their duty, repulsed the savages, and carried off their own dead and disabled comrades. Lieutenant Johnston was shot in the forehead, and fell; but the ball having merely grazed the skull without penetrating, he suffered no serious consequence from the wound. For this intrepid act, and other achievements during the campaign, he was rewarded with a captaincy by brevet; and, in 1846, he became full captain by seniority.

In 1847, having been brevetted lieutenant-colonel of volti-geurs, he accompanied General Scott to Mexico, where he won additional laurels. In a reconnoissance at Cerro Gordo, venturing too near the enemy's works, he received three musket balls, which like to have terminated his military career. But

"Man is immortal till his work is done,"

and Providence had other use for the brave lieutenant-colo-nel. With the aid of a good constitution and a skilful sur-geon, he recovered, to gather new glory at Molina del Rey, and experience another severe wound at Chapultepec.

After the Mexican war he was made colonel, and subse-quently became quartermaster-general of the United States army. This office he resigned at the commencement of our present struggle, and took a position among the troops of his native state. Soon afterward, however, he offered his services to the Confederate government, was appointed major-gen-eral by President Davis, and sent to take charge of the Army of the Shenandoah. Amid great difficulties, he protected an extensive line of frontier on the Upper Potomac; and by a series of skilful movements, with ten thousand men, foiled, defeated, and held at bay for a long time, a force of twenty thousand. He prevented Patterson's junction with McClellan at Winchester, repulsed him with heavy loss at Falling Water, and afterward marched to join Beauregard at Manas-sas. In that terrific conflict he put the enemy to disastrous rout, reoccupied the country almost to Arlington Heights, and held his position about Centreville through the autumn and winter.

In the spring of 1862 the enemy, inflated with his successes along the southern seaboard, on the Tennessee, the Cumberland, and the Mississippi, with an army of two hundred and twenty thousand, splendidly equipped, and confident almost to madness, made a second attempt, under the command of McClellan, to march over our little army at Manassas, and take up his quarters in the Confederate capital. He advanced early in March, "breathing out threatening and slaughter;" but Johnston had foiled him, by withdrawing his whole force to the neighborhood of Richmond, without the loss of a single life, or the abandonment of anything important to the government.

The little Napoleon now resolved to approach Richmond by another route, and so transported "The Grand Army" to the Peninsula. Johnston was ready to receive him there. He repulsed him with great slaughter at Williamsburg; met him again upon the Chickahominy; drove him back, broken and shattered, to his gunboats; and the disaster to the Federal arms would doubtless have been much greater, had not our hero received a wound which came nigh costing the Confederate cause one of its bravest champions.

Through the mercy of God, however, he is again in the field, and at the head of the Army of the West. His advent in Tennessee revived the hopes of our suffering citizens, and inspired our soldiers with new confidence and courage. It is understood that he selected the battle-ground before Murfreesboro', and suggested the disposition of the troops and the plan of the battle. The result reflected fresh credit upon his skill and fresh glory upon our arms.

Last May, under orders from Richmond, he went to take command, in person, of our forces on the Mississippi. The failure of that campaign, with the loss of Vicksburg and Port Hudson, is attributed to the insubordination of General Pemberton, who is alleged to have disobeyed every order of

his superior officer, suffered himself unnecessarily to be besieged, and then shamefully surrendered the city.

On General Bragg's retirement from the Army of Tennessee, General Johnston succeeded to the command. No appointment could have been more gratifying to the troops and their
officers. His appearance at their head inspired them with new
confidence and zeal, and never were they in better heart for
battle than to-day.

My personal acquaintance with General Johnston being
but slight, I beg leave to quote another's estimate of his
character and abilities as a military commander:

"The career of General Johnston has been such as the
most illustrious chieftain might envy. A quick genius, a solid
judgment, invincible firmness, imperturbable self-reliance,
a will as resolute as that of 'the first bald Caesar,' a penetra-
tion which no device can baffle, a perseverance which no
difficulty can subdue, a courage which no danger can shake,
quickness of conception, promptness of action, endurance
almost superhuman, and reticence as perfect as the grave—
all these we take to be characteristics of a great commander;
and in a high degree General Johnston possesses them all.
For proof we need not go beyond the events of the last
twelve months. He divined all the designs of Patterson, as if
by intuition. With a force not half as strong as him, he
thwarted all his plans and baffled all his enterprises. With
the promptness of lightning he flew to reinforce Beauregard,
as soon as he discovered that he was to be attacked. He suffered a clamor to be raised against him for not attacking
McClellan, rather than permit the secret of his weakness to
be known. In front of an army five times as strong as his
own, he never suffered himself to be betrayed into a false
movement, or lost for a single moment that perfect reliance
upon his own resources which is the mark, as it is most

fortunate property, of a strong understanding. He found the army a brave, but little more than half-disciplined militia; he left it a host of veterans, able to contend with any body of equal numbers that ever trod the earth. We believe that he will live to render services even more brilliant than any he has yet rendered to his country."

A small matter sometimes furnishes the key to a great character. I conclude this sketch with a scene in General Johnston's room at the Lamar House, during his visit at Knoxville, last spring. The hero was surrounded with gallant officers who had called to pay their respects, and conversation was at its floodtide, when a gentle tap was heard at the door. An officer, shining with stars and gold lace, opened it; and there stood an aged negress, with a coarse sun-bonnet upon her head and a cotton umbrella under her arm. "Is this Mr. Johnston's room?" asked the American lady of African descent. The glittering officer replied in the affirmative. "Mr. Joe Johnston's room?" "Yes." "Well, I wants to see him." And in she marched, *sans cérémonie*, and familiarly tapped the great military chieftain upon the shoulder. He turned and clasped her ebony hand in his, while she for a moment silently perused his features, and then exclaimed, with a sad voice, half-suppressed by emotion, "Massa Joe, you's gittin old." The conversation which followed is not to be recorded. Suffice it to add that, as the general held the old slave by the hand and answered her artless questions, large tears rolled down his cheeks; and the gay officers around him "albeit unaccustomed to the melting mood," found use for their pocket cambric. The sable visitant who made the stern commander of the armies of the West weep like a child was old Judy Paxton, who had "toted" Joe in her arms when he was not a general, and nobody dreamed that he ever would be.

Dinner at the Oriental

CAPTAIN FITZGERALD Ross returned to Richmond in December, 1863. In this passage he gives some interesting insights into the public social life of the population-swollen capital and the dietary hardships of its citizens.

Early in December we proceeded to Richmond, accompanied by Captain Fearn. We had been introduced to the conductor of the train, who secured us comfortable seats, and our hospitable friends at Wilmington had provided us with a large hamper of provisions of all sorts—a very useful precaution before a long railroad journey in the present state of affairs. Thus our travels were not so unpleasant as they might otherwise have been. Thirty hours of railway brought us to our destination, and we took up our old quarters at the Ballard House. Richmond now presented a very different aspect from what it had done in summer. Congress, as well as the State Legislature of Virginia, was in session; the shops were full of stores, and crowded with purchasers; hosts of furloughed officers and soldiers perambulated the streets;

236

hotels, restaurants, and bar-rooms were crowded with guests, and the whole city presented a lively appearance.

There was some outcry, even from the pulpits, against the gaieties that were going on, but General Lee was reported to have said that the young ladies were quite right to afford the officers and soldiers on furlough as much amusement as possible; and balls, tableaux vivants, and all kinds of social gatherings, were the order of the day.

Gambling, however, as an unmitigated vice, has lately been checked by the Virginia Legislature. They debated a little whether to legalise gambling, and by making it a public amusement to check gamblers by public opinion, or whether to put it down by severe measures, and decided for the latter. All gamblers caught in the fact were to be heavily fined, and the banker to be flogged. Corporal punishment is not otherwise generally popular in this country, and has been abolished even in the army, where it is so necessary for the protection of the good soldiers, who under the lockup and imprisonment system are punished by extra duty for the faults of unworthy comrades, to whom a term of imprisonment is generally a matter of indifference, if not of positive satisfaction. Good soldiers are never flogged, and there is no more hardship or disgrace to them in bad ones being thus punished than there is to good people in murderers being hanged. And there is another consideration with regard to flogging, namely, that in time of war many men have to be shot for offences for which otherwise a sound flogging would be an adequate punishment, and, as as example, a sufficient preventive.

Colonel Brien and Major Von Borcke met us at the hotel, and carried us off to the "Oriental Saloon," when we had a capital supper, and sat talking till a late hour.

As the South is supposed just now to be in a starving condition, I will insert here the bill of fare of the Oriental Saloon, together with a little bill or two for meals partaken at that establishment:—

ORIENTAL, 8TH JANUARY 1864

BILL OF FARE.

SOUPS.

Per Plate.
Dols.

Beef, ... 1.50
Chicken.
Macaroni.
Vegetable.
Clam.
Oyster.
Terrapin.
Turtle.
Mock turtle.

FOWLS.

Roast turkey, ... 3.50
Roast goose.
Roast ducks.
Roast chickens, ... 3.50

FISH.

Rock fish, ... 5.00
Chub.
Shad.
Perch.
Herrings.
Crabs and lobsters.

MEATS.

Plate.

Roast Beef, ... 3.00
Roast mutton, ... 3.00
Roast pork, ... 3.00
Roast lamb, ... 3.00
Roast veal, ... 3.00

STEAKS.

Dish.

Beef steaks, ... 3.50
Pork steaks, ... 3.50
Mutton chops, ... 3.50
Veal cutlets, ... 3.50
Venison steaks, ... 3.50

SUNDRIES.

Ham and eggs, ... 3.50
Boiled eggs, ... 2.00
Poached eggs, ... 2.00
Scrambled eggs, ... 3.00
Fried eggs, ... 3.00
Omelette, ... 3.00

OYSTERS.

Fried oysters, ... 5.00
Scalloped oysters, ... 5.00
Roasted oysters, ... 5.00
Raw oysters, ... 3.00

BIRDS.

Partridge, ... 3.50
Sora.
Robin.
Snipe.
Plover.
Woodcock.

VEGETABLES.

Cabbage, ... 1.00
Tomato.
Green pease.
Black-eyed pease.
Cucumbers.
Onions, ... 1.00
Lettuce.
Squashes.
Snaps.
Lima beans.
Irish potatoes, ... 1.00
Sweet potatoes, ... 1.00
Salad, ... 2.00
Asparagus.
Celery, ... 2.00

	Cup.
Pure coffee, ...	3.00
Pure tea, ...	2.00
Fresh milk, ...	2.00

WINES.

	Bottle.
Champagne, ...	50.00
Madeira, ...	50.00
Port, ...	25.00
Claret, ...	20.00
Cher[r]y, ...	35.00

LIQUORS.

	Drink.
French brandy, ...	3.00
Apple brandy, ...	2.00
Peach brandy, ...	2.00
Holland gin, ...	2.00
Rye whisky, ...	2.00

MALT LIQUORS.

	Bottle.
Porter, ...	12.00
Ale, ...	12.00
Half a bottle, ...	6.00
Fine havana, ...	1.00
Other brands of a fine quality.	

CIGARS.

Bread, 50 cents—Butter, 1 dol.—Hot rolls, 1 dol. 50 cents.

GAME OF ALL KINDS IN SEASON

Terrapins served up in every style.

PETER K. MORGAN, Sen., Proprietor.

ORIENTAL SALOON, 15TH JAN. 1864.

	Dols.		Dols.
Soup for nine, ...	13.50	5 bottles of madeira, ...	250.00
Venison steak, nine, ...	31.50	6 bottles claret, ...	120.00
Fried potatoes, ...	9.00	1 urn cocktail, ...	65.00
7 birds, ...	24.00	Jelly, ...	20.00
Baked potatoes, ...	9.00	Cake, ...	20.00
Celery, ...	13.50	1 dozen cigars, ...	12.00
Bread and butter, ...	14.00		———
Coffee, ...	18.00	Wines and desserts,	487.00
Apples, ...	12.00	Dinner, ...	144.50
	———		
Dinner, ...	144.50	Total, ...	631.50

These, it is true, are most remarkable for the nominal high prices of everything, but it must be remembered that the reason the paper money here is worth so little is that there is such a profusion of it. Indeed, the country has been swamped with bank-notes. For a time, such was the confidence of the people that they would eventually pay their debt, that paper was only at a small discount; but in the spring of this year (1863) Congress passed a measure enabling the Government to issue fifty millions of dollars a-month in paper money, without pledging any material guarantee for its eventual redemption, and since then the currency has naturally become more and more worthless. At present Congress is engaged in passing a measure to correct all this; the whole floating debt is to be funded, and a new currency issued on sounder principles.

But to return to the question of starvation in the Southern States, for it is true that many people here apprehended such a misfortune. I have no opportunity of seeing much of what goes on in the private houses of the poorer people, and can only judge from what I see at hotels, and eating and boarding-houses. Here, not hundreds, but thousands upon thousands of people take their meals, and one may fairly conclue that what is set before them is what they are accustomed to expect at their own homes.

I confess I never saw much universal profusion, and, I may say, waste. Hot meats and cold meats, venison pies, fish, oysters (prepared in half-a-dozen different ways), eggs, boiled, poached, "scrambled," and in omelettes, hot rolls and cakes, several kinds of bread, fruit in the season, &c., &c., are served up for breakfast, with "Confederate" (*i.e.*, artificial) coffee and tea, at hotels and boarding-houses, in quantities sufficient to satisfy an army of hungry soldiers.

At three o'clock a proportionate amount of food is served up for dinner, and the supper at eight is little less abundant. And for lodging and this board, a sum about equivalent to two shillings or half-a-crown has to be paid. At the eating-houses on the railroad, where the trains stop for meals, the supply is similar.

Accustomed to this extraordinary plenty, many families may now complain at having to content themselves with less than their former profusion, and yet the country is evidently very far from the starvation which the Yankees so charitably reckon upon as one of their chief auxiliaries in destroying the population of the South.

The Close of '63

IN REVIEWING the events of 1863, *The Southern Illustrated News* could still find "nothing in any part of
them which, for a moment, should stimulate gloom or
relax our energy." Here is the paper's brief summary of
military prospects at the end of the year and its report
of the military activities of the immediate past.

The old year has whirled into the grand mausoleum of
eternity, but the ties which united the living pages of its
glory to our hearts have not been sundered. We look back with
pride, it may be mingled with some sadness, to the brilliant
victories at Fredericksburg, the capture of Winchester, the
magnificent though indecisive field of Gettysburg, the complete repulse of the enemy at Charleston, in his grand attack
with plated ships and guns of unprecedented calibre and
range, the bloody battles which ended after many victories,
to our abandonment of Wagner and left glorious, but still
victorious, old Sumter in ruins. Glancing toward the far West,
though we find that we have lost Arkansas Post and been
repulsed at Helena, we have to glory in the hard fought bat-

tle of Prairie Grove; at the skillful evasion of an overpower-
ing force in lower Louisiana; the brilliant success at Bra-
shear City, Milliken's Bend, and many successes of minor
importance in Western Louisiana. Texas has been preserved
almost intact, expelling the foe with shame and blood in the
matchless repulses at Galveston and Sabine Pass. The gravest
reverses of the year have been sustained by us in Mississippi,
and resulted in the capture of Vicksburg and Port Hudson.
Yet these, says the Secretary of War in his report, were, to
the enemy, bloody acquisitions, and to us errors, not unre-
deemed by much of glory and vengeance. Our brave soldiers
succumbed only to privation and exhaustion, and whatever
may have been lost to the country, they at least lost not
honor. But the chief hopes of the enemy have proven more
elusive than the forebodings of our own people; the Mississippi remains under Confederate embargo still. In Tennessee
the campaign has been conducted with more varied fortunes.
By some unaccountable circumstance—treachery it is presumed—Cumberland Gap fell into the hands of the enemy,
and opened up East Tennessee. At Chickamauga, soon after,
the superior prowess of our arms was established in what
ranks among the grandest victories of the war; but it was
followed by another and more uneven battle, which gave to
the enemy his lost ground. The brilliant assaults of Longstreet upon the enemy's fortified positions at Knoxville, close
the catalogue of the leading events of the year. Truly we find
nothing in any part of them which, for a moment, should
stimulate gloom or relax our energy.

The events of the past two weeks have been of minor importance. The holidays passed off joyously and quietly. In
Northern Virginia, Gen. Rosser wound up a successful raid,
far within the enemy's lines, in time to enjoy a Christmas
dinner with his friends in camp; but his trail was followed

by the "vengeful enemy," who wreaked their ire upon the harmless shoemakers and hard working citizens of the two quiet little "alpine villages" of Sperryville and Luray. The main force of the enemy still remains north of the Rappahannock, while their pickets extend below Culpeper C. H. as far as Mitchell's station.

In Tennessee various raids have been made by Gen. Wheeler to the severe injury of the enemy's transportation, but no fighting of importance has occurred. All is quiet at Chattanooga. In East Tennessee the enemy is kept constantly alert by our army, and at present his pickets extend twelve miles east of Knoxville.

The most gentlemanly act the enemy have done during the war was performed in Charleston harbor on the evening of the 1st inst.— They fired a couple of shots over the ruins of Sumter, and when the evening gun of the brave, dismantled, but defiant old pile, boomed over the waters, they lowered their flag respectfully. But this is no offset to their inborn malignity. On Christmas day, and during the whole week, they fired at intervals into the city, doing, however, but little damage. The batteries on Johnson and Morris Islands have been playing occasionally, with unappreciable results. The last noticeable movements of the enemy are confined to the Inlet, where they were landing heavy guns, to be placed upon extensive earthworks opposite immortal little Secessionville.

General Kirby Simth has taken the field against the enemy in Arkansas. In Texas considerable excitement was created along the southwest coast by exaggerated reports of the invasion of Banks' army. The latter had siezed upon several small and defenceless villages, and stolen a large quantity of cattle.

The patients in the hospitals in Richmond were treated

on New Year's day to liberal contributions of food and raiment from the citizens, which will give them occasion to
remember the people—the ladies especially—of the metropo-
lis long.

The new Governor of Virginia, Major-General William
Smith, was duly inaugurated at the Capitol, on the 1st inst.
He rendered the occasion especially interesting by a patri-
otic speech, full of encouragement to the people of the Old
Dominion.

Congress continues to work with energy upon the various
matters before it. The most important measure of immediate
interest it has perfected, is the act annulling the exemptions
of persons who have furnished substitutes. The President
has fixed his signature to the act and it is now one of "the
laws of the land."

1864

President Davis' Address
to the Soldiers

ONE OF THE FIRST generally discernible signs of the doubt which was privately seeping into Confederate minds about the eventual success of the Confederacy was the whistling-Dixie sort of attitude which is represented in the next item.

It is President Davis' address to the soldiers in February, 1864, a stirring and genuinely optimistic document. Perhaps its optimism is an indication that the President was losing touch with the realities of the Confederacy's situation, for the conditions that called for such an address were, verily, a portent of hard times acoming.

Soldiers of the Army of the Confederate States:

In the long and bloody war in which your country is engaged, you have achieved many noble triumphs. You have won glorious victories over vastly more numerous hosts. You have cheerfully borne privations and toil to which you

249

were unused. You have readily submitted to restraints upon your individual will, that the citizen might better perform his duty to the state as a soldier. To all these you have lately added another triumph—the noblest of human conquests— a victory over yourselves.

As the time drew near when you who first entered the service might well have been expected to claim relief from your arduous labors, and restoration to the endearments of home, you have heeded only the call of your suffering country. Again you come to tender your service for the public defence—a free offering, which only such patriotism as yours could make—a triumph worthy of you and of the cause to which you are devoted.

I would in vain attempt adequately to express the emotions with which I received the testimonials of confidence and regard which you have recently addressed to me. To some of those first received, separate acknowledgements were returned. But it is now apparent that a like generous enthusiasm pervades the whole army, and that the only exception to such magnanimous tender will be of those who, having originally entered for the war, cannot display anew their zeal in the public service. It is, therefore, deemed appropriate, and, it is hoped, will be equally acceptable, to make a general acknowledgement, instead of successive special responses. Would that it were possible to render my thanks to you in person, and in the name of our common country, as well as in my own, while pressing the hand of each war-worn veteran, to recognize his title to our love, gratitude and admiration.

Soldiers! By your will (for you and the people are but one) I have been placed in a position which debars me from sharing your dangers, your sufferings and your privations in the field. With pride and affection, my heart has accompanied you in every march; with solicitude, it has sought to minister to your every want; with exultation, it has marked your every heroic achievement. Yet, never in the toilsome march, nor in the weary watch, nor in the desperate assault, have you rendered a service so decisive in results, as in this last display of the highest qualities of devotion and self-sacrifice which can adorn the character of the warrior-patriot.

Already the pulse of the whole people beats in unison with yours. Already they compare your spontaneous and unanimous offer of your lives, for the defence of your country, with the halting and reluctant service of the mercenaries who are purchased by the enemy at the price of higher bounties than have hitherto been known in war. Animated by this contrast, they exhibit cheerful confidence and more resolute bearing. Even the murmurs of the weak and timid, who shrink from the trials which make stronger and firmer your noble natures, are shamed into silence by the spectacle which you present. Your brave battle-cry will ring loud and clear through the land of the enemy, as well as our own; will silence the vain-glorious boastings of their corrupt partisans and their pensioned press, and will do justice to the calumny by which they seek to persuade a deluded people that they are ready to purchase dishonorable safety by degrading submission.

Soldiers! The coming Spring campaign will open under auspices well calculated to sustain your hopes. Your resolution needed nothing to fortify it. With ranks replenished under the influence of your example, and by the aid of your representatives, who give earnest of their purpose to add, by legislation, largely to your strength, you may welcome the invader with a confidence justified by the memory of past victories. On the other hand, debt, taxation, repetition of heavy drafts, dissensions, occasioned by the strife for power, by the pursuit of the spoils of office, by the thirst for the plunder of the public treasury, and, above all, the consciousness of a bad cause, must tell with fearful force upon the overstained energies of the enemy. His campaign in 1864, must, from the exhaustion of his resources, both in men and money, be far less formidable than those of the last two years, when unimpaired means were used with boundless prodigality, and with results which are suggested by the mention of the glorious names of Shiloh and Perrysville, and Murfreesboro' and Chickamauga, and the Chickahominy and Manassas, and Fredericksburg and Chancellorsville.

Soldiers! Assured success awaits us in our holy struggle for liberty and independence, and for the preservation of all that renders life desirable to honorable men. When that success shall be reached, to you—your country's hope and pride—under Divine Providence, will it be due. The fruits of that success will not be reaped by you alone, but your children and your children's children, in long generations to come, will enjoy blessings derived from you, that will preserve your memory ever-living in their hearts.

Citizen-defenders of the homes, the liberties and the altars of the Confederacy! That the God, whom we all humbly worship, may shield you with his Fatherly care, and preserve you for safe return to the peaceful enjoyment of your friends and the association of those you most love, is the earnest prayer of your Commander-in-Chief.

JEFFERSON DAVIS.

RICHMOND, February 9th, 1864.

Gaiety as Usual in Mobile

L IFE IN THE CITIES of the deep South went on in more
normal fashion than life in besieged Richmond. Even
in blockaded Mobile there was less disruption of the
usual social life of the city, and, as in Richmond, there
was a wartime heightening of such gaieties as weddings
and balls. Here is Fitzgerald Ross's account of his visit to
the Gulf City in the winter 1863–64, an account which
mixes his reports of social activities and military preparations in an interesting historical cocktail.

Mobile had suffered very little from the war, and still carried on a brisk commerce with the outer world in spite of
the blockade. It is pleasantly situated on a broad plain, and
has a beautiful prospect of the bay, from which it receives
refreshing breezes. Large vessels cannot come directly to
the city, but pass up Spanish River six miles round a marshy
island into Mobile river, and then drop down to Mobile.

We took up our quarters at the Battle House, an enormous
caravanserai; and after a refreshing bath, and a capital break-

fast at a French restaurant, we sallied forth for a walk in the city.

Colonels Walton and Deas, who are well known here, were greeted by friends almost at every step, and we presently adjourned to the Manassas Club, where our arrival was celebrated with a "cocktail." We then paid our respects to Admiral Buchanan and to General Maury, who commands the military department of the Gulf.

In the evening we went to a grand wedding-party and ball, where all the beauty of Mobile was assembled; and the reports I had heard of the charms of the fair sex at Mobile I found to be not at all exaggerated. This was the last ball of the season, as Lent was about to commence, but they had been very gay here during the carnival. There is always a great deal of social intercourse at Mobile, and I shall ever cherish amongst my most agreeable recollections of the South the pleasant hours spent with the genial inhabitants of that city. It is usual to pay visits in the evening between seven and ten o'clock.

We were not much pleased with our accommodation at the hotel, and were removing to a boarding-house; but Colonel Scheliha, now Chief Engineer of the Department of the Gulf, whom I met in the West, insisted upon my taking up my quarters with him, which I accordingly did. He also placed his horses at my disposal, and we had many rides together. The Colonel is engaged in erecting a new line of forts round Mobile, which are perfect models of strength and judicious arrangement. They are built entirely of sand, with revetments of turf alone. The turf on the embankments is fastened down to the sand by slips of the Cherokee rose, an exceedingly prickly shrub, which when grown will become a very disagreeable obstacle to a storming party. Though I must not say much more about them, I may mention, as a proof of the solidity of these works, that the parapets are 25 feet wide, the traverses against splinters of shell are 18 feet wide, against enfilading fire, 32 feet wide. Besides these forts there are two other lines of defence at Mobile, which will soon be one of the most strongly fortified places in the world. The forts in the harbour, which are built on artificial islands, were being much strengthened; and everything was being done now with great energy, as it was reported that the Yankees designed to attack the city.

Sherman had advanced upon Jackson, but it was not supposed that an attack by land would be made from that quarter, as the country through which the Yankees would have to pass was poor and thinly populated, so that they would find it difficult to obtain supplies. To attack Mobile by land they would have to make Pascagoula their base.

One day we went down the bay to visit the outer defences in a magnificent river-steamer. The Governor of Alabama, Admiral Buchanan, General Maury, and other gentlemen and ladies, were of the party. A very good band of music from one of the regiments of the garrison played, and dancing was soon got up in the splendid saloon. They dance the "finale" of the quadrille here with all sorts of figures—one of them like the last figure in the Lancers, walking round and giving the right and left hand alternately. Admiral Buchanan, who was looking on, joined in this, and naturally by doing so created a great deal of confusion and merriment, at which he was in high glee. He is immensely popular, and the young ladies all call him a charming old gentleman, although he is at least ten years too young to be an admiral in England.

We landed at Fort Morgan and went over the place. I confess I did not like it at all. It is built in the old style, with bricks here, there, and everywhere.

Now when bricks begin to fly about violently by tons'
weight at a time, which is the case when they come in contact with 15-inch shells, they make themselves very unpleasant to those who have trusted to them for protection. This
was conclusively shown at Fort Sumter.

Fort Gaines, which we did not visit, was, they told me, a
much better place, lately finished and strengthened on newer
principles; but all agreed that these two forts were a very
inadequate defence for the bay, into which the Yankees
might enter whenever they chose to make the attempt.

Governor Ward made a speech to the garrison, and com-
plimented the men who had lately re-enlisted for the war.
At the commencement of the present struggle the soldiers
only enlisted for three years, and in the whole army the
term of enlistment was now drawing to a close. This was
very awkward, as these men could not be dispensed with,
and Congress would have been obliged to pass some law on
the subject. But it was spared all trouble. The men knew
as well as the Government that they were "bound to fight
it out," and came forward voluntarily, re-enlisting with great
enthusiasm for "ten years," "forty years," some even for
"ninety-nine years," or "the war." The alacrity with which
the army has come forward on this occasion has caused much
good feeling, and the few who before were inclined to croak
and despond are now again as confident as ever of ultimate
success.

From Fort Morgan we went on to Fort Powell, a beautiful
little sandwork in Grant's Pass. This is an inlet to the bay,
through which, in former days, steamers used to take a short
cut to New Orleans, paying a toll to a Mr Grant, who had
deepened the channel for them, and who was rewarded by
a large fortune for his enterprise. Fort Powell, which was
only just being completed, had six guns, Fort Morgan about

fifty. There were still strong rumours of a contemplated attack upon Mobile, but General Maury told me he did not believe in them. . . .

Whilst at Mobile we visited the men-of-war in the harbour, of which the Tennessee was the most formidable. The great difficulty is how to get this ship over the Dog River bar, which has never more than nine feet of water, whilst the Tennessee draws full thirteen. They have therefore to raise her four feet by "*camels*," which with the dearth of mechanical appliances in the South is a very difficult operation, and Admiral Buchanan almost despaired of succeeding.

Apropos of the detention of the rams in England, Admiral Buchanan told me that during the war between the Brazils and Buenos Ayres, some sixteen years ago, he himself commanded and took out to Rio Janeiro one of two ships of war which were built at Baltimore for the Brazilians. He had given a grand entertainment—I think he said to 500 persons —on board his ship, before leaving Baltimore, and no secret was made of his destination. The Minister of Buenos Ayres at Washington was perfectly aware of what was going on, but never dreamed of making a complaint to the United States Government, and had he done so it would most certainly have been disregarded. . . .

Were it not for the friendly neutrality of the British Government towards the North, the Confederates would have had a fleet, and the war in consequence would have been over long ago.

Although the Confederates think that they have been very unhandsomely and unfairly treated by the British Government, and comment freely upon the "extraordinary conduct" of Earl Russell, I may say here that they appreciate very highly the sympathy of Englishmen, which they believe to be entirely with them; and I never in the South heard an unpleasant remark made about the people of England, whom they believe to be misrepresented by their present Foreign Secretary.

A few days after our excursion down the bay, Fort Powell was attacked by a fleet of gunboats, and underwent some shelling; but after a day or two, finding they could make no impression, the Yankees retired.

There is a capital hard "shell road," so called from being made of oyster-shells, which runs alongside the bay for some seven miles. It is the favourite drive for carriages at Mobile. At the end is a house where refreshments are taken. We drove there one day, and were in the house whilst the firing at Fort Powell was going on. When the heavy Brooks gun in the fort was fired, it shook the windows so as to make them jingle, although the distance was near thirty miles. Owing to scarcity of stone, there are very few good roads in the Southern States, except near the mountains. The sand is often so deep that horses can hardly get along. For traffic they have railways, and as Southerners, male and female, prefer riding to driving, they care little for their roads. The shell road at Mobile, however, is excellent, and at New Orleans I am told they have some equally good made of the shell of the coquille.

I met a gentleman here, the fidelity of whose negro servant (slave) deserves to be put on record. He had had to fly in haste from Natchez on the Mississippi, when that place was occupied by the Yankees, and had left very important papers and a large sum of money securely hidden at his house there. Not being able to return himself to his home, he sent his negro servant, who, with a good deal of trouble, dodged his way in and out of the Federal lines, and brought his master all his important papers and ten thousand dollars in gold (two thousand pounds). How many white servants could be trusted with a similar mission? . . .

We had decided to return by steamer up the Alabama river as far as Montgomery, as it was a much pleasanter mode of travelling than by rail. The steamers all over this continent are splendid vessels, and we were very comfortable on board our boat. The country through which we passed was fertile and cultivated, and produces much cotton.

The cultivation of cotton in America is of comparatively recent date. Colonel Deas told me, that in 1774 his grandfather, who then resided in England, wrote out to his agents in Charleston, and directed them to attempt the cultivation of a sufficient amount of cotton to supply the negroes on his plantation with homespun. At that time the great staple in the Southern States was indigo, the cultivation of which is now so entirely discontinued that they were not able to make the naval uniform in the Confederacy blue, as every one knows a naval uniform ought to be. It is now the same colour as the military uniform. I believe the reason that seamen dress in blue, is because it is the only colour which is not stained by salt water.

At Selma a large body of soldiers came on board our boat, and for the rest of our journey to Montgomery we were crowded. However, the colonels and myself took refuge in "Texas," a glass shed built high over the centre of every river-steamer, whence the vessel is piloted. The cabins below this, and above the grand saloon, where the officers of the vessel are accommodated, also belong to "Texas." Here we had chairs, plenty of room, and a fine view.

The soldiers belonged to Hardee's corps, which had been sent to reinforce General Polk, but they were now no longer required, as Sherman had retreated. He fortunately never reached the rich country about Demopolis, but the already desolate country his army passed through he devastated in the most frightful manner, both coming and going, and everybody says he deserves to be hanged.

After a short stay at Montgomery we proceeded on our journey and reached Macon the next morning. There is a magnificent railroad station here and a capital hotel, the Brown House, where we breakfasted. At the station there were a large number of Yankee prisoners, who had been picked up during Sherman's retreat.

We slept that night at Savannah and went on to Charleston next morning. Here we made a two days' rest, and I took up my quarters with Mr Ch., finding a dinner-party assembled as usual, and old friends among the guests. One of them, as a parting gift, made me a present of an enormous cigar-case full of Havannah cigars, a princely benefaction under present circumstances in Dixie, when Havannah cigars are not to be purchased at any price.

Soon after we reached Wilmington my two friends and travelling companions returned to Richmond, their leave of absence having expired, whilst I with much regret prepared to say farewell to "the sunny South." A few pleasant days flew quickly by, and then with C., whose business called him to Nassau, I embarked in the Hansa, a noble ship, which was now to run the blockade for the eighteenth time.

It was exhilarating enough when, the moon having set at midnight, we slipped out of Cape Fear river, and dashed at full speed through the blockading fleet. It was pitch dark, and not even a cigar was allowed to be alight on deck. For nearly an hour we kept peering through the night to discover whether any Yankee ship lay in our way, but we passed unobserved, and then all immediate danger was over.

The next day we saw a large number of cotton bales floating in the sea, and on arriving at Nassau we heard that they had been thrown overboard by the Alice, which had left the night before us, and had been chased for a whole day by a Yankee cruiser. A little schooner was engaged in picking them up, and as a single bale is worth 40£ she was no doubt making a good thing of it. We performed our voyage to Nassau in about sixty hours, and were loudly cheered as we steamed into the harbour.

The Consequence of Desertion

DESERTION was a serious problem in both the Union and Confederate armies. In the Confederate Army particularly, where enlistments had been lengthened and men were long separated from their homes, extended absences without leave were commonplace. To aid in planting or harvesting a crop, to alleviate a family crisis, or simply to renew home ties, men often left the camps without the formality of permission. Most of them returned after a suitable lapse of time—sometimes to be punished, but about as often, to be accepted back into their former status without too much questioning.

The laxity exercised in disciplining such cases, however, did not apply in cases of true desertion.

On Febraury 1, 1864, the Confederates under Brigadier General R. F. Hoke forced the passage of Batchelor's Creek near Newbern, North Carolina, and attacked the Yankee-held town. In the pursuit toward the city a large number of prisoners were taken, among whom were a number who proved to be Confederate deserters. But let us hear the story in the words of Chaplain John Paris, who less than a month later preached the remarkable sermon which follows:

"Among the prisoners taken, were about fifty native North Carolinians, dressed out in Yankee uniform, with muskets upon their shoulders. Twenty-two of these men were recognized as men who had deserted from our ranks, and gone over to the enemy. Fifteen of them belonged to Nethercutt's Battalion. They were arraigned before a court martial, proved guilty of the charges, and condemned to suffer death by hanging.

"It became my duty to visit these men in prison before their execution, in a religious capacity. From them I learned that bad and mischievous influences had been used with every one to induce him to desert his flag, and such influences had led to their ruin. From citizens who had known them for many years, I learned that some of them had heretofore borne good names, as honest, harmless, unoffending citizens. After their execution I thought it proper, for the benefit of the living, that I should deliver a discourse before our brigade, upon the death of these men, that the eyes of the living might be opened, to view the horrid and ruinous crime and sin of desertion which had become so prevalent."

You are aware, my friends, that I have given public notice that upon this occasion I would preach a funeral discourse upon the death of the twenty-two unfortunate, yet wicked and deluded men, whom you have witnessed hanged upon the gallows within a few days. I do so, not to eulogize or benefit the dead. But I do so, solely, for the benefit of the living; and in doing so, I shall preach in my own way, and according to my own manner, or rule. What I shall say will either be true or false. I therefore request that you will watch me closely; weigh my arguments in the balance of truth; measure them by the light of candid reason, and compare them by the Standard of Eternal Truth, the Book of God; what is wrong, reject, and what is true, accept, for the sake of the truth, as responsible beings.

Of all deserters and traitors, Judas Iscariot . . . is undoubtedly the most infamous, whose names have found a place in history, either sacred or profane. No name has ever been more execrated by mankind: and all this has been justly done. . . .

Well may it be said that this man is the most execrable of all whose names stand on the black list of deserters and traitors that the world has furnished from the beginning until now.— Turning to the history of our own country, I find written high on the scroll of infamy the name of Benedict Arnold, who at one time stood high in the confidence of the great and good Washington. What was his crime? Desertion and treason. He too hoped to better his condition by selling his principles for money, to the enemies of his country, betraying his Washington into the hands of his foes, and committing the heaven-insulting crime of perjury before God and man. Verily, he obtained his reward; an immortality of infamy; the scorn and contempt of the good and the loyal of all ages and all countries.

Thus, gentlemen, I have brought before you two grand prototypes of desertion, whose names tower high over all on the scroll of infamy. And I now lay down the proposition, that every man who has taken up arms in defence of his country, and basely deserts or abandons that service, belongs in principle and practice to the family of Judas and Arnold. But what was the status of those twenty-two deserters whose sad end and just fate you witnessed across the river in the old field? Like you they came as volunteers to fight for the independence of their own country. Like you they received the bounty money offered by their country. Like you they took upon themselves the most solemn obligations of this oath: "I, A.B. do solemnly swear that I will bear true allegiance to the Confederate States of America, and that I will serve them honestly and faithfully against all their enemies or opposers whatsoever, and observe and obey the orders of the Confederate States, and the orders of the officers appointed over me, according to the rules and articles for the government of the Confederate States, so help me God."

With all the responsibilities of this solemn oath upon their souls, and all the ties that bind men to the land that gave them birth, ignoring every principle that pertains to the patriot, disowning that natural, as well as lawful allegiance that every man owes to the government of the State which throws around him the aegis of its protection, they went boldly, Judas and Arnold-like, made an agreement with the enemies of their country, took an oath of fidelity and allegiance to them, and agreed with them for money to take up arms and assist in the unholy and hellish work of the subjugation of the country which was their own, their native land! These men have only met the punishment meted out by all civilized nations for such crimes. To this, all good men, all true men, and all loyal men who love their country, will say, Amen!

But who were those twenty-two men whom you hanged upon the gallows? They were your fellow-beings. They were citizens of our own Carolina. They once marched under the same beautiful flag that waves over our heads; but in an evil hour, they yielded to mischievous influence, and from motives or feelings base and sordid, unmanly and vile, resolved to abandon every principle of patriotism, and sacrifice every impulse of honor; this sealed their ruin and enstamped their lasting disgrace. The question now arises, what are the influences and the circumstances that lead men into the high and damning crimes of perjury and treason? It will be hard to frame an answer that will fit every case. But as I speak for the benefit of those whom I stand before to-day, I will say I have made the answer to this question a matter of serious inquiry for more than eighteen months. The duties of my office as Chaplain have brought me much in contact with this class of men. I have visited twenty-four of them under sentence of death in their cells of confinement, and with death staring them in the face and only a few short hours between them and the bar of God, I have warned them to tell the whole truth, confess everything wrong before God and man, and yet I have not been able to obtain the full, fair and frank confession of everything relating to their guilt from even one of them, that I thought circumstances demanded, although I had baptized ten of them in the name of the Holy Trinity. In confessing their crimes, they would begin at Newbern, where they joined the enemy, saying nothing about perjury and desertion. Every man of the twenty-two, whose execution you witnessed, confessed that bad or mischievous influences had been used with him to influence him to desert. All but two, willingly gave me the names of their seducers. But none of these deluded and ruined men seemed to think he ought to suffer the penalty of death, because he had been persuaded to commit those high crimes by other men.

But, gentlemen, I now come to give you my answer to the question just asked. From all that I have learned in the prison, in the guard house, in the camp, and in the country,

I am fully satisfied, that the great amount of desertions from our army are produced by, and are the fruits of a bad, mischievous, restless, and dissatisfied, not to say disloyal influence that is at work in the country at home. If in this bloody war our country should be overrun, this same mischievous home influence will no doubt be the prime agent in producing such a calamity. Discontentment has, and does, exist in various parts of the State. We hear of these malcontents holding public meetings, not for the purpose of supporting the Government in the prosecution of the war, and maintenance of our independence, but for the purpose of finding fault with the Government. Some of these meetings have been dignified with the name of "peace meetings;" some have been ostensibly called for other purposes, but they have invariably been composed of men who talk more about their "rights," than about their duty and loyalty to their country. These malcontents profess to be greatly afflicted in mind about the state of public affairs. In their doleful croakings they are apt to give vent to their melancholy lamentations in such words as these: "The country is ruined!" "We are whipt!" "We might as well give up!" "It is useless to attempt to fight any longer!" "This is the rich man's war and the poor man's fight;" &c. Some newspapers have caught the mania and lent their influence to this work of mischief; whilst the pulpit, to the scandal of its character for faith and holiness, has belched forth in some places doctrines and counsels through the ministrations of unworthy occupants, sufficient to cause Christianity to blush under all the circumstances. I would here remark, standing in the relation which I do before you, that the pulpit and the press, when true and loyal to the Government which affords them protection, are mighty engines for good; but when they see that Government engaged in a bloody struggle for existence, and show themselves opposed to its efforts to maintain its authority by all constitutional and legal means, such a press, and such pulpits should receive no support for an hour from a people that would be free. The seal of condemnation should consign them to oblivion.

Office Board of Examiners—Examination of a Conscript.

Such sentiments as we have just alluded to, are sent in letters to our young men in the army, by writers professing to be friends; often with an urgent and pressing invitation to come home; and some have even added that execrable and detestable falsehood, the quintessence of treason, "the State is going to secede." Letters coming into our camps on the

Rappahannock and Rapidan sustain this position. What are the effects produced upon our young men in the ranks? With the illiterate, they are baleful indeed. The incautious youth takes it for granted that the country is ruined and that the Government is his enemy. The poisonous contagion of treason from home gets hold in his mind and steals into his feelings. This appeal from home has overcome him. The young man of promise and of hope once, now becomes a deserter. Is guilty by one false step of the awful crimes of perjury and desertion. The solemn obligations of his oath are disregarded; he takes to the woods, traverses weary roads by night for days, until he reaches the community in which he claims his home; but for what? To engage in any of the honorable vocations of life? No, gentlemen. But to lie hidden from the face of all good, true and loyal men. But for what purpose? To keep from serving his country as a man and a citizen. To consume the provisions kept in the country for the support of the women and children, families of soldiers who are serving their country, indeed; and lastly, to get his living in part, at least, by stealing and robbing. And here allow me to say, I am not sufficiently skilled in language to command words to express the deep and unutterable detestation I have of the character of a deserter. If my brother were to be guilty of such a high crime, I should certainly make an effort to have his name changed to something else, that I, and my children after me, might not feel the deep and lasting disgrace which his conduct had enstamped upon it.

I hold, gentlemen, that there are few crimes in the sight of either God or man, that are more wicked and detestable than desertion. The first step in it is perjury. Who would ever believe such an one in a court of justice again? The second, is treason. He has abandoned the flag of his country; thus much he has aided the common enemy. These are startling crimes, indeed, but the third is equally so. He enstamps disgrace upon the name of his family and children.

From amidst the smoke and flames of Sinai God has declared that He "is a jealous God, visiting the iniquities of the fathers upon the children unto the third and fourth generations of them that hate me." The infamy that the act of disloyalty on the part of a father places his children in after him, is a disability they cannot escape: it was his act, not theirs; and to them it has become God's visitation according to the text quoted above. The character of infamy acquired by the tories of the revolution of 1776, is to this day imputed to their descendants, in a genealogical sense. Disloyalty is a crime that mankind never forget and but seldom forgive; the grave cannot cover it.

Many cry out in this the day of our discontent, and say, "we want peace." This is true, we all want peace, the land mourns on account of the absence of peace, and we all pray for peace. You have often heard me pray for peace, but I think you will bear me witness to-day that you have never heard me pray for peace without independence. God forbid that we should have a peace that brought no independence. . . .

I think you will bear me witness that I have never been hopeful of an early peace in my intercourse among you. But to-day I fancy that I can discover a little cloud, in the political heavens as large as a man's hand at least, that seems to portend peace. Take courage, then, companions in arms. All things around us to-day bid us be of good courage. History fails to tell us of ten millions of freemen being enslaved, who had determined to be free. A braver or more patriotic army than we have, never followed their chief to victory. Their endurance challenges the admiration of the world. When I have seen our brave men in winter's cold and summer's heat, marching from battle-field to battle-field, bare-footed as they were born, and without a murmur, I could not doubt our final success. *Such men as these, were never born to be slaves.* Again, when I have turned my eye home-ward from the camp, and witnessed the labors of our fair country women, in preparing clothing to meet the wants of the suffering in the field and witnessed their untiring devo-tion to the relief of the sick and wounded in the hospitals, I knew that the history of no country, and of no age afforded anything like a parallel, and my faith assured me we never were born to be the slaves of Yankees. Then let your trust to-day be strong in the God of nations.

Surely, then, no man can be found in all our land who owes allegiance to his country, that is so lost to himself, and to all that is noble and patriotic, as to say, "I am for the Union as it was." Such an one could only merit the good man's scorn, and desire the tory's infamy for himself, and disgrace for his children. . . .

Then, to-day, in the light of this beautiful Sabbath sun, let us take courage, and with renewed trust in God, resolve to do our whole duty as patriots and soldiers, and leave the event to the Arbiter of nations. *Amen!*

Theatricals in the Army

BUT CAMP MORALE could be good as well as bad, and it is surprising to find that in most cases Confederate morale was exceptionally good. Soldier amusements were not provided by any government or nationally organized agency. There were various state and local relief societies in the Confederacy, but for their own welfare and amusements the men in the armies were left pretty much to their own devices.

Camp amusements consisted of card playing, gambling of every conceivable description, snowballing and swimming in season, occasional ball games, and entertainment by amateur talent among the soldiers themselves. Bands were not widespread in the Confederate Army, but there were a few. Portable musical instruments, however, provided entertainment in almost every camp. There were occasional performances of amateur theatricals. Such a performance is described in the following communication to *The Southern Illustrated News*.

THEATRICALS IN THE ARMY.

A correspondent in the army writes to us as follows:

CAMP GREGG'S BRIGADE, FIELD'S DIVISION, ⎫
ZOLLICOFFER, EAST TENNESSEE, April 15, 1864.⎰

Mr. Editor:—As a portion of your valuable journal is devoted to the drama, I take the liberty to ask a small space therein, in order to bring before the public an enterprise in this far-famed corner of the Confederacy—vulgarly called "East Tenn."

I dare say a majority of your readers will be surpised to learn that the drama (not Ogden's legitimate) is prospering among Longstreet's war-worn veterans, Such is the case, however, as I shall soon show. Mrs. Bailey, a member of the *quondam* "Bailey Troupe," being on a visit to her husband, leader of the 3d Arkansas band, kindly tendered her efforts toward relieving the dull monotony of camp life. Thereupon, Mr. J. A. Bailey, calling to his assistance his brother, Geo. A. Bailey, together with several members of "Hood's Minstrels," determined to give a theatrical performance. "Where there's a will there's a way;" and despite the weather—April weather—lack of conveniences, &c., they at once set to work to extemporize a *stage* under the broad canopy of Heaven.

The spot selected for this model "Temple of the Muses" is, as the accompanying drawing [not published] shows, a natural amphitheatre, close to the track of the East Tenn. & Va. railroad, and about one mile from Zollicoffer. The *stage* consisted of planks used for shipping horses on the cars, and was kindly furnished by an obliging quartermaster. The *infernal regions* from which "Banquo's Ghost" issues forth to astonish "Macbeth," were, of course, omitted. The back scenery was formed by a tent-fly from General Anderson's head-quarters; the ladies dessing-room, to the left, by a wall-tent, captured at Lenoir Station, from Burnside & Co., and the gentlemen's *ditto*, by a so-called *A* tent. As to boxes, parquette, reserved seats, and other modern improvements, our opera-house was almost destitute; a dozen or so of benches, borrowed from a neighboring church, supplying the whole. In fact, "standing seats" were found more convenient, and the hill in front served as an admirable substitute for these sometimes indispensable articles.— Tallow candles, screened by a board as reflector, supplied the place of footlights; but "pale-faced Luna," who was expected to shed her benign rays over the assembled multitude, deemed it proper to hide her features behind a veil of sable clouds, and the audience was thus thrown into darkness. I am thus explicit in detailing the minutiae of this novel theatre as I consider it important for future reference as a guide to all who intend to seek "pleasure under difficulties."

The first performance was given on the 5th April, and commenced at the hour usually designated as "early candle light," the band of the 3d Arkansas playing the overture— "La Sonnambula."

The programme opened with, "The Soldier Boy's Courtship," Mr. George A. Bailey (soldier boy) being *the* character par excellence; his side-splitting humor convulsing the "house," and instituting him, at once, the favorite.— "The Soldier Lad I Adore," was sung by Mrs. Bailey, with exquisite taste and feelings and failed not to carry every heart with it. "Highland Fling," danced by Mr. D. Stetter, of "Hood's Minstrels," in Ethiopian costume, (female) was executed to perfection—so much so, that no one would have imagined the little drummer of the 4th Texas to be sailing under false colors. Mrs. Bailey followed in that charming ballad, "Annie of the Vale," in which, if possible, she surpassed her first effort. Mr. George A. Bailey, who has already proved himself complete master of the humorous, appeared next, with unbounded success in the execution of a comic hornpipe; in fact, we have seen but few to equal him, and still fewer to surpass him. The farce of "Lucy Long," in which "Hood's Minstrels" appeared as a body was well rendered. Messrs. Chandler and Jett brought out the negro's character in a manner which might make the "Buckley's" look to their laurels. Albert Pike's "Fine Arkansas Gentleman" was sung next by Mr. G. A. Bailey, and here again his well-modulated voice, comic gestures, and inimitable performance, carried the audience by *storm*, as we soldiers say. The performance concluded with "P. T. Barnum's ball," the principal character (negro Pete) being sustained by Mr. Jett, in his usual excellent style. His dance with the soldier, (Mr. G. B.) especially, was most humorous, and brought down the "house" as well as himself, for he was skillfully tripped by his nimble antagonist. Such, Mr. Editor, was one of our most pleasant nights in camp, and we do not think that this performance has ever been equalled in the army.

The performers, each and all, deserve the thanks of their fellow-soldiers, and especially Mrs. Bailey, who, by her fine acting and vocal powers, elevated the whole affair to the rank of a first class entertainment.

All hail to the Messrs. Baileys and Hood's Minstrels.— Long may they meet the plaudits with which they were greeted is the wish of one who, with many others, varied camp life by a pleasant evening among the Muses.

NEMO

The Bishop-General, Leonidas Polk

S HERMAN left his camp near Chattanooga May 8, 1864, to begin his campaign against Atlanta. Among the Confederate generals opposing him was the celebrated churchman-warrior, General Leonidas Polk. By June 14 the Confederates had fallen back to a range of small mountains just north and west of Marietta. It was here that General Polk was killed by a shot from a Yankee battery.

General Johnston expressed the feelings of the country in the General Field Order he published on the day of Polk's death:

"COMRADES! You are called to mourn your first captain, your oldest companion-in-arms. Lieutenant-General Polk fell to-day at the outpost of this army—the army he raised and commanded—in all of whose trials he has shared—to all of whose victories he contributed.

"In this distinguished leader we have lost the most courteous of gentlemen, the most gallant of soldiers.

"The christian, patriot soldier, has neither lived nor died in vain. His example is before you—his mantle rests with you."

Here is a portion of the sketch of General Polk which Chaplain Cross had written in December, 1863, for his book *Camp and Field*.

Lieutenant-General Polk is a man of brilliant mind; well informed on all subjects; lively and imaginative; prompt, ardent, and energetic; remarkably neat in personal appearance; dignified, yet courteous, in manner; as brave in battle as eloquent in discourse; and looks as much the general as the bishop.

A good story was told of him soon after he entered the army, which went the rounds of the Southern newspaper press. On a journey he entered a hotel where he was a stranger. The proprietor met him at the door, and saluted him as "Judge." "You mistake me, sir," said the bishop; "I am no judge." "General, then, perhaps," rejoined the publican. "And no general," was the reply. "Bishop, then, I am sure," exclaimed his host. "Very well," said the traveller; "but why do you take me for judge, general, or bishop?" "Why, sir," answered the other, "having kept a hotel for a long series of years, and seeing constantly so many strangers, I have accustomed myself to the study of character, and am seldom wrong in my judgment. As soon as you entered my house, I perceived that you were a professional gentleman; and it needed no second look to assure me that, whatever your profession, you must be at the head of it."

Perhaps the story is not true, but it *might* be. No officer in the Confederate army has more the port of a leader than Lieutenant-General Polk. Manifestly, he was made to command.

The following is furnished me in a letter by the Rev. Dr. Quintard, the general's chaplain and intimate friend. I give it in his own words:

"The other day, as we were riding out and talking very familiarly on various subjects, General Polk mentioned a singularly incident that occurred to him some years ago. His oldest son—now Captain Hamilton Polk—when in college, purchased a walking-stick for his father. Wishing his father's name and Episcopal seal engraved upon the head of the cane, he carried it to an engraver in New York and gave him a picture of the bishop's seal, as printed in the 'Church Almanac.' The seal was a simple shield, having for its device a cross in the centre, with key and crosier laid across it. On calling for the cane, young Polk found that the engraver, by some strange hocus-pocus, had engraved, plainly and distinctly, a sword in place of a key. Now you may speculate on that to your heart's content; for it has the advantage over most stories, of being true."

I have the best authority for saying that the remarkable yarn, first spun in the Chattanooga Rebel, of the presentation to the bishop, by his brother, of a bowie-knife and a brace of pistols as an outfit for him after his consecration to the Episcopate, was a sheer facbrication.

To the same category, doubtless, belongs a certain story of him in connection with the Battle of Perryville. It is said that General Cheatham, in a furious charge, exhorted his troops to drive the Yankees to a certain place supposed to be not far from every battle-field; and that General Polk, dashing by, waved his sword and shouted, "Drive them, my brave fellows! drive them where General Cheatham told you to drive them!"

The following, however, did actually occur on that bloody field. Near the close of the day a large force appeared on our right, enfilading General Polk's corps with terrible effect. Thinking them to be some of our own troops who had mistaken him for the enemy, he ordered his men to suspend their action and rode forward alone. Approaching the force in question, he was surprised to find them in Federal uniform. With great presence of mind he rode near the general in command and cried, with an authoritative voice, "Cease firing, general! Don't you see that you are slaughtering our own men?" The officer, with a somewhat doubtful and puzzled look, responded, "Excuse men, sir; but who are you? I have not the honor of knowing you." To which General Polk replied, "You cease firing, and in five minutes you shall hear from me." Then, putting spurs to his horse, he galloped back to his command and shouted, "Boys, they are your enemies! Fire!" The instant crash which followed was as if all the thunders of heaven had united their voices; and when the blue battle-cloud rose, the enfilading foe had disappeared, but the ground where he had stood was heaped with the wounded and the dead.

Bishop Polk, though he has laid aside his lawn, has not put off his religion. As far as practicable in the army, he hallows the Sabbath, and avails himself of every opportunity of attending public worship. At Harrodsburg, two days before the battle, he invited Dr. Quintard to accompany him to the Episcopal church, which is one of the most beautiful in the West. As they walked up the aisle alone, the general exclaimed, with emotion, "O for the days when we went up to the house of the Lord and compassed His altar with the voice of praise and thanksgiving!" Reaching the chancel, he said to the doctor, "Can we not have prayers?" and they kneeled down and poured out their hearts to God; and the general left the sanctuary with a face all bathed in tears. Such soldiers do not fight for fame.

A Plea for the Reliable Gentleman

EVEN WITH THE WAR reaching deeper and deeper into the South, the Confederates could still laugh at themselves, though the humor was sometimes sardonic.

Here is a typical sketch by a Confederate humorist, a sketch that has application not only to the war of the Confederates but to all wars. The article appeared in *The Southern Illustrated News* with an illustration by the distinguished Confederate artist, W. L. Sheppard. Although unsigned, "A Plea for the Reliable Gentleman" was probably written by Dr. George W. Bagby.

A PLEA FOR THE RELIABLE GENTLEMAN.

"Adde parum parvo, magnum acervo erit."

If the barbarities of this "cruel" war are to be summed up at its close, none will strike a then calm and refrigerated public as more unprovoked and inhuman in their character than those which have been perpetrated upon that innocent and unoffending man now known as "The Reliable Gentleman," whose name has become a reproach in the house of his friends—if he has any—and a jest in the mouth of his enemies. An unfriendly press, which took him by the hand at the commencement of the war, has turned upon him with a merciless ferocity, and an unthinking people, taking the cue, have pursued him with unrelenting inhumanity. He is represented as wandering about on the railroads, with his carpet-bag full of the most marvellous stories with which to gull his fellow-citizens and take in unsuspecting newspaper reporters. Even his private character has been made the subject of animadversion, and we not unfrequently see allusions in the press to incorrect rumors which it says must have originated with The Reliable Gentleman, after taking "one snifter too many."

Now I know the charges against him are grave enough. After a heavy outlay of the old currency, I have succeeded in obtaining a copy of them. Among the more serious, I find that last spring he, in company with one Louis Napoleon, did recognize and declare free and independent, the Confederate States of America, and that shortly after The Reliable Gentleman, at the head of fifty thousand French troops, was on the Rio Grande, carpet-bag in hand, awaiting an opportunity to cross. A few weeks after he ran out of England with seven iron-clads, and was to break the blockade at Charleston all to flinders—if he ever reached it—which he didn't. On the 3d of July last, I find him charged with taking forty thousand prisoners at Gettysburg, but, owing to some difficulty in getting transportation for his carpet-bag or some other serious cause, failing to bring them into the Confederate lines. A few days before that, through his instrumentality, Grant lost sixty thousand men before Vicksburg by a "slow fever," and virtually gave up the siege. In another specification, he is accused of having arrived nine times at Spottswood Hotel, in company with a delegation from Illinois, empowered to form a treaty of peace with the Confederacy. He is charged, also, with having re-captured New Orleans (with the aid of the Mobile papers) almost every week since its fall, and with spending what time he had to spare from this operation in leading brigades of deserters from the Yankee army who were "tired of the war," and had thrown down their arms. In an exodus of this kind, other brigades have been represented as falling upon him fiercely, but only to result in those other brigades being "totally destroyed" by those centurions who had thrown down their arms. In the flanking business, his conduct (if the indictment were true, which I utterly deny) would appear to have been peculiarly flagrant. In company with some distinguished general, he is always on the enemy's flank, having just gotten through Snickers' Gap, or some other gap, in time to get a favorable opportunity to open on the unsuspecting foe, of whose artillery he has already pocketed two or three dozen pieces by way of an eye-opener. In those flank movements it is alleged that he is always with "the cavalry in hot pursuit," from which hot pursuit nothing is ever heard "at the War Department." The captured artillery is generally found to be entirely used up in those caloric chases, and is not sent down to the armory. These I believe may be set down as the more serious of the charges. His captures of immense wagon trains and some minor matters are omitted. Now against all these on behalf of The Reliable Gentleman, I put in an *alibi*. I shall contend that that much abused gentleman had no agency in the circulation of these reports, that he has been sitting down quietly at home, and that it is the Public which has deceived itself. Taking this Public for my jury, I shall submit the following statement of facts as evidence:

A few weeks since I traveled the entire length of one of the railroads in Virginia. I carried no baggage, with the exception of two baskets of postage stamps, given me by the conductor in taking my fare out of a Confederate I. O. U., and having nothing about me that any of the passengers could steal, I looked around with an unclouded mind. As we approached a station where a good deal of artillery had been encamped, I descried a tall countryman, (exempt from conscription, probably an account of his having no shoes and very few pantaloons that I could see,) sitting on a worm-fence. Just as we reached the station, this exempt, in reply to a question from a neighbor, used these remarkable words: "Yes! old Dillory moved it 'bout 9 o'clock this morning."

"Eh! what's that?" ejaculated a nervous gentleman in front of me; "all the artillery moved? 'Here, my friend, (to the man on the fence) do you know whether Captain Three-bars' battery went?'"

(Man on the fence)—"Cappen w-h-a-t?"

(Old gent, cars now moving off)—"Captain Three-bars' bat—"

Here the man was out of sight. "Bless my soul, this is too bad; I've got a son in that battery."

Here the old gentleman explained to his neighbor on the next seat that the man had said that all the artillery had moved up to the front at 9 o'clock, "and" he added, "they must be fighting by this time!"

At the next station, a countryman who was on the cars got off, and rushing up to a party of his chums at the grocery door, breathlessly jerked out the following information: "Fighting like thunder in front—commenced at 9 o'clock—been going it all day—Captain Three-bars killed—battery cut all to pieces—his father's on the train now—old man takes it mighty hard—we got the best of it—drove 'em ten miles—lots of prisoners."

Two stations below this the report had grown into such dimensions as to include Lieut. Gen Blanks' corps in the fight, and the capture of several thousand prisoners, the several being soon changed into the definitive numeral seven as a more satisfactory statement. A wounded cavalryman on the cars, (who *had* been in the skirmish the day before) was set upon and besieged with questions. He could not tell much of the "scrummage," as he had been wounded early in the day, and brought off, but though all might have happened which was stated, as "they was 'gaging in right peert, when he left."

I need not occupy your space with a detailed statement of how the rumor grew. When we reached the end of the road, the newspaper reporters rushed upon the scene, and in a remarkably short time had every thing every body knew, and a great deal they didn't know, winding up by carrying off the cavalryman bodily. The daily journals next morning contained the following:

"Highly Important from the Army—Heavy engagement Yesterday—Large Captures of Prisoners—Threebars' Battery Cut to Pieces:

"The city was much excited last evening by rumors of a heavy engagement which took place yesterday morning on the Cross-it-or-die river, in which our troops were victorious, routing the enemy with great slaughter, and taking seven thousand prisoners. From a conversation with a gentleman who was wounded in the action, and other passengers who came down on the train, we are enabled to give a brief but Gen. Blank. The infantry fighting commenced at daybreak, reliable account. The corps engaged on our side was that of and our artillery, which was ordered up at 9 o'clock, arrived on the ground in admirable condition, and opened fire about 11 o'clock. The fighting on both sides was of a most determined character, but an irresistible charge of our men broke the lines of the enemy, and the cowardly foe retreated in

great confusion, leaving 7,000 prisoners, including many field
officers, in our hands.

"Capt. Threebars' battery bore a most gallant part in the
action, and was literally cut to pieces. It repulsed seven distinct charges of three whole divisions of the enemy, the men
fighting with their rammers after their ammunition gave out.
One private killed twenty-seven of the enemy, including
three lieutenant colonels, with a priming wire. A gallant fellow, acting as No. 3 at the gun, used a thumb-stall so effectually that the ground for miles around him was strewed with
the slain. Capt. Threebars set a noble example to his men,
standing by his guns until pierced by nineteen 100-pounder
Parrot shells. His body was brought down on the train last
evening in charge of his afflicted father.

"The prisoners may be expected here some time this morning. No official details of this engagement had been received
at the war department last night, though something from
Gen. Blank may be expected during the day."

Now did The Reliable Gentleman do this? I respectfully
submit not; and gentlemen of the jury you will agree with
me. Well, now, let me read you an extract from the same
journals published the day after:

"It appears that the statements brought to this city night
before last by 'the reliable gentleman,' about the fight that
morning, were grossly exaggerated, so much so, indeed, that
that most veracious (?) gentleman is supposed to have been
under the effects of a drop too much when he communicated
the intelligence."

I am sure that if I were to rest the case of my client here,
my jury immediately upon retiring would find itself guilty of
murder in the first degree, and insist on being hung. This,
however, is not the object of The Reliable Gentleman, and to
calm the remorse of the jury I will cite a case to show that it

is not only in war matters that rumors grow without much aid, but that they thrive finely even in the social circle. I have a friend named Smith, a sober, amiable, peaceable man, who, I don't think, would intentionally hurt a chicken. Not long ago Smith threw a rock, and accidentally hitting Mrs. Jones' cat in his garden, killed it. He afterwards put the cat over the fence. Now, here is what I heard of Smith's character in company a few weeks afterwards: I heard that he drank; that he had a violent temper; that when this temper was up he was worse than an Indian, and didn't make anything of executing a war dance on top of the dinner-table, which he immediately followed up by falling upon his family and tomahawking a couple of them by way of keeping his hand in; that only a few weeks before he had seized a brickbat, knocked his neighbor, Mrs. Jones, off her fence, and then thrown her body over into the next yard!

With this conclusion, which I flatter myself is a settler, I rest the case of The Reliable Gentleman with a High-minded, Honorable, Intelligent and Just Public.

The Jews in Richmond

As a minority in the South (though they contributed the most distinguished member of President Davis' Cabinet) the Jews were attacked as speculators and shirkers. Here is Maximilian Michelbacher's defense of his people, published as a preface to the eminent rabbi's sermon delivered on one of the days of national prayer recommended by the President.

Brethren of the House of Israel: It is due to you, to whom I always speak of your faults, without fear, favour or affection, to say: I have carefully investigated your conduct from the commencement of this war to the present time, and I am happy in coming to the unbiassed conclusion, that you have fulfilled your duties as good citizens and as men, who love their country. It has been charged by both the ignorant and the evil-disposed against the people of our faith, that the Israelite does not fight in the battles of his country! All history attests the untruthfulness of this ungracious charge, generated in the cowardly hearts and born between the hypocritical lips of ungenerous and prejudiced foes. The Israelite

287

has never failed to defend the soil of his birth, or the land of his adoption—the Emperors of France and Russia will bear evidence to the verity of this assertion. In respect to those Israelites, who are now in the army of the Confederate States, I will merely say, that their patriotism and valor have never been doubted by such men as have the magnanimous souls of Lee, Johnston, Jackson and others of like manhood. The recorded votes and acts of the Israelites of this Confederacy, amply prove their devotion to the support of its Government. They well understand their duties as citizens and soldiers, and the young men do not require the persuasion of conscription to convert them into soldiers, to defend, as they verily believe, the only free government in North America. Many of our young men have been crippled for life, or slain upon the field of battle, in the service of the Confederate States, and there are several thousands yet coursing the campaigns of the war against those enemies of our Confederacy, who are as detestable to them, as were the Philistines to David and his countrymen.

The humanity and providence of the Israelite for the distressed families of the soldiers of our army, have allayed the pangs of poverty and brought comfort to households, wherein before were only seen hopelessness and misery. In this you have performed your duties as Israelites and as citizens—and, for this, may the God of our fathers shower upon you all the blessings which He confers upon His favourite children!

There is another cry heard, and it was even repeated in the Halls of Congress, that the Israelite is oppressing the people —that he is engaged in the great sin of speculating and extorting in the bread and meat of the land. To discover the character of this accusation, I have made due inquiry—the information I have acquired upon this head, from sources that extend from the Potomac to the Rio Grande, plainly present the fact, that the Israelites are not speculators nor extortioners. As traders and as merchants, they buy merchandise and sell the same *immediately*; the merchandise is never put aside, or hoarded to enhance its value, by withdrawing it from the market. Flour, meal, wheat, corn, bacon, beef, coal and wood are hardly ever found in the mercantile magazines or storehouses of the Israelite—he buys some of these articles for his own consumption, but he buys none of them to sell again—he does not extort—it is obvious to the most obtuse mind that the high prices of the Israelite would drive all his customers into the stores of his Christian neighbours; but is such the effect of the price of the Israelite's goods?

The peculiar characteristic of the Jewish merchant is seen in his undelayed, rapid and instant sales; his temperament does not allow him, by hoarding his goods, to risk time with his money, which, with him, is as restless as the waves of the sea that bears the ships that convey the manufactured goods of his customers. I thank God, that my investigation has proved to me that the cry against the Jew is a false one—this cry, though cunningly devised after the most approved model of villainy, will not subserve the base and unjust purpose of hindering the virtuous indignation of a suffering people, from tracing the true path of the extortioner, and awarding to him, who deals in the miseries, life and blood of our fellow-citizens, that punishment, which the traitor to the happiness and liberties of his country deserves to have measured unto him.

Spending the Seed Corn

As Sherman's army drove deep into Georgia, all the resources of the Confederacy and of the state were called upon to check the advance on Atlanta. President Davis relieved General Johnston as commander of the Confederate troops defending the city and replaced him with General John B. Hood. Time proved the inadequacy of the President's supposed remedy for a grave situation, but public opinion was demanding a general who would cease the withdrawals toward the city he was protecting and give issue to the campaign.

Georgia's governor, Joseph Emerson Brown, who had been among the severest critics of the administration, was now forced to use the men he had withheld from the Confederate Army by special state exemptions. Whole-hearted cooperation with General Hood might have done much to lighten the fix in which the Confederates found themselves, but, even on the brink of disaster, Governor Brown could make the transfer of men and ordnance to the use of the Confederacy full of difficulties.

Among local troops which participated in the futile defense of Atlanta was the body of cadets from the Georgia

Military Institute, a small school near Marietta which died with the war. The service of the cadets was inconsiderable, but it was typical of the spirit with which teenagers and old men alike came to the defense of their homes.

The Georgia cadets were typical of the spirit with which the whole people of the Confederacy waged war. The feats of individual youngsters are legion and uncounted. In Virginia another group of cadets, young soldiers from "Stonewall" Jackson's V.M.I. won a hard fight at New Market on May 15, 1864. The reports on the two groups of schoolboy soldiers follow.

Headquarters Battalion of Cadets,
And Georgia Military Institute,
Milledgeville, Oct. 27th, 1864.

Maj. Gen. H. C. Wayne,
    Adj. and Inspector General of Georgia.

Sir—Your order of the 12th, May 1864, to report myself to General Jos. E. Johnston commanding the Army of Tennessee and "to hold the corps of Cadets in readiness, to obey his orders during the present emergency," was joyfully received and promptly executed. The Cadets of the Georgia Military Institute, have sought active field service from the beginning of the war. This desire had become almost a passion. Under its influence we had lost our higher classes and might have lost the existence of the Institute, but for the hopes inspired by your reply to the petition of last year and their positive realization in your order of May 12th.

The service of the Battalion has been as follows. On the 27th of May, under a special field-order from General Johnston we reported to you in Atlanta, where you were organizing the Militia. By your order the Battalion was sent to West Point, where we remained until the third (3d) of July, when by order of Maj. General G. W. Smith, we reported for duty at Turner's Ferry on the Chattahoochee. There for the first time, the Cadets exchanged shots with the enemy. I remember with pride that the style of their march across the river on the afternoon of the 6th, under fire, elicited applause from veterans.

On the 12th July the following special order from General Johnston, detached the Battalion from General Smith's command, viz:

Headquarters Army of Tennessee,
July 12th, 1864, 11 A.M.

General:

General Johnston directs you to send the Battalion of Georgia State Cadets, Maj. Capers commanding, to West Point, Georgia, without delay.

Most respectfully, your obedient servant,

(Signed)   A. P. Mason,
Major & A. A. G.

On the 25th July the Battalion was ordered back to the division; and marched to position in the trenches of Atlanta, in the night of the 27th.

On the 14th August the Battalion was ordered here by his Excellency the Governor.

In no single instance, whatever may have been the duties

assigned them or the position occupied by them, have our expectations been disappointed in either the bearing or efficiency of the command. There was fatigue and blood and death in their ranks but no white feather.

Considering the nature of our services in the trenches and on the picket lines of Atlanta, we have reason to be grateful to God that our list of casualties is so small. . . .

Very respectfully,
Your obedient servant,

F. W. Capers,
Major Commanding.

✧   ✧   ✧   ✧   ✧

Head Quarters, Corps Cadets,
July 4, 1864.

General:

In obedience to General Orders, No. —, head quarters, Virginia Military Institute, June 27th, 1864, I have the honor to submit the following report of the operations of the corps of cadets, under my command in the field, from May 11th to June 25th, inclusive.

In obedience to orders from Maj. Gen. Breckinridge, communicated through you, at 7 A.M. on the morning of May 11th, the corps of cadets, consisting of a battalion of four companies of infantry, and a section of three inch rifle guns, took up the line of march for Staunton. The march to Staunton was accomplished in two days. I preceded the column, on the second day, some hours, for the purpose of reporting to Gen. Breckinridge, and was ordered by him to put the cadets in camp one mile south of Staunton. On the morning of the 13th I received orders to march at daylight on the road to

A gallant boy my love was born:
The Yankee name he holds in scorn;
He's always faithful, loving, brave,
And risks his life this land to save.
He knows right well how oft my thoughts
Hover around him day and night;
How oft to Heaven I upward look,
And pray for him, my life! my light!

George Dunn & Comp'y, Publishers, Richmond, Va.

294

I shall be a son of Mars
When Iv'e been at many wars,
When I show my cuts and scars
    To the sound of the drum.
But this nasty, weary drill.
Of it I have had my fill,
And if I had my will,
    To it would never come.
       [ARDENT RECRUIT

George Dunn & Comp'y, Publishers. Richmond, Va

Harrisonburg, taking position in the column in rear of Echols' brigade. We marched eighteen miles, and encamped—moved at daylight on the 14th, marched sixteen miles, and encamped. At 12 o'clock on the night of the 14th, received orders to prepare to march immediately, without *beat* of drum, and as noiselessly as possible. We moved from camp at half past one o'clock, taking position in the general column, in rear of Echols' brigade, being followed by the column of artillery under the command of Major McLaughlin. Having accomplished a distance of six miles, and approached the position of the enemy, as indicated by occasional skirmishing with his pickets in front, a halt was called, and we remained on the side of the road two or three hours, in the midst of a heavy fall of rain. The general having determined to receive the attack of the enemy, made his dispositions for battle, posting the corps in reserve. He informed me that he did not wish to *put the cadets in,* if he could avoid it, but that should occasion require it, he would use them very freely. He was also pleased to express his confidence in them, and I am happy to believe that his expectations were not disappointed, for when the tug of battle came, they bore themselves gallantly and well.

The enemy not making the attack as was anticipated, or not advancing as rapidly as was desired, the line was deployed into column, and the advance resumed. Here I was informed by one of Gen. Breckinridge's aids, that my battalion, together with the battalion of Col. G. M. Edgar, would constitute the reserve, and was instructed to keep the section of artillery with the column, and to take position, after the deployments should have been made, 250 or 300 yards in rear of the front line of battle, and to maintain that distance. Having begun a flank movement to the left, about two miles south of New Market, the nature of the ground was such as to render it impossible that the artillery should continue with the infantry column. I ordered Lieut. Minge to join the general artillery column in the main road, and to report to Major McLaughlin; after that, I did not see the section of artillery until near the close of the engagement. Major McLaughlin, under whose command they served, was pleased to speak of the section in such complimentary terms, that I was satisfied they had done their duty. Continuing the advance on the ground to the left of the main road, and south of New Market, at 12½ P.M. we came under the fire of the enemy's batteries. Having advanced a quarter of a mile under the fire, we were halted, and the column was deployed, the march up to this time having been by flank in column. The ground in front was open, with skirts of woods on the left. The General's plans seem to have undergone some modification. Instead of one line, with a reserve, he formed his infantry in two, artillery in rear and to the right; the cavalry deployed and guarding the right flank, left flank resting on a stream. Wharton's brigade of infantry constituted the first line; Echols' brigade the second; the battalion of cadets, brigaded with Echols, was the last battalion but one from the left of the second line, Edgar's battalion being on the left. The lines having been adjusted, the order to advance was passed. As Wharton's line ascended a knoll, it came in full view of the enemy's batteries, which opened a heavy fire, but not having gotten the range, did but little damage. By the time the second line reached the same ground, the Yankee gunners had gotten the exact range, and their fire began to tell on our line with fearful accuracy. It was here that Captain Hill and others fell. Great gaps were made through the ranks; but the cadet, true to his discipline, would close in to the centre to fill the interval, and push steadily forward. The alignment of the battalion, under this terrible fire, which strewed the ground with killed and wounded for more than a mile, on open ground, would have been creditable even on a field day.

The advance was thus continued until, having passed Bushong's house, a mile or more beyond New Market, and still to the left of the main road, the enemy's batteries, at 250 or 300 yards, opened upon us with canister and case shot, and their long lines of infantry were put into action at the same time. The fire was withering. It seemed impossible that any living creature could escape; and here we sustained our heaviest loss, a great many being wounded, and numbers knocked down, stunned, and temporarily disabled. I was here disabled for a time, and the command devolved upon Capt. H. A. Wise, company A. He gallantly pressed onward. We had before this gotten into the front line. Our line took a position behind a fence. A brisk fusillade ensued; a shout; a rush—and the day was won. The enemy fled in confusion, leaving killed, wounded, artillery and prisoners in our hands. Our men pursued in hot haste, until it became necessary to halt, draw ammunition, and re-establish the lines for the purpose of driving them from their last position on Rude's hill, which they held with cavalry and artillery to cover the passage of the river, about a mile in their rear. Our troops charged and took the position without loss. The enemy withdrew, crossed the river, and burnt the bridge. The engagement closed at 6½ P.M. The cadets did their duty, as the long list of casualties will attest. Numerous instances of gallantry might be mentioned—but I have thought it better to refrain from specifying individual cases, for fear of making invidious distinctions, or from want of information, withholding praise where it may have been justly merited. It had rained almost incessantly during the battle, and at its termination the cadets were well nigh exhausted. Wet, hungry, and many of them shoeless—for they had lost their shoes and socks in the deep mud through which it was necessary to march—they bore their hardships with that uncomplaining resignation, which characterizes the true soldier. . . .

I am, General, very respectfully,
Your obedient servant,

S. Ship,
Lieut. Col. and Commandant

Maj. Gen. F. H. Smith, Superintendent

Peace Negotiations

A N *Address* of the Confederate Congress in 1864
summed up the situation and reiterated the South's
desire for peace. It was interpreted by amateur peace-
makers as an invitation to negotiations to end the war.
The most important of several abortive attempts at peace
was the mission of Colonel James F. Jacquess and J. R.
Gilmore to Richmond.

Jacquess and Gilmore came with the knowledge of
Lincoln, but they were not sent by him. Their representations gained them an audience with President Davis,
but the conversations reached a stalemate on Davis' in-
sistence on the already published Confederate conditions
for peace—terms which had not altered from the outbreak
of the war.

The conferees in Richmond agreed upon secrecy, but
accounts of the conference were printed in the North,
and Secretary of State Judah P. Benjamin felt free to
release to the public the letter he had written Commissioner James M. Mason in Paris as a report of the
conference.

DEPARTMENT OF STATE. ⎱
Richmond, Va., August 25, 1864. ⎰

Sir,—Numerous publications which have recently appeared
in the journals of the United States on the subject of informal
overtures for peace between two Federations of States now at
war on this continent, render it desirable that you should be
fully advised of the views and policy of this Government on a
matter of such paramount importance. It is likewise proper
that you should be accurately informed of what has occurred
on the several occasions mentioned in the published statements.

You have heretofore been furnished with copies of the
manifesto issued by the Congress of the Confederate States,
with the approval of the President, on the 14th June last, and
have doubtless, acted in conformity with the resolution which
requested that copies of this manifesto should be laid before
foreign governments. "The principles, sentiments, and purposes, by which these States have been, and are still actuated," are set forth in that paper with all the authority due
to the solemn declaration of the Legislative and Executive
Departments of this Government, and with a clearness which
leaves no room for comment or explanation.—In a few sentences it is pointed out that all we ask is immunity from interference with our internal peace and prosperity "and to be
left in the undisturbed enjoyment of those inalienable rights
of life, liberty, and the pursuit of happiness, which our common ancestors declared to be the equal heritage of all parties
to the social compact. Let them forbear aggressions upon us,
and the war is at an end. If there be questions which require
adjustment by negotiation, we have ever been willing, and
are still willing, to enter into communication with our adversaries in a spirit of peace, of equity, and manly frankness."

The manifesto closed with the declaration that "we commit our cause to the enlightened judgment of the world, to the sober reflections of our adversaries themselves, and to the solemn and righteous arbitrament of Heaven."

Within a very few weeks after the publication of this manifesto, it seemed to have met with a response from President Lincoln. In the early part of last month a letter was received by General LEE from Lieutenant-General GRANT, in the following words:

"Headquarters Armies of the United States,
"City Point, Va., July 8, 1864.

"General R. E. LEE, commanding Confederate forces near Petersburg, Virginia:

"GENERAL,—I would request that Colonel JAMES F. JACQUESS, Seventy-third Illinois volunteer infantry, and J. R. GILMORE, Esq., be allowed to meet Colonel ROBERT OULD, Commissioner for the Exchange of Prisoners, at such a place between the lines of the two armies as you may designate. The object of the meeting is legitimate with the duties of Colonel OULD as Commissioner.

"If not consistent for you to grant the request here asked, I would beg that this be referred to President DAVIS for his action.

"Requesting as early an answer to this communication as you may find it convenient to make, I subscribe myself,

"Very respectfully, Your ob't serv'nt,

"U. S. GRANT.
"Lieutenant-General, U. S. A."

On the reference of this letter to the President, he authorized Colonel Ould to meet the persons named in General Grant's letter; and Colonel Ould, after seeing them, returned to Richmond, and reported to the President, in the presence of the Secretary of War and myself that Messrs. Jacquess and Gilmore had not said anything to him about his duties as Commissioner for Exchange of Prisoners, but that they asked permission to come to Richmond for the purpose of seeing the President; that they came with the knowledge and approval of President Lincoln, and under his pass; that they were informal messengers, sent with a view of paving the way for a meeting of formal commissioners authorized to negotiate for peace, and desired to communicate to President Davis the views of Mr. Lincoln, and to obtain the President's views in return, so as to arrange for a meeting of commissioners. Colonel Ould stated that he had told them repeatedly that it was useless to come to Richmond to talk of peace on any other terms than the recognized independence of the Confederacy, to which they said that they were aware of that, and that they were, nevertheless, confident that their interview would result in peace. The President, on this report of Colonel Ould, determined to permit them to come to Richmond under his charge.

On the evening of the 16th of July, Colonel Ould conducted these gentlemen to a hotel in Richmond, where a room was provided for them, in which they were to remain under surveillance during their stay here, and the next morning I received the following letter:

"SPOTSWOOD HOUSE
"RICHMOND, VA., JULY 17, 1864.

"*Hon.* J. P. BENJAMIN, *Secretary of State of Confederate States of America:*

"DEAR SIR,—The undersigned, JAMES F. JACQUESS, of Illinois, and JAMES R. GILMORE, of Massachusetts, most respectfully solicit an interview with President DAVIS. They visit Richmond as private citizens, and have no official character or authority; but they are fully possessed of the views of the United States Government relative to an adjustment of the differences now existing between the North and the South and have little doubt that a free interchange of views between President DAVIS and themselves would open the way to such *official* negotiations as would ultimate in restoring PEACE to the two sections of our distracted country.

"They therefore ask an interview with the President, and, awaiting your reply, are

> "Most truly and respectfully,
> > "Your obedient servants,
> >
> > "JAMES F. JACQUESS,
> > "JAMES R. GILMORE."

The word "official" is underscored, and the word "peace" doubly understored, in the original.

After perusing the letter, I invited Colonel Ould to conduct the writers to my office; and on their arrival, stated to them that they must be conscious they could not be admitted to an interview with the president without informing me more fully of the object of their mission, and satisfying me that they came by request of Mr. Lincoln. Mr. Gilmore replied that they came unofficially, but with the knowledge, and at the desire, of Mr. Lincoln; that they thought the war had gone far enough; that it could never end except by some sort of agreement; that the agreement might as well be made now as after further bloodshed; that they knew by the recent address of the Confederate Congress that we were willing to make peace; that they admitted that proposals ought to come from the North, and that they were prepared to make these proposals by Mr. Lincoln's authority; that it was necessary to have a sort of informal understanding in advance of regular negotiations, for if commissioners were appointed without some such understanding, they would meet, quarrel, and separate, leaving the parties more bitter against each other than before; that they knew Mr. Lincoln's views, and would state them if pressed by the President to do so, and desired to learn his in return.

I again insisted on some evidence that they came from Mr. Lincoln; and in order to satisfy me, Mr. Gilmore referred to the fact that permission for their coming through our lines had been asked officially by General Grant in a letter to General Lee, and that General Grant in that letter had asked that this request should be referred to President Davis. Mr. Gilmore then showed me a card, written and signed by Mr. Lincoln requesting General Grant to aid Mr. Gilmore and friend in passing through his lines into the Confederacy. Colonel Jacquess then said that his name was not put on the card for the reason that it was earnestly desired that their visit should be kept secret; and he had come into the Confederacy a year ago, and had visited Petersburg on a similar errand, and that it was feared if his name should become known, that some of those who had formerly met him in Petersburg would conjecture the purpose for which he now came. He said that the terms of peace which they would offer to the President would be honorable to the Confederacy; that they did not desire that the Confederacy should accept any other terms, but would be glad to have my promise, as they gave theirs, that their visit should be kept a profound secret if it failed to result in peace; that it would not be just that either party should seek any advantage by divulging the fact of their overture for peace, if unsuccessful. I assented to this request, and then, rising, said: "Do I understand you to state distinctly that you come as messengers from Mr. Lincoln for the purpose of agreeing with the President as to the proper mode of inaugurating a formal negotiation for peace, charged by Mr. Lincoln with authority for stating his own views and receiving those of President Davis?" Both answered in the affirmative, and I then said that the President would see them at my office the same evening at 9 P.M.; that, at least, I presumed he would, but if he objected, after hearing my report, they should be informed. They were then recommitted to the charge of Colonel Ould, with the understanding that they were to be reconducted to my office at the appointed hour unless otherwise directed.

This interview, connected with the report previously made by Colonel Ould, left on my mind the decided impression that Mr. Lincoln was averse to sending formal commissioners to open negotiations, lest he might thereby be deemed to have recognized the independence of the Confederacy, and that he was anxious to learn whether the conditions on which alone he would be willing to take such a step would be yielded by the Confederacy; that with this view he had placed his messengers in a condition to satisfy us that they really came from him, without committing himself to anything in the event of a disagreement as to such conditions as he considered to be indispensable. On informing the President, therefore, of my conclusions, he determined that no question of form or etiquette should be an obstacle to his receiving any overtures that promised, however remotely, to result in putting an end to the carnage which marked the continuance of hostilities.

The President came to my office at 9 o'clock in the evening, and Colonel Ould came a few moments later, with Messrs. Jacquess and Gilmore. The President said to them that he had heard, from me, that they came as messengers of peace from

Mr. Lincoln; that as such they were welcome; that the Confederacy had never concealed its desire for peace, and that he was ready to hear whatever they had to offer on that subject.

Mr. Gilmore then addressed the President, and in a few minutes had conveyed the information that these two gentlemen had come to Richmond impressed with the idea that this Government would accept a peace on the basis of a reconstruction of the Union, the abolition of slavery, and the grant of an amnesty to the people of the States as repentant criminals. In order to accomplish the abolition of slavery, it was proposed that there should be a general vote of all the people of both federations, in mass, and the majority of the vote thus taken was to determine that as well as all other disputed questions. These were stated to be Mr. Lincoln's views. The President answered, that as these proposals had been prefaced by the remark that the people of the North were a majority, and that a majority ought to govern, the offer was, in effect, a proposal that the Confederate States should surrender at discretion, admit that they had been wrong from the beginning of the contest, submit to the mercy of their enemies, and avow themselves to be in need of pardon for crimes; that extermination was preferable to such dishonor.

He stated that if they were themselves so unacquainted with the form of their own government as to make such propositions, Mr. Lincoln ought to have known, when giving them his views, that it was out of the power of the Confederate Government to act on the subject of the domestic institutions of the several States, each State having exclusive jurisdiction on that point, still less to commit the decision of such a question to the vote of a foreign people; that the separation of the States was an accomplished fact: that he had no authority to receive proposals for negotiation except by virtue of his office as President of an independent confederacy; and on this basis alone must proposals be made to him.

At one period of the conversation, Mr. Gilmore made use of some language referring to these States as "rebels" while rendering an account of Mr. Lincoln's views, and apologized for the word. The President desired him to proceed, that no offence was taken, and that he wished Mr. Lincoln's language to be repeated to him as exactly as possible. Some further conversation took place, substantially to the same effect as the foregoing, when the President rose to indicate that the interview was at an end. The two gentlemen were then recommitted to the charge of Colonel Ould, and left Richmond the next day.

This account of the visit of Messrs. Gilmore and Jacquess to Richmond has been rendered necessary by publications made by one or both of them since their return to the United States, notwithstanding the agreement that their visit was to be kept secret. They have, perhaps, concluded that as the promise of secrecy was made at their request, it was permissible to disregard it. We had no reason for desiring to conceal what occurred, and have therefore, no complaint to make of the publicity given to the fact of the visit. The extreme inaccuracy of Mr. Gilmore's narrative will be apparent to you from the foregoing statement.

You have no doubt seen, in the Northern papers, an account of another conference on the subject of peace, which took place in Canada, at about the same date, between Messrs. C. C. Clay and J. P. Holcombe, Confederate citizens of the highest character and position, and Mr. Horace Greeley, of New York, acting with authority of President Lincoln. It is deemed not improper to inform you that Messrs. Clay and Holcombe, although enjoying, in an eminent degree, the confidence and esteem of the President, were strictly accurate in their statement that they were without any authority from this Government to treat with that of the United States on any subject whatever. We had no knowledge of their conference with Mr. Greeley, nor of their proposed visit to Washington, till we saw the newspaper publications. A significant confirmation of the truth of the statement of Messrs. Gilmore and Jacquess, that they came as messengers from Mr. Lincoln, is to be found in the fact that the views of Mr. Lincoln, as stated by them to the President, are in exact conformity with the offensive paper addressed to "whom it may concern," which was sent by Mr. Lincoln to Messrs. Clay and Holcombe by the hands of his private secretary, Mr. Hay, and which was properly regarded by those gentlemen as an intimation that Mr. Lincoln was unwilling that this war should cease while in his power to continue hostilities.

I am, very respectfully,
Your obedient servant,

J. P. BENJAMIN,
Secretary of State.

HON. JAMES M. MASON, Commissioner to the Continent, &c., &c., &c., PARIS

Victories in the Indian Territory

THE WAR in the West was sometimes forgotten in the rush of political and military activity in Virginia and Georgia and has almost as often been overlooked by historians of the war. It raged with its particular kind of guerrilla fury and produced its particular kind of heroes and heroism. The Confederates made good use of the Indian troops and worked with them effectively in the Indian Territory.

Events in the fall of 1864 called forth three General Orders which were printed in pamphlet form so that the soldiers of the West could send them to their families as mementos of a memorable campaign.

CIRCULAR.

HEAD QUARTERS, DIST. IND. TER'Y.⎱
Fort Towson, C. N., Oct. 17th, 1864. ⎰

There having been many applications within the last few days for copies of Gen'l Orders No. 61, current series from these Head Quarters, the Major General Commanding this

310

military District has ordered that another supply embracing General Orders No. 81 current series from Head Quarters Trans-Mississippi Department, and General Orders No. 26, current series from Gen'l Cooper's Head Quarters, be printed for the use of the troops of this District, to enable them to furnish copies to their friends at home.

By Order of   MAJOR GEN'L. MAXEY

T. M. Scott, A. A. Gen'l.

HEAD QUARTERS INDIAN DIVISION.}
Camp Bragg. Sept. 30th, 1864.

GENERAL ORDERS}
No. 26.

I. The thanks of this command are hereby tendered to the gallant officers and men, of Gano's & Watie's Brigades and Howell's Battery, for the signal successes they have gained over the enemy within his lines, and in rear of his fortifications, north of the Arkansas River by destroying his Forage Camps and capturing a magnificent train of 255 loaded wagons, and other property (valued at one and one half millions of dollars in U. S. currency) a large proportion of which they secured and brought out, marching over 300 miles in fourteen days, engaging the enemy victoriously four times, with small loss on our side in numbers. We mourn the death of the honored few, among them the promising young soldier, Adjt. D. R. Patterson of he Seminole Regiment whose career of usefulness was suddenly terminated at Cabin Creek, while at the side of the gallant Chieftain John Jumper charging the enemy's right. The enemy lost 97 killed, many wounded and 111 prisoners. The brilliancy and completeness of this expedition has not been excelled in the history of the war. Firm, brave and confident, the officers had but to order and the men cheerfully executed. The whole having been conducted, with perfect harmony between the war-worn veterans, Stand Watie, the chivalrous Gano and their respective commands, ending with the universal expression that they may again participate in like enterprises. The commanding Genl. hopes that they, and the rest of the command may soon have an opportunity to gather fresh laurels on other fields.

II. In the departure of Genl. Gano he takes the best wishes of the Comdg. Gen'l. and it is a matter of pride to record, in General Orders, the gallant bearing, energy and promptness which has characterized that officer in the execution of every order and instruction—from his brilliant dash at Diamond Grove, to the splendid achievement at Cabin Creek. While the circumstances attending require his immediate transfer, the Comdg. Gen'l hopes that it may be of short duration.

By Command of   BRIG. GEN'L. D. H. COOPER.

T. B. HEISTON, Capt. A. A. Gen'l.

———

HEAD QUARTERS, DIST. IND. TER'Y.⎫
Fort Towson C. N., Oct. 7th, 1864.   ⎭

GENERAL ORDERS⎫
No. 61   ⎭

The Major General Commanding announces with pride and pleasure the series of brilliant victories on the 16th, 17th, 19th and 20th ultimo, north of the Arkansas River, by the Troops under the leadership of the gallant and chivalrous Gano, and the noble old hero Stand Watie, accompanied by Howell's Battery.

Of this expedition Gen. Gano in his official Report says:

"For three days and nights our boys were without sleep, except such as they could snatch in the saddle or at watering places.

"They dug down banks, cut out trees, rolled wagons and Artillery up hill and down by hand, kept cheerful and never wearied in the good cause, and came into Camps, all rejoicing on the 28th.

"We were out fourteen days, marched over four hundred miles, killed ninety-seven, wounded many, and captured one hundred and eleven prisoners, burned six thousand tons of hay, and all the reapers and mowers, destroyed altogether (from the Federals) one and a half millions of dollars worth of property, bringing safely into our lines nearly one third of that amount estimated in Green Back."

Officers and men behaved gallantly. Of Gen. Watie, he says, "Gen. Watie was by my side, cool and brave as ever."

Of the whole command he says: "The men all did their duty and laid up for themselves imperishable honors."

Throughout the expedition I am rejoiced to say perfect harmony and good will prevailed between the white and Indian troops, all striving for the common good of our beloved country.

For gallantry, energy, enterprise, dash and judgment, and completeness of success, this raid has not been surpassed during the war.

The Major General Commanding deems this a fit occasion to say that not the least of the glorious results of this splendid achievement is the increased cheerfulness and confidence of all in their prowess, and ability to whip anything like equal numbers. Throughout the year the MORALE of the command has been steadily on the increase. For the Troops of the Indian Territory, this has been a year of brilliant success.

Your Arkansas campaign is part of the recorded history of the country.

Since your return, almost every part of the command has been engaged.

A steam boat laden with valuable stores has been captured, a regiment has been almost demolished in sight of the guns of Fort Smith, the survivors captured and the camp destroyed.

Many guns and pistols have been taken,—mail after mail has been captured,—hay camps almost without number have been destroyed and the hay burned; horses, mules and cattle have been wrested from the enemy and driven into our lines. Vast amounts of Sutlers Stores have been captured. Wagons have been burned in gun shot of Fort Smith; the enemy has been virtually locked up in his Forts, and your successes have culminated in this most glorious victory, over which the Telegraph informs us the enemy is *now* wailing.

In our rejoicings let us not forget our gallant comrades in arms who have offered up their lives upon their country's altar of Freedom, priceless sacrifices to their country's redemption. If there be widows and orphans of these gallant men seek them out and deliver this poor tribute to their worth.

And let us remember the sufferings of our wounded, and offer them the tears of sympathy.

Soldiers! There is a cruel enemy still cursing your country. There is still work to do. You have proven what you can do —Remember that strict and cheerful obedience to orders, strict discipline, and thorough drill, will render you still more efficient as soldiers of the holy cause. Your Commanding General has every confidence in your ability and willingness to take and perform any part you may yet have in the ensuing campaign.

II. It is ordered that this order be read at the head of every regiment and battalion, and company of artillery, and at every post in this District.

III. A copy will be forwarded of this order and the commendatory order of Brig. Gen. D. H. Cooper, to the Head Quarters Trans-Mississippi Department.

S. B. MAXEY.
Maj. Gen'l. Comdg.

Official,
    M. L. BELL   A. A. Gen'l.

HEAD QUARTERS, TRANS-MISS. DEPARTMENT,
Shreveport, La., Oct. 12th, 1864.

GENERAL ORDERS, }
    No. 81   }

The General Commanding announces to the army the complete success of one of the most brilliant raids of the war.

The expedition under Brigadier Generals Gano and Stand Watie, penetrating far within the enemy's lines, has captured his forage camp and train, destroyed five thousand tons of hay, and brought out one hundred and thirty captured wagons, loaded with stores, after destroying as many more, which were disabled in the action.

These, with one hundred and thirty-five prisoners, and more than two hundred of the enemy killed and wounded, attest the success of the expedition.

The celerity of the movement, the dash of the attack, and their entire success, entitle the commands engaged to the thanks of the country.

By command of   GEN'L. E. KIRBY SMITH.

S. S. ANDERSON, A. Ad't. Gen'l.

Sherman in Atlanta

S HERMAN had whipped Hood at Peachtree Creek in late July. Hard battles around the city sealed the fate of Atlanta. After the battle at Jonesboro on September 2, Atlanta's ordnance stores were fired and Hood's soldiers marched out of the city to the plaintive strains of "Lorena."

Inspired by a visit from President Davis, Hood set to harassing Sherman's lines of communication and promised a drive to the north through Tennessee. Unperturbed, Sherman prepared to continue his March Through Georgia as a March to the Sea. The following informal report of Yankee doings in Atlanta was published on Turnwold Plantation (near Eatonton, Georgia)—in the line of march toward Savannah—just the day before Sherman turned his men south from Atlanta.

Eatonton, Ga., Nov. 4, 1864.

J. A. Turner, Esq.,

Dear Sir:— At your request, I have written down all the points of interest, furnished me by my friend, connected with her leaving Atlanta, &c. I have written it hastily, and leave it for you to condense, as you may deem proper. Hoping its publication may prove of some interest to your readers, I proceed, as follows:

I had pleasure of meeting with a very intelligent lady, a few days since, one of the exiles from Atlanta, under the late order of Gen. Sherman, banishing the citizens from that place, who furnished me with some facts, which may prove of interest to your readers. As soon as the yankees obtained possession of the city, the officers began to hunt up comfortable quarters, and the lady of whom I speak, found herself under the necessity of taking three of them as boarders, or of submitting to the confiscation of her house to the purpose of sheltering our foe. Those who boarded with Mrs. —— proved to be very gentlemanly fellows, and rendered her service in protecting her from the intrusion of the private soldiers, besides aiding her in disposing of her cows, and hogs, when she was compelled to leave. A neighbor of hers, whose husband had rendered himself obnoxious to the yankees, by his service to the south, was ordered by a yankee general, to vacate her premises, in two hours, and a guard was stationed to prevent her from moving her effects. This lady appealed to Gen. Sherman, who immediately ordered the removal of the guard, and permitted her to remove, or sell, any, or all, of her furniture, and other valuables, at her discretion. The lady with whom I conversed, was under the necessity of calling upon Gen. Sherman, after the publication of the edict of banishment, and she represents him as being very kind, and conciliatory in his deportment towards her, and others who visited him. He expressed much regret at the necessity which compelled him to order the citizens of Atlanta from their homes, but stated, in justification of his course, that he intended to make Atlanta a second Gibraltar; that when he completed his defensive works, it would be impregnable; and as no communication could be held with their friends, in the south, they (the citizens) would suffer for food; that it was impossible for him to subsist his army, and feed the citizens, too, by a single line of railroad; and that as he intended to hold Atlanta, at all hazards, he thought it was humanity to send them out of the city, where they could obtain necessary supplies. He took the little child of my friend in his arms, and patted her rosy cheeks, calling her "a poor little exile," and saying he was sorry to have to drive her away from her comfortable home, but that war was a cruel, and inexorable thing, and its necessities compelled him to do many things, which he heartily regretted. in conversation with the lady, he paid a just and well merited tribute to the valor of our arms. He remarked, that it would be no disgrace to us, if we were finally subjugated—as we certainly would be—as we had fought against four or five times our number, with a degree of valor which had excited the admiration of the world; and that the United States government would gain no honor, nor credit, if they succeeded in their purposes, as they had thus far failed, with five men in the field, to our one. He regarded the southern soldiers as the bravest in the world, and admitted, that in a fair field fight, we could whip them two to our one, but he claimed for himself, and his compeers, the credit of possessing more strategic ability than our generals. "You can beat us in fighting, madam," said he, "but we can out-manœuvre you; your generals do not work half enough; we work day and night, and spare no labor, nor pains, to carry out our plans."

Referring to his evacuation of the trenches, around the city, he asked the lady, if they did not all think he was retreating; and when she replied that some did think so, he laughed heartily at the idea and remarked, "I played Hood a real *yankee trick*, that time, didn't I? He thought I was running away, but he soon had to pull up stakes, and run himself." (I wonder whose turn it is to laugh now?)

The lady, from whom these facts were obtained, says that Sherman had a vast number of applications from ladies, and others, in reference to their moving, and that, as far as she could learn, he was very patient, gentlemanly, and obliging, as much so as he could be to them consistently with his prescribed policy. He permitted her to bring out her horse, and rockaway, although his army was greatly needing horses at the time; and, also, to send her provisions to some suffering relatives within his lines. She speaks in high terms of the discipline of the yankee army; says that the privates are more afraid of their officers than our slaves are of their masters, and that, during her stay, there was no disorderly conduct to be seen anywhere, but that quiet, and good order, prevailed throughout the city.

An instance of yankee kindness deserves to be mentioned here: A widow lady, whose husband had been a member of the masonic fraternity, died, shortly after the occupation of the city by the enemy. The yankee officers gave her remains a decent and respectable burial, and took her three orphan children, and sent them to their own homes, to be educated at some masonic institute, at the north.

From the facts which I report, on the authority of a lady

of unquestioned veracity, and respectability, it will be seen that our barbarous foes are not entirely lost to all the dictates, and impulses of humanity. Would to God that the exhibition of it were more frequent in their occurrence.

Respectfully, yours,

Geo. G. N. MacDonell.

In a Yankee Prison

O F THE THOUSANDS of Confederates who spent months
or years in Federal prisons at Point Lookout, Fort
Warren, Johnson's Island, Elmira, and other prison pens
during the war, only three told their stories in books for
the homefolks. One of these was Anthony M. Keiley, a
prominent citizen of Petersburg, who was taken prisoner
early in 1864 and spent five months at Point Lookout and
Elmira before he was exchanged through the lines.

Keiley's account of his experiences paints little prettier
a picture of the Yankee camps that the Union soldiers'
stories did of Andersonville, Millen, Salisbury, and other
Southern prisons. In the chapter that follows he describes
the routine at Point Lookout, Maryland.

The routine of prison-life at Point Lookout was as follows:
Between dawn and sunrise a "reveille" horn summoned us
into line by companies, ten of which constituted each division—of which I have before spoken—and here the roll was
called. This performance is hurried over with as much haste
as is ascribed to certain marital ceremonies in a poem that it

would be obviously improper to make more particular allusion to—and those whose love of a nap predominates over fear of the Yankees usually tumble in for another snooze. About 8 o'clock the breakfasting begins. This operation consists in the forming of the companies again into line, and introducing them under lead of their Sergeants, into the mess-rooms, where a slice of bread and a piece of pork or beef—lean in the former and fat in the latter being contraband of war— are placed at intervals of about twenty inches apart. The meat is usually about four or five ounces in weight. These we seized upon, no one being allowed to touch a piece, however, until the whole company entered, and each man was in position opposite his ration (universally *and properly* pronounced *raytion*, among our enemies, as it is almost as generally called, with the "a" short among ourselves). . . . The men then busy themselves with the numberless occupations, which the fertility of American genius suggests, of which I will have something to say hereafter, until dinner time, when they are again carried to the mess-houses, where another slice of bread, and rather over a half pint of a watery slop, by courtesy called "soup," greets the eyes of such ostrich-stomached animals, as can find comfort in that substitute for nourishment. About sundown the roll is again called, on a signal by the horn, and an hour after, "taps" sounds, when all are required to be in their quarters—and this, in endless repetition and without a variation, is the routine life of prison.

The Sanitary Commission, a benevolent association of exempts in aid of the Hospital Department of the Yankee army, published in July last, a "Narrative of Sufferings of United States Officers and Soldiers, Prisoners of War," in which a parallel is drawn, between the treatment of prisoners on both sides, greatly to the disadvantage of course, of "Dixie."

Among other statements, in glorification of the humanity of the Great Republic, is one on page 89, from Miss Dix, the grand female dry nurse of Yankee Doodle, who by the by, gives unpardonable offence to the pulchritude of Yankeedom by persistently *refusing to employ any but ugly women as nurses*—the vampire—which affirms that the prisoners at Point Lookout, "were supplied with vegetables, with the best of wheat bread, and fresh and salt meat three times daily in abundant measures."

Common gallantry forbids the characterization of this remarkable extract in harsher terms than to say it is untrue *in every particular*.

It is quite likely that some Yankee official at Point Lookout, made this statement to the benevolent itinerant, and her only fault may be in suppressing the fact that she *"was informed,"* &c., &c. But it is altogether inexcusable in the Sanitary Commission, to attempt to palm such a falsehood upon the world, knowing its falsity, as they must. For my part, I never saw any one get enough of any thing to eat at Point Lookout, except the soup, and a tea spoonful of that was *too much* for ordinary digestion.

These digestive discomforts are greatly enhanced by the villainous character of the water, which is so impregnated with some mineral as to offend every nose, and induce diarrhoea in almost every alimentary canal. It colors every thing black in which it is allowed to rest, and a scum rises on the top of a vessel if it is left standing during the night, which reflects the prismatic colors as distinctly as the surface of a stagnant pool. Several examinations of this water have been made by chemical analysis, and they have uniformly resulted in its condemnation by scientific men, but the advantages of the position to the Yankees, so greatly counterbalance any claim of humanity, that Point Lookout is likely to remain a prison camp until the end of the war, especially as there are wells outside of "the Pen," which are not liable to these charges, the water of which is indeed perfectly pure and wholesome, so that the Yanks suffer no damage therefrom. I was not surprised therefore on my return to the Point, after three months absence, to find many preparations looking to the permanent occupancy of the place. It has already served the purposes of a prison, since the 25th of July, 1863, when the Gettysburg prisoners, or a large portion of them, were sent thither from the "Old Capitol," Fort McHenry and Fort Delaware, and the chances are that it will play the part of a jail until the period of the promised redemption of our National Currency.

Another local inconvenience is, the exposed location of the post. Situated on a low tongue of land jutting out into the bay, and, as I have before remarked, but a few inches above ordinary high tide, it is visited in winter by blasts whose severity has caused the death of several of the well-clad sentinels, even, altho' during the severest portion of the winter of 1863-4, they were relieved every thirty minutes— two hours being the usual time of guard duty. And when a strong easterly gale prevails for many hours in winter, a large portion of the camp is flooded by the sea, which finds convenient access by means of ditches constructed for the drainage of camp. When this calamity befalls the men, their case is pitiable indeed. The supply of wood issued to the prisoners during the winter was not enough to keep up the most moderate fires for two hours out of the twenty-four, and the only possible way of avoiding freezing, was by unremitting devotion to the blankets. This, however, became impossible when everything was afloat, and I was not surprised, therefore, to hear some pitiable tales of suffering during the past winter from this cause.

This latter evil might be somewhat mitigated but for a barbarous regulation peculiar, I believe, to this "pen," under which the Yanks stole from us any bed clothing we might possess, *beyond one blanket!* This petty larceny was effected through an instrumentality they call *inspections.* Once in every ten days an inspection is ordered, when all the prisoners turn out in their respective divisions and companies in *marching order.* They range themselves in long lines between the rows of tents, with their blankets and haversacks—those being the only articles considered orthodox possessions of a rebel. A Yankee inspects each man, taking away his extra blanket, if he has one, and appropriating any other superfluity he may chance to possess, and this accomplished, he visits the tents and seizes everything therein that under the convenient nomenclature of the Federals, is catalogued as "contraband,"—blankets, boots, hats, anything. The only way to avoid this, is by a judicious use of greenbacks,—and a trifle will suffice—it being true, with a few honorable exceptions, of course, that Yankee soldiers are very much like ships: to move them, you must "slush the ways."

In the matter of clothing, the management at Point Lookout is simply infamous. You can receive nothing in the way of clothing without giving up the corresponding article which you may chance to possess; and so rigid is this regulation, that men who come there bare-footed have been compelled to beg or buy a pair of worn out shoes to carry to the office in lieu of a pair sent them by their friends, before they could receive the latter. To what end this plundering is committed I could never ascertain, nor was I ever able to hear any better, or indeed any other reason advanced for it than that the possession of extra clothing would enable the prisoners to bribe their guards! Heaven help the virtue that a pair of second-hand Confederate breeches could seduce!

As I have mentioned the guards, and as this is a mosaic chapter, I may as well speak here as elsewhere of the method by which order is kept in camp. During the day the platform around the pen is constantly paced by sentinels chiefly of the Invalid (or, as it is now called, the Veteran Reserve) Corps, whose duty it is to see that the prisoners are orderly, and particularly, that no one crosses "the dead line." This is a shallow ditch traced around within the enclosure, about fifteen feet from the fence. The penalty for stepping over this is death, and although the sentinels are probably instructed to warn any one who may be violating the rule, the order does not seem to be imperative, and the negroes, when on duty, rarely troubled themselves with this superfluous formality. These were on duty during my stay at the Point, every third day, and their insolence and brutality were intolerable.

Besides this detail of day guard, which of course is preserved during the night, a patrol makes the rounds constantly from "taps," the last *horn* at night, to "reveille." These were usually armed with pistols for greater convenience, and as they are shielded from scrutiny by the darkness, the indignities and cruelties they oftentimes inflict on prisoners, who for any cause may be out of their tents between those hours, especially when the patrol are black, are outrageous. Many of these are of a character which could not by any periphrase be decently expressed,—they are, however, precisely the acts which a set of vulgar brutes, suddenly invested with irresponsible authority, might be expected to take delight in, and, as it is of course impossible to recognize them, redress is unattainable, even if one could brook the sneer and insult which would inevitably follow complaint. Indeed, most of the Yankees do not disguise their delight at the insolence of these Congoes.

To the Friends of the Southern Cause

THE EFFORTS of the Southern women in support of the war were seldom formally organized, but they were priceless. Their services in feeding and aiding traveling soldiers in the Wayside Homes and Hospitals supplied an essential need not taken care of by the government. Their work with the sick and wounded released men for service in the field. And their help in keeping up individual morale was inestimable.

In late 1864 the good ladies of South Carolina planned a bazaar to raise money and collect supplies for the use of the soldiers. This is the circular in which they set forth the objects of their Soldiers' Relief Association.

To the Friends of the Southern Cause at Home.

In May last we addressed our friends abroad. This appeal is to those at home. We will be satisfied if our second appeal shall be as successful at the first—if our home people respond as well as strangers have done. Our first Circular was sent to Nassau and Europe. It set forth the greatness and duration of our struggle—the vast expenditures of money and the sacrifice of life by our ruthless foe for our subjugation. But while it was showed how vain were his efforts, it set forth also our great sacrifices, and explained to those whose want of local knowledge rendered information necessary how much exertion was required to provide for the comfort and well-being of our soldiers and seamen in health and in sickness. We devoted attention especially to Wayside Homes and Hospitals, and explained to our distant friends how essential they had proved in a country having such a large area as ours—with so many soldiers in the field and so many battles being fought, and with so many sick and wounded passing to and fro. And, finally, we mentioned that one of the most honorable missions of the war—the care for the sick and wounded—had been confided, to a considerable extent, to our females, and that we had accepted the trust in humble dependence upon the Divine guidance, and with it would labor to the end. That in the discharge of these duties we felt the need of many articles, such as bed clothing, groceries, shoes, for the seamen, etc., and that in aid of this object we intended during the fall to hold a bazaar in the city of Columbia, where we would collect articles of domestic use, such as sugar, tea, coffee, candles, soap, crockeryware, cooking utensils, shoes, blankets, gloves, and articles of clothing for both sexes and for children; and after devoting such of them as were necessary to the use of the Homes and Hospitals, we would sell the remainder at reasonable prices.

We appealed to our foreign friends to send us any of the articles enumerated or any others that occurred to them—or if they preferred it to remit funds in aid of our plans. The response to this appeal, as we remarked in the outset, has been most encouraging. In Nassau and in Liverpool our friends have been particularly zealous, and the undersigned are already in possession of such contributions as inspire them with every hope of success. This, however, cannot be complete without the co-operation of our friends at home, and it is the object of this paper to solicit your warmest efforts in an enterprise which commends itself to the heart of every patriot. We cannot expect to succeed in so large a work without the active assistance of all classes; but that of the planters and farmers is indispensable. It will be remembered that in these times every product of the farmer is in great demand. These we solicit of every kind. There is nothing that the farmer produces and manufactures, from a bale of cotton or barrel of flour or fresh and salt meat to a straw broom or a wooden bowl, that will not be acceptable. Pickles, catsups, vinegar, syrup, are all useful and valuable for hospital purposes.

We would especially invite attention to the numberless articles of a useful and fancy kind which the taste and ingenuity of the ladies have developed during the war, as for instance straw and palmetto bonnets and hats, cloth hats, knitting of every description, crochet and tatting, camp bags, tobacco pouches, pin and needle cases. And, in a word, to all the handiwork of the busy fingers which have plied so industriously in obedience to the promptings of earnest hearts in the cause of our country.

Such of these as are perishable will be sold, the remainder will be devoted to the use of the Hospitals and Homes. So large an undertaking has required time and preparation, which has resulted in postponement heretofore. As the bazaar will have for sale articles comprised in the separate departments of business, for example, dry goods, groceries, fresh and salt meats, fancy articles, etc., all to be sold in separate departments, there was no building in Columbia but the

State House that would answer our purpose. It had been our expectation to have had our sales opened in November, but the delays of the blockade and the sitting of the Legislature have compelled a postponement until January. Before that time the public will be duly informed through the newspapers of all the necessary arrangements. For the present we desire to let it be known that such a scheme as we have described is, we hope, in successful progress, and to invite our friends to give it their earnest consideration and that generous support to which it is so well entitled from every motive of humanity and patriotism.

> Mrs. Dr. John Fisher, Columbia.
> Mrs. M. A. Snowden, Charleston.
> Miss Eliza P. Hayne, Charleston.
> Mrs. F. H. Elmore, Columbia.
> Mrs. A. W. Leland, Columbia.
> Mrs. D. E. Huger, Charleston.
> Mrs. A. M. Manigault, Charleston.
> Miss L. S. Porter, Charleston.

Columbia, S. C., November 5, 1864.

Discipline in Lee's Army

E VEN THE SOLDIERS under so noble a commander as General Lee were not immune to the faults that have been the faults of soldiers since wars began. As supplies became scarcer in the Confederate Army, scrounging became more and more an acceptable, and necessary, way of procuring necessities. It was inevitable that some soldiers should overstep the bounds of discipline in appropriating stores for their own use. Here is General Lee's order against such practices.

HEAD QUARTERS ARMY OF NORTHERN VA.
12th December, 1864.

GENERAL ORDERS,⎱
    No. 71   ⎰

The General Commanding has heard with pain and mortification that outrages and depredations amounting in some cases to flagrant robbery, have been perpetrated upon citizens living within the lines, and near the camps of the army. Poor and helpless persons have been stripped of the means of subsistence and suffered violence by the hands of those upon whom they had a right to rely for protection. In one instance an atrocious murder was perpetrated upon a child by a band of ruffians whose supposed object was plunder.

The General Commanding is well aware that the great body of the army which so unselfishly devotes itself to the defence of the country, regards these crimes with abhorrence; and that they are committed by a few miscreants unworthy of the name of soldiers. But he feels that we cannot escape the disgrace that attends these evildoers, except by the most strenuous exertions on our part to restrain their wickedness and bring upon them the just punishment of their offences. This can only be accomplished by the united efforts of those good and true men who are no less desirous of being esteemed for virtue by their countrymen, than of being respected for courage by their enemies. Laws and orders will prove ineffectual unless sustained by the hearty cooperation of those who feel that the existence of the evil is a reproach to themselves. The aid of all such is earnestly and confidently invoked to remove this stain from the fair name of the army. Let each man guard its honor as zealously as his own, regarding those who bring reproach upon it, as enemies of his own reputation, and remembering that to withhold information that might lead to the detection of these criminals is to become morally a participant of their guilt.

The attention of officers is particularly directed to this subject. Their responsibility is greatest, for upon their care and vigilance necessarily depend, in a great degree, the prevention and detection of unlawful acts by these men.

Those commanding regiments, companies, or in charge of camps, hospitals, or detachments, will be required to account for all who fail to attend the roll calls under existing orders, or for such of their officers and men as may be arrested absent from their commands without proper authority, by the guards and pickets of the army.

Corps commanders will habitually keep out patrols to arrest all who are improperly absent and to protect the persons and property of those residing in the vicinity of their commands. When arrested the parties, themselves, and the officers responsible for their conduct will be brought to trial without delay.

By command of General LEE.

W. H. TAYLOR,
A. A. General.

In Sherman's Wake

As 1864 drew to a close General Hood was in Tennessee on a daring and disastrous campaign. Sherman had left Atlanta undefended to march to the coast. With the bulk of the Confederate Army in Tennessee with Hood, Wheeler's Cavalry was all that stood before Sherman to block his advance. Wheeler's troops were not strong enough to provide anything more than harassing actions, but for individual courage and determination they were unmatched.

The first of the next pair of selections is General Joe Wheeler's address to his troops at the close of 1864, thanking them for past braveries and exhorting them to renewed endeavor.

As Wheeler's men, as well as Sherman's, had of necessity to live off the country in which they were fighting, their presence in Georgia was almost as much feared as that of the Yankees themselves. "The whole land mourns, on account of Wheeler's cavalry," wrote Joseph Addison Turner in *The Countryman*. "Here in middle Georgia, they are dreaded fully as much, if not more, than the yankees." The second of these selections concerning

Wheeler's Cavalry is a letter published in *The Country-man* in January, 1865, which describes the passage of both the Yankees and the Confederates through Scriven County, Georgia.

HEAD QUARTERS, CAVALRY CORPS,
December 31st, 1864.

My brave Soldiers:

The close of the year terminates a campaign of eight months, during which you have engaged in continuous and successful fighting.

From Dalton to Atlanta you held the right of our army. Opposed almost continuously by a force of infantry ten times your number, you repulsed every assault, inflicting upon the enemy a loss in killed and wounded numerically greater than your entire strength. Every attempt on the part of the enemy to turn or strike our right flank was met and repulsed by your valor and determined courage. It should be a proud reflection to you all, that during the entire campaign, the Army of Tennessee never lost a position by having the flank turned which it was your duty to protect.

During every movement of our lines, you have been between our infantry and the enemy hurling back his exulting advance, and holding his entire army at bay until our troops had quietly prepared to receive and repulse his gigantic assaults. Having failed by other means to drive our army from the position in front of Atlanta, he now sends three heavy columns of cavalry to destroy our communications, to release prisoners of war, and march in triumph with them through our country. You promptly strike one column and drive it back discomfited; then quickly assailing the two others, you defeat them and complete their destruction and capture. This, alone, cost the enemy more than five thousand men, horses, arms and equipment, besides material, colors and cannon. This was due to your valor, and is without parallel in the history of this war.

Having been detached and sent to the rear of the enemy you captured his garrison, destroyed his stores and broke his communications more effectually and for a larger period than any other cavalry force, however large, has done.

During Sherman's march through Georgia you retarded his advance and defeated his cavalry daily, preventing his spreading over and devastating the country.

During the last five months you have traveled nearly three thousand miles, fighting nearly every day, and always with success. You must have been victorious in more than fifty pitched battles, and a hundred minor affairs placing a number of the enemy *hors du combat* fully four times the greatest number you ever carried into action.

I desire, my brave soldiers, to thank you for your gallantry, devotion and good conduct. Every charge I have asked you to make, has been brilliantly executed. Every position I have asked you to hold, has been held until absolutely untenable. Your devotion to your country fills my heart with gratitude. You have done your full duty to your country and to me; and I have tried to do my full duty to you. Circumstances have forced upon you many and great deprivations. You have been deprived of the issues of clothing and many of the comforts and conveniences which other troops have enjoyed and have borne all without a murmur.

Soldiers of Kentucky, Tennessee, Texas and Arkansas! you deserve special commendation for your sacrifices and fortitude. Separated from your homes and families you have nobly done all that gallant devoted men could do. Soldiers from Alabama and Georgia! your homes have nearly all been over-run and destroyed, yet without complaint you have stood to your colors like brave and patriotic men. Your country and your God will one day reward you.

The gallant Kelly whom we all loved so well is dead. Many other brave spirits whose loss we deeply feel sleep with him. They fell—the price of victory.

Allen, Humes, Anderson, Dibbrell, Hagan, Crews, Ashby, Harrison and Breckenridge, and many other brave men whose gallantry you have so often witnessed are here still to guide and lead you in battles yet to be fought and victories yet to be won.

Another campaign will soon open in which I only ask you to fight with the same valor I have always seen you exhibit upon the many fields where your determined courage has won victory for our cause.

J. WHEELER,
Major General.

    ❁   ❁   ❁   ❁   ❁

Mobley's Pond, Scriven Co., Ga.

Mr. Countryman:—I accidentally met with a number of your delightful paper, The Countryman, and felt, while reading it, that I had met an old friend, so much rejoiced was I to again hear from a section of country where I have left some dear friends. Being deprived entirely of a mail, I have, for some time past, felt much anxiety about the welfare of the people of Milledgeville, and vicinity—having heard the yankees de-stroyed much property—but trust the rumors are somewhat exaggerated. Allow me to congratulate you, on such a lucky deliverance of your Countryman from the hands of the northern vandals.

I have been residing in Scriven county, for several weeks past, and thought, if there was any place secure from the enemy, it was here. It seems no place is so safe, but they can compass it out. They passed through this part of the country, committing great depredations, such as burning gin-houses, corn-cribs, and even dwellings of those who had not courage to meet the dreaded foe. Some have no corn left; others were more fortunate, as the yankees were in a considerable hurry, and could not visit every place. Watches and money were carried off in large quantities. One wealthy farmer suffered much by them. He buried his valuables in the graveyard, but was betrayed by one of his servants; so they carried off his gold, and silver, his watches, and a large amount of confederate money, and bonds. Many have suffered in like manner. All the stock was killed, and carried off, in some places.

I must tell you how shamefully Gen. Wheeler's men acted. Though they have a wide-spread reputation of being the greatest horse thieves in the country, they never acted worse than they have recently. While the enemy were burning and destroying property, on one side of Briar creek, they were stealing horses, and mules on the other. Only a few yankees crossed over on our side, and there was a large force of Wheeler's men dodging about, who could have captured, and killed all the enemy, and saved much property.

Some of the neighbors ran themselves, and stock to Carolina, for safe keeping; some took to the swamps, while only a few were captured. Some were exceedingly lucky, having returned home safely, after being politely stripped of everything, and paroled by their blue-coated friends; while others, not so fortunate, are sojourning with them still, and, report says, are penned up at night like hogs, feeding on roasted potatoes. One of the citizens was severely whipped. They found him armed, and gave him two hundred lashes. He has not since been heard from.—It is now getting more quiet. The past two weeks have been very exciting. The roads were strewn with dead horses, and several dead yankees have been found. At last accounts, the enemy had surrounded Savannah. Fort McAllister has fallen. It is only thirty miles from here to Savannah, and when an engagement is going on, we hear the cannon very distinctly. . . .

Respectfuly yours,

BERTHA.

1865

"Forbid It Heaven!"

ACTIVITY in Virginia was slowed to a mire truce by winter, but operations in the deep South continued. Sherman took Savannah in time to offer it to President Lincoln as a Christmas gift. Though the people of Charleston feared that their city, the birthplace of secession, was next and would receive a particularly thorough "Shermanizing," the astute old redhead turned northeast and headed for Columbia.

Despite the threats to the cities of their heartland, the soldiers of the South were not yet officially downhearted. Here are the resolutions passed by McGowan's Brigade, one of the most distinguished units of South Carolina soldiers.

RESOLUTIONS

Adopted by McGowan's Brigade, South Carolina Volunteers.

The soldiers and officers of McGowan's Brigade do
Resolve, 1st. That the war in which we are engaged is a war of self-defence; that in the beginning, nearly four years ago, we took up arms in defence of the right to govern ourselves, and to protect our country from invasion, our homes from desolation, and our wives and children from insult and outrage.

2d. That the reasons which induced us to take up arms at the beginning have not been impaired, but, on the contrary, infinitely strengthened by the progress of the war. Outrage and cruelty have not made us love the perpetrators. If we then judged that the enemy intended to impoverish and oppress us, we *now know* that they propose to subjugate, enslave, disgrace and destroy us.

3d. As we were actuated by principle when we entered the service of the Confederate States, we are of the same opinion still. We have had our share of victories, and we must expect some defeats. Our cause is righteous and must prevail. In the language of General Greene, during the darkest hours of the Revolution, when he was struggling to recover South Carolina, then entirely overrun and suffering under the scourge of Tarl[e]ton, "Independence is certain, if the people have the fortitude to bear and the courage to persevere."

4th. To submit to our enemies now, would be more infamous than it would have been in the beginning. It would be cowardly yielding to power what was denied upon principle. It would be to yield the cherished right of self-government, and to acknowledge ourselves wrong in the assertion of it; to brand the names of our slaughtered companions as traitors; to forfeit the glory already won; to lose the fruits of all the sacrifices made and the privations endured; to give up independence now nearly gained, and bring certain ruin, disgrace and eternal slavery upon our country. Therefore, unsubdued by past reverses, and unawed by future dangers, we declare our determination to battle to the end, and not to lay down our arms until independence is secured. Is life so dear, or peace so sweet, as to be purchased at the price of chains and slavery? Forbid it Heaven!

"Humiliation Spreads Her Ashes"

B UT THERE WAS NOTHING in the South to stem the tide
sweeping over her. William Gilmore Simms, the dean
of Southern literary men, was then a resident of Columbia. As the city rose from the ashes left in Sherman's wake
he published, first in the *Daily Phoenix* and then in a
pamphlet printed on paper originally intended for Confederate bank notes, a remarkable account of the "sack
and destruction" of the city.

"It has pleased God," begins Simms' introduction, "in
that Providence which is so inscrutable to man, to visit
our beautiful city with the most cruel fate which can ever
befall States or cities. He has permitted an invading army
to penetrate our country almost without impediment; to
rob and ravage our dwellings, and to commit three-fifths
of our city to the flames. . . . The schools of learning,
the shops of art and trade, of invention and manufacture;
shrines equally of religion, benevolence and industry;
are all buried together, in one congregated ruin. Humiliation spreads her ashes over our homes and garments, and
the universal wreck exhibits only one common aspect of
despair. It is for us, as succinctly but as fully as possible,

and in the simplest language, to endeavor to make the melancholy record of our wretchedness as complete as possible."

Here is a portion of Simms' account.

The end was rapidly approaching. The guns were resounding at the gates. Defence was impossible. At a late hour on Thursday night, the Governor, with his suite and a large train of officials, departed. The Confederate army began its evacuation, and by daylight few remained who were not resigned to the necessity of seeing the tragedy played out. After all the depletion, the city contained, according to our estimate, at least twenty thousand inhabitants, the larger proportion being females and children and negroes. Hampton's cavalry . . . lingered till near 10 o'clock the next day, and scattered groups of Wheeler's command hovered about the Federal army at their entrance into the town.

The inhabitants were startled at daylight, on Friday morning, by a heavy explosion. This was the South Carolina Railroad Depot. It was accidentally blown up. Broken open by a band of plunderers, among whom were many females and negroes, their reckless greed precipitated their fate. This building had been made the receptacle of supplies from sundry quarters, and was crowded with stores of merchants and planters, trunks of treasure, innumerable wares and goods of fugitives—all of great value. It appears that, among its contents, were some kegs of powder. The plunderers paid, and suddenly, the penalties of their crime. Using their lights freely and hurriedly, the better to *pick*, they fired a train of powder leading to the kegs. The explosion followed, and the number of persons destroyed is variously estimated, from seventeen to fifty. It is probable that not more than thirty-five suffered, but the actual number perishing is unascertained.

At a nearly hour on Friday, the commissary and quartermaster stores were thrown wide, the contents cast out into the streets and given to the people.. The negroes especially loaded themselves with plunder. All this might have been saved, had the officers been duly warned by the military authorities of the probable issue of the struggle. Wheeler's cavalry also shared largely of this plunder, and several of them might be seen, bearing off huge bales upon their saddles.

It was proposed that the white flag should be displayed from the tower of the City Hall. But General Hampton, whose command had not yet left the city, and who was still eager to do battle in its defence, indignantly declared that if displayed, he should have it torn down.

The following letter from the Mayor to General Sherman was the initiation of the surrender:

MAYOR'S OFFICE
COLUMBIA, S. C., February 17, 1865.

TO MAJOR-GENERAL SHERMAN: The Confederate forces having evacuated Columbia, I deem it my duty, as Mayor and representative of the city, to ask for its citizens the treatment accorded by the usages of civilized warfare. I therefore respectfully request that you will send a sufficient guard in advance of the army, to maintain order in the city and protect the persons and property of the citizens.

Very respectfully, your obedient servant,

T. J. GOODWYN, Mayor.

At 9 o'clock, on the painfully memorable morning of the 17th February, (Friday,) a deputation from the City Council, consisting of the Mayor, Aldermen McKenzie, Bates and Stork, in a carriage bearing a white flag, proceeded towards the Broad River Bridge Road. Arriving at the forks of the Winnsboro Road, they discovered that the Confederate skirmishers were still busy with their guns, playing upon the advance of the Federals. These were troops of General Wheeler. This conflict was continued simply to afford the main army all possible advantages of a start in their retreat. General Wheeler apprised the deputation that his men would now be withdrawn, and instructed them in what manner to proceed. The deputation met the column of the Federals, under Captain Platt, who send them forward to Colonel Stone, who finally took his seat with them in the carriage. The advance belonged to the 15th corps.

The Mayor reports that on surrendering the city to Colonel Stone, the latter assured him of the safety of the citizens and of the protection of their property, *while under his command.* He could not answer for General Sherman, who was in the rear, but he expressed the conviction that he would fully confirm the assurances which he (Colonel Stone) had given. Subsequently, General Sherman did confirm them, and that night, seeing that the Mayor was exhausted by his labors of the day, he counselled him to retire to rest, saying, "Not a finger's breadth, Mr. Mayor, of your city shall be harmed. You may lie down to sleep, satisfied that your town shall be as safe in my hands as if wholly in your own." Such was very nearly the language in which he spoke; such was the substance of it. He added: "It will become my duty to destroy some of the public or Government buildings: but I will reserve this performance to another day. It shall be done to-

morrow, provided the day be calm." And the Mayor retired
with this solemnly asserted and repeated assurance.

About 11 o'clock, the head of the column, following the
deputation—the flag of the United States surmounting the
carriage—reached Market Hall, on Main street, while that of
the corps was carried in the rear. On their way to the city,
the carriage was stopped, and the officer was informed that a
large body of Confederate cavalry was flanking them. Colonel Stone said to the Mayor, "We shall hold you responsible
for this." The Mayor explained, that the road leading to
Winnsboro, by which the Confederates were retreating, ran
nearly parallel for a short distance with the river road, which
accounted for the apparent flanking. Two officers, who arrived in Columbia ahead of the deputation, (having crossed
the river at a point directly opposite the city,) were fired
upon by one of Wheeler's cavalry. We are particular in men-
tioning this fact, as we learn that, subsequently, the incident
was urged as a justification of the sack and burning of the
city.

Hardly had the troops reached the head of Main street,
when the work of pillage was begun. Stores were broken open
within the first hour after their arrival, and gold, silver, jewels
and liquors, eagerly sought. The authorities, officers, soldiers,
all seemed to consider it a matter of course. And woe to him
who carried a watch with a gold chain pendant; or who wore
a choice hat, or overcoat, or boots or shoes. He was stripped
in the twinkling of an eye. It is computed that, from first to
last, twelve hundred watches were transferred from the
pockets of their owners to those of the soldiers. Purses shared
the same fate; nor was the Confederate currency repudiated. . . .

At about 12 o'clock, the jail was discovered to be on fire
from within. This building was immediately in rear of the

Market, or City Hall, and in a densely built portion of the city. The supposition is that it was fired by some of the prisoners—all of whom were released and subsequently followed the army. The fire of the jail had been preceded by that of some cotton piled in the streets. Both fires were soon subdued by the firemen. At about half-past 1 P. M., that of the jail was rekindled, and was again extinguished. Some of the prisoners, who had been confined at the Asylum, had made their escape, in some instances, a few days before, and were secreted and protected by citizens.

No one felt safe in his own dwelling; and, in the faith that General Sherman would respect the Convent, and have it properly guarded, numbers of young ladies were confided to the care of the Mother Superior, and even trunks of clothes and treasure were sent thither, in full confidence that they would find safety. Vain illusions! The Irish Catholic troops, it appears, were not brought into the city at all; were kept on the other side of the river. But a few Catholics were collected among the corps which occupied the city, and of the conduct of these, a favorable account is given. One of them rescued a silver goblet of the church, used as a drinking cup by a soldier, and restored it to the Rev. Dr. O'Connell. This priest, by the way, was severely handled by the soldiers. Such, also, was the fortune of the Rev. Mr. Shand, of Trinity (the Episcopal) Church, who sought in vain to save a trunk containing the sacred vessels of his church. It was violently wrested from his keeping, and his struggle to save it only provoked the rougher usage. We are since told, on reaching Camden, General Sherman restored what he believed were these vessels to Bishop Davis. It has since been discovered that the plate belonged to St. Peter's Church in Charleston.

And here it may be well to mention, as suggestive of many clues, an incident which presented a sad commentary on that

confidence in the security of the Convent, which was entertained by the great portion of the people. This establishment,
under the charge of the sister of the Right Rev. Bishop Lynch,
was at once a convent and an academy of the highest class.
Hither were sent for education the daughters of Protestants,
of the most wealthy classes throughout the State; and these,
with the nuns and those young ladies sent thither on the
emergency, probably exceeded one hundred. The Lady Superior herself entertained the fullest confidence in the immu-
nites of the establishment. But her confidence was clouded,
after she had enjoyed a conference with a certain major of
the Yankee army, who described himself as an editor, from
Detroit. He visited her at an early hour in the day, and announced his friendly sympathies with the Lady Superior and
the sisterhood; professed his anxiety for their safety—his purpose to do all that he could to insure it—declared that he
would instantly go to Sherman and secure a chosen guard;
and, altogether, made such professions of love and service, as
to disarm those suspicions, which his bad looks and bad manners, inflated speech and pompous carriage, might otherwise
have provoked. The Lady Superior with such a charge in her
hands, was naturally glad to welcome all shows and prospects
of support, and expressed her gratitude. He disappeared, and
soon after re-appeared, bringing with him no less than eight
or ten men—none of them, as he admitted, being Catholics.
He had some specious argument to show that, perhaps, her
guard had better be one of Protestants. This suggestion staggered the lady a little, but he seemed to convey a more potent
reason, when he added, in a whisper: *"For I must tell you,
my sister, that Columbia is a doomed city!"* Terrible doom!
This officer, leaving his men behind him, disappeared, to
show himself no more. The guards so left behind were finally
among the most busy as plunderers. The moment that the

inmates, driven out by the fire, were forced to abandon their house, they began to revel in its contents,

Quis custodiet ipsos custodes?—who shall guard the guards —asks the proverb. In a number of cases, the guards provided for the citizens were among the most active plunderers; were quick to betray their trusts, abandon their posts, and bring their comrades in to join in the general pillage. The most dextrous and adroit of these, it is the opinion of most persons, were chiefly Eastern men, or men of immediate Eastern origin. The Western men, including the Indiana, a portion of the Illinois and Iowa, were neither so dextrous nor unscrupulous—were frequently faithful and respectful; and, perhaps, it would be safe to assert that many of the houses which escaped the sack and fire, owed their safely to the presence or the contiguity of some of these men. But we must retrace our steps.

It may be well to remark that the discipline of the soldiers upon their first entry into the city, was perfect and most admirable. There was no disorder or irregularity on the line of march, showing that their officers had them completely in hand. They were a fine looking body of men, mostly young and of vigorous formation, well clad and well shod, seemingly wanting in nothing. Their arms and accoutrements were in bright order. The negroes accompanying them were not numerous, and seemed mostly to act as drudges and body servants. They groomed horses, waited, carried burdens, and, in almost every instance under our eyes, appeared in a purely servile, and not a military capacity. The men of the West treated them generally with scorn or indifference, sometimes harshly, and not unfrequently with blows.

But if the entrance into town and while on duty, was indicative of admirable drill and discipline, such ceased to be the case the moment the troops were dismissed. Then, whether by tacit permission or direct command, their whole deportment underwent a sudden and rapid change. The saturnalia soon began. We have shown that the robbery of the persons of the citizens and the plunder of their homes commenced within one hour after they had reached the Market Hall. It continued without interruption throughout the day. Sherman, at the head of his cavalry, traversed the streets everywhere—so did his officers. Subsequently, these officers were everywhere on foot, yet beheld nothing which required the interposition of authority. And yet robbery was going on at every corner—in nearly every house. Citizens generally applied for a guard at their several houses, and, for a time, these guards were alloted them. These might be faithful or not. In some cases, as already stated, they were, and civil and respectful; considerate of the claims of women, and never trespassing upon the privacy of the family; but, in numbers of cases, they were intrusive, insulting and treacherous—leaving no privacy undisturbed, passing without a word into the chambers and prying into every crevice and corner.

But the reign of terror did not fairly begin till night. In some instances, where parties complained of the misrule and robbery, their guards said to them, with a chuckle: "This is nothing. Wait till tonight, and you'll see h-ll."

Among the first fires at evening was one about dark, which broke out in a fithy purlieu of low houses, of wood, on Gervais street, occupied mostly as brothels. Almost at the same time, a body of the soldiers scattered over the Eastern outskirts of the city, fired severally the dwellings of Mr. Secretary Trenholm, General Wade Hampton, Dr. John Wallace, J. U. Adams, Mrs. Starke, Mr. Latta, Mrs. English, and many others. There were then some twenty fires in full blast, in as many different quarters, and while the alarm sounded from these quarters a similar alarm was sent up almost simultaneously from Cotton Town, the Northermost limit of the city, and from Main street in its very centre, at the several stores or houses of O. Z. Bates, C. D. Eberhardt, and some others, in the heart of the most densely settled portion of the town; thus enveloping in flames almost every section of the devoted city. At this period, thus early in the evening, there were few shows of that drunkenness which prevailed at a late hour in the night, and only after all the grocery shops on Main street had been rifled. The men engaged in this were well prepared with all the appliances essential to their work. They did not need the torch. They carried with them, from house to house, pots and vessels containing combustible liquids, composed probably of phosphorous and other similar agents, turpentine, &c.; and, with balls of cotton saturated in this liquid, with which they also overspread floors and walls, they conveyed the flames with wonderful rapidity from dwelling to dwelling. Each had his ready box of Lucifer matches, and, with a scrape upon the walls, the flames began to rage. Where houses were closely contiguous, a brand from one was the means of conveying destruction to the other.

The winds favored. They had been high throughout the day, and steadily prevailed from South-west by West, and bore the flames Eastward. To this fact we owe the preservation of the portions of the city lying West of Assembly street.

The work, begun thus vigorously, went on without impediment and with hourly increase throughout the night. Engines and hose were brought out by the firemen, but these were soon driven from their labors—which were indeed idle against such a storm of fire—by the pertinacious hostility of the soldiers; the hose was hewn to pieces, and the firemen, dreading worse usage to themselves, left the field in despair. Meanwhile, the flames spread from side to side, from front to rear, from street to street, and where their natural and inevitable progress was too slow for those who had kindled them, they helped them on by the application of fresh combustibles and more rapid agencies of conflagration. By midnight, Main street, from its Northern to its Southern extremity, was a solid wall of fire. By 12 o'clock, the great blocks, which included the banking houses and the Treasury buildings, were consumed; Janney's (Congaree) and Nickerson's Hotels; the magnificent manufactories of Evans & Cogswell —indeed every large block in the business portion of the city; the old Capitol and all the adjacent buildings were in ruins. The range called the "Granite" was beginning to flame at 12, and might have been saved by ten vigorous men, resolutely working.

At 1 o'clock, the hour was struck by the clock of the Market Hall, which was even then illuminated from within. It was its own last hour which it sounded, and its tongue was silenced forevermore. In less than five minutes after, its spire went down with a crash, and, by this time, almost all the buildings within the precinct were a mass of ruins.

Very grand, and terrible, beyond description, was the awful spectacle. It was a scene for the painter of the terrible. It was the blending of a range of burning mountains stretched in a continuous series of more than a mile. Here was Ætna, sending up its spouts of flaming lava; Vesuvius, emulous of like display, shooting up with loftier torrents, and Stromboli, struggling, with awful throes, to shame both by its superior volumes of fluid flame. The winds were tributary to these convulsive efforts, and tossed the volcanic torrents hundreds of feet in air. Great spouts of flame spread aloft in canopies of sulphurous cloud—wreaths of sable, edged with sheeted lightnings, wrapped the skies, and, at short intervals, the falling tower and the tottering wall, avalanche-like, went down with thunderous sound, sending up at every crash great billowy showers of glowing fiery embers.

Throughout the whole of this terrible scene the soldiers continued their search after spoil. The houses were severally and soon gutted of their contents. Hundreds of iron safes, warranted "impenetrable to fire and the burglar," it was soon satisfactorily demonstrated, were not "Yankee proof." They were split open and robbed, yielding, in some cases, very largely of Confederate money and bonds, if not of gold and silver. Jewelry and plate in abundance was found. Men could be seen staggering off with huge waiters, vases, candelabra, to say nothing of cups, goblets and smaller vessels, all of solid silver. Clothes and shoes, when new, were appropriated—the rest left to burn. Liquors were drank with such avidity as to astonish the veteran Bacchanals of Columbia; nor did the parties thus distinguishing themselves hesitate about the vintage. There was no idle discrimination in the matter of taste, from that vulgar liquor, which Judge Burke used to say always provoked within him "an inordinate propensity to sthale," to the choicest red wines of the ancient cellars. In one vault on Main street, seventeen casks of wine were stored away, which, an eye-witness tells us, barely sufficed, once broken into, for the draughts of a single hour —such were the appetites at work and the numbers in possession of them. Rye, corn, claret and Madeira all found their way into the same channels, and we are not to wonder, when told that no less than one hundred and fifty of the drunken creatures perished miserably among the flames kindled by their own comrades, and from which they were unable to escape. The estimate will not be thought extrava-

gant by those who saw the condition of hundreds after 1
o'clock A. M. By others, however, the estimate is reduced to
thirty; but the number will never be known. Sherman's
officers themselves are reported to have said that they lost
more men in the sack and burning of the city (including
certain explosions) than in all their fights while approaching
it. It is also suggested that the orders which Sherman issued
at daylight, on Saturday morning, for the arrest of the fire,
were issued in consequence of the loss of men which he had
thus sustained.

One or more of his men were shot, by parties unknown, in
some dark passages or alleys—it is supposed in consequence
of some attempted outrages which humanity could not endure; the assassin taking advantage of the obscurity of the
situation and adroitly mingling with the crowd without. And
while these scenes were at their worst—while the flames were
at their highest and most extensively raging—groups might
be seen at the several corners of the streets, drinking, roaring, revelling—while the fiddle and accordeon were playing
their popular airs among them. There was no cessation of
the work till 5 A. M. on Saturday.

A single thought will suffice to show that the owners or
lodgers in the houses thus sacrificed were not silent or quiet
spectators of a conflagration which threw them naked and
homeless under the skies of night. The male population, consisting mostly of aged men, invalids, decrepits, women and
children, were not capable of very active or powerful exertions; but they did not succumb to the fate without earnest
pleas and strenuous efforts. Old men and women and children were to be seen, even while the flames were rolling and
raging around them, while walls were crackling and rafters
tottering and tumbling, in the endeavor to save their clothing and some of their most valuable effects. It was not often

that they were suffered to succeed. They were driven out headlong.

Ladies were hustled from their chambers—their ornaments plucked from their persons, their bundles from their hands. It was in vain that the mother appealed for the garments of her children. They were torn from her grasp and hurled into the flames. The young girl striving to save a single frock, had it rent to fibres in her grasp. Men and women bearing off their trunks were seized, despoiled, in a moment the trunk burst asunder with the stroke of axe or gun-butt, the contents laid bare, rifled of all the objects of desire, and the residue sacrificed to the fire. You might see the ruined owner, standing woebegone, aghast, gazing at his tumbling dwelling, his scattered property, with a dumb agony in his face that was inexpressibly touching. Others you might hear, as we did, with wild blasphemies assailing the justice of Heaven, or invoking, with lifted and clenched hands, the fiery wrath of the avenger. But the soldiers plundered and drank, the fiery work raged, and the moon sailed over all with as serene an aspect as when she first smiled upon the ark resting against the slopes of Ararat.

"The Glory of History Is Honour"

EDWARD A. POLLARD was a remarkable and forceful Confederate editor. Although he violently opposed nearly everything that President Davis ever did, his loyalty to the South cannot be questioned. Pollard was the chief contemporary historian of the Confederacy and is well remembered for his year-by-year history of the war and for his pamphlets on individual battles.

In May, 1864, Pollard undertook to go to England to work with his publishers in London on his forthcoming volume about the war. (Publishing conditions in Richmond had deteriorated so that his book was a project beyond the capacities there.) Passage on blockade runners to Bermuda cost at that time $8,000 in Confederate money ($400 in gold), but Pollard had the good fortune to sail as the guest of the captain of the British owned *Greyhound*. His good fortune, however, was short-lived. The *Greyhound* was captured by Union blockaders, and Pollard was sent to Fort Warren, the Union prison in Boston harbor. He stayed there until August, when he was released on parole. After four months as a prisoner at large he was returned to the Confederacy.

Pollard prepared a short book of his experiences as a prisoner, *Observations in the North*, which vies with Keiley's prison narrative for the honor of the last Confederate book published in Richmond. But the publication of the book took some time, and, inveterate reporter that he was, he put out as an interim message to his countrymen a small pamphlet reviewing the political situation and urging continued resistance. Although he urged resistance and put up a front of optimism, here in Pollard's open letter is the first real statement of the Confederacy as "The Lost Cause." "The glory of history," he says, "is indifferent to events; it is simply Honour."

The grand conclusion to which the observations I made in the North last summer lead is this: that if we can ever regain substantially nothing more than the *status quo* of seven months ago; if we can ever present to the North the same prospect of a long war we did then, and put before them the weary task of overcoming the fortitude of a brave people, we shall have peace and independence in our grasp. It is a vulgar mistake that to accomplish our success in this war we have to retrieve all of the past and recover by arms all the separate pieces of our territory. It is to be remembered that we are fighting on the defensive, and have only to convince the enemy that we are able to protect the vital points of our country to compel him to a peace in which all is surrendered that he has overrun, and all the country that he holds by the ephemeral and worthless title of invasion, falls from him as by the law of gravitation. The price of our peace has come to be now but a moderate measure of endeavour—a measure

I am persuaded only large enough to convince the Yankee of another link drawn out in the prolongation of the war. Let but his present animated hope of dispatching the Confederacy in a few months be exploded, and I predict that peace will be the result; for he will have then an occasion of discouragement far greater than that of last summer, as each later prolongation of the war will bring with it a larger tax on patience and a new train of necessities—among them the dreaded one of *conscription*, no longer to be put off by the present comfortable expedients which have reached their *maximum* in the substitution of the foreigner and the negro.

My friends, it is not extravagant to say that the time has come when only such endeavour as will put us in anything like the situation we were a few months ago—or only such proof of endurance as will convince the North of another lease of the war—will assure us peace and independence. I wish that I could insert this conviction in every fibre of the Southern mind. The task before us is not very great. If we can only regain the situation of last summer, or even if we can only give a proof to the enemy that we are not at the extremity of our resources or at the last limits of resolution —that we are able and determined to fight this war indefinitely, we have accomplished the important and vital conditions of peace. And I believe we can easily do the first— recover substantially, in all important respects, the losses of the past few months, and even add to the *status quo* of last summer new elements of advantage for us. Defeat Sherman at any stage short of Richmond and it re-opens and recovers all the country he has overrun. Leave him if you please the possession of the seaports; but these have have no value to us as ports of entry and are but picket posts in our system of defences. His campaign comes to nought if he cannot reach Grant; nothing left of it but the brilliant zig-zag of a raid,

vanishing as heat lightning in the skies. Follow the consequences of Sherman's misadventure. Grant's army of mon-
grels alone, without the looked for aid from the Carolinas,
can no more take Richmond than it can surmount the sky.
If that army is the only assailant of Richmond, then the ctiy
never was more feebly threatened. It is true that Grant is
within a few miles of our capital, when, this time last year,
he was on the Rapidan. But that is a fool's measure of danger;
for in each case we have the same army shielding Richmond,
and whether that shield is broken ten or a hundred miles
away is of no importance to the interest it covers. Again,
Grant had on the Rapidan the finest army the enemy had
ever put in the field. He has now on the lines around Richmond the poorest army that has ever been assembled under
the Yankee flag; and the last dregs of the recruiting offices
have been sifted out to make it.

Is there anything really desperate in our situation, unless
to fools and cowards who draw lines on paper to show how
the Yankees are at this place and at that place, and think
that this cob-web occupation of the country, where the
enemy has no garrisons and no footholds, indicates the extent
of Yankee conquest and gives the true measure of the remnant of the Confederacy! And yet this is too much the popular fashion of the time in estimating the military situation.
Men are drawing for themselves pictures of despair out of
what are to those who think profoundly and bravely no more
important than the passages of the hour—

> Light and shade
> Upon a waving field, chasing each other.

I am determined to express the truth, no matter how painful to myself or unwelcome to others. In the first periods of
this war who was not proud of the Confederacy and its

heroic figure in history! Yet now it is to be confessed that a large portion of our people have fallen below the standards of history, and hold no honourable comparison with other nations that have fought and struggled for independence. It is easy for the tongue of the demagogue to trip with flattery on the theme of war; but when we come to the counsels of the intelligent the truth must be told. We are no longer responding to the lessons and aspirations of history. You speak of the scarcity of subsistence. But Prussia in her wars, drained her supplies until black bread was the only thing eat in the king's palace; and yet, under Frederick, she won not only her independence, but a position among the Five Great Powers of Europe. You speak of the scarcity of men. Yet with a force not greater than that with which we have only to hold an invaded country and maintain the defensive, Napoleon fought his splendid career, and completed a circle of victories that touched the boundaries of Europe.

It is enough then to sicken the heart with shame and vexation that now, when of all times, it is most important to convince the enemy of our resolution—now, when such a course, for peculiar reasons, will insure our success—there are men who not only whine on the streets about making terms with the enemy, but intrude their cowardice into the official places of the Government, and sheltered by secret sessions and confidential conversations, roll the word "reconstruction" under the tongue. Shame upon the Congress that closed its doors that it might better consult of dishonoura ble things! Shame upon those leaders who should encourage the people and yet have broken down their confidence by private conversations, and who, while putting in newspapers some cheap words of patriotism, yet in the same breath suggest their despair by a suspicious cant about trusting in Providence, and go off to talk submission with their intimates

in a corner! Shame upon those of the people who have now
no other feeling in the war than an exasperated selfishness;
who are ready to sink, if they can carry down in their hands
some little trash of *property*; who will give their sons to the
army, but not their precious negro slaves; who are for hurrying off embassies to the enemy to know at what price of dishonour they may purchase some paltry remnant of their
possessions! Do these men ever think of the retributions of
history?

When Cato the Younger was pursued to Utica by the victorious arms of Caesar, Plutarch relates of him on this occasion certain conversation and sentiments which singularly
apply to our own condition in a besieged city, and may
almost be taken as repeated in the streets of Richmond:

"One of the Council," writes Plutarch, "observed the expediency
of a decree for enfranchising the slaves, and many commended the
motion. Cato, however, said: 'He would not do that, because it was
neither just nor lawful; but such as their masters would voluntarily
discharge, he would receive, provided they were of proper age to
bear arms.' This many promised to do; and Cato withdrew, after having ordered lists to be made out of all that should offer. . . . All of
the patrician order with great readiness enfranchised and armed their
slaves; but as for the three hundred, who dealt in traffic and loans of
money at high interest, and whose slaves were a considerable part of
their fortune, the impression which Cato's speech had made upon them
did not last long. As some bodies readily receive heat, and as easily
grow cold again when the fire is removed, so the sight of Cato warmed
and liberalized these traders; but when they came to consider the
matter among themselves, the dread of Caesar soon put to flight their
reverence for Cato and for virtue. For thus they talked: 'What are we,
and what is the man whose orders we refuse to receive? Is it not
Caesar, into whose hands the whole power of the Roman empire is
fallen? And surely none of us is a Scipio, a Pompey, or a Cato. Shall
we, at a time when their fears make all men entertain sentiments beneath their dignity—shall we, in Utica, fight for the liberty of Rome

with a man against whom Cato and Pompey the Great durst not make a stand in Italy? Shall we enfranchise our slaves to oppose Caesar, who have no more liberty ourselves than that conqueror is pleased to leave us? Ah! what wretches that we are! Let us at last know ourselves, and send deputies to intercede with him for money.' . . . They told Cato that they had resolved to send deputies to Caesar to intercede first and principally for him. If that request should not be granted, they would have no obligation to him for any favour to themselves, but as long as they had breath would fight for Cato. Cato made his acknowledgments for their regard, and advised them to send immediately to intercede for themselves. 'For me,' said he, 'intercede not. It is for the conquered to turn suppliants, and for those who have done an injury to beg pardon. For my part, I have been unconquered through life, and superiour in the things I wished to be; for in justice and honour I am Caesar's superiour.' "

The arguments of the traders and time-servers in Utica are not unknown in Richmond. But shall we not also find in this city something of the aspirations of Cato—a determination, even if we are overcome by force, to be unconquered in spirit, and, in any and all events, to remain superiour to the enemy—in honour.

I do not speak to you, my countrymen, idle sentimentalism. I firmly believe that the great Commonwealth of Virginia, and this city, which has a peculiar title to whatever there is of good and illustrious report in this war, have been recently, and are yet in some measure on the verge of questions which involve an interest immeasurably greater than has yet been disclosed in this contest—that of their historical and immortal honour.

My friends, this is not rubbish. The glory of History is indifferent to events: it is simply Honour. The name of Virginia in this war is historically and absolutely more important to us than any other element of the contest; and the coarse time-server who would sell an immortal title of honour as a trifling sentimentalism, and who has constantly in his mouth the phrase of "substantial interests," is the inglorious wretch who laughs at history and grovels in the calculations of the brute.

Those who have lived entirely in the South since the commencement of this war have little idea of the measure of honour which Virginia has obtained in it, and the consideration she has secured in the eyes of the world. One away from home finds even in intercourse with our enemies, that the name of Virginia is an ornament to him, and that the story of this her heroic capital—the record of Richmond—is universally accepted in two hemispheres as the most illustrious episode of the war. Honour such as this is not a piece of rhetoric or a figure of speech; it is something to be cherished under all circumstances, and to be preserved in all events.

It is scarcely necessary to say that I regard subjugation but as the vapour of our fears. But if remote possibilities are to be regarded, I have simply to say, that in all events and extremities, all chances and catastrophes, I am for Virginia going down to history, proudly and starkly, with the title of a subjugated people—a title not inseparable from true glory, and which has often claimed the admiration of the world—rather than as a people who ever submitted, and bartered their honour for the mercy of an enemy—in our case a mercy whose *pittance* would be as a mess of pottage weighed against an immortal patrimony!

The issue I would put before you is: No Submission; No State Negotiations with the Enemy; No Conventions for such objects, however proper for others. Let Virginia stand or fall by the fortunes of the Confederate arms, with her spotless honour in her hands.

If Virginia accepts the virtuous and noble alternative, she saves in all events, her honour, and by the resolution which it implies, may hope to secure a positive and glorious victory; and I, among the humblest of her citizens, will be proud to associate myself with a fate which, if not happy, at least can never be ignoble. But, if she chooses to submit, and make terms for Yankee clemency, the satisfaction will at least remain to me of not sharing in the dishonour of my native State, and of going to other parts of the world, where I may say: "I, too, was a Virginian, but not of those who sold the jewels of her history for the baubles and cheats of her conquerours."

EDWARD A. POLLARD

"Great Disasters Have Overtaken Us"

TIME WAS RUNNING OUT for the Confederacy. For accounts of the last days of the war we must turn to later publications. The Confederates were no longer able, physically or spiritually, to publish them. And there was little point in doing so. The propaganda value of accounts of a nation in its death throes would have been nil. And transportation had become so disrupted that publications could no longer be distributed to a wide audience.

Grant opened his spring campaign against the Richmond-Petersburg line, and the Virginia defense finally gave way. Richmond was evacuated on April 2 and Lee surrendered to Grant at Appomattox Court House on April 9. Only Johnston blocked Sherman's path toward joining his army with that of Grant. Resistance in the East was no longer effective. President Davis and the remnants of his Cabinet were fleeing south and west.

For there was still a forlorn hope in the West. If the President could make his way across the Mississippi and join the troops of General Edmund Kirby Smith, all might not yet be lost. In one of the very last of Confederate

$100,000

REWARD!

IN GOLD.

Hez quarters Cav. Corp.,
Military Divi ion Mississippi,
Macón Ga., May 6, 1865.

One Hundred Thousand Dollars Reward

in Gold, will be paid to any person or persons who wil apprehend and deliver JEFFERSON DAVIS to any of the Military authorities of the United States.

Several millions of specie, reported to be with him, will become the property of the captors.

J. H. WILSO

370

publications General Kirby Smith urged his troops to maintain the hopes of the dying nation.

Head Quarters Trans-Miss. Department,

SHREVEPORT, LA., APRIL 21 1865.

SOLDIERS OF THE TRANS-MISSISSIPPI ARMY:

The crisis of our revolution is at hand. Great disasters have overtaken us. The Army of Northern Virginia and our Commander-in-Chief are prisoners of war. With you rest the hopes of our nation, and upon your action depends the fate of our people. I appeal to you in the name of the cause you have so heroically maintained,—and in the name of your fire-sides and families so dear to you,—in the name of your bleeding country whose future is in your hands. Show that you are worthy of your position in history. Prove to the world that your hearts have not failed in the hour of disaster, and that at the last moment you will sustain the holy cause which has been so gloriously battled for, by your brethren east of the Mississippi.

You possess the means of long resisting invasion. You have hopes of succor from abroad—protract the struggle, and you will surely receive the aid of nations who already deeply sympathize with you.

Stand by your colors—maintain your discipline. The great resources of this Department, its vast extent, the numbers, the discipline, and the efficiency of the Army, will secure to our country terms that a proud people can with honor accept, and may, under the Providence of God, be the means of checking the triumph of our enemy and of securing the final success of our cause.

E. KIRBY SMITH,
General.

Secession Runs Its Course

JOHNSTON surrendered to Sherman near Hillsboro, North Carolina. President Davis met with the remaining members of his Cabinet for the last time at Washington, Georgia, May 4. Here he talked optimistically of re-establishing the government in Kirby-Smithdom west of the Mississippi. But the midshipmen who had accompanied him from Richmond as his guard were released from their assignment, and the Cabinet was allowed to disperse to take their chances individually.

Two days later, from his headquarters at Macon, Federal General J. H. Wilson issued an order that was soon posted on the buildings and fences in the heart of the Confederacy:

"One hundred thousand dollars reward in gold, will be paid to any person or persons who will apprehend and deliver Jefferson Davis to any of the military authorities of the United States. Several million of specie, reported to be with him, will become the property of the captors."

Four days later President Davis was captured at Irwinville, Georgia.

Secession had run its course.

Index